To Dad & Gr
from
Dann, Nina, & Nadia

NAVAL BATTLES OF WORLD WAR II

By the same Author

By Human Error
Coronel and the Falklands
Cowan's War, British naval operations in the Baltic, 1918–1920
The Battle of Jutland
Charlie B, a biography of Admiral Lord Beresford
Naval Battles of the First World War
Nelson the Commander
Battle of the River Plate
The Loss of the 'Prince of Wales' and 'Repulse'

NAVAL BATTLES
OF WORLD WAR II

Geoffrey Bennett

With a foreword by
Admiral Arleigh Burke USN

B. T. Batsford London & Sydney

For ADMIRAL OF THE FLEET SIR ALGERNON WILLIS,
GCB, KBE, DSO
on whose staff I had the honour to serve during a
significant part of the Second World War

First published 1975
© Geoffrey Bennett 1975

ISBN 0 7134 2997 6

Printed in Great Britain by
Willmer Brothers Limited, Birkenhead

for the publishers B. T. Batsford Ltd
4 Fitzhardinge Street, London W1H 0AH
and 23 Cross Street, Brookvale, NSW 2100
Australia

Contents

List of Illustrations

The illustrations are between pages 118 and 119

List of Maps and Diagrams

Acknowledgements

I am much indebted to the following for reading the manuscript of this book in whole or in part, and for their invaluable advice: Admiral Arleigh Burke, USN, Dr. J. E. de Courcy Ireland, Captain W. R. Lapper, RN, Captain Donald Macintyre, RN, Douglas H. Robinson, MD, and Captain Stephen Roskill, RN. They have helped me to avoid errors of fact, false interpretations and wrong-headed judgements. For such as remain, or with which the reader is unable to agree, I alone am responsible.

I have also to thank the respective authors, publishers, etc., for permission to quote from the following works: *War Memoirs* by Admiral of the Fleet Sir Algernon Willis (private and unpublished); *The Two-Ocean War* by Samuel Eliot Morison (Little, Brown & Co., Boston, Mass.); *Wings of the Morning* by Ian Cameron (David Higham Associates and Hodder & Stoughton, London); *Everyman's History of the Sea War* by A. C. Hardy (Nicholson & Watson, London); *Enemy in Sight* by Esmond Knight, in *Tales of the Fighting Navy* (William Blackwood & Sons, London); *The Bismarck Episode* by Captain Russell Grenfell (David Higham Associates and Faber & Faber, London); *The Second World War* by Winston S. Churchill (Cassell & Co., London and Houghton Mifflin Co., Boston, Mass.); *The Sinking of the Scharnhorst* by R. B. Ramsden, in *Sea Tales from 'Blackwood'* (William Blackwood & Sons, London); *A Sailor's Odyssey* by Admiral of the Fleet Viscount Cunningham of Hyndhope (Hutchinson & Co., London), by permission of the author's Estate; *Battle of Matapan* by S. W. C. Pack, and *Battle of the Atlantic* by Donald Macintyre (both B. T. Batsford, London); and *The War at Sea, 1939–1945* by Captain S. W. Roskill (H.M. Stationery Office, London; Crown copyright).

The sheer quantity of the records of World War Two now available, and the great number of books which have been written about its naval side during the past 30 years (not only in English but in French, German, Italian and Japanese), are such that a comprehensive bibliography would require a volume to itself, whilst a select one would involve an invidious task. None has therefore been included in this book. But two indispensable works must be mentioned: *The War at Sea, 1939–45*, by Captain S. W. Roskill, DSC, RN, published in four volumes by HM Stationery Office, London, and *History of the United States Naval Operations in World War II*, by Samuel Eliot Morison, published in fifteen volumes by Little, Brown & Co., New York.

GEOFFREY BENNETT
LUDLOW 1975

*   *   *

The Author and Publishers wish to thank the following for permission to reproduce the illustrations in this book: Author's collection (4, 5); Imperial War Museum (1–3, 7–12, 14–18, 20–23, 25–31, 38, 39); National Maritime Museum (6); Press Association (13); US Navy Department (19, 24, 32–37).

Foreword   by Admiral Arleigh Burke, USN

whose brilliant handling of Destroyer Squadron 23 during the Solomons campaign, 1942–43, won him the nickname '31-knot Burke', who was Chief of Staff to the Admiral Commanding Task Force 58 during the later part of World War Two in the Pacific, and who crowned some forty years service in the United States Navy with the appointment of Chief of Naval Operations, 1955–61.

This book will be intensely interesting to any person who is at all curious about naval warfare. It will be – or at least it should be – absorbing for all men who may find themselves in positions with command responsibility in the future. It will bring back poignant memories to those who have already participated in naval battles.

This book is valuable because it is written with an insight into naval operations which can be acquired only with experience in battle. Captain Bennett's long service in the Royal Navy has given him the background to assess correctly the causes for success or failure in the naval engagements he describes.

He has brought out clearly the elements that are needed for a Navy to meet its responsibilities. It takes years to build a ship and it must operate for several decades. An erroneous concept, a faulty design in a weapons system, may very well cause failure in battle and possibly the loss of a war. By the examples he recounts he has shown the need for effective organisation of a Navy so that proper routines can be established in peacetime that will become automatic in war – and will work in war.

He has demonstrated the value of intelligence and the necessity for quick, accurate analysis of the scarce information available and the importance of its rapid dissemination to commanders who can do something about it – and the grievous misfortunes that too frequently occur when information is misinterpreted by, or withheld from, the operating commander. He has shown the absolute need for professionalism throughout the Navy for it to operate effectively in war. There must be knowledge, experience and skill in all ranks and ratings from the commander-in-chief to an ammunition passer. Each man must know thoroughly his own job and those of his associates, so that everybody knows what the ship or unit can do, and be able to depend on it doing what it should amid the stress and casualties of battle.

Most importantly, he correctly stresses the crucial role of the commanders. He has emphasized that they must have the high degree of professionalism, skill, knowledge, physical stamina and all the other qualities required by all Navy men to meet the demanding requirements of successful naval battles. He has shown that the outcome of many of these has been largely determined by the talents of the commanders. Those who have won their battles when the odds were against them have all had fundamental characteristics in common. Each one had the ability to make correct decisions under great stress. Each knew the importance of timing – of surprise. They knew when to act – usually right now. Each had evaluated the capabilities – and limitations – of his own force and he demanded – and got – full performance. And most of all, each one had courage, boldness, persistence, the confidence of his people – and a little bit of luck.

Neither timid nor reckless men should go to sea.

A*

Introductory Notes

Throughout this book, except where otherwise indicated, references to *Britain* (in strict terms 'Great Britain'), the *British/Royal* Navy etc., include the erstwhile British Dominions and their Navies. This literary convenience in no way belittles their contribution to the Allied cause.

The classification *cruiser* is used for all such vessels even though some Navies continued to subdivide them into armoured cruisers, heavy cruisers, light cruisers etc.

The classification *destroyer* includes flotilla leaders and vessels typed by some Navies as torpedoboats.

The term *U-boat* is used for Italian and Japanese submarines as well as for German.

To simplify comparisons between gun and torpedo armaments, those normally measured in centimetres are given their nearest equivalent in inches.

The number of destroyers and submarines credited to the various Fleets in Part One, and the losses which they are stated to have suffered during World War Two, are the best available figures.

Differences between individual ships' data as given in Part One, and as given in subsequent Parts, are the consequences of modernization, alterations in armament etc.

The following differences in nomenclature should be noted. During World War Two the British Navy was divided into *geographical fleets*. Its cruisers and larger ships were normally organized in *squadrons*, its destroyers and smaller vessels in *flotillas*, both being split into *divisions*. Ships of all types required for specific operations were organised as *lettered forces* (occasionally into lettered groups).

Other Navies were similarly organised with the exception of the USA's. Her geographical fleets were also *numbered*, her cruisers and larger ships were organised in *divisions*, and her destroyers and smaller vessels in *squadrons* which were split into divisions. Ships of all types required for specific operations were organised as numbered *task forces* which were divided into *task groups*, and sub-divided into *task units*.

Quotations from contemporary reports and other sources have been abridged for reasons of space without the use of ellipses, and, where essential, edited without disfiguring them with square brackets.

Notes will be found on the last page of each chapter.

PART 1: IN WHICH THE SCENE IS SET

1 *Montevideo*

'History is bunk,' declared Henry Ford. Winston Churchill held a different view: 'History is the one sure guide to the future—that and imagination!' In truth, history enshrines the wisdom of the ages; and in no field is this more valid than war, a thesis for which there is ample evidence in the first of the many naval battles fought in World War Two.

Admirals Graf von Spee and Franz von Hipper served their country well; one vanquished a British squadron off Coronel in November 1914, the other came near to destroying Beatty's battlecruisers at Jutland. The Third *Reich* bestowed the former's name on a pocket-battleship. Among Hipper's staff officers on 31 May 1916 was Commander Erich Raeder. The Armistice of November 1918 required Imperial Germany to surrender all her U-boats, and to submit the bulk of her surface ships to internment at Scapa Flow. The Versailles Treaty left her with a minuscule Navy manned by 15,000 officers and men, among whom was Raeder, and he had a special reason to learn from his country's defeat. The futility of the Kaiser's attempt to seize Britannia's trident by building a fleet of dreadnoughts was clear enough; and so was the near-success of Germany's unrestricted U-boat campaign in 1917. But not until Raeder was assigned the task of writing two volumes of *Der Krieg zur See*, the German official history, did he appreciate the achievements of the handful of surface warships which were overseas at the beginning of hostilities; the stranglehold which the cruiser *Emden* imposed on British commerce in the Indian Ocean, and the numerous Allied capital ships and cruisers which were required to compass the destruction of von Spee's East Asiatic Squadron. And he did not forget this lesson when he reached the peak of his profession in 1929.

As head of the *Reichsmarine* Admiral Raeder inherited Germany's solution to the problem of building useful replacements for her old predreadnoughts on a Treaty limit of 10,000 tons. The first pocket-battleship had just been laid down at Kiel. When completed as the *Deutschland* with six 11-inch guns and a speed of 26 knots, she would outgun all existing cruisers and outrun all capital ships except four British and four Japanese battlecruisers. (Not until after she was commissioned in 1933 was it appreciated that Germany had only achieved so much by exceeding the Versailles Treaty limit by more than two thousand tons, by which time other events made protest useless.) Moreover, with diesel engines giving her an endurance of 9,000 miles at 19 knots, her potential for ocean warfare was so clear that Raeder ordered two sister ships whose names commemorated the German C-in-C at Jutland, Reinhard Scheer, and the victor at Coronel.

He would have ordered more but for Hitler's seizure of power in 1933, his subsequent repudiation of the Versailles Treaty, and his negotiation of an agreement with Britain which allowed Germany to build up to 35 per cent of her surface tonnage, and to achieve parity with submarines. Raeder then ordered two 32,000 ton battlecruisers, two 41,700 ton battleships and five 8-inch cruisers, all with the endurance needed for ocean warfare, before Hitler's abrogation of the Anglo-German naval agreement allowed him to plan a larger, balanced fleet of as many as 13 capital ships, four aircraft-carriers and 33 cruisers, plus 250 U-boats.

Few of these surface vessels were, however, destined to be completed. Hitler's rape of Czechoslovakia in the spring of 1939 required Raeder to prepare for an early war with France and Britain. But against their 23 capital ships, eight aircraft-carriers, and more than 80 cruisers, what could he do with only two battlecruisers, three pocket-battleships and eight cruisers, plus 57 U-boats, barely enough to keep a dozen on patrol? His answer was contained in the *Reichsmarine*'s battle instructions issued in May 1939; the greater part of his Fleet would be deployed in the North Sea and the Baltic, but enemy maritime trade was also to be attacked, not only by U-boats around the British Isles but by pocket-battleships operating much further afield.

As soon as Raeder knew the date of Hitler's intended *blitzkrieg* attack on Poland, he sent his ships to their war stations. On 21 August the *Admiral Graf Spee* sailed from Wilhelmshaven under the command of Captain H. Langsdorff. The *Deutschland* followed her three days later. Keeping close to the Norwegian coast until far to the north, and making the best use of darkness, both vessels rounded the Faroes without being seen by Britain's Home Fleet or by the Royal Air Force's Coastal Command. When Whitehall and the Quai d'Orsay declared war on 3 September, the *Deutschland* and her supply ship were away to the south of Greenland, while the *Graf Spee* with hers, the *Altmark*, was to the west of the Cape Verde Islands heading for the South Atlantic.

Because Hitler hoped that his lightning conquest of Poland might be followed by a negotiated peace with France and Britain, both ships were initially ordered to refrain from hostile acts. Not until 26 September were they released for the 'disruption and destruction of enemy merchant shipping by all possible means, making sudden appearances in widely separated areas'. Unfortunately for Raeder's plans, the *Deutschland*'s subsequent activities were more of an embarrassment than a help to Germany. After sinking one British freighter on 5 October, she seized the US *City of Flint,* then on the 14th sank the Norwegian *Lorenz W. Hansen,* two neutrals among only three victims in as many weeks. The *Deutschland* was ordered home.

In sharp contrast, the *Graf Spee* began by sinking the British SS *Clement* off Pernambuco on 30 September. Five days later Langsdorff seized the SS *Newton Beech* on the Cape-UK route; on 7 October he sank the SS *Ashlea,* and 24 hours later the SS *Huntsman,* in the same waters. Having refuelled from the *Altmark,* the *Graf Spee* then made a second foray against the Cape-UK route, sinking the SS *Trevanion* on 22 October. Her radio operator was the first to clear a raider report since the attack on the *Clement*; and just as that impelled Langsdorff to shift his hunting ground, this persuaded him to take the *Graf Spee* round into the Indian Ocean. But 10 days on the Cape-Australia route produced no prey, so he turned north for the Mozambique Channel and there, on 15 November, sank the SS *Africa Shell.* Next day he sighted the Dutch *Mapia* but respected her neutrality. Judging that he had done enough to alert the enemy of his presence, he headed back to his refuelling area in the South Atlantic.

There, on 23 November, he wrote these fateful words:

> The *Graf Spee* having now steamed 30,000 miles, should continue to cause damage and disruption to enemy shipping for as long as possible in order to tie down the greatest possible enemy forces. But her machinery requires a dockyard overhaul. Commerce raiding is therefore nearing an end, and the necessity for avoiding damage by an enemy warship no longer pressing. If the *Graf Spee* closed the range her powerful armament should at least so damage an opponent as to eliminate him as a shadower. The *Graf Spee* will therefore operate again on the Cape route until about 6 December. She will then cross the Atlantic and operate against the River Plate traffic before returning to Germany in the New Year.

Leaving all but the principal officers from his victims on board the *Altmark,* to be landed at some neutral port, Langsdorff again headed for the African coast where, on 2 December, he sank the SS *Doric Star* after she had cleared a raider report. Having thus stirred a hornet's nest, he steered west to find next day another victim, the SS *Tairoa.* Three days later the *Graf Spee* refuelled from the *Altmark* for the last time before, on 7 December, sinking the SS *Streonshalh.* This, after 10 weeks of cruising, brought his bag up to nine merchant ships totalling some 50,000 tons, from which to Langsdorff's credit not one life had been lost. The *Streonshalh*'s papers told him that Allied shipping leaving the Plate steered some 300 miles to the east before turning north for Freetown.

When Berlin radioed that four British merchant ships were expected to sail from Montevideo on the 10th, Langsdorff set course for this focal area.

Next day, by an unhappy chance, his single floatplane cracked a cylinder on returning from a reconnaissance flight. Because the *Graf Spee*'s stock of spares was exhausted, she could not be catapulted on the 13th to give him prior warning of what he was to see for himself as that morning dawned clear and cloudless. He believed that British cruisers in South American waters were patrolling singly: instead 'at about 0552, there appeared off the starboard bow at first two and then four thin masts, and by 0600 enough of the superstructure of the right hand ship could be seen to identify her as HMS *Exeter*. At 0610 the two smaller vessels were identified as HMS *Ajax* and HMNZS *Achilles*.'

Britain's First Sea Lord and Chief of Naval Staff, Admiral Sir Dudley Pound, another veteran of Jutland, and the commander of the Royal Navy's South American Division, Commodore Henry Harwood, had also studied history. Both recognized that 'nothing could paralyse our seaborne trade so certainly and immediately as a successful attack by surface raiders'. As soon as Pound and Admiral Jean François Darlan, who headed the French Ministry of Marine, knew from the attacks on the *Stonegate* and *Clement* that two German corsairs must be at large in the Atlantic, nine British and French hunting groups were formed on 5 October, each fast enough to catch a pocket-battleship and with the power to cripple if not sink her. As Raeder expected, these called for as many as four capital ships, five aircraft-carriers and 17 cruisers, whilst four more capital ships and as many large cruisers were required to safeguard North Atlantic convoys. With the need to keep a strong force at Scapa Flow to guard against a break-out by Germany's battlecruisers and cruisers (as the *Scharnhorst* and *Gneisenau* made a half-hearted attempt to do in November, only to return to Wilhelmshaven because they encountered the armed merchant cruiser *Rawalpindi* between the Faroes and Iceland), this would have placed a heavy strain on both countries' naval resources but for Italy's and Japan's reluctance to support their Axis partner. Mussolini was waiting to be sure of a German victory before showing his hand; Japan was locked in conflict with China. Britain and France were, therefore, able to withdraw the majority of their ships from the Mediterranean and the Far East to reinforce their squadrons in the Atlantic and Indian Oceans.

Force G, which comprised the 8-inch cruisers *Cumberland* and *Exeter* and the 6-inch cruisers *Ajax* and *Achilles*, was under Harwood's command. To watch the French fleet in Toulon Nelson needed all his ships-of-the-line. To protect trade flowing past Gibraltar, he could spare only three 32-gun frigates; and their commander's chief concern was a single French ship-of-the-line, the 74-gun *Aigle* based on Cadiz. Yet Nelson

The cruise of the *Admiral Graf Spee*, 21 August–13 December 1939.
Key: **A**: ss *Clement* (5051 GRT) sunk; **B**: ss *Newton Beech* (4651 GRT) captured and then sunk; **C**: ss *Ashlea* (4222 GRT) sunk; **D**: ss *Huntsman* (8106 GRT) sunk; **E**: ss *Trevanion* (5299 GRT) sunk; **F**: ss *Africa Shell* (706 GRT) sunk; **G**: ss *Doric Star* (10086 GRT) sunk; **H**: ss *Tairoa* (7983 GRT) sunk; **J**: ss *Streonshalh* (3895 GRT) sunk.

advised Captain John Gore: 'Your intentions of attacking that ship are very laudable, but I do not consider your force by any means equal to it'. Like Hawke and Howe, he judged that a single 'battleship' was more than a match for a squadron of 'cruisers'. And this was still the accepted view in the Dreadnought era: when Rear-Admiral Ernest Troubridge, commanding four British cruisers, was charged with failing to bring the battlecruiser *Goeben* to action in August 1914, the court martial decided that he 'was justified in considering the *Goeben* a superior force and in abandoning the chase'. Pound remembered the Admiralty's inept orders to Troubridge's superior in the Mediterranean, which impelled the Court to give this verdict. There was no doubting those which he issued to his hunting groups; even those which comprised no more than cruisers were to 'find, fix and strike'. And Harwood had no wish to suffer the stigma of guilt to which the Admiralty had subjected Troubridge, despite his acquittal.

For more than two months, for all of which Harwood's force patrolled the east coast of South America, the Allied hunting groups failed to find their foe. At the beginning of December Harwood's flagship, the *Ajax*, Captain C. H. Woodhouse, was watching the River Plate and the New Zealand manned *Achilles*, Captain W. E. Parry, was off Rio de Janeiro, while the *Cumberland*, Captain W. H. Fallowfield, and *Exeter*, Captain F. S. Bell, guarded the Falklands against the enemy attacking Port Stanley by way of avenging von Spee's defeat in 1914. These dispositions were changed when Harwood received the *Doric Star*'s raider report. Convinced that the *Graf Spee* would soon attack the rich traffic in his area, he calculated that Langsdorff could reach Rio by 12 December, the Plate by the 13th, and the Falklands by the 14th. Opting for the second of these, he ordered the *Exeter* and the *Achilles* to rendezvous with the *Ajax* 150 miles to the east of the Plate at 0700 on the 12th, whilst the *Cumberland* remained at the Falklands for a self-refit and for their protection.

Next morning Harwood's three ships were steaming in single line ahead on a mean course of 060 degrees, at 14 knots to conserve fuel. Although the *Exeter* and *Ajax* each carried two aircraft, none was launched for a dawn patrol. According to the *Exeter*'s observer: 'I'm afraid we were not very air-conscious in those days!' But Harwood had to conserve his planes' engine-hours when the *Ajax*'s second machine was already unserviceable; so it was not until soon after dawn that his insight into Langsdorff's mind was proved as sure as Nelson's into Brueys' in 1798. When smoke was sighted at 0614 on 13 December bearing 320 degrees, the *Exeter* was ordered to close and investigate. Two minutes later Bell signalled: 'I think it is a pocket-battleship'.

According to Langsdorff's memorandum, 'if the *Graf Spee* was to close the range her powerful armament would at least so damage an opponent

TABLE 1: Ships involved in the Battle of the Plate

Ship	Displacement (tons)	Speed (knots)	Guns	Torpedo tubes	Aircraft	Thickest armour
Admiral Graf Spee	12,100	26	6 11in 8 6in	8 21in	One	5½in
Exeter	8,390	32	6 8in	6 21in	2 spotter-reconnaissance amphibians	3in
Ajax	6,985	32	8 6in	8 21in	2 spotter-reconnaissance floatplanes	4in
Achilles	7,030	32	8 6in	8 21in	None	4in
(Cumberland	9,750	31	8 8in	8 21in	1 search floatplane	5in)

as to eliminate him as a shadower'. *An* opponent—but Langsdorff was faced with three. He might have turned away and engaged his assailants with the *Graf Spee*'s 11-inch guns for as long as possible before they could overhaul her and get her within range of their smaller weapons. But in December 1914, in these same waters, HMS *Invincible* and *Inflexible* had had to fire 80 per cent of their 12-inch shells to sink SMS *Gneisenau* and *Scharnhorst*. By closing his opponents the *Graf Spee*'s heavy guns should soon score damaging hits, especially on vessels as lightly protected as British cruisers, without expending too much of her irreplaceable ammunition. At 0600 Langsdorff increased to full speed and altered course towards the enemy: 15 minutes later, when the range was down to 20,000 yards, he turned to port to bring both turrets to bear on HMS *Exeter* and opened fire.

Though faced with a more heavily armed and better protected vessel, Harwood had other compensating advantages besides a higher speed; he had a force which could be divided and engage from different bearings with a larger number of guns that could maintain a higher rate of fire. On 12 December he had signalled: 'My policy with three cruisers versus one pocket-battleship. Attack at once. By day act as two units. First Division [*Ajax* and *Achilles*] and *Exeter* diverged to permit flank marking [*i.e.* spotting the other division's gun fire from a flank]. First Division will concentrate gunfire.' With these instructions Bell needed no further orders: already diverging from the *Ajax* and *Achilles* he had only to ring for full speed, swing the *Exeter* round to 280 degrees to bring her three turrets to bear and at 0620, two minutes after the *Graf Spee*, open fire. Meantime, Harwood ordered the *Ajax* and *Achilles* to increase speed and turn to 340 degrees to close the range; and at 0621, when this was down to 19,400 yards, the First Division likewise opened fire, the *Achilles* conforming with the *Ajax*'s movements three to four cables astern.

The *Graf Spee*'s third salvo straddled the *Exeter,* one shell bursting short amidships, its splinters killing the starboard torpedo tube's crew,

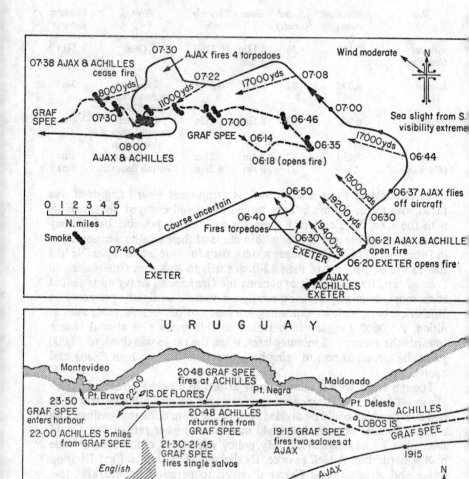

2 *Above* The Battle of the Plate (0614–0800 hrs)
  Below The *Graf Spee*'s approach to Montevideo

and damaging both her aircraft before they could be launched so that they had to be jettisoned. This left only the *Ajax*'s serviceable floatplane for spotting duties, but although this was successfully catapulted at 0637, some 15 minutes elapsed before radio communication was established. For a very different reason the *Exeter* was unable to flank mark the First Division's gunfire: after firing eight salvoes, and surviving a German shell that went through the deck without exploding, she received a direct hit on B turret which not only put it out of action but swept the bridge with splinters that killed nearly all who were there, and wrecked the wheelhouse communications. Suffering from a facial wound, Bell had now to fight his ship from her secondary conning position abaft the after funnel, with the handicap of having to pass all orders to the after steering position through an improvised chain of messengers.

Whilst the *Exeter* now received two more damaging hits, her opponent did not escape punishment. One of Bell's 8-inch shells struck the *Graf Spee*'s control tower, and by 0630 Langsdorff was so worried by the *Ajax*'s and *Achilles*'s gunfire that he ordered his 11-inch guns to shift target. These two British cruisers were then straddled by heavy shells but, by weaving, avoided anything more damaging than splinters from bursts short. Bell used this brief respite to fire, first his starboard torpedoes, then his port. To avoid these, as well as the *Ajax*'s and *Achilles*'s rapid salvoes at a range that was down to 13,000 yards, Langsdorff altered course 150 degrees away under cover of smoke. He also re-directed his main armament on to its original target, when the *Exeter,* after achieving her second hit on the *Graf Spee*, was struck by two more 11-inch shells, one of which put 'A' turret out of action, while the other started a fierce fire amidships. This severed her fire-control circuits and put all her gyro repeaters out of action, leaving Bell with nothing better than a boat's compass with which to con his ship.

Fortunately for the *Exeter,* although the battle was far from being over, Langsdorff's decision to turn away only 20 minutes after first opening fire was the action of a beaten man. Confronted by three cruisers whose commander had determined to attack instead of being content to shadow, he lacked the resolution to continue his intended close range action. He could have swung the *Graf Spee* right round to the south-west and given the *coup de grâce* to the *Exeter* which had only one turret left in action. Instead, although the 6-inch shells of the *Ajax* and *Achilles* failed to penetrate the *Graf Spee*'s armour, Langsdorff so feared the damage they were doing to her superstructure, and the casualties they were inflicting on the exposed crews of her secondary armament, that he changed his tactics to engaging these two cruisers at long range, now some 17,000 yards. This allowed the *Exeter* to continue the fight, despite an 11-inch hit which flooded several compartments forward and caused a seven degree list. Not until 0729, when electricity supply to 'Y' turret failed, did a gallant Captain Bell, 61 of whose officers and men had been killed and 23 wounded, break off the action. Twenty minutes later, according to the much-damaged *Exeter*'s log: 'Enemy disappeared to westward pursued by *Ajax* and *Achilles*.'

By 0710 Harwood tired of engaging his enemy at long range and turned more directly in pursuit to the westward at full speed. To thwart this move, Langsdorff made another drastic alteration to port under cover of smoke; next, at 0720, he turned back to starboard when, with the range down to 11,000 yards, the *Ajax* was quickly straddled by three 11-inch salvoes. But Harwood's flagship also scored hits on her opponent which started a fire amidships. Five minutes later an 11-inch shell struck the *Ajax* aft, putting both 'X' and 'Y' turrets out of action. Almost simultaneously, Woodhouse turned to starboard and fired four torpedoes at 9,000 yards. Langsdorff swung his ship to port to avoid this salvo, then turned back to fire his own starboard torpedoes, but the tracks were seen by the *Ajax*'s aircraft in time to warn Harwood to avoid them.

These turns apart, the action continued with the *Graf Spee* heading west and the two British cruisers in hot pursuit until 0738 when, with the range down to 8,000 yards, Harwood learned that the *Ajax* had fired 80 per cent of her ammunition. Assuming that the *Achilles* had expended a similar quantity, and because the *Graf Spee*'s shooting remained disturbingly accurate, one salvo bringing down the *Ajax*'s main topmast and all her radio aerials, he decided to break off the action until after dark. At 0740, after a brisk engagement that had lasted an hour and twenty minutes, the *Ajax* and *Achilles* turned away to the east, a decision to which Harwood held even though he subsequently established that it was only the *Ajax*'s foremost turret which had fired so much ammunition.

Langsdorff, who had suffered two splinter wounds, made no attempt to round on his adversaries: he kept the *Graf Spee* heading west at 24 knots, whilst the *Ajax* and *Achilles* followed at the safe distance of 15 miles. The pocket-battleship had by now expended 60 per cent of her ammunition, and since the two British 6-inch cruisers retained their speed advantage, he had no confidence in his chances of crippling them with what remained. Even if he did so, the *Graf Spee* would be left with too little with which to face an encounter with Britain's Home Fleet when she tried to return to Germany. Then there were the *Graf Spee*'s casualties, none of them fortunately among her 62 British prisoners: in addition to 36 dead, she had six seriously wounded who needed hospital treatment, as well as 53 with lesser injuries.

More important was the damage inflicted by three 8-inch and 17 6-inch British shells. Although only one had pierced the armoured deck, and none had affected her immediate battleworthiness, the *Graf Spee* had a large hole in her bows which would have to be repaired before she faced winter weather in the North Atlantic; and much of her superstructure, including her galleys and bakery, and the plant for purifying the fuel and lubricating oil for her engines, had been wrecked beyond repair by the ship's resources. But these factors are not enough to explain Langsdorff's decision to take the *Graf Spee* into the neutral port of Montevideo. His apologists contend that his judgement was impaired by his wounds; the truth lies in the skill and tenacity of his opponents; they had shown that the British Navy of 1939 had lost neither the fighting ability nor the courage with which, in the past, it had so often gained a victory against odds.

Around 0800 Harwood ordered the *Ajax*'s floatplane to locate the *Exeter* and ascertain why she did not answer radio calls. She was soon found, 'obviously hard hit', ablaze amidships and 'in no condition to fight another action'. She did not, however, need immediate assistance.

At 0916 Harwood ordered the *Cumberland* to leave the Falklands at full speed. Despite the handicap of boilers opened up to repair brickwork, she sailed from Port Stanley as soon as 1000, because Fallowfield had raised steam on his own initiative when, around 0630, his ship intercepted signals indicating that the rest of Force G was in action. Even so, it was a long haul to the mouth of the Plate, 36 hours at 30 knots.

At 1005 *Achilles* closed in to 23,000 yards and drew two 11-inch salvoes from the *Graf Spee*, of which the second fell close alongside: Parry immediately made smoke and turned away, to resume shadowing from a safer range.

An hour later Harwood received a signal from the *Exeter*: having rigged jury aerials, Bell was able to report that only one gun in 'Y' turret remained in action, and that his ship was so far down by the bows that her speed was limited to 18 knots. To this there could be only one reply: the *Exeter* was ordered to proceed to Port Stanley as best she could without straining her bulkheads.

The *Ajax* and *Achilles*, whose combined casualties totalled, almost miraculously, only 11 killed and 5 injured, shadowed the *Graf Spee* throughout the rest of the day. At 1915, more than an hour after first sighting the coast of Uruguay, Langsdorff fired two salvoes at the *Ajax* at a range of 26,000 yards, causing her to turn away under smoke. Long before this he had signalled Berlin his intention to enter Montevideo, to which Raeder had replied: 'Agreed'. But not until 1900 was Harwood sufficiently sure of his enemy's destination to order the *Achilles*, which had suffered no damage except for splinters, to follow her if she went west of Lobos Island, while the *Ajax* turned south in case she doubled back that way.

Just after sunset at 2048, the *Graf Spee*, still more than 50 miles from her intended haven, fired three salvoes to ensure that the *Achilles* kept her distance, to which she replied with five. As darkness fell Parry closed in to 10,000 yards to maintain touch, when his ship was the target for three final salvoes as, between 2130 and 2145 the *Graf Spee* passed to the north of English Bank. By 2200 the pocket-battleship was clearly silhouetted against the lights of Montevideo; and Parry saw her drop anchor in that neutral city's roads shortly before midnight.

Harwood could not touch her there, and he had no idea how long she would stay. One of his ships had two of her turrets out of action, and he could not expect the *Cumberland* to join him for another 24 hours. The best he could do was to patrol to seaward of the Plate, the *Achilles* in a sector north of English Bank, and the *Ajax* to the south, and await the enemy's next move. Meantime, there could be no doubt as to who had won; Harwood's achievement was recognized by his immediate promotion to rear-admiral, the award of the KCB, and by these words from Pound: 'Your action has reversed the findings of the Troubridge court martial and shows how wrong that was'. In the New York *Herald Tribune* Walter Lippman wrote: 'The defeat of the *Graf Spee* is pleasing to all the Americas'.

Intense activity in Montevideo, and widespread movements by British naval units followed. For the Government of Uruguay, for British and German diplomats, for Whitehall and the Wilhelmstrasse, and for the C-in-C South Atlantic, Admiral Sir D'Oyly Lyon, in his Freetown headquarters, as well as for Harwood and Langsdorff, the problem was for how long should, or would, the *Graf Spee* remain in Montevideo Roads? Lyon signalled the 8-inch cruiser *Dorsetshire* to leave Cape Town for the Plate. Pound ordered her sister-ship, the *Shropshire*, to follow, and diverted the battlecruiser *Renown* and the aircraft-carrier *Ark Royal* of Force K to Rio de Janeiro for fuel, where they would be joined by the 6-inch cruiser *Neptune* before hurrying south. To guard against the *Graf Spee* escaping round the Cape into the Indian Ocean, the aircraft-carrier *Eagle*, the 8-inch cruiser *Cornwall* and the 6-inch cruiser *Gloucester* were sent to Durban. An overwhelming concentration was thus directed towards the estuary of the Plate. But such were the distances that many of these ships had to steam—2,500 miles in the case of the *Ark Royal* and *Renown,* more than 3,500 for the *Dorsetshire* and *Shropshire*—that there was no possibility of achieving it before 19 December.

The Government of Uruguay had to interpret and enforce International Law. The Hague Convention allowed a belligerent warship to prolong her stay in a neutral port for more than 24 hours only if she had suffered damage, in which case she might 'carry out such repairs as are absolutely necessary to render her seaworthy, but may not add to her fighting force. The neutral Power shall decide what repairs are necessary'. The German Minister, Otto Langmann, pressed for the *Graf Spee* to be allowed to stay for 15 days: Langsdorff needed to make his ship seaworthy, but he wanted also to make her battleworthy. The British Minister, Eugene Millington-Drake, argued that since the *Graf Spee* had steamed at high speed for some 300 miles after the battle, she was clearly seaworthy and should not be allowed to remain for more than 24 hours. Langmann was told that Uruguay's technical experts would inspect the *Graf Spee*'s damage: Millington-Drake was reminded that in World War One the cruiser *Glasgow* had been allowed to dock in Rio for the best part of a week after the battle of Coronel.

The inspection took place on the 14th, after Langsdorff had freed his British prisoners and landed his dead and wounded. But before the Uruguayan Government had reviewed their experts' report, Harwood signalled Millington-Drake that he wanted the *Graf Spee* detained until his force was augmented by more than the *Cumberland,* by taking advantage of a *caveat* in the Hague Convention: 'a belligerent warship may not leave a neutral port less than 24 hours after the departure of a merchant ship flying the flag of her adversary.' So, whilst his naval attaché hastened to arrange for the ss *Ashworth* to leave Montevideo that evening, Millington-Drake had to ask for the pocket-battleship to be prevented from sailing before 1800 on the 16th.

This embarrassing *volte-face* was, however, superfluous: the Uruguyan Government decided to grant the *Graf Spee* an extension of 72 hours. But for Langsdorff this was a far from satisfactory solution: according to his sources the Plate was *already* blockaded by the *Renown* and *Ark Royal*, and his gunnery officer believed he could see these ships from the *Graf Spee*'s control tower. When he signalled this news to Berlin, he added that there was 'no prospect of breaking out into the open sea and getting through to Germany. If I can fight my way through to Buenos Aires I shall endeavour to do so'. But as this 'might result in destruction without possibility of causing damage to the enemy, request instructions whether to scuttle the ship or submit to internment'. Raeder answered: 'Attempt by all means to extend the time in neutral waters. Approved [to fight your way through to Buenos Aires if possible]. No internment in Uruguay. Attempt effective destruction if ship scuttled.'

Again Langmann pressed for the *Graf Spee*'s stay to be extended, but to no effect. Uruguay's determination to respect International Law, coupled with Millington-Drake's pressure, proved too strong. Early on the 17th Langsdorff accepted his fate: since the *Führer* had forbidden internment, the *Graf Spee* would leave Montevideo that evening. Before this, Harwood had judged from reports being broadcast by US radio commentators, who had flown to Montevideo, that he could rely on receiving news of any movement by the enemy. This had allowed him to concentrate the *Ajax, Achilles* and *Cumberland* ready to engage the *Graf Spee* as soon as she left territorial waters, using the same 'divided tactics' as on the 13th. 'My object destruction,' he signalled his captains; even so he estimated that the *Graf Spee* had a 70 per cent chance of escaping. But this was far from being Langsdorff's assessment; because he supposed the *Renown* and *Ark Royal* to be waiting for him, he believed he had no chance of breaking out. He would not send his officers and men to almost certain death; that might be the British tradition, as the gallant *Exeter* was destined to prove on 1 March 1942 after she had again been severely damaged in the battle of the Java Sea, but it was not the German.

Early on 17 December the pocket-battleship's secret documents and equipment were destroyed; scuttling charges were placed in several of her larger compartments; finally, 700 of her crew were transferred to the *Tacoma*, a German tanker lying in the Roads. Shortly after 1800 Langsdorff gave the order to weigh. Watched by a crowd of many thousands the *Graf Spee* left Montevideo, followed by the *Tacoma*. Four miles out she altered course sharply to the west, then stopped and again dropped anchor. There the time-fuses were set and Langsdorff and his skeleton crew left their ship in her own boats.

> It was a glorious evening with a vivid sunset [wrote the *Ajax*'s gunnery officer]. We were closed up and loaded, ready for whatever might come. We received the news that she had sailed. We could hear the Yankee broadcasters describing us as the suicide squadron with their little pop-guns! And then, enormous moment, at 2000, *Ajax*'s plane radioed '*Graf Spee* has just blown herself up'. We continued to close and gradually the burning hulk came up on the horizon. The Germans had made a very thorough job of it. She burned fiercely. Towards midnight we approached within a few miles of the pyre, then turned away.

Harwood and his officers and men could at last relax, secure in the certainty that the battle which they had fought four days before, had ended, as was always Nelson's ambition, in the annihilation of the enemy.

As the pocket-battleship sank in water so shallow that the tangled wreckage of her control tower, turrets and superstructure remained shrouded in smoke and fire, the *Tacoma* took Langsdorff and his skeleton crew on board. But her attempt to head for Buenos Aires was frustrated by an Uruguayan warship, which persuaded her to return to Montevideo after the *Graf Spee*'s crew had transferred to Argentine tugs. They expected to be welcomed in Buenos Aires and treated as shipwrecked seamen: instead Langsdorff was attacked by the press for not having gone down with his ship, whilst the Argentine Government decided that the *Graf Spee*'s complement should be interned instead of being allowed their freedom. So that evening he wrote three letters, to his wife, to his parents, and to the German Ambassador. According to the last of these:

> I reached the grave decision to scuttle the *Graf Spee* to prevent her falling into the hands of the enemy. With the ammunition remaining, any attempt to break out to open water was bound to fail. It was clear that this decision might be misinterpreted. Therefore I decided to bear the consequence. A captain cannot separate his own fate from that of his ship. I can do no more for my ship's company. I can only prove by my death that the fighting Services of the Third *Reich* are ready to die

for the honour of their flag. I shall meet my fate with firm faith in the cause and the future of the nation and my *Führer*.

Langsdorff then drew his revolver: he was found next morning lying dead on the German ensign.[1] His crew were held in internment camps until the Argentine joined the Allies in March 1945, when they became prisoners of war until February 1946, when some 900 were returned to Germany on board the liner *Highland Monarch*, escorted—a nice touch of irony—by HMS *Ajax*.

The *Altmark*'s ruthless Captain Dau ignored Langsdorff's order to land his 299 British prisoners in a neutral port: he waited far to the south until, on 22 January 1940, Berlin advised that it would be safe to run for home. He crossed the Equator on the 31st and eleven days later passed through the Denmark Strait: three more and the *Altmark* reached neutral Norway's territorial waters. A Norwegian torpedoboat boarded her on 15 February, but Dau refused to allow his ship to be searched; and because she was a naval auxiliary, the Norwegian captain decided that he could do no more. But the Royal Navy was determined to spare Dau's captives the rigours of a German prison camp. Learning on the evening of the 15th that the *Altmark* was off Bergen, Admiral Sir Charles Forbes, commanding Britain's Home Fleet, signalled Captain Q. D. Graham of the cruiser *Arethusa*, who was retiring with five destroyers from a sortie into the Skagerrak: '*Altmark* your objective'.

She was spotted next day, steaming down the Leads inside Norway's off-shore islands. Graham promptly ordered his destroyers to go after her, but these were prevented from boarding by Norwegian torpedoboats steaming close alongside until Dau had turned his ship into Jösing Fiord. She was there when, as darkness fell, Captain P. L. Vian came up in the *Cossack*. Informing the senior Norwegian officer that there were British prisoners on board, he demanded the right to search for them. The Norwegian replied that his orders were to resist, and trained his torpedo tubes on the *Cossack*. Vian sought the Admiralty's instructions: they came three hours later:

> Unless Norwegian torpedoboat undertakes to convoy *Altmark* to Bergen with a joint Anglo-Norwegian guard onboard and a joint escort, you should board *Altmark*, liberate the prisoners and take possession of ship. Suggest to Norwegian captain that honour is served by submitting to superior force.

For a man of Vian's character these words were enough. The Norwegian warships were soon persuaded to withdraw, leaving the *Cossack* to turn into Jösing Fiord. Dau turned a blinding searchlight on the British destroyer's bridge, then went full speed astern in an attempt to ram her. But to no avail; a damaging collision was avoided when the *Altmark* grounded by the stern. This allowed the *Cossack* to go alongside and send

over an armed boarding party. The *Graf Spee*'s guards offered resistance:
six were killed and six wounded before they escaped ashore. Then the
Altmark's hatches were broken open. 'Any British down there?' 'Yes,'
came a tremendous yell, 'We're all British.' The reply has become part of
the British tradition. 'Come on up then; *the Navy's here*!' The *Altmark*
had to be left in Jösing Fiord until Dau could free her stern and, under
cover of darkness, complete his return to Germany, while the *Cossack*
carried her prisoners, 13 officers and 286 seamen, back to the safety of
Leith.

The *Ajax* had already returned to England for repairs, and the *Achilles*
to New Zealand. And when the much-damaged *Exeter* finally reached
Plymouth Sound, Churchill gave this verdict to her company on the battle
which all three ships had fought so bravely:

> In this sombre dark winter the brilliant action in which you played a
> memorable part, came like a flash of light and colour on the scene,
> carrying with it an encouragement to ourselves and to our Allies. We
> congratulate you upon the fortune which enabled you to fight an action
> in the old style which will long be told in song and story, carrying us
> back to the great sea days of olden times. You have lost good comrades
> and shipmates, but you have come back having faithfully accomplished
> a worthy cause, with your honours gathered and your duty done.

The battle of the Plate may be counted a small one, but its place in any
selection from the many naval engagements of World War Two is assured
for more reasons than as an illustration of how much may be gained from
a study of history. It was not only the first naval action but one of the last
to be fought between ships alone, without radar's farseeing eye and in
which neither submarines nor strike aircraft were involved. Secondly, it
ensured that many months elapsed before Hitler again permitted Raeder
to risk his surface warships by allowing them out into the Atlantic to prey
upon the Allies' trade routes.

But long before the Plate there were other battles of a very different
kind which had as profound an effect upon the course of World War
Two; battles which took the form of prolonged arguments between ship,
aircraft and weapon designers, of fierce conflicts between Admiralties and
treasuries, above all of diplomatic negotiations between the principal
maritime Powers. To these this book now turns.

NOTES

[1] I am indebted to the American historian, Douglas H. Robinson, for this
lucid justification for Langsdorff's suicide: 'It is entirely consistent with
the *Götterdämmerung* complex. The Germans have a neurotic and patho-

logical sense of honour which the British, with their sense of humour, cannot comprehend. In Langsdorff's place a Britisher would have fought the ship till she sank regardless of superior numbers, and if he had survived, would have come aboard his captor's ship with a joke on his lips. For a German, the thought of losing a precious symbol of the *Reich* implied such overwhelming personal disgrace that suicide offered the only proper atonement. All the mystique with which the German invests such woolly abstract concepts as *Volk, Reich, Blut* and *Boden,* extends to the warship as a symbol of the national spirit—one reason why the High Seas Fleet was scuttled at Scapa in 1919.'

Contrast this with the story of the British submarine *Seal*. Driven aground in the Skaggerak by German patrol craft in May 1940, Lieutenant-Commander R. Lonsdale surrendered in order to avoid the useless sacrifice of the lives of his crew, a decision wholly in accord with the traditions of the world's Navies in the days of fighting sail. After five years as a prisoner-of-war Lonsdale was subjected to the customary ordeal of trial by court martial and honourably acquitted.

2 *Washington and London*

The first and most important of these battles of words was fought in Washington, D.C.

'The first satisfactory survey of the naval side of the war', was the kindly verdict of an eminent American chronicler[1] of post-1880 British naval history, of this author's *Naval Battles of the First World War*. Such a tribute by one who has added lustre to the crown worn by his compatriot, Admiral Alfred Mahan, has encouraged the production of this volume. But it cannot take the same form. Not only was World War One ended in four and a half years while World War Two continued for six, but if one omits fleeting encounters (such as that between units of the British and German Fleets on 17 November 1917), single ship actions and other minor engagements, there were less than half-a-dozen sea battles between 4 August 1914 and 11 November 1918.

In sharp contrast World War Two included some 40 sea battles. This book must, therefore, choose *some* of them; because they were major ones, because they had a marked effect on the course of the war, or because they are of other special interest. And there can be no space for such maritime operations as the seaborne invasions of North Africa, Italy, Normandy and the Pacific islands, notwithstanding their magnitude and their importance. So this volume is not intended to be a 'survey of the naval side of the war'.

There are other differences. In World War One the principal actors on the maritime stage were the great battle fleets of Britain and Germany: the Navies of Austria, France, Italy, Japan, Russia and Turkey played lesser roles, whilst the United States did not become involved until 1917. But in World War Two the Fleets of Britain, France, Germany, Italy, Japan and the United States all took part in one or more battles. (The Soviet Fleet was chiefly employed defending Leningrad in the Baltic, and in support of the Soviet Army along the Black Sea coast.) Secondly, the naval side of World War One could be divided into three phases without significant chronological overlap—overseas, British Home waters, and under the sea—because the first of these virtually ended off the Falkland

Islands in December 1914, and the second at Jutland on 31 May 1916, whilst the third did not really begin until after this date. The battles of the Second World War are, however, best divided into those fought in the Atlantic and the Mediterranean, and those fought in the Pacific Ocean, which overlap, the first covering September 1939 to May 1945 and the second from December 1941 to September 1945.

There is a further reason why this book must accord with its title. In the century which elapsed between the war against Napoleon and World War One, steam replaced sail, armoured hulls superseded wooden walls, 12-inch and larger guns succeeded 24- and 32-pounder cannon, submarines and aircraft were evolved, and the mine, torpedo and radio invented. Any comparison between the ships and weapons with which Jellicoe and Beatty fought Scheer and Hipper and those with which Nelson vanquished Villeneuve is, therefore, otiose. Moreover, although underwater weapons modified naval strategy—Cornwallis's and Nelson's close blockades of Brest and Toulon had to be replaced by Jellicoe's and Beatty's more distant one from Scapa Flow and Rosyth—the ship-of-the-line, in its dreadnought form, still reigned supreme. And in 1918 naval tactics were dominated as much by the gun as they had been by the cannon 100 years before.

But space must be found to explain why in 1939 the major Fleets were so small compared with those of 1805 and 1914. It must also chronicle the considerable changes in those Fleets between 1939 and 1945, notably the extent to which the aircraft-carrier replaced the battleship as the principal unit of naval power, and the technical progress which was so much greater than during World War One, notably such innovations as sonar and radar. For all these were of consequence to the naval battles of World War Two, explaining why, for example, the *Bismarck* was hunted down within a week in 1941, whereas von Spee's squadron was at large for four months in 1914, and why no comparison is possible between Jellicoe's tactics at Jutland and those with which Fletcher and Spruance vanquished Yamamato and Nagumo at Midway.[2]

To understand why the Fleets of the chief protagonists in World War Two were so small at the outset, one must go back to the year 1920; for it was then, some 12 months after the Treaty of Versailles, that the victorious Allies first determined their peacetime naval strengths. Britain, France, Italy, Japan and the USA did not have to take Austria or Germany into account. The last remnants of the Hapsburg Empire no longer extended to the Adriatic coast. The Peace Conference had deprived Germany of all but six pre-dreadnoughts, as many obsolescent cruisers and 24 destroyers, numbers which were not to be exceeded, with new construction restricted to battleship replacements as small as 10,000 tons and cruisers of 6,000 tons, when the existing ones were 20 years old, and to destroyers of 800 tons when these were 15.

For the remaining naval Powers the prime consideration was the number of capital ships to be retained, because the dreadnought was still queen of the maritime chess board. Britain had declared war in 1914 with 33; in November 1918 she emerged victorious with as many as 44, plus one under construction. By 1920 this figure had been reduced to 29 of which these were the most modern:

TABLE 2: Britain's Capital Ships in 1920

Class	No.	Completion date	Displacement (tons)	Main armament	Speed (knots)	Thickest armour
'Queen Elizabeth'	5	1915–16	27,500	8 15in	24	13in
'Renown'	2	1916	26,500	6 15in	32	6in
'Royal Sovereign'	5	1916–17	25,750	8 15in	21	13in
'Hood'	1	1920	41,200	8 15in	32	8in

Twenty-nine was the minimum number needed to defend Britain's world-wide interests against the fast-growing battle fleets of Japan and the USA. The latter was no longer willing to depend upon being able to use the seas under the protection of Britain's naval power, as she had done for more than a century. The former, though bound to Britain by an alliance dating from 1902, had made clear her intention of becoming the dominant nation in the Far East by her notorious Twenty-One Demands on China in 1915. Jellicoe had returned from a tour of the Dominions to recommend a British Far East Fleet headed by 16 capital ships: the Admiralty would require all of 29 to provide such a force in addition to fleets in Home waters and the Mediterranean. And to maintain this number they planned to lay down four 48,000 ton battlecruisers with nine 16-inch guns in 1921, to be followed by four 48,500 ton battleships with nine 18-inch guns.

Britain's cruiser force numbered 110 in 1914, 130 in 1918. By 1920 these were reduced to 90, the most numerous being the 4,000–5,000 tons 'C' and 'D' classes armed with 6-inch guns which had been the eyes of the Grand Fleet in the North Sea. But there were also five 'Hawkins', planned in 1917 to meet a possible German cruiser threat to the Allies' trade routes, which mounted seven 7·5-inch guns on 9,850 tons. Britain's 230 destroyers in August 1914 had grown to nearly 500. After the Armistice these were cut back to 200, almost all of the 1,075 tons 'S' and 'T' class with three 4-inch and four torpedo tubes, and the 1,275 tons 'V' and 'W' class with four 4-inch or 4·7-inch guns and six tubes. Britain's 80 sub-marines in 1914 had likewise increased to 165 in 1918, before being cut back to 100 in 1920. The best of these were the 13/10 knot[3] 'H' class of 440/500 tons[4] with four tubes and the 17/10 knot 'L' class of 890/1,080 tons with a 4-inch gun in addition to six tubes.

Britain had evolved during World War One the first of a new type of warship, one with hangars in which to stow wheeled aircraft and a flight deck from which they could fly off and land on. Two of these aircraft-carriers were in service in 1920, the 14,000 tons *Argus* carrying 20 planes, and the 22,450 tons *Furious* stowing 33. But the 22,600 tons *Eagle* was being built to carry 21 planes, and the 10,850 tons *Hermes* to carry 15. Moreover, the heavy cruisers *Courageous* and *Glorious* were earmarked for conversion in the same way as the *Furious*. With a prospective total of six, Britain's lead with this type of vessel was unchallenged; no other country had an aircraft-carrier in its Fleet, although Japan and the USA were each planning one.

By 1914 the USA had completed only ten dreadnoughts, but when a world war raised the need to protect her interests, to the extent of contemplating hostilities against Britain before Germany's flagrant disregard for the rights of neutrals tipped the scales, she increased this number, by 1918 to 16, and by 1920 to 19, of which these were the latest:

TABLE 3: The USA's Latest Capital Ships in 1920

Class	No.	Completion date	Displacement (tons)	Main armament	Speed (knots)	Thickest armour
'Nevada'	2	1916	27,500	10 14in	20	13½in
'Pennsylvania'	2	1916	31,400	12 14in	21	14in
'New Mexico'	3	1917–18	32,000	12 14in	21	14in
'California'	2	1920	32,300	12 14in	21	14in

There were also four 32,600 tons 'Maryland' class battleships building with eight 16-inch guns, which were to be followed by six of 43,200 tons with twelve 16-inch guns, and six 33 knot, 43,000 tons battlecruisers with eight 16-inch guns. Thus, after scrapping her six oldest dreadnoughts, the USA would have 29, as many as Britain, but most of them more heavily armed.

On the other hand the US cruiser force was singularly inadequate: in 1920 only 12 obsolete vessels with a best speed of 22 knots. Moreover, only ten more were under construction, the 7,050 tons 'Omahas' with 12 6-inch guns. Contrariwise, the US destroyer force numbered 300 vessels, most of these being 1,180 tons 'flush deckers' with four 4-inch guns and 12 torpedo tubes, whilst her submarine force numbered 120 boats comparable with the British 'H' and 'L' classes.

Japan, which had only emerged as a world Power at the turn of the century, but which had then proved her Fleet in the Russo-Japanese War, joined the Allies in 1914 with four dreadnoughts, a number increased by 1920 to the nine in Table 4, page 22. But as many as 16 more were projected; two 33,720 tons 'Mutsu' battleships armed with eight 16-inch guns, six larger ones with ten 16-inch guns, four battlecruisers with ten

TABLE 4: Japan's Capital Ships in 1920

Class	No.	Completion date	Displacement (tons)	Main armament	Speed (knots)	Thickest armour
'Settsu'	1	1912	21,400	12 12in	20	12in
'Kongo'	4	1913–15	27,500	8 14in	27	8in
'Fuso'	2	1915–17	30,600	12 14in	22	12in
'Ise'	2	1917–18	31,260	12 14in	23	12in

16-inch guns, and four of 41,000 tons likewise with ten 16-inch guns. In a few years' time Japan would have 24 such mighty dreadnoughts.

Her cruiser force was, however, as inadequate as the USA's; in 1920 a dozen vessels, all obsolete and slow, with six more under construction of 5,000–6,000 tons with seven 5·5-inch guns and eight torpedo tubes. Nor had Japan built the destroyers needed for a balanced fleet; she had fewer than 50, all smaller than the British 'S' boats; whilst her 50-odd submarines included few of ocean-going size.

The French and Italian Fleets were not of the same order. The former, which by 1914 had ceased to be the serious rival to Britain's that it had appeared to be 30 years earlier, had declined still further during World War One because France's dockyards had to give priority to meeting the needs of her hard-pressed Army. By 1920 only seven dreadnoughts, headed by the 23,500 tons 'Bretagne' class with 10 13·5-inch guns, had been completed, with little more to support them than a dozen obsolete cruisers, and a score of small destroyers, with double that number of submarines. Italy's Fleet was even smaller, with only five completed dreadnoughts, headed by the 22,700 tons 'Andrea Doria' class with 13 12·5-inch guns, supported by 12 cruisers, half of them obsolete, the others of only 3,500 tons with six 4·7-inch guns, 50 destroyers, and half that number of submarines.

All this is summed up in the following table indicating the sizes which these five Fleets seemed likely to achieve by the mid-1920s:

TABLE 5: The Forecast Fleets of the Principal Powers in 1925–6

Type	Britain	USA	Japan	France	Italy
Capital ships	29	29	24	7	5
Aircraft-carriers	6	1	1	—	—
Cruisers	90	20	20	12	12
Destroyers	200	300	50	20	50
Submarines	100	120	50	40	25

From this table two facts stand out. Although the Royal Navy's supremacy would remain with most vessels, not so with the type on which victory depended: her battle fleet would be no stronger than the USA's.

Even so, she was faced with having to maintain a larger battle fleet than she could afford after she had been impoverished by the immensity of her struggle with Imperial Germany. Secondly, because Britain needed to divide her capital ships between Home waters, the Mediterranean and the Far East, and the USA to divide hers between the Atlantic and the Pacific, Japan could meet either with a larger force.

However, World War One had done more than compel the USA to abandon its traditional policy of isolation. President Wilson had conceived the League of Nations as a means of settling future international problems. Unfortunately, Congress rejected membership of this potentially useful organization. (Few now remember that, in order to do so, Congress refused to ratify the Treaty of Versailles) with the anomalous consequence that the USA continued to be legally at war with Germany for more than two years longer than Britain, France, Italy and Japan—until Congress ratified a separate peace treaty on 18 October 1921.) The next administration could not, therefore, use the League to safeguard America's Philippine possessions and her considerable interests in China against Japan's hegemony over the western Pacific, which had been strengthened by the Versailles decision to grant her the lion's share of Germany's island colonies. Secretary of State Evans Hughes' solution was to invite the nine Powers concerned to attend a conference in Washington, DC.

There, Britain, France, Japan and the USA agreed to respect each other's rights in the Pacific. Britain accepted that this must end the Anglo-Japanese alliance, in part because Japan had proved a reluctant ally throughout the recent war, in part to facilitate the most important outcome of the conference. Determined to effect a drastic reduction in defence expenditure, whilst placating the element of US opinion which, for reasons of prestige, would not accept a Fleet smaller than Britain's, Hughes startled the delegates with proposals for limiting the Navies of the five principal maritime Powers. The outcome, after Britain's and Japan's considerable objections had been overcome, was the Washington Naval Treaty signed on 6 February 1922.

By this, the first disarmament treaty in all history, capital ships were limited to the following: Britain, 20, both by scrapping and by dropping her planned new ones, but with the concession that, because hers were older and less heavily armed than the USA's, two new ones might be built within the limitations detailed below: the USA, 18, by scrapping, and by completing only three 'Marylands' of her new construction programme: Japan, 10, by converting the *Settsu* to a target ship and completing only two 'Mutsus' out of her massive building programme: France, 7 (in fact 6 because one, lost by accident in 1922, was not replaced): Italy, 6 (in fact 5 because one, sunk in 1916 but subsequently refloated, was never restored to service).

B

With the aforementioned exception of two by Britain, no new capital ships were to be built except as replacements for existing ones when these were 20 years old. This would allow France and Italy to lay down new vessels in 1927, but save Britain, Japan and the USA from doing so until 1931. No new capital ship was to exceed 35,000 tons, nor mount guns larger than 16-inch. No existing capital ship was to be reconstructed, except with deck armour against air attack and anti-torpedo bulge protection not exceeding 3,000 tons. Total replacement tonnage was not to exceed: Britain and the USA, 525,000 tons; Japan 315,000 tons; France and Italy, 175,000 tons—known as the 5:5:3:2:2 ratio.

The total tonnages of aircraft-carriers were not to exceed: Britain and the USA, 135,000 tons; Japan, 81,000 tons; France and Italy, 60,000 tons. Each might build two vessels of up to 33,000 tons; the remainder were limited to 27,000 tons. None was to have an armament heavier than eight 8-inch guns, nor be replaced until it was 20 years old. No other warships were to be built in excess of 10,000 tons, nor have guns larger than 8-inch.

Japan was only persuaded to accept a smaller battle fleet than Britain's and the USA's because the other Powers agreed with her not to improve their existing bases, nor to establish new ones, in their Pacific possessions. These included British Hong Kong, but not Singapore; Japan's Formosa and the Pescadores, also the mandated Mariana, Caroline and Marshall Islands; and the USA's Aleutian Islands and Guam, but not the Hawaiian Islands. The restriction on the size and armament of 'other warships', in particular of cruisers and destroyers, which was satisfactory in so far as it would prevent the development of mini-battleships, and allow Britain to retain her 'Hawkins' class, but which was otherwise needlessly large, was the best compromise which the Conference could achieve in the face of France's implacable demand for total tonnages of cruisers and destroyers much in excess of those acceptable to the other Powers.

Up to the year 1930 this Treaty, which was to remain in force until the end of 1946 or until two years after any of its contracting Powers should give notice to terminate it, had the following consequences. Disillusioned by the enormity of the casualties which her Army had suffered in Flanders into believing that there could never be another major war, Britain signed away her long-held conviction that her island freedom, her world-wide Empire, and her vast seaborne trade depended on maintaining an adequate battle fleet. She was left with too few capital ships to provide a force in the Far East in addition to those she needed nearer home. She recognized Japan as a potential enemy only to the extent of starting to build a major naval base at Singapore, which would be defended by 15-inch guns against attack from the sea for the 90 days needed to bring a fleet east from the Mediterranean. (Defences were not provided against an overland attack across the Johore Strait, because it was believed that no army could make any progress through the Malayan jungle.)

No new capital ships were laid down, except for the 33,900 tons *Nelson* and *Rodney*, completed in 1927 with nine 16-inch guns, with armour as thick as 16 inches, and a speed of 23 knots. The clause limiting the reconstruction of existing ships was not so strictly observed. British capital ships had their bridges and control positions enlarged, a modification which required the *Queen Elizabeth*'s two funnels to be trunked into one. In US battleships not only were cage masts replaced by tripods in order to allow for larger bridges and control positions, but the elevation of their main armament guns was raised in order to increase their range from the previously accepted maximum of 24,000 yards to as much as 38,000 yards, a significant improvement in their offensive power against which Britain protested in vain. Japan went further; her capital ships, especially the 'Kongo' class battlecruisers, were extensively modernized, a breach of the Treaty which she successfully cloaked in secrecy until it was too late for the other signatories to protest.

Britain built up her aircraft-carrier strength to six by converting the 22,450 tons *Courageous* and *Glorious*, armed with 16 4·7-inch dual-purpose (DP) guns, each to carry 48 planes. But the USA, after converting the 11,050 tons collier *Langley* in 1922, did no more than complete two of her abandoned battlecruisers, each to carry 72 aircraft and eight 8-inch guns on a nominal 33,000 tons, but in fact more than 36,000. The Japanese likewise exceeded the Treaty limits; after completing the 7,470 tons *Hosho* to carry 21 aircraft, they converted the 38,200 tons *Kaga* and the 36,500 tons *Akagi* each to carry 90 aircraft and ten 8-inch guns, as well as laying down the 10,600 tons *Ryujo*. Except for France which produced the 22,100 tons *Béarn* to carry 40 aircraft, no other country built this type of ship.

Inevitably, all five Powers built cruisers of the maximum size with the largest gun allowed. Britain laid down seven 'Kents' of 9,880 tons armed with eight 8-inch guns, followed by six similar 'Londons', before a reaction set in against such expensive ships, the *York* and *Exeter* being designed to mount six 8-inch guns on 8,250 tons. The USA built two 9,100 tons 'Pensacolas' with ten 8-inch guns, then laid down six 'Northamptons' and two 'Indianapolis' mounting nine 8-inch guns on 9,950 tons. Japan laid down two 'Furatakas' and two 'Aobas' which mounted six 8-inch guns on some 7,000 tons, then four 'Myokos' and four 'Takaos' with ten 8-inch guns which violated the Treaty to the extent of displacing 13,380 tons. The French built three 7,300 tons 'Duguay-Trouins' with eight 6-inch guns, before laying down two 'Tourvilles', four 'Suffrens', and the *Algérie*, all of 10,000 tons, all with eight 8-inch guns, to match Italy's decision to build two 'Trentos' and four 'Zaras' of this nominal[5] size and armament, before reverting to the 5,200-ton 'Condottieris' with eight 6-inch guns and the high speed of 37 knots.

Britain had no need to begin a replacement programme of nine destroyers a year until 1928. Evolved out of the 'V's' and 'W's', these displaced 1,350 tons and mounted four 4·7-inch guns and eight torpedo tubes. For a comparable reason (her numerous 'flush-deckers' completed after the Armistice) the USA deferred a replacement programme until after 1930. Japan completed 34 of 1,300 tons mounting four 4·7-inch guns and six tubes, plus 12 of 820 tons mounting three 4·7-inch guns and four tubes, before beginning 24 of the 'Fubuki' class which displaced 2,090 tons and were armed with six 5-inch guns and nine tubes. She was not alone in building such large vessels: in addition to completing 26 of the 'Simoun' and 'Alcyon' classes, which were similar to the British, the French laid down the 2,126 tons 'Tigres' with five 5-inch guns, and followed them with many more of 2,440 tons and a speed of nearly 40 knots to outmatch Italy's twelve 'Navigatoris' of 1,940 tons and 38 knots armed with six 4·7-inch guns.

Britain began replacing her ageing submarine force with nine of the 15/9 knot 'O' class, which were improved 'Ls' of 1,350/1,870 tons, followed by six of the slightly larger 'P' class. The USA was content to build only six new boats, but the Japanese completed more than 50, of which the 16/8 knot 'RO60' class of 996/1,322 tons with one 3-inch gun and six 21-inch tubes, and the 20/8 knot 'I153' class of 1,800/2,300 tons with one 4·7-inch gun and eight tubes, were typical. Italy built four of around 1,450/1,904 tons and 12 of around 900/1,000 tons, a programme that was more than matched by France.

In this same period, 1922–30, outside the orbit of the Washington Treaty but of consequence to the Second World War, a new German Fleet was born. Four cruisers were completed within the Versailles limits, three 'Karlsruhes' of 6,650 tons armed with nine 6-inch guns plus the slightly smaller *Emden*. But 12 new destroyers exceeded the Treaty limits; armed with three 4-inch guns and six tubes, these displaced 933 tons. More significant, however, were two other German developments. As soon as 1922 a 'top secret' submarine construction office was established at The Hague under cover of a Dutch firm; and in 1928 the prototype of a new class of U-boat emerged from a Spanish yard, followed by another from a Finnish one. By 1930 Germany was ready to start production of these craft as soon as the ban imposed at Versailles might be overcome. How she solved her other pressing problem, the replacement of her obsolete pre-dreadnoughts, has been told in Chapter One.

The following table (which should be compared with Table 5 on page 22) summarizes the Fleets of the principal Powers involved in World War Two as they were in 1930, the figures in parenthesis indicating ships under construction:

TABLE 6: The World's Principal Fleets in 1930

Type	Britain	USA	Japan	France	Italy	Germany
Battleships	16	18	6	6	4	—
Battlecruisers	4	—	4	—	—	—
Pocket-battleships	—	—	—	—	—	(1)
Aircraft-carriers	6	3	3 (1)	1	—	—
Cruisers with 7·5 and 8-inch guns	20 (3)	5 (5)	8 (4)	6	2 (4)	—
Other cruisers	40	10	21	9	6 (5)	6 (1)
Destroyers	146 (10)	230	120	70 (10)	75 (15)	25
Submarines	50 (10)	100 (6)	60 (10)	60 (35)	65 (10)	—

But this picture, in which Britain's Navy just—but only just—retained the premier place that it had held for nearly a century and a half, was not to stand for long.

The ink was no sooner dry on the Washington Treaty than the maritime Powers began further discussions on total tonnage limits for cruisers and, potentially more important, on the abolition of submarines. A conference held at Geneva in 1927 failed to reach agreement; but the achievements of the next one were substantial because the world was by then in the trough of a severe economic depression. Britain and the USA needed to escape the expense of laying down the new capital ships to which they would be entitled in a year's time, just as France and Italy had yet to begin their authorized replacements. By the London Naval Treaty, signed by the five Washington Powers on 22 April 1930, not only did Britain, Japan (reluctantly) and the USA agree to defer laying down new capital ships until 1936, and France and Italy decide to lay down no more than the two which they were already allowed, but the first three Powers accepted further reductions: Britain to 15, by scrapping the *Tiger* and three 'Iron Dukes', retaining the *Iron Duke* herself as a demilitarized training ship; the USA to 15, by scrapping two 'Utahs' and retaining the *Wyoming* as a training ship; and Japan to 9, by disarming the battlecruiser *Hiei*.

The extent to which Britain reduced her numerical strength (by five ships) as compared with the USA (by three ships) and, even more so, with Japan (by only one) will be noted. But this was far from being her only step towards finally sacrificing the vestiges of her naval supremacy. A myopic Labour Government over-rode the Admiralty's insistence on a minimum of 70 cruisers, and accepted the limits tabulated on next page. For Britain this involved more than accepting a smaller number of 8-inch cruisers than the USA, and the need to replace the 7·5-inch guns in her 'Hawkins' class with smaller ones. Since an adequate vessel armed with 6-inch guns could not be built on less than 5,000–6,000 tons, her total cruiser strength would be cut to 50. Fortunately these limits were not to be effective until the end of 1936, by which time much had happened to deter

Type	Britain	USA	Japan
With guns larger than 6-inch	Not more than 15, totalling 146,800 tons	Not more than 18, totalling 180,000 tons	Not more than 12, totalling 108,400 tons
With 6-inch or smaller guns	192,200 tons	143,500 tons	100,450 tons
Total	339,000 tons	323,500 tons	208,850 tons

such a drastic reduction. France and Italy resisted the Conference's attempt to limit their cruiser strengths by refusing to accept a figure as low as 100,000 tons.

In the same ratio of 3:3:2, Britain and the USA agreed total tonnage limits for destroyers of 150,000, and Japan 105,000, with none exceeding 1,850 tons or armed with guns larger than 5-inch. Britain's only compensation for reducing her strength to below 100 vessels was a clause allowing the unlimited construction of ships such as sloops, which were not to exceed 2,000 tons, mount more than four guns up to 6-inches, nor have a speed greater than 20 knots. But, as with cruisers, France and Italy rejected any limit on their destroyers.

In their desire to achieve the abolition of submarines, Britain, Japan and the USA agreed total tonnage limits as low as 52,700, with none exceeding 2,000 tons surface displacement, which required each of them to cut their forces to some 35 boats. But, again, neither France nor Italy would accept any restriction on what they insisted was an essential weapon for a lesser naval Power. However, all five signatories confirmed that 'with regard to merchant ships, submarines must conform to the rules of International Law to which surface vessels are subject'—a clause of singularly little value to the future since the one Power, Germany, which had consistently violated it during the First World War was no party to it.

All this would have reduced the Fleets of the principal Powers to the following by the end of 1936:

TABLE 7: The Forecast Fleets of the Principal Powers in 1936-7

Type	Britain	USA	Japan	France	Italy	Germany
Battleships	12	15	6	6	5	—
Battlecruisers	3	—	3	—	—	—
Pocket-battleships	—	—	—	—	—	3
Aircraft-carriers	6	4	4	1	—	—
8-inch cruisers	15	16	12	8	10	—
Other cruisers	35	10	17	12	14	8
Destroyers	160	220	120	65	80	24
Submarines	35	35	35	110	75	—

But events proved most of these figures to be of little more than academic interest, because the London Treaty was not destined to be the only decisive influence on naval developments during the 1930s.

Germany's decision to build pocket-battleships impelled France to lay down the battlecruiser *Dunkerque*, of 26,500 tons armed with eight 13-inch guns, followed three years later by her sister-ship, the *Strasbourg*. Not to be outdone, Italy laid down two 'Littorios' which, by exceeding the Washington Treaty limit by more than 6,000 tons, carried enough armour as well as nine 15-inch guns at 28 knots to be typed as fast battleships.

In 1933 Japan gave fresh indications of her intention to dominate the Far East by occupying Manchuria in defiance of the League of Nations from which she then withdrew. She followed this with notice to terminate her adherence to the Washington and London Treaties so that she might begin building up her Fleet to equality with Britain and the USA. Fascist Italy's hostility impelled France to emulate Japan's example early in 1935. So the five-Power conference called in December of that year to limit future capital ships to 35,000 tons with no guns larger than 14-inches, and future cruisers to 8,000 tons with nothing bigger than 6-inches, had only limited success, especially after Japan had withdrawn her deputation and publicly announced that she intended to ignore all restrictions.

Of more immediate importance, Nazi Germany, having repudiated the Versailles Treaty, negotiated an agreement with Britain, which limited her surface tonnage to 35 per cent of Britain's, but with parity in submarine tonnage. Next, in 1935 Italy waged war against Abyssinia in defiance of the League. By requiring Britain to concentrate the bulk of her Fleet at Gibraltar and Alexandria to deal with a second-class naval Power, this made abundantly clear the extent to which the Treaties, and the no-war-for-ten-years rule (enunciated by the British Cabinet for the guidance of the Services Ministries reasonably enough in 1919, but in 1928 imposed on a continuing basis by a Treasury headed, with fearful irony for the future, by none other than Winston Churchill, and not revoked until 1933) had dangerously eroded her naval strength.

Belatedly, but before the London Treaty had become fully effective, she began to rearm, not because of Japan's potential threat to her Far East possessions, but chiefly to protect her homeland against a Germany whose *Führer* made his aggressive intentions clear in 1936 by his seizure of the Rhineland. Not long afterwards the USA also began to build up her Fleet, chiefly with an eye to Japan, who, having embarked on a war of aggression in China in 1937, recklessly bombed and sank the American gunboat *Panay* and two tankers on their 'lawful occasions' in the river Yangtse. All this and more, notably Germany's seizure of Austria in 1938, which prompted the Munich crisis in September, had the following consequences up to the outbreak of the Second World War.

Britain quickly laid down five 35,000 tons 'King George V' class fast battleships armed with ten 14-inch guns and 16 5·25-inch DP guns instead of the previously accepted separate low-angle (LA) and anti-aircraft (AA) secondary armaments. These were followed, after Japan had rejected the Treaty limits, by four 40,000 tons 'Lions' which were to mount nine 16-inch guns. The USA's programme was headed by two 'North Carolina's' and four 'South Dakotas', fast battleships of 35,000 tons whose construction was fortuitously delayed for long enough for their main armament to be changed from 14-inch guns to nine 16-inch. Even so, they were outclassed by Japan's four 'Yamatos' whose immense size, 64,800 tons, and heavy armament of nine 18-inch guns, was for long concealed from the rest of the world. In the same years France began four 'Richelieus' of 35,000 tons with eight 15-inch guns, and Italy a second group of two 'Littorios', while Germany turned from pocket-battleships to building two 'Scharnhorst' battlecruisers of 31,800 tons with nine 11-inch guns, followed by two 'Bismarcks', fast battleships of 41,700 tons with eight 15-inch guns, and the first of six projected vessels of 56,000 tons with eight 16-inch guns.

Simultaneously, Britain began to modernize her existing capital ships by giving them more armour, increasing the range of their 15-inch guns, mounting 5·25-inch DP weapons in place of separate LA and AA secondary armaments, replacing their tripod masts and tops and their armoured conning towers with massive bridge structures as in the 'Nelsons', and by giving them new engines and boilers. The *Warspite* and *Renown* were completed before war broke out; the *Queen Elizabeth* and *Valiant* were finished in 1940. The USA, having already partially modernized the *Arkansas,* two 'Texas', two 'Oklahomas' and two 'Pennsylvanias', now increased their AA armament to 12 5-inch, and modernized her three 'New Mexicos'. France rebuilt her three 'Bretagnes', Italy her two 'Cavours' and two 'Andrea Dorias'. But Japan did most in the time available; not only were all her nine capital ships extensively modernized, but the demilitarized *Hiei* was restored to combat service. All this is summarized in the following Table 8 for September 1939 in which ships in parenthesis are those building. Not until 1935 could Britain lay down a new aircraft-carrier, the *Ark Royal* of 22,000 tons with 16 4·5-inch DP guns and as many as 72 aircraft in her two hangar decks. But she was followed by four of the 'Illustrious' class, which were similar vessels embodying a significant innovation, a hangar with $4\frac{1}{2}$-inch side armour and a 3-inch deck: this halved their aircraft capacity but was to have a value all its own when the war came. The 14,750 tons *Unicorn* designed to carry 35 planes, was also begun. The USA's first addition to her small carrier force was kept within the Washington limits, the *Ranger* which managed to stow as many as 86 planes on a displacement of only 14,500 tons. But with the expiry of the Treaties, three 20,000 tons 'Yorktowns' were laid down, each to carry 100 aircraft, followed by a reversion to the 'Ranger'

TABLE 8: Capital Ships of the Principal Powers in 1939

Type	Britain	USA	Japan	France	Italy	Germany
Battleships completed before 1936 and *not* modernized	Barham Malaya Ramillies Resolution Revenge Royal Oak Royal Sovereign Nelson Rodney **9**	California Tennessee Colorado Maryland West Virginia — — — **5**	— — — — — — — —	Courbet Océan Paris — — — — **3**	— — — — — — — —	— — — — — — — — —
Ditto modernized or being modernized	Queen Elizabeth Valiant Warspite — — — — **3**	Arkansas New York Texas Nevada Oklahoma Pennsylvania Arizona New Mexico Mississippi Idaho **10**	Fuso Yamashiro Hyuga Ise Mutsu Nagato — **6**	Bretagne Lorraine Provence — — — **3**	Conte di Cavour Giulio Cesare Andrea Doria Caio Duilio — — **4**	— — — — — —
Battlecruisers completed before 1936 and *not* modernized	Repulse Hood **2**	— —	— —	— —	— —	— —

B*

TABLE 8—continued

Type	Britain	USA	Japan	France	Italy	Germany
Battle cruisers completed before 1936 and modernized	*Renown* —	— —	*Haruna* *Hiei* *Kirishima* *Kongo*	— —	— —	— —
	1	—	4			
Fast battleships to be completed after 1935	*King George V* *Prince of Wales* *Duke of York* *Anson* *Howe* 4 'Lions'	*North Carolina* *Washington* *South Dakota* *Indiana* *Massachusetts* *Alabama*	*Yamato* *Musashi* — —	*Clemenceau* *Gascogne* *Jean Bart* *Richelieu* —	*Littorio* *Vittorio Veneto* *Impero* *Roma* —	*Bismarck* *Tirpitz* 2 unnamed —
	9	6	2	4	4	4
Battle cruisers completed after 1935	— —	— —	— —	*Dunkerque* *Strasbourg*	— —	*Gneisenau* *Scharnhorst*
				2		2
Pocket-battleships	— — —	— — —	— — —	— — —	— — —	*Deutschland* *Admiral Graf Spee* *Admiral Scheer*
						3
Totals	15 (+9)	15 (+6)	10 (+2)	8 (+4)	4 (+4)	5 (+4)

type in the USS *Wasp*, while the *Langley* was reduced to an aircraft tender. Japan completed the 10,600 tons *Ryujo* to carry 48 planes and two 'Soryus' of some 16,000 tons, each for 73 planes. Significantly, but unnoticed by the other Powers, four high speed oilers and five NYK liners were designed so that they could be speedily converted into aircraft-carriers. France laid down the *Joffre* and *Painlevé* of 18,000 tons, each with space for 40 aircraft. Germany began the *Graf Zeppelin* of 23,000 tons to carry 40 planes. Italy continued to find no use for this type of ship, as is shown in Table 9 summarizing these programmes up to September 1939.

Having built eight 7,000 tons 'Leanders' armed with eight 6-inch guns, Britain began four 5,220 tons 'Arethusas' with only six in order to provide a sufficient number of cruisers within the London tonnage limits. Rearmament produced eight 9,100 tons 'Southamptons' mounting 12 6-inch guns, followed by two slightly larger 'Edinburghs'. The 1935–36 Conference required a new design, 11 'Fijis' with the same armament on 8,000 tons, but which in the event displaced 8,800. At the same time, to counter the growing threat of air attack, a new class of 11 'Didos' was begun with ten 5·25-inch DP guns on 5,770 tons. Older cruisers retained in service included not only the post-war 8-inch vessels but 23 of the 'C', 'D' and 'E' classes (of which six were rearmed as AA cruisers with eight 4-inch AA guns), plus three 'Hawkins',[6] of which the *Effingham* was rearmed with nine 6-inch guns.

After completing her allowance of 8-inch cruisers by building seven 'Astorias' plus the *Wichita*, the USA laid down nine 10,000 tons 'Brooklyns' armed with as many as 15 6-inch guns. Japan, having already fulfilled her 8-inch quota, built four 'Mogamis' mounting 15 6-inch guns on as little as 8,400 tons, but after denouncing the Treaties, these were followed by two 11,215 tons 'Tones' mounting eight 8-inch guns. In the same period Japan began to add to her stock of smaller cruisers by laying down four 6,652 tons 'Aganos' mounting six 6-inch guns. France completed the 5,886 tons cruiser-minelayer *Emile Bertin* and six 7,600 tons 'La Galissonnières', all with nine 6-inch guns; then laid down the *De Grasse* to have the same armament on 8,000 tons. Italy, having completed six 5,200 tons 'Condottieris' with eight 6-inch guns, laid down four larger ones with the same armament followed by two with ten 6-inch. Germany completed the 6,710 tons *Leipzig* and the 6,980 tons *Nürnberg*, both armed with nine 6-inch guns, before laying down the 13,900 tons *Admiral Hipper* and *Blücher* with eight 8-inch, followed by the *Lützow*, *Prinz Eugen* and *Seydlitz* with the same armament on 14,800 tons.

All this is summarized in Table 10 for September 1939.

The large destroyers built by other Powers impelled Britain to lay down 16 1,870 tons 'Tribals' with eight 4·7-inch guns but only four torpedo tubes, followed by the 1,690 tons 'J' and 'K' classes with six 4·7-inch DP guns and eight tubes. To provide vessels faster than her 34 sloops for

TABLE 9: Aircraft-carriers of the Principal Powers in 1939

Type	Britain	USA	Japan	Italy	France	Germany
Aircraft-carriers built up to 1930	Argus Furious Eagle Hermes Courageous Glorious	Lexington Saratoga	Hosho Kaga Akagi Ryujo		Béarn	(Graf Zeppelin)
Aircraft-carriers laid down after 1930	Ark Royal (Illustrious) (Victorious) (Formidable) (Indomitable)	Ranger Yorktown Enterprise (Hornet) (Wasp)	Hiryu Soryu (Shokaku) (Zuikaku)		(Joffre) (Painlevé)	
Ships laid down for rapid conversion into aircraft-carriers			(9)			
Totals	7 (+4)	5 (+2)	6 (+2+9)		1 (+2)	(1)

TABLE 10: Cruisers of the Principal Powers in 1939

Type	Britain	USA	Japan	France	Italy	Germany
Cruisers laid down before 1922	3 'Hawkins' Adelaide 13 'C' class 8 'D' class 2 'E' class 27	10 'Omaha' — — — 10	2 'Tenryu' 5 'Kuma' 6 'Nagaro' Yubari 14	— — — —	Taranto Bari — 2	— — — — —
Post-Washington cruisers with guns larger than 6-inch	13 'County' 2 'Cathedral' — — 15	2 'Pensacola' 6 'Northampton' 2 'Indianapolis' 7 'Astoria' Wichita 18	2 'Furataka' 2 'Aoba' 4 'Myoko' 4 'Takao' 2 'Tone' 14	2 'Duquesne' 4 'Suffren' Algérie 7	2 'Trento' 4 'Zara' Bolzano 7	Admiral Hipper Blücher (Lützow) (Prinz Eugen) (Seydlitz) 2 (+3)
Post-Washington cruisers with 6-inch or smaller guns	8 'Leander' 4 'Arethusa' 8 'Southampton' 2 'Edinburgh' (11 'Dido') (11 'Fiji') 22 (22)	9 'Brooklyn' — — — 9	4 'Mogami' 3 'Sendai' (4 'Agano') — — 7 (4)	3 'Duguay Truin' Jeanne d'Arc Emile Bertin 6 'La Galissonnière' (De Grasse) 11 (1)	12 'Condottieri' — — — 12	Emden 3 'Karlsruhe' Leipzig Nürnberg 6
Totals	64 (+22)	37	35 (+4)	18 (+1)	21	8 (+3)

trade protection, 15 'V' and 'W' destroyers were rearmed with AA guns, and a new 'Hunt' class of 900–1,100 tons destroyer escorts armed with four or six 4-inch AA guns, was begun. The USA began her replacement programme in 1932 with eight 1,395 tons 'Farraguts' with five 5-inch guns and eight tubes, followed by eight 1,850 tons 'Porters' mounting as many as eight 5-inch guns. Next, however, came 18 1,500 tons 'Fannings' with five 5-inch DP weapons and 12 tubes; then five improved 'Porters'. By September 1939 there were building 22 1,500 tons 'Cravens', 12 1,570 tons 'Sims' and the first of the 1,620 tons 'Benson-Livermores', all with DP guns.

Japan built destroyers such as the 1,580 tons 'Shiratsuyus' with five 5-inch DP guns and the 2,033 'Kageros' with six, both with eight tubes, whilst continuing to find a use for small ones of some 800 tons, mounting three 4·7-inch guns and three tubes. France added to her 2,100 tons 'Tigres' as many as 24 more 37 knots vessels of some 2,500 tons, mounting five 5·5-inch guns and laid down seven 'Mogadors' of nearly 3,000 tons to mount eight 5·5-inch guns plus ten tubes. She also built more conventional destroyers of 1,378–1,772 tons mounting four or six 5-inch guns and six or seven tubes, and small boats of 600–1,010 tons with two or four 4-inch guns and two or four tubes. Italy having completed 15 large vessels, turned to building the 1,640 tons 'Maestrales' with four 4·7-inch guns and six tubes; also a sizeable number of small ones, such as the 800 tons 'Spica' class with three 4-inch guns and four tubes. In 1934 Nazi Germany began the 38 knots 2,200 tons 'Leberecht Maass' class mounting five 5-inch guns and eight tubes.

After completing three 'R' class (repeat 'Ps') submarines, three 'Thames' with the high surface speed of 22 knots, and six larger minelayers submarines, Britain concentrated on three new types, chiefly for operations in the confined waters of the North Sea and Mediterranean; the 670/960 tons 'S' class with one 3-inch gun and six tubes, the 1,090/1,575 tons 'T' class with one 4-inch gun and 10 tubes, and the 540/730 tons 'U' class with one 3-inch gun and only four tubes. With an eye to the Pacific, the USA laid down 30 larger boats, mostly of the fast 'S' class of 1,435/2,210 tons with one 4-inch gun and eight tubes, and the 'T' class of 1,475/2,370 tons with one 5-inch gun and 10 tubes. Japan was so much concerned to provide her boats with an endurance of 16,000 miles and the ability to remain at sea for 90 days, that she concentrated on fast types ranging from 1,570/2,330 tons with one 4-inch gun and six torpedo tubes, up to as much as 2,525/3,583 tons with one 5·5-inch gun and six tubes. Moreover, to improve their scouting role, a number of these carried a small floatplane in a hangar before or abaft the conning tower.

France's advocacy of submarines for a lesser naval Power was matched by her building programme. Boats laid down ranged from 558/787 tons with one 3-inch gun and three torpedo tubes for coastal work, by way of 1,384/1,570 tons ocean patrol types with one 4-inch gun and eleven tubes, up to the 3,250/4,304 tons submarine cruiser *Surcouf* with two 8-inch guns and 12 tubes, plus a floatplane carried in a hangar abaft the conning tower. Italy was even more prolific with new submarines, chiefly of two types, 700/840 tons boats with one 4-inch gun and six tubes, and 1,500/2,000 tons large ones with two 4·7-inch guns and eight tubes. But Germany restricted her initial programme to boats of only 250/330 tons with speeds of 13/7 knots armed with three torpedo tubes, and larger ones of 500/650 tons with speeds of 16/8 knots, with one 3·5-inch gun and five tubes, of which 57 were completed by September 1939, with as many more on the slips.

The states of the Fleets of the six major maritime Powers when Britain and France declared war on Germany were, therefore, as follows:

TABLE 11: The Fleets of the Principal Powers in 1939

Type	Britain	France	USA	Germany	Italy	Japan
Capital ships	15 (9)	8 (4)	15 (6)	5 (4)	4 (4)	10 (2)
Aircraft-carriers	7 (4)	1 (2)	5 (2)	(1)	—	6 (2+9)
Cruisers	64 (22)	18 (1)	37	8 (3)	21	35 (4)
Destroyers	192 (28)	70 (30)	214 (38)	48 (14)	112 (4)	104 (18)
Submarines	59 (14)	78 (27)	95 (10)	57 (50)	104 (11)	57 (13)

Comparison with Table 7 on p 28 shows considerable increases over the numbers to which the Treaties had aimed to reduce these Fleets. But none could compare in size, especially in capital ships and cruisers, with the great Fleets with which Britain and Germany had gone to war in 1914.

NOTES

[1] Arthur Marder in *From the Dreadnought to Scapa Flow*.

[2] One more difference deserves a footnote. The author was only a child during World War One, but he served ashore and afloat in the Royal Navy throughout World War Two.

[3] The first figure is the surface speed and the second the speed when submerged.

[4] The first figure is the surface displacement and the second the displacement when submerged.

[5] 'Nominal' because the 'Zaras' exceeded the Treaty limit by some 1,500 tons as Britain discovered in 1936 when, to Mussolini's embarrassment, the *Gorizia* suffered an internal explosion whilst anchored off Tangier and had to be docked at Gibraltar for emergency repairs.

[6] Of the original five, the *Raleigh* was lost by stranding in fog on the coast of Newfoundland, and the *Vindictive* underwent successive conversion into an aircraft-carrier, then into a cadet training ship, and finally into a repair ship.

3 World War Two

The major Fleets were not destined to remain so small for very long. There were more naval battles during World War Two than those which were won and lost on the high seas. A very different but nonetheless vital one was fought in the shipyards of the maritime Powers.

Britain completed her five 'King George V' class battleships, but cancelled her four 'Lions' because their slips could not be spared when it was unlikely that the ships would be finished before the end of hostilities. The *Vanguard* was laid down in the hope that, by using the four 15-inch turrets removed from the *Courageous* and *Glorious*, she might be completed in time.

TABLE 12: Capital Ships Built by Britain During World War Two

Ship	Completion date	Displacement (tons)	Main armament (guns)	Speed (knots)	Thickest armour
Prince of Wales	3/1941				
King George V	11/1941				
Duke of York	11/1941	38,000	10 14in	29	16in
Anson	6/1942				
Howe	8/1942				
Vanguard	(1946)	44,500	8 15in	30	16in

Britain's losses included the *Royal Oak* torpedoed as soon as 14 October 1939 by *U47*, in which Lieutenant Güther Prien skilfully navigated one of the entrances to Scapa Fow, the *Hood* sunk by the *Bismarck* off Iceland on 23 May 1941, the *Barham* torpedoed by Lieutenant von Tiesenhausen in *U331* off the Libyan coast on 25 November 1941, and the *Prince of Wales* and *Repulse* sent to the bottom of the South China Sea by Japanese aircraft on 10 December 1941. With the *Royal Sovereign* loaned to the USSR (and renamed *Archangelsk*) from early in 1944, Britain's capital ship strength was reduced to 14, with one more on the stocks.

In sharp contrast she not only commissioned her four 'Illustrious' class aircraft-carriers and the *Unicorn,* but recognized their now vital role to the extent of laying down nine more armoured ones, plus as many as 24 of a simpler design, of which two and six respectively were operational before VJ day.

TABLE 13: Aircraft-carriers Built by Britain During World War Two

Ship or class	No.	Completion date	Displacement (tons)	Speed (knots)	Aircraft capacity
Fleet carriers:					
Illustrious	1	5/1940			
Formidable	1	11/1940			
Victorious	1	5/1941	23,000	31	36
Indomitable	1	10/1941			
Indefatigable	1	5/1944	26,000	32	72
Implacable	1	8/1944			
'Audacious'	4	—	36,800	31	100
'Gibraltar'	3	—	45,000	32	100+
Light fleet carriers:					
Unicorn	1	3/1943	14,750	24	35
'Colossus'	10	6 in 1945	13,190	25	48
'Majestic'	6	—	14,000	24	34
'Hermes'	8	—	18,300	29	50

Using merchant ship hulls and machinery, mostly built in the USA under Lend-Lease, as many as 43 escort carriers were also commissioned, the majority being of the 17 knots, 11,420 tons 'Ruler' class which carried 24 planes. Although intended for convoy work, these were also used for such tasks as providing fighter protection over the Salerno beachhead in 1943, and to help drive the Germans out of the Aegean in 1944.

Losses included the *Courageous* torpedoed by Lieutenant-Commander Schuhart in *U29* in the South-Western Approaches as soon as 17 September 1939, the *Glorious* to gunfire from the *Gneisenau* and *Scharnhorst* off Norway on 8 June 1940, the *Ark Royal* torpedoed to the east of Gibraltar by Lieutenant-Commander F. Guggenberger in *U81* on 13 November 1941, the *Hermes* sunk off Ceylon by Japanese planes on 9 April 1942, the *Eagle* torpedoed by Lieutenant-Commander H. Rosenbaum in *U73* to the east of Gibraltar on 11 August 1942, and four escort carriers, plus one transferred to the French. So, having begun the war with seven aircraft-carriers, Britain ended it with this number of fleet carriers, plus as many building, seven light fleets plus 18 building, and 38 escort carriers, a remarkable achievement, especially when one considers not so much the large number of planes needed for them, because most were provided by the USA under Lend-Lease, but the many trained pilots required to fly them, all British.[1]

As well as completing her 11 'Fiji' and 11 'Dido', Britain laid down eight 'Minotaurs' which sacrificed one triple 6-inch turret for a heavier AA armament, and completed five modified 'Didos' which likewise sacrificed one 5·25-inch turret.

TABLE 14: Cruisers Built by Britain During World War Two

Class	No.	Completion date	Displacement (tons)	Main armament (guns)	Speed (knots)
'Fiji'	11	5 in 1940 3 in 1942 3 in 1943	8,000	12 6in	33
'Minotaur'	8	1 in 1944 2 in 1945	8,800	9 6in	32
'Dido'	11	8 in 1940 2 in 1941 1 in 1943	5,450	10 5·25in DP	33
Modified 'Dido'	5	1943	5,770	8 5·25in DP	33

Britain's losses numbered five 8-inch cruisers (the *York* torpedoed in Suda Bay, Crete, by Italian one-man torpedoboats on 26 March 1941, the *Exeter* by Japanese gunfire after the battle of the Java Sea, on 1 March 1942, the *Cornwall* and *Dorsetshire* by Japanese aircraft off Ceylon on 5 April 1942, and HMAS *Canberra* in the battle of Savo Island on 9 August 1942) and 25 smaller ones (three in 1940, eight in 1941, nine in 1942, one in 1943, and four in 1944). Britain was thus left with the same number of cruisers, 64, as that with which she began the war, but with only five more on the stocks. In truth, at no stage of the war did she have enough, for all that this figure came near to the Admiralty's minimum of 70. Though fewer might be required for fleet work because aircraft performed the scouting duties for which such ships had been needed in World War One, many more were required for trade protection. To remedy this in 1939 Britain requisitioned 56 passenger liners for quick conversion into armed merchant cruisers mounting from six to nine 6-inch guns, of which 15 were lost before they could be released for other duties, notably as troopships.

If Britain was short of cruisers, how much more was this true of destroyers. The USA came to her help in August 1940 by 'trading' 50 of her old 'flush deckers' (of which 10 were lent to the USSR in 1944) in return for the right to establish bases in British western Atlantic possessions. In her own yards Britain completed eight 'Ls', plus eight 'Ms' and eight 'Ns', likewise armed with six 4·7-inch guns and eight or 10 torpedo tubes. She then ordered 10 flotillas, each of eight boats, mostly of 1,730 tons armed with four 4·7-inch guns and eight tubes, and acquired one similar flotilla building for the Brazilian and Turkish Navies, before laying down four more flotillas armed with four 4·5-inch DP weapons, three of which were still on the stocks on VJ day. Moreover, in 1942 the Admiralty realized that none of these was adequate for operations in the Pacific; they lacked the necessary endurance and required a more powerful AA armament. The following were, therefore, ordered: 40 2,400 tons 'Battles' with four or five 4·5-inch DP guns and 10 tubes, 20 1,980-tons 'Weapons' with six 4-inch AA guns and 10 tubes, eight 2,000 tons 'Gs' with four 4·5-inch DP guns and 10 tubes, and 20 2,610 tons 'Darings' with six 4·5-inch DP guns and 10 tubes; but of all these only five 'Battles' were complete by VJ day. As many as 86 'Hunt' class destroyer escorts were also built for convoy work, whilst the old 'V' and 'W' boats were adapted for this task by the removal of their quarterdeck gun and one set of tubes so that they could mount an AA gun and carry more depth charges, or by the removal of one boiler, reducing their speed to 24 knots, to allow space for more fuel tanks and increase their endurance.

Against so many additions must be set these considerable losses: four in 1939, 36 in 1940, 22 in 1941, 53 in 1942, 17 in 1943, 20 in 1944, three in 1945—a total of 155. Although 20 were also transferred to the Dutch, Greek and Polish Navies, Britain ended hostilities with the satisfactory figure of 268, with 93 more on order.

For much of the war Britain was content to build her already proven submarine classes. Forty-two 'S' boats, as many 'Ts', and 68 'Us' (of which some were given 'V' names), were completed between September 1939 and September 1945, with 38 more on the stocks. Because none of these was really suitable for Pacific operations, 46 of a new 1,120/1,620 tons 'A' class of 18/8 knots, armed with one 4-inch gun and 10 tubes, were ordered, but too late to be completed before VJ day. Losses numbered one in 1939, 23 in 1940, 10 in 1941, 16 in 1942, 15 in 1943, five in 1944, and one in 1945, a total of 71. Seven World War One 'H' boats had to be scrapped, whilst a dozen other boats were transferred to Allied Navies: nonetheless, by VJ day Britain had as many as 122 submarines, plus 80 more on order.

The story of the French Fleet during World War Two is a chequered one. For the first nine months, up to France's surrender, her ships and submarines fought with Britain's against Germany, and for the final two and a half years, after the Allies had reached agreement with the French authorities in North Africa, they again fought against the Axis Powers. During the intervening period a handful of vessels fought on under the Cross of Lorraine, whilst others sought refuge in British ports or accepted immobilization in Alexandria and at Martinique, but the majority were deployed between Toulon and French ports in North Africa to serve the interest of the puppet Vichy Government. The consequences were tragic: new construction was brought to a virtual standstill whilst her Fleet suffered greater losses by Allied action than by the Axis, notably during the British bombardment of Mers-el-Kébir on 3 July 1940, and in vain attempts to repel the Allied landings in North Africa on 8 November 1942. The latter impelled Hitler to send his troops into Vichy France when, rather than that they should fall into German hands or sail to join the Allies, Admiral Darlan ordered all his ships lying in Toulon and Hyères to be scuttled on 27 November 1942.

Of France's new capital ships only the *Richelieu* was finished in time to sail for Dakar before the Germans captured Brest, though the *Jean Bart* escaped on two shafts to Casablanca where, with only one turret mounted, she served as a floating fort until she was so severely damaged during the US attack in November 1942 that she could not be repaired until the war was over. The *Bretagne* was sunk in Mers-el-Kébir by the gunfire of Britain's Force H in July 1940; the *Provence* and *Dunkerque* were effectively scuttled in Toulon in November 1942; the salvaged *Océan* and *Strasbourg* were sunk by Allied aircraft during 1944; the *Courbet* was expended to help form the artificial harbour off the Normandy beach-head in 1944. Thus France, which had begun the war with eight capital ships, plus four on the stocks, emerged from her ordeal with only three, plus the unfinished *Jean Bart*.

The *Béarn*, after being released from Martinique early in 1943, was judged to be too slow for further use as an aircraft-carrier and was converted into a transport: in her place France acquired the escort carrier *Dixmude*. Only three 8-inch cruisers survived the war (the *Algérie*, *Colbert*, *Foch* and *Dupleix* were scuttled in Toulon), plus five 6-inch cruisers and the unfinished *De Grasse* (five having been lost). In addition to completing eight new destroyers before the débâcle of June 1940, France gained seven built later in the USA, but since her losses numbered 57, she was left with only 28. Similarly, although she acquired three submarines from Britain, her losses numbered 59, leaving only 20, albeit with three hulls remaining on the stocks.

Germany lost all her capital ships of which, in addition to three pocket-battleships, only the following were finished:

TABLE 15: Capital Ships Built by Germany Post-1935

Ship	Completion date	Displacement (tons)	Main armament (guns)	Speed (knots)	Thickest armour
Gneisenau	1938	} 31,800	9 11in	32	14in
Scharnhorst	1938				
Bismarck	1941	41,700	8 15in	29	14in
Tirpitz	1941	42,900	8 15in	29	14in

The *Admiral Graf Spee* was scuttled after the battle of the Plate; the *Bismarck* and *Scharnhorst* succumbed to the guns of Britain's Home

Fleet, the former in the Atlantic on 27 May 1941, the latter off North Cape on 26 December 1943; the *Tirpitz* and *Admiral Scheer* were destroyed by RAF bombs, the first in Tromsö Fiord on 12 November 1944, the second at Kiel on 9 April 1945; the already damaged *Gneisenau* and *Deutschland* (renamed *Lützow* in 1940) were scuttled, the one in Gdynia on 29 March 1945 and the other in Swinemünde on 16 April 1945.

Germany never acquired a naval air arm. Construction of the *Graf Zeppelin* was suspended in 1940 and the unfinished hull was scuttled at Stettin in 1945; a sister ship was scrapped on the slips within a year of her keel being laid down at the end of 1939; conversion of the cruiser *Seydlitz* was never completed. The 8-inch cruiser *Prinz Eugen* was finished in 1940, but construction of her two sister-ships was abandoned, the *Lützow* after her transfer to the USSR in 1940. Nine 6-inch vessels laid down after 3 September 1939 were scrapped before launching. The 8-inch cruiser *Blücher* succumbed to Norwegian guns and torpedoes in Oslo Fiord on 9 April 1940, but the *Admiral Hipper* survived until she was scuttled on 3 May 1945. Two 6-inch cruisers were lost in 1940 and one in 1945 when three surrendered to the Allies.

To provide ships to prey upon the Allied trade routes Germany skilfully converted 11 18-knots merchant vessels into disguised commerce raiders armed with six 6-inch guns and four torpedo tubes, of which—to cite three—the *Atlantis* sank or captured 22 vessels totalling 145,697 tons in the Atlantic, Indian and Pacific Oceans during a cruise that lasted from 31 March 1940 until 22 November 1941, when she was sunk by the 8-inch cruiser *Devonshire*, and the *Kormoran* which sank the Australian 6-inch cruiser *Sydney* in the Indian Ocean on 19 November 1941 before she herself succumbed, whereas the *Komet* after sinking only six ships during her first 15 months' cruise in the Pacific, was sunk in the English Channel on 14 October 1942 at the outset of her second.

In the destroyer category Germany completed 45 vessels after the outbreak of war, many armed with 6-inch guns, before abandoning another score whilst they were still on the stocks; but her losses numbered 62 so that only 31 surrendered to the Allies. Her surface fleet was, indeed, always so small that it could not hope to win the war at sea. It was, nonetheless, of a size that required Britain to keep a battle fleet based on Scapa Flow, both to maintain control of her Home waters and to counter any sortie against Atlantic or Arctic convoys, with the consequence that, when Italy joined the war and France surrendered, she could not match the Japanese Navy in the Far East in addition to deploying fleets at both ends of the Mediterranean.

The saga of Germany's U-boats is a very different one: in the hope that these might gain the victory which they had come near to winning in 1917–18, Raeder and his successor, Admiral Karl Dönitz, devoted the bulk of their ship-building resources to their mass-production. Most typical was the 769/871 tons Type VIIC of 18/7 knots with one 3·5-inch gun and five torpedo tubes. Not until 1944, too late for any to be finished before VE day, did they turn to building the 1,621/1,819 tons Type XXI with the same armament but the very different speeds of 15/17 knots.

Consider these figures:

TABLE 16: German U-boats Built and Lost During World War Two[2]

Year	Number commissioned	Number lost	Final strength
1939	64	9	55
1940	54	26	83
1941	202	38	247
1942	238	88	397
1943	290	245	442
1944	230	264	408
1945	93	139	362
Totals	1,171	809	—

Two hundred more were building when Germany surrendered. Sixty-five worked in the Mediterranean, some 40 in the South Atlantic and 30 in the Indian Ocean. Almost all the rest were employed in the Western Approaches and across the Atlantic to the shores of North America. They sank nearly 3,000 Allied vessels grossing over 14 million tons. They lost 27,491 officers and men out of a force of some 55,000. To defeat them, especially in the crucial year of the battle of the Atlantic, 1943, Britain and the USA had to build, requisition, convert and man not only a large number of escort carriers and destroyers, but an armada of other anti-submarine craft—sloops, frigates, corvettes, trawlers etc.—as well as building an enormous number of new merchant ships to replace those which were lost.

Italy added three fast battleships to her capital ship strength (the *Impero* was still unfinished by the armistice of 1943 after which she was used by the Germans as a target ship and sunk in 1945):

TABLE 17: Italian Capital Ships Completed During World War Two

Ship	Completion date	Displacement (tons)	Main armament (guns)	Speed (knots)	Thickest armour
Littorio (renamed *Italia* in July 1943)	8/1940	41,377	9 15in	28	14in
Vittorio Veneto	8/1940	41,167	9 15in	28	14in
Roma	11/1942	41,650	9 15in	30	14in

Up to the armistice Italy lost only one battleship beyond repair, the *Cavour* in the British attack on Taranto on 12 November 1940, but the

Roma was sunk by German aircraft on 9 September 1943 when on her way to surrender to the Allies.

In July 1941 a large liner was taken in hand for conversion into Italy's first carrier, the *Aquila,* to suffer the same fate as the *Impero.* A smaller liner, on which conversion into an escort carrier was begun in November 1942, fared no better. Late in 1939 13 3,747 tons cruisers of the 'Capitani Romani' class were laid down, to be armed with eight 5·5-inch guns and with the high speed of 43 knots. One was finished in 1942 and two in the early months of 1943, by which time work on five more had been abandoned. Of the remainder, one hull was sunk by a British 'chariot' (human torpedo) in Palermo, two were destroyed by Allied air attack and another scuttled at the time of the armistice, leaving two to be completed after the war. Two 6,000 tons vessels building for Siam were requisitioned for service as AA cruisers and armed with six 5·5-inch guns, only to be scuttled in September 1943 when 60 per cent complete. Other cruiser losses were heavy; all seven 8-inch vessels (the *Fiume, Pola* and *Zara* at the battle of Matapan on 28 March 1941, the *Trento* to a torpedo from the British submarine *Umbra,* Lieutenant S. L. C. Maydon, on 15 June 1942, the *Trieste* by Allied air attack on 19 April 1943, the *Gorizia* scuttled at the time of the armistice, and the *Bolzano* sunk whilst in German hands by an Italo-British 'chariot' attack on Spezia on 21 June 1944), and eight out of 14 6-inch vessels (one in 1940, three in 1941, two in 1942 and two in 1943).

Some 50 destroyers were laid down after Italy joined the war, but only six had been completed by the time of the armistice, after which a dozen more were finished by the Germans. Losses were very heavy, as many as 74 in action with British forces before the armistice and some 30 more as a consequence of that débâcle. Twelve submarines of 2,190/2,600 tons were designed for transporting essential war materials from Japan, of which only two were finished. Twelve new boats of 714/860 tons were completed in 1941–42; so, too, were eight of 905/1,068 tons. Losses exceeded 90 before the armistice and numbered nearly 20 after it. Thus Italy emerged from World War Two with a Fleet cut down to five battle-ships, 13 cruisers, some 30 destroyers and half that number of sub-marines, which she was required to surrender by the terms of a peace treaty which divided them between the Allies. The USSR exacted her pound of flesh, notably the battleship *Guilio Cesare* (renamed *Novorossisk*) and the 6-inch cruiser *Duca D'Aosta* (renamed *Stalingrad*), but Britain, France and the USA allowed her to keep their shares in return for the help which she gave to the Allies during the latter part of the war.

Japan completed only two 'Musashi' battleships; a third was converted into an aircraft-carrier, and the fourth cancelled. Two planned 32,000 tons battlecruisers were also cancelled.

TABLE 18: Japanese Capital Ships Completed During World War Two

Ship	Completion date	Displacement (tons)	Main armament (guns)	Speed (knots)	Thickest armour
Yamato	12/1941	64,170	9 18in	27	20in
Musashi	12/1942				

All but one of her 12 capital ships were lost; the *Hiei* and *Kirishima* by US air and surface attack off Guadalcanal in November 1942, the *Mutsu* by an accidental magazine explosion in June 1943, the *Fuso, Yamashiro* and *Musashi* by gunfire and torpedoes in the battle of Leyte Gulf in October 1944, the *Kongo* by the submarine *Sealion II*, Commander E. T. Reich, on 7 April 1945, and the *Haruna,* plus the *Hyuga* and *Ise* (which had been converted into hybrid aircraft-carriers) by US carrier planes whilst in Kure dockyard in July 1945. Only the *Nagato* survived to surrender on VJ day.

Japan completed, chiefly by converting other vessels, notably liners and fast tankers, the large number of aircraft-carriers, listed in Table 19 on the next page.

To these 25 aircraft-carriers, there must be added the hybrid battleships *Hyuga* and *Ise,* each of which had a hangar and flight deck substituted for her two after turrets in 1943. There were, moreover, another dozen vessels undergoing conversion at the time of Japan's surrender. But although she entered the war with a carrier force stronger than the USA's, and although her shipyards completed nearly a score of new ships after the crucial attack on Pearl Harbour, she suffered losses so crippling, first in 1942 and subsequently in 1944, that only three finished vessels remained to be surrendered on VJ day.

In sharp contrast there were few additions to Japan's cruiser force. In 1939–40 she rearmed her four 'Mogamis' with 10 8-inch guns, which increased their displacement to 12,400 tons. Her four 6-inch 'Aganos' were finished in 1942–43; but of the small handful laid down post-1939 only the *Oyodo*, a modified 'Agano' of larger tonnage with six 6-inch guns, was completed in 1943. Four 8-inch cruisers were lost to US forces in 1942 (the *Mikuma* in the battle of Midway, the *Kako* in the battle of Savo Island, the *Furataka* in the battle of Cape Esperance, and the *Kinugasa* in the battle of Guadalcanal), eight in 1944 (the *Atago, Chikuma, Chokai, Maya, Mogami* and *Suzuya* in the battles of Leyte Gulf, the *Nachi* by US carrier aircraft in Manila Bay, and the *Kumano* by the same means off Luzon), and in 1945 three to British forces (the *Haguro* torpedoed in a night destroyer attack off Penang on 16 May, the *Ashigara* torpedoed off Sumatra on 8 June by Commander A. R. Hezlet in the submarine *Trenchant,* and the *Takao* whilst berthed in the Johore Strait on 31 July when the British midget submarines *XE1* and *XE3*

TABLE 19: Japanese Aircraft-carriers

Ship	Displacement (tons)	Speed (knots)	Aircraft capacity	Fate
Completed before 7/12/41				
Hosho	7,470	25	21	
Kaga	38,200	28	90	Sunk in battle of Midway 4/6/42
Akagi	36,500	31	91	do.
Ryujo	10,600	29	48	Sunk in battle of East Solomon Sea 24/8/42
Hiryu	17,300	34	73	Sunk in battle of Midway 4/6/42
Soryu	15,900	34	73	do.
Shokaku	25,675	34	84	Sunk in battle of Philippine Sea 19/6/44
Zuikaku	25,675	34	84	Sunk in battles of Leyte Gulf 25/10/44
Completed after 7/12/41				
Shoho (1942)	11,262	28	30	Sunk in battle of Coral Sea 8/5/42
Zuiho (1942)	11,262	28	30	Sunk in battles of Leyte Gulf 25/10/44
Chuyo (1942)	17,830	21	27	Sunk by US submarine Sailfish 4/12/43
Taiyo (1942)	17,830	21	27	Sunk by US submarine Rasher 18/8/44
Unyo (1942)	17,830	21	27	Sunk by US submarine Barb 16/9/44
Hiyo (1942)	24,140	25	53	Sunk in battle of Philippine Sea 20/6/44
Junyo (1942)	24,140	25	53	
Rhyho (1942)	13,360	26	31	
Chiyoda (1943)	11,190	29	30	Sunk in battles of Leyte Gulf 25/10/44
Kaiyo (1943)	13,600	24	24	Sunk by US bombers in Beppu Bay 10/8/45
Shinyo (1943)	17,500	22	33	Sunk by US submarine Spadefish 17/11/44
Chitose (1944)	11,190	29	30	Sunk in battles of Leyte Gulf 25/10/44
Taiho (1944)	29,300	33	53	Sunk in battle of Philippine Sea 19/6/44
Shinano (1944)	64,800	27	47	Sunk by US submarine Archerfish 29/11/44
'Unryu' class (1 in 1944 3 in 1945)	17,150	34	65	Unryu sunk by US submarine Redfish 19/12/44 Amagi, Aso and Ikoma destroyed by US aircraft in Kure dockyard 24/7/45

skilfully navigated the 40 mile passage to the British-built dockyard and gained two VCs for their tiny crews), and two to US carrier aircraft whilst in Kure dockyard (the Aoba and Tone, both in July), leaving only the already heavily damaged *Myoko* to be surrendered in September 1945. Smaller cruiser losses were as heavy; two in 1942, two in 1943, 13 in 1944 and three in 1945, leaving only two to be surrendered.

Japan augmented her destroyer force with 20 'Yugumos' of 2,077 tons armed with six 5-inch guns and eight torpedo tubes, 12 'Akitsukis' of 2,701 tons armed with eight 4-inch guns and four tubes, and 40 'Matsus' of 1,262 tons armed with three 5-inch guns and four tubes. But against these she lost four in the last month of 1941, 16 in 1942, 33 in 1943, 61 in 1944, and 17 in 1945, so that few more than 50 remained to be surrendered.

With submarines Japan fared little better. She added as many as 150, ranging from the small 'Ha201' class of 377/440 tons and 10/13 knots, armed with two torpedo tubes and intended for coast defence, to the giant 'I400' class of 5,223/6,560 tons and 18/6 knots, armed with one 5·5-inch gun and eight tubes, plus a catapult and a hangar large enough to stow three small torpedo-bomber planes. Most were, however, of around 2,500/3,500 tons and 23/8 knots, armed with one 5·5-inch gun and six to eight tubes, with stowage for one catapult-launched plane or one or more midget submarines. A number was also specially built or converted for running supplies to Japanese forces in their occupied Pacific islands when US operations made it too hazardous to employ surface craft. Losses numbered three in 1941, 16 in 1942, 27 in 1943, 53 in 1944 and 30 in 1945, so that 78 remained to be surrendered.

The USA followed her two 'North Carolina' and four 'South Dakota' battleships with six 'Iowas', of which four were finished, and six 'Alaska' class battlecruisers, of which two were completed by VJ day.

TABLE 20: Capital Ships Built by the USA During World War Two

Ship	Completion date	Displacement (tons)	Main armament	Speed (knots)	Thickest armour
North Carolina	8/1941	35,000	9 16in	28	18in
Washington	3/1942				
South Dakota	8/1942	35,000	9 16in	28	18in
Indiana	10/1942				
Massachusetts	/1942				
Alabama	11/1942				
Iowa	2/1943	45,000	9 16in	33	19in
New Jersey	5/1943				
Missouri	6/1944				
Wisconsin	4/1944				
Alaska	6/1944	27,500	9 12in	33	13in
Guam	9/1944				

Losses beyond repair were limited to the *Oklahoma* and *Arizona* in the attack on Pearl Harbour on 7 December 1941. The USA was, therefore, left with as many as 25 capital ships at the end of the war in the Pacific, plus three on the stocks.

Only the three 'Yorktown' aircraft-carriers were completed before the USA was drawn into the war. Not until Pearl Harbour was the value of this type of vessel fully appreciated when she pressed on with an augmented construction programme begun in 1940:

TABLE 21: Aircraft-carriers Built by the USA During World War Two

Ship or class	No.	Completion date	Displacement (tons)	Speed (knots)	Aircraft capacity
Fleet carriers:					
Yorktown	1	1939	19.900	34	100
Enterprise	1	1939	19,900	34	100
Hornet	1	1941	20,000	34	100
Wasp	1	1941	14,700	29	84
'Essex'	32	1 in 1942	27,100	33	100
		6 in 1943			
		6 in 1944			
		4 in 1945			
'Midway'	3	—	45,000	33	137
Light fleet carriers:					
'Independence'	9	5 in 1943	11,000	33	45
		4 in 1944			
'Saipan'	2	—	14,500	33	48

In addition the USA commissioned nearly 80 escort carriers similar to the British manned 'Ruler' class.

Her losses were heavy in 1942; the veteran *Lexington* at the battle of Coral Sea on 8 May, the *Yorktown* by the Japanese submarine *I168* on 7 June after the battle of Midway, the *Wasp* torpedoed by *I19* south of Guadalcanal on 15 September, and the *Hornet* at the battle of Santa Cruz on 26 October. Thereafter they were limited to the light fleet *Princeton* at the battles of Leyte Gulf on 24 October 1944, plus six escort carriers. Since many new ships were cancelled on the stocks when victory seemed assured, the USA ended World War Two with a total of 20 fleets plus 11 building, eight light fleets plus two building, and some 70 escort carriers with 10 building.

Cruisers laid down, a few after the outbreak of war in Europe, mostly after Pearl Harbour, were of the four types listed in Table 22 on page 51.

Losses were limited to seven 8-inch vessels (the *Houston* to Japanese gun and torpedo fire in the Sunda Strait on 1 March 1942, the *Astoria*, *Quincy* and *Vincennes* likewise off Savo Island on 9 August 1942, the *Northampton* torpedoed during the battle of Tassafaronga on 30 November 1942, the *Chicago* torpedoed by Japanese aircraft in the Solomon Islands on 30 January 1943, and the *Indianapolis* torpedoed by

TABLE 22: Cruisers built in the USA during World War Two

Class	No.	Completion date	Displacement (tons)	Main armament (guns)	Speed (knots)
'Baltimore'	24	2 in 1943 3 in 1944 8 in 1945	13,600	9 8in	33
'Des Moines'	4	—	17,000	9 8in	33
'Cleveland'	40	5 in 1942 7 in 1943 8 in 1944 6 in 1945	10,000	12 6in	33
'Atlanta'	11	4 in 1942 1 in 1943 2 in 1944 1 in 1945	6,000	16 or 12 5in DP	32

the Japanese submarine *I58* in the Philippine Sea on 29 July 1945), plus the 6-inch *Helena* in 1943, and the 5-inch *Atlanta* and *Juneau* in 1942. Allowing for 19 ships whose construction was cancelled when victory was assured, the USA ended the war with 74 cruisers, plus 13 on the stocks.

With the construction of destroyers the USA surpassed all other combatants. The 'Craven' and 'Sims' classes were completed before Pearl Harbour, and by the end of 1943 the number of 'Benson-Livermores' in commission had risen to 96. These were followed by 179 of the larger 'Fletcher' class of 2,050 tons armed with five 5-inch guns and 10 torpedo tubes, and 58 of the 'Allen M. Summer' class of 2,200 tons armed with six 5-inch guns and 10 tubes. The first of the 2,425 tons 'Gearing' class, with the same armament, were then laid down, but none was finished by VJ day. Beginning in 1941, five classes of destroyer escorts were built, the 1,400 tons 'Buckleys' of 23 knots with three 3-inch guns and three torpedo tubes contributing the largest number. In all some 400 were commissioned, excluding 56 converted into high-speed transports: the rest were cancelled in June 1944. Losses numbered 25 in 1941–42, 17 in 1943, 24 in 1944 and 16 in 1945, a total of 82. After allowing for the 50 'four stackers' transferred to Britain in 1940, the USA emerged from World War Two with the massive total of 850 destroyers, with another 105 on the stocks.

Having completed 16 'S' class and 12 'T' class submarines before Pearl Harbour, the USA met her war needs with the 1,525/2,415 'Gato' class of 20/10 knots armed with one 5-inch gun and ten tubes, of which 165 were commissioned before VJ Day, leaving 30 on the stocks, and the 1,570/2,415 'Tench' class with the same speed and armament, of which only half-a-dozen reached completion, leaving 30 on the stocks. Losses were relatively few, 8 in 1941–42, 17 in 1943, 19 in 1944 and 8 in 1945, a total of 42. The USA's submarine force at the end of World War Two numbered 242, with 60 building.

All this, the transformation of the world's major Fleets during World War Two, is summed up in the following table in which figures in parenthesis are ships under construction.

TABLE 23: The Fleets of the Principal Maritime Powers during World War Two

Type	Date	Britain	France	USA	Germany	Italy	Japan
Capital	3.9.39	15	8	15	5	4	10
ships	6.40[a]	14	9	15	4	4	10
	12.41[b]	13	8	16	5	5	10
	31.12.42	15	6	19	5	6	10
	9.43[c]	15	6	21	5	6	9
	31.12.44	14	3	25	3	5[g]	5
	5.45[d]	14	3	25	0	5[g]	4
	9.45[e]	14(1)	3(1)	25(3)	–	5[g]	1
Aircraft-	3.9.39	7	1	5	0	0	6
carriers	6.40[a]	6	1	5	0	0	7
(all types)	12.41[b]	11	1	8	0	0	8
	31.12.42	11	1	5	0	0	10
	9.43[c]	23	0	36	0	0	10
	31.12.44	48	0	62	0	0	3
	5.45[d]	46	1	82	0	0	6
	9.45[e]	52(25)	1	99(23)	–	0	2
Cruisers	3.9.39	64	18	37	8	21	35
	6.40[a]	64	18	37	6	21	35
	12.41[b]	67	18	37	6	14	35
	31.12.42	57	12	39	6	16	29
	9.43[c]	63	12	45	6	15	27
	31.12.44	61	9	60	6	13[g]	8
	5.45[a]	61	9	70	3	13[g]	8
	9.45[e]	64(5)	9(1)	74(13)	–	13[g]	3
Destroyers	3.9.39	192	70	214	48	112	104
	1945[f]	268(93)	28	850(105)	31	30[g]	53
Submarines	3.9.39	59	78	95	57	104	57
	1945[f]	122(80)	20(3)	242(60)	362(200)	16[g]	78

Notes: a. i.e. immediately prior to France's surrender.
  b. i.e. immediately before the Japanese attack on Pearl Harbour.
  c. i.e. immediately before the Italian surrender.
  d. i.e. immediately before the German surrender.
  e. i.e. immediately before the Japanese surrender.
  f. i.e. for Germany immediately before her surrender, for the other nations immediately before Japan's surrender.
  g. Almost all under Allied control.

From these figures three points stand out. First, the USA achieved its cherished ambition, the world's strongest Fleet, whilst Britain's was relegated to second place. Secondly, the Fleets of Germany and Japan were annihilated, and those of France and Italy much reduced in strength. Last but not least, as much as anywhere on the high seas World War Two was won in the shipyards of the USA and Britain which, in addition to building and repairing so many warships and merchant ships, also created the armadas of landing craft of diverse size and kind needed for amphibious operations. Although these fall outside the limits of this book, without them the Allied armies could not have invaded Italy in 1943 and France in 1944, nor the Japanese-held Pacific islands from 1942 onwards, which leaves the sobering reflection that had the war against Germany continued for longer than May 1945, it might have been won in the submarine construction yards of the Third *Reich*.

NOTES

[1] The Royal Navy's Fleet Air Arm was also required to provide the aircrews for 19 large merchant ships (Macships) which, for convoy protection, were fitted with flight decks and carried fighter and A/S patrol aircraft in addition to their normal cargo.

[2] *U-Boote im Einsatz (U-boats in action)* by Bodo Herzog. Another authority gives a total of 1,162 commissioned and 785 sunk, with 156 surrendered and 221 scuttled by their crews on VE Day.

4 *Progress, 1919 - 1945*

Man needed four centuries to transform the *Henri Grâce à Dieu* into the *Warspite*, which not only survived 'Hell-Fire-Corner' at Jutland but helped save the day when the Allied armies were in difficulties on the Salerno beach-head in September 1943. Contrariwise, man was given little more than 100 years to produce the airships of 1914 out of the Montgolfiers' balloon, and only 10 in which to devise better war planes than the aircraft in which the Wright brothers first flew. It is not, therefore, surprising that Scheer's Zeppelins and Jellicoe's floatplanes were fragile and slow. But although the weather denied to both their allotted role on 31 May 1916, such primitive machines were used at sea in World War One to an extent exemplified by Britain's strength in 1918; 2,300 fighters, spotter-reconnaissance machines and torpedo-bombers, some to operate from the Grand Fleet's aircraft-carriers and off the turrets of its dreadnoughts, but many more from 100 shore stations around Britain and the Mediterranean, chiefly for anti-submarine (A/S) patrol and convoy escort.

The Treaty of Versailles denied Germany all forms of warplane for more than a decade. Public apathy and stringent peacetime limits on defence expenditure, coupled with a continuing belief in the big gun as the paramount weapon, reduced the naval air arms of the other maritime Powers to the low figures required to equip the small number of aircraft-carriers in their Fleets, plus a mere handful of shore-based planes. These factors also discouraged the development of machines much better than the 'sticks and string' Sopwith Camels of the Royal Naval Air Service in 1917. Nonetheless, France, Japan and the USA so far recognized the need for shore-based as well as carrier-borne planes for use with their Fleets as to treat them as integral components. Their Navies were free to develop and provide the most suitable machines and, as important, to train their crews in their maritime tasks. Japan took the fullest advantage of this freedom : in December 1941 hers was the largest, best equipped and best trained naval air arm, with more than 1,200 planes of which half were carrier-borne—with near-disastrous consequences for both Britain, whose

Fleet Air Arm counted only 340 planes and Coastal Command only 194 in 1939, and the USA who, by 1941, counted fewer than 1,000, both carrier-borne and shore-based for maritime tasks.

In sharp contrast, the Fleets of Germany and Italy were handicapped by being wholly dependent on their *Luftwaffe* and *Regia Aeronautica,* for which maritime operations were always of secondary importance[1]—fortunately for the Allies in view of the success with which the former sometimes attacked the British Fleet, notably in the Mediterranean. Britain was only marginally better off, her Fleet being dependent on the Royal Air Force for all except the crews of its ship-borne planes until a few months before the outbreak of World War Two. After 20 years of bitter argument to reverse the 1918 absorption of the RNAS into a separate RAF, the Admiralty then regained control of its ship-borne machines, but too late to develop and produce adequate ones of its own. Throughout the coming war most of the Fleet Air Arm's needs had to be met either by modifying RAF machines (*e.g.* the Seafire fighter which was a Spitfire adapted for carrier work) or from the USA. But for shore-based planes Britain's Fleet continued to be wholly dependent on Coastal Command which was so much the Cinderella of the RAF that, for example, in September 1939 it could provide nothing for maritime operations outside Home waters except for a single reconnaissance squadron in the Mediterranean. It was as slow to meet the Royal Navy's need for shore-based long range fighters and strike aircraft. And even after the Government conceded the strength of the Navy's case half way through World War Two, to the extent of giving it operational control of all maritime aircraft, Coastal Command was denied many of the long-range planes for which the Admiralty appealed to the Air Ministry again and again in order to ensure victory in the crucial battle of the Atlantic, on which all other operations against Germany depended. In the damning words of one distinguished British admiral, referring more specifically to the early years of the conflict: 'The war effort was impeded by the RAF giving absolute priority to bombing Germany, co-operation with the other Services taking very much second place'.[2]

Typical of the aircraft available for working with the British Fleet in September 1939 were the following (* indicates ship-borne machines):

TABLE 24: Typical British Maritime Aircraft in 1939

Type	Year entered service	Purpose	Max. speed (mph)	Max. range miles	Armament	Weapon load (lbs)
Anson	1936	Reconnaissance	188	790	2 mg	360
Sea Gladiator*	1936	Fighter	253	410	4 mg	—
Skua*	1937	Fighter and dive-bomber	225	760	5 mg	740
Swordfish*	1937	Torpedo-bomber and spotter-reconnaissance	138	546	2 mg	1,610
Walrus*	1937	Spotter-reconnaissance	135	600	2 mg	—

C

How much better were the planes available on the same date for co-operation with the German Fleet:

TABLE 25: Typical German Maritime Aircraft in 1939

Type	Year entered service	Purpose	Max. speed (mph)	Max. range (miles)	Armament	Weapon load (lbs)
Arado 196*	1936	Reconnaissance and anti-submarine	193	980	2 cn 2 mg	220
Focke Wulf 200K	1937	Reconnaissance bomber	235	2,430	2 cn 4–6 mg	3,300
HE 111	1936	Reconnaissance and anti-shipping	252	1,280	1 cn 5 mg	5,512
JU 88	1939	Fighter-bomber	280	1,056	5 mg	3,960
Messerschmitt 109	1939	Fighter-bomber	357	568	2 cn 2 mg	—
Stuka	1938	Dive-bomber	239	370	3 mg	1,102

But subsequent years transformed this picture. As reconnaissance aircraft took over the cruiser's scouting role, as torpedo-bombers were recognized as the paramount maritime weapon, and fighters as the best defence against them, rugged all metal, propellor-driven machines of high speed and considerable range came into service. (The jet engine was invented too late for many to be available before VJ day.) Not for these the single Lewis gun and the puny 50–120 lb bombs or 14-inch torpedoes of World War One; they were armed with 20 mm cannon and, later, with rockets, and carried bombs ranging from armour-piercing 500 to 1500 pounders for dropping on shipping from high altitudes or, with greater effect, by dive bombing, up to the six-ton 'Tallboys' with which the RAF destroyed the *Tirpitz* in November 1944. Potentially more dangerous were the radio-guided bombs developed by Germany during the war, such as the FX 1400 3,000 pounders with which the *Luftwaffe* sank the *Roma* in 1943, and the HS 293 1,100 pounders with which it menaced Atlantic convoys.

Aircraft also carried 18-inch torpedoes for attacking surface ships, or depth charges which proved more destructive than bombs against U-boats which hurriedly submerged. And from the autumn of 1944 a desperate Japan sought to stem the Allied advance with a special *kamikaze* corps. Inspired by the warrior spirit of *Bushido* these pilots flew bombed-up or explosive-filled planes into their targets. As many as 1,465 struck more than 400 US ships around Okinawa between 6 April and 22 June 1945, sinking 21 and disabling 56 of them. The wisdom of Britain's decision to armour the flight decks of her aircraft-carriers was then demonstrated.

The British carriers [proved] the value of [armoured] steel [flight] decks, which American naval architects had rejected on account of their weight. A *kamikaze* crashing a steel 'flat-top' crumpled up like a scrambled egg, and did no damage beyond its immediate vicinity; but a *kamikaze* crashing an American wooden [flight] deck started serious fires and its bombs penetrated the ship's interior. On the other hand, the Royal Navy carriers were short on fuel capacity and had to retire [from the operational area] to refuel [more often than those of the US Navy].[2]

In addition to aircraft-carriers, most capital ships and cruisers were fitted with one or two catapults for launching from one to four spotter-reconnaissance amphibians or floatplanes. Such ships built after 1935 had small hangars in which to stow these planes, either amidships abaft the bridge structure or below the quarterdeck. But catapult aircraft were so seldom used after the first years of World War Two, not least because their recovery under way in waters in which submarines could be lurking, presented difficulties, that by 1943 most had been landed, and ships built after this date were not so equipped.

Too many different types of maritime aircraft were produced during World War Two for all to be listed, but the following table gives a representative selection in ascending order of maximum take-off weight (* indicates ship-borne machines):

TABLE 26: Typical World War Two Maritime Aircraft

Type	Country of origin	Year entered service	Purpose	Max. speed (mph)	Max. range (miles)	Armament	Weapon load (lbs)
Zeke* (Zero)	Japan	1939	Fighter-bomber	351	1,194	2 cn 2 mg	132
Wildcat*	USA	1940	Fighter-bomber	318	850	6 mg	—
Seafire*	Britain	1942	Fighter-bomber	352	465	2 cn 4 mg	500
Kate*	Japan	1937	Torpedo-bomber	235	608	1 mg	1,764
Judy*	Japan	1942	Dive-bomber	357	944	3 mg	1,235
Val*	Japan	1941	Dive-bomber	239	913	3 mg	816
Dauntless*	USA	1941	Dive-bomber and reconnaissance	245	1,110	4 cn 2 mg	2,250
FW 190	Germany	1941	Fighter	426	519	4 cn 2 mg	—
Fulmar*	Britain	1940	Fighter	280	800	8 mg	—
Albacore*	Britain	1940	Torpedo-bomber	161	930	3 mg	1,610
Hellcat*	USA	1942	Fighter	380	945	6 mg	—
Corsair*	USA	1943	Fighter-bomber	446	1,005	6 mg	2,000
Jill*	Japan	1943	Torpedo-bomber and reconnaissance	299	1,085	2 mg	1,764
Avenger*	USA	1942	Torpedo-bomber	271	1,215	3 mg	2,000
Barracuda*	Britain	1943	Torpedo-bomber and reconnaissance	228	686	2 mg	1,620
Firefly*	Britain	1943	Fighter-bomber and reconnaissance	316	1,300	4 cn	2,000
Helldiver*	USA	1943	Dive-bomber	295	1,165	2 cn 2 mg	1,000
Nell	Japan	1940	Bomber	232	2,722	1 cn 3 mg	1,764
Beaufort	Britain	1939	Torpedo-bomber and reconnaissance	265	2,000	4 mg	1,500
Beaufighter	Britain	1940	Anti-shipping strike	333	2,000	4 mg	1,500
Betty	Japan	1941	Bomber	272	3,765	2 cn 4 mg	2,205
Whitley	Britain	1937	Reconnaissance and anti-submarine	222	1,650 (470)	5 mg	3,300 (7,000)
Wellington	Britain	1938	Bomber and reconnaissance	255	1,540	6 mg	4,500

TABLE 26:—*continued*

Type	Country of origin	Year entered service	Purpose	Max. speed (mph)	Max. range (miles)	Armament	Weapon load (lbs)
B25	USA	1941	Bomber	272	1,350	12 mg	3,000
DO 217	Germany	1940	Bomber and reconnaissance	320	1,428	1 cn 5 mg	8,818
Catalina	USA	1936	Patrol and reconnaissance	175	3,000	4 mg	4,000
BV 138	Germany	1940	Reconnaissance	170	2,670	2 cn 2 mg	660
Flying Fortress	USA	1941	Bomber	317	2,000	13 mg	17,600
Liberator	USA	1941	Bomber and reconnaissance	290	2,100	10 mg	8,800
Sunderland	Britain	1938	Reconnaissance	213	2,980	12 mg	2,000
HE 177	Germany	1942	Bomber	317	2,500	2 cn 6 mg	12,346
Superfortress	USA	1943	Bomber	358	4,100	1 cn 10 mg	20,000

By 1945 the Navies of Britain and the USA had each built up first line strengths of more than two thousand such planes. Conversely, the first line strengths of Germany and Japan were well below their peaks, and dwindling fast, although a desperate Japan, having put her final faith in *kamikaze,* still had as many as 5,350 of these dangerous weapons, after expending 2,550.

From aircraft, the latest naval weapon, to guns, the oldest. In the decade before World War One Britain's Captain Percy Scott and America's Captain W. Sims revolutionized naval gunnery. But there was no comparable progress in the post-1919 era prior to the introduction of radar in the middle of World War Two. Guns were given horizon range by increasing their elevation, and radio allowed effective concentration firing by two or more ships. Otherwise surface ship gunnery continued to be as prodigiously wasteful of ammunition as it was in World War One—notwithstanding the strong pull which Britain's Whale Island Gunnery School and Washington's Bureau of Ordnance (the 'Gun Club') had for the more able officers in the Royal and United States Navies, who considered themselves the élite of their respective Services and held a near-monopoly of the better appointments both afloat and ashore. The irony of this lies in the reality of World War Two, in which very few of the more important posts were achieved by members of these cliques.

Be this as it may, Navies recognized the air threat to the extent of augmenting the AA armaments of cruisers and larger warships. In the older dreadnoughts eight 4-inch guns replaced the two 3-inch with which they had been armed in World War One: new and modernized ones mounted up to 20 5- or 5·25-inch. And these long-range weapons were augmented by close-range ones such as the four and eight barrel ('Chicago piano') 2 pdr pompoms. But to design an accurate AA fire control system for use with time-fused shells proved an intractable problem: the USA's tachymetric equipment was the best solution;

Britain's goniographic High Angle Control System could do little better than put up a deterrent barrage.

Next communications. The introduction of thermionic valves for radio transmitters and receivers, in place of arcs, sparks and crystal detectors, followed by the discovery of the properties of short waves, provided world-wide communication between ships and shore stations (in 1914 Admiral Graf von Spee was obliged to send a cruiser into Pearl Harbour to cable his progress to Berlin: in 1939 the *Admiral Graf Spee* was in direct radio touch) and allowed many more channels to be used for signals within a fleet and with its aircraft. Britain's discovery that high power transmissions on the very low frequency of 16 khz could be received by submerged submarines, allowed them to receive orders without risking sighting by enemy patrols. (As the High Seas Fleet hurried back to the Jade on 1 June 1916, it passed safely over three bottomed British submarines which knew nothing of Jutland until they returned to Yarmouth on the 9th.)

All Navies replaced ciphers using various systems of substitution and transposition with new ones employing subtractor tables which were believed to provide adequate security for their radio signals. Most Navies also developed and installed cipher machines, such as the German Enigma, which not only gave added security but were quicker to use; but the British rejected them as being too sensitive and complicated for shipboard use.

The most important between-the-wars innovation was a British secret. From 1914 to 1918 Allied A/S vessels were handicapped for lack of any mean for detecting a submerged U-boat. An Allied Submarine Detection Investigation Committee tried to find a solution; hence the name Asdic by which the instrument was first called. But not until after World War One did Britain achieve the break-through, a means by which a cone of super-sonic pulses could be transmitted through the sea, and their reflection (echo) received from a submerged object. By 1939 all her destroyers were fitted with it. The secret was passed to France early in 1939, and in 1940 to the USA who had previously developed a similar but not so effective instrument whose name, Sonar, was taken into Allied use.

Germany acquired asdic gear from France after her surrender and passed its secrets, after a considerable delay, to Italy and Japan. And with sonar many submarines were detected and sunk during World War Two. But it was not the panacea which Britain optimistically believed it to be in 1939. Its range was, at best, only a mile; and because it could not pierce a temperature inversion, because it was subject to interference in rough weather, and because it could not be used by a ship steaming at more than 20 knots, skilful U-boat commanders were able to elude detection, and torpedo such important ships as the *Barham, Eagle* and *Ark Royal*. Moreover, since sonar gave only the bearing and range of a submarine, not its depth, it was still necessary to fire a pattern of depth charges set to explode at various depths, and usually many patterns to achieve a kill. A further crucial shortcoming was its inability to detect a surfaced submarine. (It could also be 'deceived' by *Pillenwerfer,* a chemical substance discharged from a U-boat's stern torpedo tubes, which produced false echoes.)

The other notable between-the-wars innovation, which proved the deadliest of weapons in the Pacific, was developed in as much secrecy by Japan. In 1920 all Navies used 21-inch torpedoes with 600 lb warheads and contact pistols, driven by compressed air impulse steam engines which gave them a maximum range of 15,000 yards, while aircraft used a similar 18-inch weapon carrying a 300 lb warhead. Neither was adequate for sinking a vessel with bulges or similar built-in underwater protection. So Britain, Germany and the USA developed magnetic pistols which would detonate below a ship's vulnerable bottom. Britain's proved their value in the airborne attack on Taranto, but in general, and especially those produced by Germany and the USA, they were too unreliable to be effective. German torpedoes were also bad depth keepers: those with contact pisols often passing harmlessly under Allied ships during the first nine months of World War Two.

Britain also envisaged an oxygen-enriched, air impulse engine with a greater range and higher speed, but failed to produce a satisfactory design. It was otherwise with Japan: early in the 1930's she produced the Long Lance, a 24-inch torpedo carrying a 1,200 lb warhead propelled by this means out to 44,000 yards. And by 1941 most of her cruisers and destroyers were able to fire them; moreover some of the former mounted as many as 24 tubes instead of the usual six to twelve, whilst many of the latter, which had space for only eight or nine tubes, carried double this number of torpedoes with rapid reloading arrangement. Equally important, the Japanese developed 18-inch torpedoes for their aircraft which could be dropped from a greater, and therefore safer, height and range than those used by the planes of other Powers.[4]

No technical innovation brought into general use after September 1939 had a greater impact on war at sea than Radar (RDF to the British until 1943). In the 1930s Britain, France, Germany and the USA, independently, and in secret, developed equipment to transmit a metric wave beam of very short radio pulses, with which the bearing and range of any ship or aircraft from which these were reflected could be measured on a cathode-ray tube. Like the Royal Air Force the British Navy saw in this a means by which high flying aircraft could be detected out to 100 miles: by the time World War Two began half-a-dozen of its capital ships and cruisers had been fitted with a set which gave this warning of enemy attack. The German Navy was concerned to develop it as a rangefinder of greater accuracy than any optical one: by August 1939 the *Graf Spee* and her sisters mounted a set, but with its range limited to 16,000 yards this was of little value at the battle of the Plate. Subsequent improvements, especially the British inventions of the strapped cavity magnetron transmitting valve and the silicon crystal receiving valve (the first transistor), with which more powerful pulses could be transmitted and received on centimetric waves, enabled ships not only to 'see' through darkness and fog, but to detect and track aircraft, ships and surfaced submarines, by measuring their bearing and range with great accuracy—and with aircraft, to estimate their height.

For surface gunnery, radar proved much more than an accurate range-finder. For so long—during World War One and the first years of World War Two—as this depended on visual observation of straddles, the proportion of hits to shells fired was seldom more than five per cent. Radar allowed individual shots to be spotted with the result that, from 1942 onwards, ships were able to hit more quickly and more often—and to do this at night without disclosing their presence by the use of searchlights or starshell.

Table 27 (page 63) lists the ship-mounted radar sets produced by Britain between 1939 and 1945.

Table 28 shows the extent to which these sets were fitted in typical British ships during the second half of the war.

Radar was also of value to maritime aircraft. By 1939 Britain had produced her first metric wave Air to Surface Vessel (ASV) sets with which her search planes could detect surface ships by night and, more important, surfaced submarines out to five miles, a range which was more than doubled when, in 1942, centimetric wave sets became available. Soon after this naval fighters were fitted with Air Interception (AI) radar sets for use at night.

The US Navy began to equip its ships with radar in 1940, subsequently developing a comprehensive range of sets similar to those used by the Royal Navy whose secrets it shared from August in that year. French warships were fitted with British or US sets when they fought on the Allied side. Germany was slower to produce a comprehensive range, chiefly because she had to wait until the fortunes of war allowed her to capture and copy a British magnetron in 1943. She never entrusted her Italian ally with her radar sets, and she delayed giving their secrets to Japan until it was too late for that nation's ships to be as well equipped as those of the Allies.

For Identification between Friend or Foe (IFF) Allied aircraft (and small surface vessels such as motor-torpedoboats) were equipped with responders, which transmitted a coded signal when triggered by a special interrogator attached to a radar set. Unhappily this was not always effective owing to the reluctance of some pilots to switch their sets on, sometimes because of a false belief that it might reveal their presence to the enemy, sometimes because under operational stress they forgot to do

TABLE 27: British Naval Radar Sets

Purpose	Type no.	Frequency (mhz)	Wavelength	Power output (kw)	Range (nautical miles)	Usual position for aerial array
Air warning, cruisers and above	79	43	7 metres	70	90 @ 20,000 ft	Masthead
As above with AA barrage predictor	279	43	7 metres	70	90 @ 20,000 ft	Masthead
Air warning, cruisers and above	281	90	3½-4 metres	350	100 @ 20,000 ft	Masthead
Air warning, destroyers and below	286*	214	1·5 metres	10	20	Masthead
Air warning, destroyers and below	291	214	1·5 metres	10	20	Masthead
Surface warning, cruisers and above	272	3,000	10 cm	90	10-25	Above bridge
Surface warning, cruisers and above	273	3,000	10 cm	90	10-25	Above bridge
Surface warning, destroyers and below	271	3,000	10 cm	90	10-25	Above bridge or on after superstructure
Surface and low air warning	277	3,000	10 cm	500	25-35	Bridge structure
Surface gunnery control	284	600	50 cm	25-50	8-12	Main armament director control tower
Surface gunnery control	274	3,000	10 cm	400	20	Main armament director control tower
AA gunnery control	285	600	50 cm	25-50	—	AA director
AA gunnery control	275	3,000	10 cm	400	—	AA director
AA barrage control of main armament	283	600	50 cm	25-50	—	AA director
Close range AA gunnery control	282	600	50 cm	25-50	—	Pompom director
Air and surface target indicating	293	3,000	10 cm	500	12	Foremast

* This was an adaptation of the RAF's and Fleet Air Arm's first ASV set.

so, with the consequence that they were shot down by their own ships' AA fire.

TABLE 28: Typical Naval Radar Outfits

Purpose	Capital ship	Aircraft-carrier	Cruiser	Destroyer	Submarine
Air warning	79	281	279	291	291
Surface warning	272	273	—	271	—
Surface and low air warning	—	—	277	—	—
Air and surface target indicating	293	—	—	—	—
Surface gunnery control	284	—	274	—	—
AA gunnery control	4/285	4/285	2/275	285	—
AA barrage control	—	—	—	—	—
Close range AA gunnery control	4/282	4/282	2/282	—	—

Unable to develop an efficient radar set for her U-boats to use when they were surfaced until near the end of the war, Germany produced in 1942 a warning receiver (Metox) to detect metric ASV transmissions. But this passive device came into service too late to be of much value before the Allies changed first to ten centimetre ASV and then to a three centimetre version. And although Germany produced a passive receiver (Naxos) to detect the former (but nothing to detect the latter before the war's end), she found a much more effective antidote in *Schnorkel* (*anglice* Snort), a between-the-wars Dutch invention which no other nation then thought to be of any significance. This allowed U-boats to run their diesel engines for battery charging whilst wholly submerged, except for the head of a vertical pipe containing special valves to prevent the ingress of water, which served the dual purpose of air inlet and exhaust. With this, Germany's U-boats were able to operate against Allied shipping during the last year of the war in waters much closer to Europe than had been possible after 1940. An even more deadly weapon would have been her development of the first true submarine, a boat fitted with engines fuelled with hydrogen peroxide, which could remain wholly submerged throughout a patrol. Fortunately for the Allies the first *Walther* boats came into service too late to be put to operational use.

Radar did more than provide accurate range for AA guns and allow them to be used at night without searchlight illumination. In the last years of the war, Britain and the USA developed sets and gun mountings which 'locked on' to enemy aircraft. Close range weapons, in particular, could then be aimed at high speed aircraft with much greater accuracy than was possible with visual sights and manually operated mountings. A more significant innovation in this field was, however, the Anglo-US development, in 1942, of the Proximity (VT) Fuse—one detonated by its own midget radar set when it came within effective distance of an enemy

C*

plane, instead of depending on the largely hit or miss method of the time fuse.

Even so, the growing danger from air attack required considerable increases in AA armaments, as is shown by the following table for one British cruiser, HMS *Belfast:*

TABLE 29: HMS *Belfast*'s AA Armaments During World War Two

Gun	On completion in 1939	On completion of repairs in 1942	By August 1945
4-inch	12	12	8
2 pdr pompom	16	16	36
40 mm Bofors	—	—	3
20 mm Oerlikon	—	14	8
0·5-inch	8	—	—

Larger warships were even more extensively rearmed, typical numbers of guns fitted by 1945 being:

TABLE 30: Typical AA Armaments in US Warships

Calibre	US 'Iowa' class battleships	US 'Essex' class aircraft-carriers
5-inch	20	10–12
40 mm	80	44–72
20 mm	50	52

The carrier-borne fighter was, however, always the best defence against air attack. By 1942 at least one aircraft-carrier able to maintain a combat air patrol (CAP) of four fighters during daylight hours, and to launch more if an enemy strike was detected, was recognized as an essential component of any major force. And by 1944 the additional need to maintain a night CAP in Pacific operations required one carrier to be detailed to provide this whilst the others rested their crews.

The Allies overcame the inherent inaccuracy of the hydrostatically fused 300 lb depth charge, dropped or mortared from the stern of a warship after it had passed over a U-boat and sonar contact had been lost, by developing an ahead-throwing underwater weapon. Anti-submarine vessels were first armed with a Hedgehog, which mortared a pattern of 24 50-lb 'bombs' at the sonar tracked position of a submarine with sufficient accuracy for some to detonate against its vulnerable hull. And by 1945 they were being armed with the similar but more effective Squid.

Germany devised the Acoustic Torpedo (Gnat) for her U-boats. These homed on to the sound of an enemy vessel's propellors, and achieved considerable successes against Allied convoys until countered by Foxer, a simple noise-making device towed astern on to which a torpedo homed more readily and harmlessly. But escorts remained vulnerable to the extent that foxer could not be used when they were steaming at more than 15 knots.

Italy developed the Human Torpedo (Chariot), a 'torpedo' with a 600 lb warhead, ridden and guided by a crew of two wearing self-contained diving suits, with which she achieved the notable success of attacking the battleships *Queen Elizabeth* and *Valiant* at their moorings in Alexandria harbour in December 1941, putting both out of action for many months. Japan produced a comparable but larger weapon, the Midget Submarine, a 10-ton boat, some 40 feet in length, with a crew of two–four, carrying two torpedoes (or saddled with two heavy charges to be placed below an anchored warship) which was carried or towed by a conventional submarine to within 50 miles of its target. But their only significant success was against the *Resolution* shortly after the British seizure of French Madagascar in 1942 to prevent it becoming a Japanese base. The four employed in the attack on Pearl Harbour were lost before they could carry out their missions.

Germany produced the comparable *Seehund*, and Britain built X-craft, but it needed three of her larger XE boats of 30 tons to pierce Tromsö Fiord in 1943 in order to put the powerful *Tirpitz* out of action for the best part of a year. The USA failed to recognize their value until *XE1* and *XE3* sank the Japanese cruiser *Takao* off Singapore dockyard in 1945, by which time it was too late to complete any for her Navy before the end of hostilities.

Widespread mining, using weapons which were a great improvement on the 'traditional' contact type, required all the maritime Powers to construct a disproportionately large number of minesweepers and to evolve and produce other counter-measures on an extensive scale. The initial 'villain' was the Magnetic Mine. Originally developed by Britain in 1918, but abandoned and virtually forgotten after the Armistice, these were first sown around the British Isles in the autumn of 1939 by German surface ships, U-boats and aircraft, where their victims included the Home Fleet flagship *Nelson* in Loch Ewe and the cruiser *Belfast* in the Firth of Forth, the latter being damaged so seriously that she was out of service for the next two years. But as soon as one of these mines was recovered from the sands off Shoeburyness on 23 November an effective antidote was quickly found. By Wiping (a quick but temporary method) or by Degaussing (running heavy electric cables round a ship above the waterline) the magnetism of a steel hull, which detonated these mines, was neutralized.

Germany's later development of the Acoustic Mine, detonated by the sound of a passing ship's propellors, and the Pressure-Influence Mine (Oyster), detonated by the change in sea pressure produced by the passage of a ship, were more effective. Although their secret was quickly known, there were no easy counter-measures, especially to the Oyster to which many Allied ships fell victims in the shallow waters of the English Channel at the time of the Normandy invasion in 1944 and afterwards.

Radio communication links—ship-shore and ship-ship—were extensively developed, especially on high frequencies (3–30 mhz) for which smaller and more efficient equipment was produced and optimum frequency prediction introduced. Navies, which had for long insisted on using only hand-operated morse (W/T), were by 1941 induced to introduce telephony (R/T or Voice) in the 2 mhz band for inter-communication between convoy escorts and with their patrolling aircraft, and in the 100–150 mhz band for use with single-seater fighter aircraft, which they soon found to be more effective than W/T or visual signalling (V/S) for inter-ship communication e.g. for manoeuvring signals (TBS = Talk Between Ships). And by the end of hostilities automatic high-speed morse (the fore-runner of radio-teletype) was coming into use. The result was much more efficient systems of command and control of all maritime units, ships, submarines and planes, operating in a sea area by a shore headquarters, and of all units within a force by its flagship, than had been available before.

High Frequency Directing Finding sets were installed in many Allied escort vessels when it was realized that U-boats were making frequent radio reports to their base. With sense-finding equipment (i.e. the ability to distinguish between a bearing and its reciprocal) and with cathode-ray tube presentation, H/F D/F (Huff-Duff) could obtain an accurate bearing of the shortest transmission and estimate its distance, which made it possible to locate a U-boat menacing a convoy when it was outside radar range (out to about 50 miles).

Shore stations provided the Navies of both sides with more radio intelligence than the British obtained and put to good use against the German High Seas Fleet in World War One. H/F D/F sets initially sited only in Britain, but later elsewhere, notably on the east coasts of Canada and the USA, fixed every U-boat transmission and, because Admiral Karl Dönitz's pack tactics against convoys required them to transmit frequent reports to his headquarters at Lorient, allowed the Allies to track them. Convoys and independently routed ships were thereby warned to change course to avoid U-boat attacks. To counter this Germany developed equipment which could 'flash' a short message in less than a second; but Allied scientists dealt with this in a far shorter time than Germany's could produce a set for intercepting convoy escort R/T tranmissions (Presskohle), which was not ready for fitting in U-boats until 1944.

Having supposed her latest ciphers to be secure against cracking, Britain was greatly disturbed to discover a few months after the outbreak of hostilities that Germany had established a 'B' Service, under the brilliant Captain Kupfer, which not only intercepted the Royal Navy's radio signals but deciphered many of them. By being known to the enemy in advance all Britain's naval operations were at risk until she could introduce more sophisticated ciphers, notably the One-time Reciphering Pad and the Type X cipher machine, both of which were in general use by the end of 1942. The USA had a 'Magic' service which cracked the Japanese diplomatic machine cipher ('Purple') in 1941. This success was, however, initially spoiled by the failure of President Roosevelt and his Service Chiefs to use this intelligence to warn their Pearl Harbour commanders to be fully prepared for a surprise Japanese attack. (They allowed them to believe that the first blow would fall on the Philippines when there was ample evidence that the Hawaiian Islands would be the target.) But 'Magic's' subsequent achievement in cracking other Japanese ciphers allowed the USA to bring enemy forces to battle on several notable occasions.

After a shaky start Britain's 'Y' organization achieved comparable results, especially after a German Enigma machine reached London in 1940.[5] As important, the lesson was well learned from the consequences of the Admiralty's failure to tell Jellicoe that Scheer was returning home by the Horns Reef channel during the night of 31 May–1 June 1916. In World War Two intelligence obtained from enemy signals was fully coordinated with operational control. It was not, however, always reliable: a signal ordering an operation might be intercepted, but a subsequent one cancelling it missed, or a false one intercepted and too readily believed. This could be the reason why Pound was so sure in June 1942 that Arctic Convoy PQ17 was in imminent danger of attack by the *Tirpitz* that he ordered it to scatter and its escort to withdraw—with tragic results when its ships were subsequently attacked by U-boats and the *Luftwaffe,* when in reality the German battleship had not left the security of Norway's fiords.

Ironclads, from the USS *Monitor* down to the dreadnoughts of World War One, were provided with armoured conning towers from which their captains fought them: they needed this protection when the optimum gun range was as short as 4,000 yards. But at the longer ranges of Dogger Bank and Jutland, imposed by the torpedo threat, they found the view through a narrow slit too restricted, and stayed on their open bridges. Conning towers were, therefore, omitted from post-1918 designs. World War One also showed the need to keep a continuous plot of other vessels of one's own fleet, and of the positions of enemy vessels reported by radio, on a scale larger than a navigational chart. Post-1918 battleships and cruisers were, therefore, provided with a separate compartment containing an automatic plotting table on which own ship's position was continuously marked by electro-mechanical means.

World War Two called for a second table on which enemy planes detected by radar were plotted, and by which fighters could be directed into contact with them, until the Plan Position Indicator (PPI) type of radar screen became available towards the end of hostilities. Out of this was evolved the Combat Information Centre (CIC) or Operations Room which processed all visual, radio and sonar intelligence and presented it on plots and radar screens from which a captain could fight his ship and control its weapons, as well as aircraft, more effectively than from the bridge.

All Navies envisaged the need to refuel their ships at sea in war, and devised means of doing so *under way* at speeds of 12–15 knots. From the outset of hostilities Germany sent supply ships overseas to replenish her surface raiders and U-boats with fuel and stores at ocean rendezvous. By 1941 Britain's convoy escorts were refuelling from tankers en route in order to increase the distance across the Atlantic for which convoys could be given A/S protection. But these achievements pale beside those of the USA. The vast distances across which her Pacific Fleet was required to operate impelled her Navy to devise means of replenishing its warships under way from a Fleet Train of support ships, not only with fuel but with aviation spirit, ammunition and other supplies.

During World War One Britain's Grand Fleet seldom remained at sea for more than a week: the endurance of its ships, especially its destroyers, was too small and coaling was impracticable at sea. By World War Two all warships were oil-fired and had more than twice the endurance of their predecessors. With these advantages, and by replenishment at sea as often as might be required, America's Third and Fifth Fleets, and in 1945 Britain's Pacific Fleet, were able to operate continuously against Japanese targets for two months, and sometimes more, without returning to harbour.

All this does no more than skim the cream off the technical progress made by the World's Navies between 1919 and 1945. It is, nonetheless, enough to make abundantly clear that the laboratories and factories of Britain and the USA contributed as much as their shipyards towards winning World War Two at sea. To quote Dönitz's telling words, written in 1943:

> For some months past the enemy has rendered the U-boat war ineffective. He has achieved this, not through superior tactics or strategy, but through his superiority in the field of science; this finds its expression in the modern battle weapon—detection. By this means he has torn from our hands our sole offensive weapon in the war against the Anglo-Saxons.

In what ways, then, were maritime strategy and tactics influenced by these technological developments, as in World War One they were changed by the torpedo, which required battleships to fight outside its range, and the mine, which enforced the distant, as opposed to close, blockade? Moreover, to what extent did the small size of the Fleets with which the Powers entered World War Two—much smaller than those with which Britain and Germany began World War One—affect maritime strategy and tactics; maritime rather than naval because World War Two was fought above the sea as well as on and below its surface?

'Strategy governs ships,' wrote Lord Fisher when Britain's Fleet was being expanded in the decade before 1914; 'weapons govern tactics.' But in World War Two the first part of this dictum was not always true for more reasons than Fleets artificially limited by the Versailles, Washington and London Treaties. The aim of the stronger Fleet is not 'command of the sea', in the sense of all five oceans. Never, in a war between maritime Powers, has this been achieved. The stronger Fleet aims only to control such sea areas as its country needs to pursue its overall strategy; to transport the sinews of war—oil and other essential raw materials, munitions, troops and the supplies required to sustain its people—to wherever they are required, and for offensive operations, both maritime and amphibious, against the enemy. It aims also to prevent the enemy from using the seas for these purposes. It achieves both by blockade (World War Two examples are the watch maintained on the northern entrance to the North Sea by Britain's Home Fleet—sometimes reinforced by US ships—assisted by the RAF's Coastal Command, and the numerous offensive patrols carried out by 288 US submarines plus 30 British and 15 Dutch in Far East waters from the beginning of 1942 onwards); by protecting its own merchant shipping (the world-wide Allied convoy system, and the Italian convoys across the central Mediterranean to north Africa); and by attacking the enemy's fleets whenever opportunity offers (the battles of Matapan and Midway).

Trade protection—the protection of merchant shipping conveying the sinews of war—merits special mention because in Britain and the USA it involved a battle of words between the supporters and opponents of convoy. The eighteenth century provided abundant evidence that this was the best form of trade protection: only by sailing merchant ships in groups could all be given warship escort. Unhappily for the twentieth century the Declaration of Paris 1856, which outlawed privateering (the chief instrument for war against trade), coupled with the Victorian laissez faire belief that government control of privately owned shipping was unacceptable even in war, led the maritime Powers to abandon convoy. This could not forsee the potentialities of submarines, nor comprehend that they might be privateers in a new guise. Britain's 1914 war plans contained no provision for convoys except for troopships. Against attacks by the handful of German cruisers overseas the Admiralty was content to deploy cruisers to patrol focal points on the trade routes.

The career of the *Emden* exposed this strategy. Whenever Captain von Müller attacked an Allied ship, all mercantile sailings were suspended over a wide area of the Indian Ocean, causing more serious delays than those inherent in the convoy system. But because these German marauders were rounded up by the end of 1914, the Admiralty saw no need to change its plans. They reckoned without Germany's decision to introduce unrestricted U-boat warfare, *i.e.* to authorize their submarines to sink merchant ships on sight contrary to International Law. Even so they issued a memorandum as late as January 1917 asserting that 'convoy is not recommended in any area where submarine attack is a possibility'. However, Germany's U-boats continued to sink so many Allied ships that by the middle of 1917 Britain was within sight of starvation. In desperation the Admiralty was compelled to try the convoy system in both the Atlantic and the Mediterranean. The result was the most dramatic turn of the tide in the whole war. In April 1917 one ship out of four leaving British ports never returned: one year later the loss rate was down to one ship out of a hundred.

Notwithstanding this clear Allied victory over Germany's U-boat fleet the convoy system was again abandoned after that war was over. In both Britain and the USA, Japan was seen to be the next most likely enemy, and in an armed conflict with her there should be no need to protect merchant shipping, except in the Far East and the Pacific. As important, convoy was judged to be a *defensive* measure, such as all naval thought, to whom the battleship remained the supreme arbiter of maritime power, found repellent. In vain did America's Admiral William Sims point out that to use escorts to search the oceans for patrolling submarines was no better than looking for a needle in a haystack; that convoys were *offensive* because, by acting as bait, they provided escorts with a real chance to sink submarines. Not only was convoy little studied and less seldom exercised between the wars, but as late as March 1935 a British Lord of the Admiralty informed Parliament that 'the convoy system will only be introduced when sinkings are so great that this country no longer feels justified in allowing ships to sail by themselves'.

Fortunately, initially for Britain and later for the Allies, by 1937 the Admiralty not only realized that a war with Germany was as likely as one with Japan, but potentially more dangerous. Moreover, although Germany then had few U-boats, and although she had recently signed an agreement which required them to conform to International Law, the Admiralty put no trust in Hitler's word. Britain's protagonists of the convoy system won the day: plans were made to introduce it on the outbreak of war and to augment her available destroyer escorts and sloops with the 'Hunt' class and other A/S vessels.

Britain was, therefore, ready to introduce convoys in September 1939—

ready, that is, with the necessary organization. But she had taken the decision too late for more than a tithe of the necessary escorts to be built. And the Air Ministry had done even less towards providing the aircraft needed to give convoys A/S cover, and nothing to give them fighter protection against bombing by the *Luftwaffe*. Moreover, the old antipathy to convoy as a defensive measure died hard. As late as September 1940 an outward bound convoy of some 30 ships was escorted by no more than a single sloop and two trawlers because, at Winston Churchill's instigation, a sizeable proportion of the then available A/S vessels was employed in hunting groups, on which the views of one distinguished escort commander, now Admiral Sir Peter Gretton, 'are unprintable, a complete waste of time'.[6]

However, the insufficiency of sea and air escorts to give convoys full protection before 1942 was also due to three other factors. These were Germany's post-1939 decision to concentrate the bulk of her naval effort on the mass-construction of a greater number of U-boats than had been conceived possible; the fall of France in 1940 which gave Germany bases in that country; and the success of Britain's A/S measure which, by forcing U-boats to operate further and further afield, required convoys to be escorted right across the Atlantic instead of only within some 500 miles of the British Isles.

Nor was Britain the only purblind nation. Although the USA's entry into World War One had provided the large number of escorts needed to introduce the convoy system in 1917, she, too, allowed this strategy to lapse largely into oblivion after victory was won. Whilst ready to use it in the Pacific in December 1941, she had no plans to employ it down her eastern seaboard, nor in the Caribbean. America's Commander-in-Chief US Fleet (Cominch) and Chief of Naval Operations (CNO), Admiral Ernest King, insisted, against all British experience and advice, that 'inadequately escorted convoys were worse than none'. As a consequence, the USA suffered potentially crippling losses of merchant ships in these waters for the best part of six months before she introduced convoys with the help of escort vessels borrowed from Britain.

The Allies also tried other strategies against Germany's U-boats. In 1940 a deep mine barrier was laid across the gap between Scotland and Iceland, but this achieved nothing. Offensive air patrols in the Bay of Biscay did little more than compel U-boats to transit this area submerged. And bombing raids on German bases and construction yards destroyed relatively few U-boats because they were so well protected by concrete shelters. In short, none of these methods justified the effort which they involved, while the aircraft used for the latter two would have been better employed on convoy protection. It is beyond doubt that it was the convoy system which won the battle of the Atlantic for the Allies— but only after 'virtually every surface and air anti-submarine lesson of the first submarine war had been relearnt in the second at immense cost in blood, tears and treasure'.[7]

Now for the strategy of the weaker Fleet. Although this may seek to gain ascendancy by surprise attack (Pearl Harbour is a notorious example from World War Two), it more usually presents the threat of a fleet-in-being (*e.g.* Germany's heavy ships based on Norway's fiords, and the British Eastern Fleet at Kilindini in 1942), and fights a *guerre de course* (*e.g.* the world-wide operations of Germany's armed merchant raiders). The unrestricted U-boat campaign falls between both stools: to Germany it was a blockade of Britain by a stronger undersea fleet; to the Allies it was the old *guerre de course* by a Fleet weak in surface vessels.

In the first years of World War Two the extent to which the British and US surface fleets and the German submarine fleet could pursue the aims of the stronger fleet was restricted by their shortage of many types of vessel. The relatively few capital ships did more than fulfil their *raison d'être* of destroying their own kind, as the *Bismarck* sank the 'mighty Hood' in 1941, and was herself reduced to a helpless wreck a few days later by HMS *King George V* and *Rodney*. In March 1941 the *Scharnhorst* and *Gneisenau* were deterred from attacking two convoys in the Atlantic by the mere sight of the *Malaya* escorting one and the *Rodney* the other, in sharp contrast to the *Admiral Hipper* which had decimated another in the previous month because it was unescorted.

Battleships' heavy guns also provided bombardment support for numerous opposed seaborne landings; and their large AA batteries, mounted on strongly armoured platforms, were invaluable for the protection of aircraft-carrier task forces. But the disastrous loss of the *Prince of Wales* and *Repulse* to Japanese planes in the Gulf of Siam in December 1941 showed that they were no longer impregnable. They could not safely operate within range of enemy aircraft without air cover, which could seldom be provided by shore-based planes because of their limited range. (The escape of the *Scharnhorst* and *Gneisenau* from Brest through the English Channel and the Straits of Dover back to Germany in February 1942 under the cover of the *Luftwaffe* was the exception which proves the rule.)

But Britain and the USA were woefully short of aircraft-carriers, which were needed for more purposes than providing fighter cover for task forces and convoys, and to fly anti-submarine patrols. From a vessel intended to support the battleship, the carrier became the dominant naval unit. Whilst a battleship's strike range was limited to that of her heavy guns (at most twenty miles), aircraft carrying torpedoes or armour-piercing bombs had an effective range of several hundred. Taranto showed this; Pearl Harbour proved it; so did the battle of the Coral Sea in April 1942, the first in all history in which major units were sunk on both sides without a single surface ship coming within sight of the enemy. So it was carriers which had to be built in large numbers, not battleships—in which respect it will be noted that weapons, as well as strategy, sometimes govern ships, just as before World War One the torpedo impelled the introduction of the torpedoboat and the torpedoboat destroyer.

There was, however, more than this in World War Two to give the lie to the first part of Fisher's dictum. Much as the Allies would have liked to pursue a strategy that was not governed by ships, it was often restricted by the lack of them. Just as their convoys could seldom be provided with adequate escorts before 1942, so in subsequent years there were never enough landing ships and craft to carry out all the seaborne invasions for which they had the troops and other resources. There is, nonetheless, much to support Fisher's wisdom. Blockade and the *guerre de course* impelled Germany to abandon almost all surface ship construction so that she could concentrate on producing more than 1,000 U-boats. And the Allies had to build very large numbers of A/S escorts and planes to provide adequate air and sea protection for their convoys. As important, because the Allies were compelled by their eviction from Continental Europe in 1940 and by geography in the Pacific, to accept the truth of another of Fisher's dicta, that a country's Army is best used as a shell to be fired by its Navy, Britain and the USA had to evolve and build an armada of specialized landing ships and craft for seaborne invasions.

Evolve is the *mot juste* because there were very few before 1940. The British can hardly be blamed for ignoring amphibious operations between the wars because they had burned their fingers so badly at Gallipoli in 1915. But they had to pay the price for this during the Norwegian campaign—which repeated many of the mistakes of 1915, such as nontactical loading of transports—and in the frontal assault on Dieppe in 1942 (which one can argue should never have been undertaken against a defended port in the light of Nelson's near-disastrous failure to take Santa Cruz). The USA was less averse to them. Fearing extinction between the wars her Marine Corps made them their special mission, developing and exercising the necessary techniques in the 1930s in conjunction with the US Navy, though the latter was as slow as the British to appreciate the need for specially designed vessels for amphibious operations.

The second part of Fisher's dictum, 'weapons govern tactics', has to be considered from two angles, of battle fleets (or forces) and carrier forces (*i.e.* those in which aircraft-carriers were the core), and of the forces used for the attack and defence of convoys.

The British Grand Fleet of World War One, which from 1917 included a squadron of US battleships, cruised in divisions in line ahead disposed abeam, for ease of manoeuvre and for their best protection by a destroyer screen against submarines. For warning of an approaching enemy they depended on cruisers spread singly at visibility distance apart some 15 miles ahead, and by battlecruisers, with their own destroyer screen and advanced cruiser screen, as much as 60 miles ahead. On making contact

with the enemy *by day,* battlecruisers and cruisers fell back on the battleships as these deployed into single line ahead for a gun duel with the
enemy battle fleet, usually on similar courses, at a range around 15,000
yards, whilst the destroyers carried out independent flotilla attacks which
impelled the enemy to turn *away* to avoid torpedoes. One emphasizes 'by
day' because the British were averse to fighting a night action, believing
that this would involve so much confusion that the outcome would be a
matter of chance.

All this, which was exemplified by Jellicoe's conduct of the battle of
Jutland, governed naval thought for most of the period between the wars,
when Japan was the likely enemy for both Britain and the USA. All three
Powers believed that they must be ready to fight a battle fleet action. To
quote Admiral of the Fleet Sir Casper John: 'The obsession with Jutland
ran through the British Navy as a deadening virus' .There were, nonetheless, two significant developments. Learning from Germany's success
during the night of 31 May–1 June 1916, effective star shell, remote
controlled searchlights and recognition signals were developed. With the
benefit of these, naval thought accepted that in some circumstances a
night action could be fought. Admiral Sir Ernle Chatfield and Sir
William Fisher so trained Britain's Mediterranean Fleet during the 1930s.
So did the USA and, to a higher standard, Japan. During World War
Two the fruits were garnered in such battles as Matapan, Savo Island and
Guadalcanal.

Secondly, whilst the embryo aircraft-carriers of World War One had
followed in the wake of the battle fleet during the approach, and operated
on its disengaged side when action was joined, in the 1930s this policy
was abandoned in favour of incorporating them into the battle fleet,
where they enjoyed the protection of the battleships and of their destroyer
screen. Not until the battle fleet deployed for a gun action were they
detached to operate on its disengaged side. And World War Two had not
long begun before it was realized that, with reconnaissance aircraft and
radar, an advanced cruiser screen was no longer needed to give warning
of the enemy. In 1943 the four battleships, two carriers and six cruisers of
Britain's Force H operated in the Mediterranean as a single compact body,
of two columns in single line ahead, with an open V close screen of three
flotillas of destroyers just one mile ahead. Only if contact with Italian
battleships appeared likely would the carriers be detached to operate clear
of the gun action, which might be on parallel or opposite courses or, more
likely, as a chase after a flying enemy.

However, this formation suffered two defects. It was evolved for
destroyers without AA guns, which were therefore best disposed as an
A/S screen against a form of attack which must come from ahead. When
destroyers mounted DP weapons they needed some other disposition if
they were to use these against air attack from any direction, as well as
providing an A/S screen. It had also been evolved out of one employed

when carriers operated only spotter-reconnaissance planes and torpedo bombers, of which the former had an endurance of several hours and the latter were not required until an enemy surface force was sighted, so that these ships needed to turn into the wind to operate their planes at relatively infrequent intervals when the whole force could alter course for this purpose.

When carriers were subsequently required, at least during daylight hours, to provide a CAP of fighters of limited endurance, they had to turn into the wind at approximately hourly intervals; and the whole force could not alter course so often, because of the time off the course being made good, and because the destroyer screen had to be moved round to each new course at speeds which expended too much of their limited fuel stowage. The British solution was to allow a carrier, with a screen of two destroyers, to operate temporarily and independently clear of the main body each time it needed to fly off or land on. But this suffered two disadvantages; insufficient A/S protection for such a valuable vessel and, if the wind was light and from a direction opposite to the force's line of advance, the carrier could become detached too far and for too long.

The US Pacific Fleet found the solution in waters in which the air threat was often more serious than that from submarines. Carriers were grouped together as the hub of a wheel whose rim was comprised of its battleships, cruisers and destroyers. This whole formation could easily be turned together into the wind whenever a carrier needed to operate aircraft. When the number of carriers available exceeded four or five the force was divided into two or more similar groups, each of which steamed in this formation, stationed from 12 to 20 miles abeam of each other. This held good for cruising and against air attack: only if Japanese battleships appeared on the scene were the battleships detached for the traditional line ahead gun action.

None of the combatant Fleets had enough destroyers to carry out the massed flotilla attacks which were so often practised between the wars. They had to be content with ordering the ships of a single flotilla, or less, to fire torpedoes as opportunity offered from different bearings, if possible more or less together, known as the 'star' method. Britain's Captain M. L. Power, after turning a Nelsonian blind eye to his C-in-C's order to withdraw from the Straits of Malacca, thus sank the Japanese 8-inch cruiser *Haguro* during the night of 14 May 1945. Incidentally, and contrary to all experience in World War One and of exercises between the wars, the best countermeasure was found to be a turn *towards* a torpedo attack which had the advantage of closing gun range instead of opening it.

The above described Circle Formation was adopted by Britain's Navy when the war in Europe, and her building programme, allowed an adequate fleet to be deployed in the Pacific. The British also adopted another US innovation: because the senior officer of the carriers was in the best position to manoeuvre a force for flying operations, he was usually designated Officer in Tactical Command (OTC) by day, this responsibility reverting to the overall commander, in a battleship or cruiser, by night, when little flying took place, and if a surface ship action developed.

The circle was, nonetheless, found to have one disadvantage. It was so compact that its radar gave too little warning of air attack for a force to fly off fighters to reinforce its CAP. Some destroyers were therefore fitted with long range air warning radar and stationed 50 miles out on an arc covering the bearings from which air attack must come. These Radar Pickets were inevitably vulnerable: although each was provided with its own CAP, as many as six were sunk and 13 seriously damaged during the 1945 Okinawa operations. A better solution was found in Aircraft Early Warning (AEW) planes; search aircraft fitted with long range air warning radar which could operate further from the force, and give even longer warning of enemy air attack, but which were less vulnerable than radar pickets.

So much for fleet tactics; now for convoys, of which slow ones steamed at 7–9½ knots and fast ones at 10–14½. Merchant ships with speeds of 17 knots or more were often allowed to proceed independently, relying on their speed to escape attack, except for liners carrying troops which were usually escorted, the notable exceptions being the handful of monster liners, such as the ss *Queen Elizabeth*, whose very high speed was considered sufficient protection. Convoys were initially limited to some 40 merchant ships on the principle that 'the larger the convoys the greater the risk': not until halfway through World War Two was it appreciated that the escort's strength should be calculated according to the total area within a convoy's boundaries, not on the number of vessels in it, so that a very large convoy required fewer escorts than two or three smaller ones, after which convoys of 100 or more vessels were formed.

Merchant ships usually steamed in columns of up to five vessels in line ahead disposed abeam. As soon as sufficient A/S escorts were available, five or more of these provided a screen against attack from ahead, whilst one or two were stationed astern to drive off any U-boat attempting to shadow the convoy from its rear. Shore-based A/S aircraft patrolled at a distance round the convoy, not only to spot U-boats but to make them submerge, which handicapped their ability to attain favourable attacking positions. Against attack by an enemy surface raider, a battleship, cruiser, or armed merchant cruiser was included in a convoy. And when Atlantic convoys were placed at risk by *Luftwaffe* bombers, a number of merchant ships was fitted with catapults to launch a single fighter, one such CAM ship being included in each convoy. This was, however, only a temporary one-shot measure: having exhausted its fuel the fighter had no alternative to ditching, its pilot being rescued by an escort. As soon as escort carriers became available, one was included in each convoy, both to give it fighter protection and to provide an A/S patrol when no shore-based one was available.

Such were the normal arrangements for most Atlantic convoys, which were at first used only within some 500 miles of the British Isles, at which distance those outward bound were dispersed to proceed independently to their various destinations. If inward bound for the UK they assembled at a designated port of departure (*e.g.* Halifax, Nova Scotia) and proceeded in formation without an A/S escort until they reached the 500 mile limit. But as Germany's U-boats were driven to operate further and further out in the Atlantic, both inward and outward bound convoys proceeded in formation, and were by 1942 provided with A/S air and surface escorts, for their whole voyage.

There were also special convoys; those which had to be fought through waters in which they were subject to heavy air or surface attack as well as by U-boats, and those carrying troops and their landing craft, tanks, ammunition and stores for amphibious landings. Examples of the former are the Allied convoys to and from Russia, which Arctic ice compelled to steer within easy range of German airfields as well as of German surface ships and U-boats operating from Norwegian fiords; and those through the Mediterranean to supply beleaguered Malta, which had to run the gauntlet of the Italian fleet and the *Regia Aeronautica*. Their escorts included AA cruisers in addition to numerous destroyers, and they were provided with a covering force of battleships, aircraft-carriers and cruisers, which operated independently from 20 to 100 miles from the convoy. Assault convoys were similarly escorted by cruisers as well as by escort carriers, and covered by task groups of battleships and fleet carriers.

U-boats were relatively few during the first year of the war, not least because of the small number in commission. But coincident with Germany's acquisition of Brest and Lorient, Dönitz realized that Britain's convoy system had filled the Atlantic with more voids than shipping, more especially because he was given little support by the *Luftwaffe*. His near decisive solution to obtaining maximum sinkings from meagre ocean reconnaissance was 'wolf-pack' tactics. His U-boats were deployed singly across the convoy routes crossing the Atlantic, and running down to the Mediterranean and further south. As soon as one sighted a convoy she reported its position, course and speed to Lorient, and thereafter shadowed and continued to report whilst Dönitz ordered as many other U-boats as were within range, to converge ahead of it. Not until a concentration had been achieved—in 1941 about six, by 1943 as many as 20—were they allowed to attack.

As opportunity offered each U-boat in turn closed the convoy to fire torpedoes, preferably from outside the screen but sometimes from inside it. Each then regained a position ahead of the convoy whilst unloading its torpedo tubes before carrying out another attack. Their submerged speed was too slow for these tactics; they were usually carried out on the surface by night when darkness provided them with some immunity from counter-measures. The screen endeavoured to frustrate these attacks. As and when a U-boat was sighted by an aircraft in the vicinity of a convoy, or when one was detected by huff-duff or radar, an escort steamed at high speed for its position, or along its bearing, compelling it to submerge. If the escort gained sonar contact, it was joined by another so that the pair could carry out co-ordinated depth-charge, hedgehog or squid attacks (*i.e.* one in contact directing the other by R/T as she ran in, and inevitably, lost contact at the crucial moment) for as long as was necessary to sink the U-boat or until it eluded them and made good its escape.

To make it more difficult for U-boats to carry out these tactics, which required them to remain on the surface for much of the time so that they could use their higher surface speed, escorts were by 1942 provided with Snowflake illuminating rockets, and A/S aircraft were fitted with the Leigh Light, both of which were intended to turn night into day. Nonetheless, slow convoys were sometimes subjected to pack tactics for more than a week, until all of the concentration of U-boats had been sunk or had expended their torpedoes, whereas fast convoys were more fortunate, because U-boats lacked the surface speed to keep touch with them for long.

To thwart these tactics, the Allies, when they had a sufficiency of ships, augmented the escorts of Atlantic convoys with Support Groups. Composed of half-a-dozen A/S vessels under an experienced escort commander, several of these were, for example, deployed in areas to the west of Ireland. As soon as the C-in-C Western Approaches, in his Liverpool headquarters, knew, often from radio intelligence, that a U-boat pack was closing a convoy, the nearest support group was ordered to join it, adding substantially to its defensive screen and, more important, its attacking power.

For an ocean convoy menaced by an enemy battleship or cruiser very different tactics were employed. If such an assailant was sighted, the convoy was ordered to scatter, *i.e.* each vessel to make off independently at her best speed away from the enemy which reduced the number which she could sink. On 5 November 1940 Convoy HX 84, of 37 ships, sighted the *Admiral Scheer* in mid-Atlantic. Captain E. S. F. Fegan, of the armed merchant cruiser *Jervis Bay*, immediately ordered it to scatter and headed his unarmoured vessel, mounting eight 6-inch guns, straight for his powerful adversary. The result was a foregone conclusion, but Fegan's dauntless courage saved all but five ships of the convoy and earned him a posthumous Victoria Cross. But to scatter a convoy *before* sighting an enemy could be disastrous, as when Pound (unhappily by then a mortally sick man[8]) ordered Convoy PQ17 to scatter, and its escorts and covering force to withdraw to the west, on 4 July 1942 on the strength of intelligence that it might be attacked by the *Tirpitz*. (He should have signalled the intelligence to the escort commander, *i.e.* the man on the spot, and left to him the action to be taken on it.) As the tragic consequence as many as 23 out of a total of 36 British and US merchant ships carrying war supplies to Archangel were sunk by German U-boats and *Luftwaffe* bombers as they made their lone way round North Cape.

Enough of the *machines* with which the Second World War was fought at sea, and of the changes which they enforced on maritime strategy and tactics. It is time to turn to the use to which the *men* of the Allied Fleets, who were increased ten fold above their peace time numbers, and their adversaries, put those machines in specific battles—men who fought in battles involving victory or defeat, life or death.

NOTES

[1] For examples of faulty co-operation between the *Luftwaffe* and the German Navy see *Hitler's Naval War* by Cajus Bekker.

[2] Admiral of the Fleet Sir Algernon Willis in his (unpublished) *War Memoirs*. A. J. P. Taylor expresses this criticism in stronger terms: 'This strategical obsession was the main cause of British misfortunes in the Second World War' (*English History, 1914–1945*).

[3] Samuel Eliot Morison in *The Two-Ocean War*.

[4] See Postscript 2 on page 247.

[5] The British were able to crack Italian ciphers from the time of the Italo-Abyssinian crisis of 1935–36, an episode which gave the German Reich its first real chance to break British ciphers. See Postscript 2.

[6] In a lecture to the Royal United Services Institute for Defence Studies in October 1972.

[7] Lieutenant-Commander D. W. Waters, RN, in *Notes on the Convoy System of Naval Warfare, Thirteenth to Twentieth Centuries*.

[8] Pound submitted his resignation in February 1943 but Churchill refused to accept it. He also declined to act on the advice of Sir Stafford Cripps, after representations by the other Sea Lords early in 1943, to the effect that Pound was no longer fit to continue his onerous duties. The Prime Minister had no wish to lose a First Sea Lord who seldom obstructed his dynamic ideas for prosecuting the war at sea. He was only compelled to accept Pound's resignation when he suffered a paralyzing stroke in August 1943. He died two months later. Churchill had by then reluctantly accepted the determined Admiral Sir Andrew Cunningham, C-in-C Mediterranean, as his successor after Admiral Sir Bruce Fraser had declined the post, saying that whilst he believed he had the confidence of his own Home Fleet, 'Cunningham has that of the whole Navy'.

PART 2: IN THE ATLANTIC AND MEDITERRANEAN

5 Narvik

The two naval actions which were fought within the brief span of four days in April 1940, known as the first and second battles of Narvik, are unique. There have been other engagements between ships in confined waters—Nelson in Aboukir Bay, 1798, Codrington at Navarino, 1827, Farragut in Mobile Bay, 1864, and Dewey in Manila Bay, 1898—but none in waters so confined as those of a Norwegian fiord whose surrounding mountains echoed every salvo with a reverberating roar.

Grand Admiral Raeder learned from Vice-Admiral Wegener's *Maritime Strategy of the Great War*, published in 1929, that if Germany had occupied Norway in 1914, Tirpitz's High Seas Fleet would have been free, within the limits of his ships' endurance, to operate against Allied trade in the north Atlantic from Norway's fiords, instead of being rendered impotent by the blockade maintained by Britain's Grand Fleet from Scapa Flow. As early as October 1939 he brought this to Hitler's attention, stressing the potentialities of Norway's fiords as advanced bases from which surface ships and U-boats might reach the trade routes without having to run the gauntlet of Britain's Home Fleet and the RAF's Coastal Command. But the *Führer* was against attacking neutral Norway for so long as it seemed possible that, after his lightning conquest of Poland had removed Britain's and France's treaty obligation to go to her aid, these two countries might be persuaded to negotiate for peace.

Raeder bided his time until Hitler's optimism had evaporated. In December he returned to the idea, adding that a German invasion of Norway should be easy because of the support to be expected from a Fifth Column led by the traitor Vidkun Quisling. In this same month of the Phoney War—so called because, except on the high seas, hostilities were quiescent—Hitler was disturbed to learn that Britain was seeking permission from Norway and Sweden to send a force of volunteers to fight with the Finns, who had suffered an unprovoked attack by Germany's co-belligerent, the USSR, on 30 November; and to land

British troops to reinforce the Norwegian garrisons of the three ports to be used for this operation, Stavanger, Bergen and Trondheim.

This news was followed by intelligence, provided by Germany's 'B' Service, that Britain's First Lord of the Admiralty, Winston Churchill, was pressing the Cabinet to allow the Home Fleet to mine The Leads— the channel inside Norway's numerous offshore islands, from Vest Fiord down to Stavanger, by which Germany obtained high-grade iron ore, mined in northern Sweden and shipped from the Norwegian port of Narvik during the winter months, when the safer route by way of Luleå and the Gulf of Bothnia was closed by ice. Hitler then authorized Raeder and General von Falkenhorst to plan an invasion which the Norwegians might oppose, notwithstanding Quisling, though not in any great strength in view of the extent to which their Armed Forces had been allowed to decline through decades of fervent neutrality, and, as a complementary necessity, a simultaneous occupation of Denmark, whose Armed Forces were even weaker than Norway's.

Soon after this, in January 1940, Britain began planning to send help to Finland and to mine The Leads even if Norway refused her agreement. When the *Altmark* incident (described in Chapter One) provided evidence that Norway would not resist German infringements of her neutrality, the date for these operations was set for mid-March. But to Hitler the *Altmark* affair was evidence that Britain would only respect Norway's neutrality for so long as it suited her: to guard against Britain occupying Norway before Germany could do so, he ordered the invasion to be at four days notice from 10 March, despite this prescient warning of possible disaster from Raeder. The operation

> . . . could only be carried out if we had naval supremacy. On the contrary we shall be carrying out the operation in the face of the vastly superior British Fleet. In spite of this, provided surprise is complete, our troops can and will be transported successfully to Norway. The most difficult operation is the return voyage which will entail breaking through the British forces.

However, by 10 March Finland had begun to negotiate an armistice with the USSR, which removed Britain's reason for occupying Norway's ports. Her plans to do this were, therefore, cancelled. But the British Cabinet could not resist Churchill's sustained arguments for mining The Leads when these were supported by the French Government. They not only authorized the mining for 5 April but, because this could be expected to provoke retaliation by Germany, added a new plan to transport 18,000 British, French and Polish troops to reinforce the Norwegian garrisons of Stavanger, Bergen, Trondheim and Narvik *if and when* 'the Germans set foot on Norwegian soil, or there is clear evidence that they intend to do so'.

This caveat, which failed to recognize the ruthlessness with which Germany waged war, was to be as fatal for the Allies as a chance last

minute postponement of the mining operation from 5 to 8 April.
Germany's 'B' Service not only told Raeder that the Allies had cancelled
their help for Finland, but enough about the mining for him to persuade
Hitler to authorize their invasion for one of the dark nights of the next
new moon period. D-day for simultaneous surprise landings in Denmark
and Norway was set for 9 April, with zero hour at 0515. For these Raeder
intended to use almost all his surface fleet (except for the pocket-
battleship *Admiral Scheer*, the 8-inch cruiser *Prinz Eugen* and the 6-inch
cruisers *Leipzig* and *Nürnberg*, which were refitting or repairing action
damage), plus the majority of Dönitz's U-boats which were withdrawn
from the Atlantic for this purpose.

The first German vessels left Hamburg on 3 April with orders to reach
Stavanger, Trondheim and Narvik before 9 April: seven freighters carry-
ing several thousand troops concealed in their holds which were to be
Trojan Horses. The main forces sailed on 7–8 April. The battlecruisers
Gneisenau, Captain H. Netzbandt flying the flag of Vice-Admiral G.
Lütjens, and *Scharnhorst*, Captain K. Hoffmann, headed north, while 31
U-boats were deployed off Vest Fiord (which leads north to Narvik),
Trondheim, Bergen, Stavanger and to the east of the Orkney and Shetland
Islands, all to cover the landings against interference by the British Fleet.

Group One, comprising 10 destroyers under Commodore F. Bonte,
carried 2,000 troops for Narvik. Group Two, comprising the 8-inch
cruiser *Admiral Hipper*, Captain H. Heye, and four destroyers, carried
1,700 troops for Trondheim. Group Three, headed by the 6-inch cruisers
Köln, flying the flag of Rear-Admiral H. Schmundt, and *Königsberg*,
carried 1,900 troops for Bergen. Group Four, headed by the 6-inch cruiser
Karlsruhe, Captain Rieve, was destined for Kristiansand. Group Five,
which included the 8-inch cruiser *Blücher*, flying the flag of Rear-Admiral
O. Kummetz, the pocket-battleship *Lützow* (ex-*Deutschland*) and the 6-
inch cruiser *Emden*, carried 2,000 troops for Oslo. Group Six, of four minesweepers carrying 150 troops, headed for the cable station at Egersund.
These were to be followed by 15 merchant ships carrying 3,761 more
troops, vehicles and stores. To refuel the German destroyers, which
would be necessary before they could return to Germany, the tankers
Kattegat and *Jan Wellen* were ordered to Narvik, and the *Skagerrak* to
Trondheim. Five more groups carried troops to Danish ports.

All this, the first major amphibious operation of the war, was meticul-
ously planned and well executed except for one disaster suffered by
Group Five, to be mentioned later, and three significant failures. Delayed
by the Norwegians' inability to provide sufficient pilots, none of the
Trojan Horses reached their destinations until after zero hour, and only
one of them even then: the rest were intercepted and sunk by Allied units.
And the U-boats achieved very little because all their torpedo attacks on
British warships failed due to faulty depth keeping mechanisms and in-

effective magnetic pistols: their bag was limited to two British submarines and six merchant ships for the loss of four of their own number.

In sharp contrast Allied reaction was hesitant, extemporized piecemeal, and ill coordinated. To begin with the Home Fleet was caught off balance, in the middle of the mining operation and preparing to land garrisons for Norway's ports. On 7 April two of its destroyers were simulating mine-laying off Kristiansand while four others laid a mine barrage off Bodö, and the minelayer *Teviot Bank* and four destroyers were en route to lay another field. To cover these ships against German interference the battle-cruiser *Renown*, Captain C. E. B. Simeon, flying the flag of Vice-Admiral William Whitworth, accompanied by eight destroyers was patrolling to the west of Trondheim. Twenty-four hours earlier the Admiralty had received sufficient reports of unusual activity in German ports, including a seaward movement by the *Gneisenau* and *Scharnhorst*, to warn the C-in-C Home Fleet, Admiral Forbes, who also received RAF reconnais-sance reports of Groups One and Two steering northwards near the Horns Reef. He had not, however, proceeded to sea to intercept the enemy because the Admiralty signalled: 'All these reports are of doubtful value and may well be only a further move in the war of nerves'. None-theless the 8-inch cruisers *Devonshire*, flag of Vice-Admiral John Cunningham, *Berwick* and *York* and the 6-inch cruiser *Glasgow*, plus six destroyers were ordered to Rosyth to embark the garrison troops.

These doubts were sufficiently resolved next day, 7 April, by an RAF report of an enemy force off the Skagerrak heading north, whereupon Forbes sailed his available ships at 2015. The battleships *Rodney* (flag) and *Valiant*, the battlecruiser *Repulse*, the 6-inch cruisers *Penelope* and *Sheffield* and 10 destroyers, plus the French 6-inch cruiser *Emile Bertin*, flying the flag of Rear-Admiral Derrien, and two destroyers, steered north from Scapa, while Vice-Admiral Sir George Edward-Collins took the 6-inch cruisers *Galatea* and *Arethusa* with eight destroyers north-east towards Stavanger. At the same time the Bergen bound convoy ON25 was recalled and its escort, the 6-inch cruisers *Manchester*, flag of Vice-Admiral Geoffrey Layton, and *Southampton* and four destroyers, were released to join Forbes. So, too, was the *Teviot Bank* recalled and her destroyers placed at Forbes' disposal, while Vice-Admiral Sir Max Horton ordered 26 of his submarines to be ready to intercept German counter-strokes. It will be noted that neither side deployed an aircraft-carrier, Germany because the *Graf Zeppelin* was still incomplete, Britain for the less adequate reason that the *Ark Royal* and the *Glorious* had been sent to the better weather of the Mediterranean to train their air-crews, while the *Furious*, which was in the Clyde was not immediately available for operations.

For much of the next day, 8 April, both the Admiralty and Forbes, whilst not entirely discounting an invasion of Norway, believed that the reported German movements presaged a break-out by the *Gneisenau* and

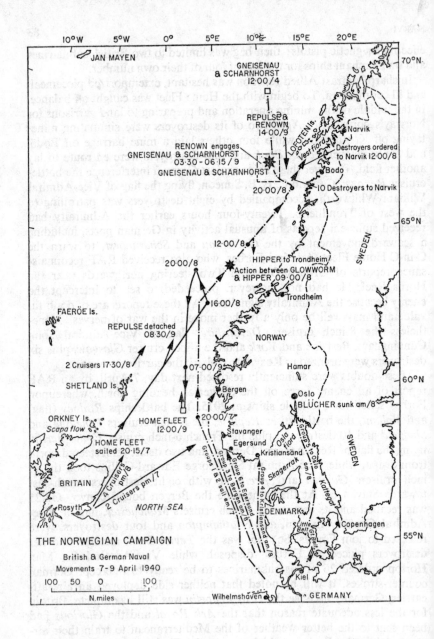

THE NORWEGIAN CAMPAIGN

British & German Naval
Movements 7-9 April 1940

100 50 0   100
N.miles

Scharnhorst into the Atlantic. Since this seemed to be confirmed by a chance incident that morning, the Home Fleet was disposed across the northern exit from the North Sea to counter it. Whitworth had left the destroyer *Glowworm* behind to search for a man lost overboard. Hurrying to rejoin the *Renown* through a dawn snowstorm, Lieutenant-Commander G. B. Roope suddenly sighted and engaged two German destroyers from Group Two. These summoned the *Hipper*, whose 8-inch guns quickly overwhelmed the British vessel. Roope sheered off for long enough to discharge his prime duty, to radio an enemy report, showing how well the Royal Navy had learned this vital lesson from such Grand Fleet's failures in World War One as the successful German raid on a Norwegian convoy on 17 October 1917. Then, because escape through such heavy seas was impossible, he turned towards his powerful opponent in the forlorn hope of torpedoing her.

When this failed, Roope headed his burning destroyer straight for the enemy cruiser, ramming her starboard bow and grinding down her side to tear off 130 feet of her armour belt and wrenching her starboard torpedo tubes from their mounting. To his credit Captain Heye withheld further fire at such a dauntless foe: he waited until the *Glowworm* blew up and sank shortly after 0900, then rescued 38 of her crew. Roope was among those who reached the *Hipper*'s side, but he was too exhausted to haul himself inboard and was drowned. Such matchless gallantry earned him a posthumous Victoria Cross, the first of three to be won during this campaign and the first to be gained by the Royal Navy during World War Two. The damage he had done was not, however, enough to prevent the *Hipper* continuing on her course for Trondheim.

Forbes responded to the *Glowworm*'s report by ordering the *Repulse, Penelope* and four destroyers to help Whitworth to make contact with the enemy. To the same end Whitworth turned the *Renown* south until the Admiralty intervened to the extent of ordering the four destroyers minelaying off Bodö to join him, which required him to turn north again in order to effect a rendezvous off Vest Fiord. Further evidence of a possible German break out into the Atlantic then came from an RAF plane which, at 1400, reported the *Hipper* and her accompanying destroyers as an enemy battlecruiser and two cruisers off Trondheim, steering *west*. But this same afternoon also provided strong evidence of the Germans' real purpose, when the Polish submarine *Orzel*, Lieutenant-Commander Grudzinski, sank the German transport *Rio de Janeiro* in the Skagerrak after giving time for her passengers and crew to take to the boats, and reported that the former were in fact uniformed German troops bound for Bergen. Nonetheless the Norwegian Government did no more than alert their coast defences—mobilization was not considered—whilst Whitehall remained sufficiently certain that the Germans intended an Atlantic operation to order Cunningham's four cruisers and six destroyers to land their troops at Rosyth—just when they could have been of real value in Norway—and to join Forbes' flag.

The evening brought two more reports; from the British naval attaché in Copenhagen of Group Five passing north through the Belt; and from the submarine *Trident* of an unsuccessful torpedo attack on the *Lützow* as she headed for Oslo Fiord. From this evidence Forbes was sure that the Germans were about to invade Norway, but he shared the Admiralty's view that a simultaneous break out was still likely and must be guarded against. To this end he turned his main fleet south, about 80 miles from the Norwegian coast, towards Edward-Collins's weak force patrolling to seaward of Bergen. But the Admiralty held different ideas: Cunningham's cruisers, plus the French *Emile Bertin,* were ordered to sweep northwards in the middle of the North Sea while Layton's and Edward-Collins' ships waited in the same area. Since this left Forbes with only his small battle force to sweep south some 60 miles from the Norwegian coast, he tried to correct these dispositions to bring the cruisers closer to Norway. But the Admiralty promptly countermanded his orders. Order, counterorder, disorder, has been well said. But in the event this Admiralty intervention during the night of 8–9 April was of no consequence. With zero hour set for 0515, it was already too late for the Home Fleet to forestall the German invasion. All 11 assault groups were nearing their respective destinations and about to land their troops on Norwegian and Danish soil.

But before this happened another of Forbes' forces encountered the enemy. Having rendezvoused at 1745 off the entrance to Vest Fiord with the destroyers whose minelaying had been cancelled, Whitworth in the *Renown* decided to stand out to sea in the hope of intercepting the German vessels which, from the false RAF report of heavy ships steering *west* off Trondheim, he, like Forbes, believed might be heading for the Atlantic. In so doing he just missed sighting Bonte's destroyers heading for Narvik; and by the time that the Admiralty signalled him to concentrate on preventing a German force proceeding to this port, he had run into an Arctic gale so strong that he had to reply that he would 'patrol the entrance to Vest Fiord when weather moderates'.

At 0230 next morning, 9 April, the sea had gone down enough for Whitworth to reverse course to the south-east. One hour later, at 0337, 50 miles to seaward of the entrance to Vest Fiord, he glimpsed to the east the distant silhouettes of the *Gneisenau* and *Scharnhorst,* steering north-west in accordance with their orders to prevent British interference with the German assault groups, more especially the one destined for Narvik. Mistaking one of the enemy ships for the cruiser *Hipper,* Captain Simeon immediately closed the range at his battlecruiser's best speed in the prevailing weather and, when it was down to 19,000 yards, opened fire. Caught at a disadvantage in the dawn light, both German vessels were taken by suprise: the *Renown*'s gun flashes, and the tall splashes raised by her 15-inch shells falling round the *Gneisenau,* were their first indication that they had encountered the enemy.

They were, however, quick to return the *Renown*'s fire with all 18 of their 11-inch guns. But the duel which then developed on parallel courses did not last for long. Although their 4·7-inch guns could inflict no significant damage, especially at long range in heavy weather, the British destroyers could not resist 'having a go'; and in the semi-darkness Admiral Lütjens supposed their gun flashes to come from the *Repulse* (which had not yet joined up with the *Renown*). After the *Renown* had received two hits which did little damage, and the *Gneisenau* three, of which one put her forward main armament control out of action, Lütjens decided against risking his country's only two capital ships against a supposedly equivalent British force, and turned away to the north-east.

Whitworth gave chase into the teeth of the gale, Simeon's ship working up to as much as 29 knots. But by disregarding the damage done to his ships by the heavy seas—both had their forward turrets put out of action —Lütjens managed to draw slowly away from his opponent. And neither side scored further hits at an ever-increasing range before, at 0615, they finally lost sight of each other. Whitworth held on for a time in the hope of regaining contact, but to no avail; and soon after 0900 he began receiving reports which required him to turn his mind from this tactical victory to other matters.

The Danes, whose Armed Forces were tiny compared with those of Germany, and who moreover suffered the disadvantages of a common frontier with the Third *Reich*, could not be expected to oppose an invasion. Groups Seven to Eleven encountered no resistance when they arrived to seize Copenhagen and other ports in Denmark, which was thus doomed to Nazi occupation for the remainder of the war. But it was otherwise with most of the groups which faced a nation directly descended from men so fearless as the Vikings. Group Five's entry into Oslo Fiord was first challenged by the patrol-boat *Pol III*, of 214 tons armed with a single gun, which was only sunk after her mortally wounded captain, W. Olsen, had successfully rammed the torpedo-boat *Albatross*. And Admiral Kummetz's subsequent attempt to land troops to capture the naval base of Horten was delayed by Captain Briseid's small minelayer *Olav Tryggvason* whose four 4·7-inch guns sank the minesweeper *R17* and further damaged the *Albatross* before she was overwhelmed.

Even so Kummetz was foolhardy enough to continue at the slow speed of 12 knots towards the Drobak Narrows, where the fiord is only 500 yards wide and was heavily defended by forts. Holding their fire until the flagship *Blücher* was at point blank range, their 8-inch and 11-inch guns seriously damaged this new 8-inch cruiser and set her ablaze. Their torpedoes then reduced her to a helpless hulk; and at 0630 she capsized and sank with the loss of more than 1,000 officers and men.

D

Before this disaster occurred, but after the *Lützow* had received three 11-inch hits, Captain A. Thiele wisely reversed course, and led the *Emden* and the rest of the group down the fiord to land their troops below the Narrows. Since von Falkenhorst's simultaneous airborne assault on the Norwegian capital was also delayed by fog, the German plan to occupy Oslo at 0515 was sufficiently disrupted to allow time for the Norwegian Royal Family and Government to make a hurried escape by a special train which left for Hamar at 0730. When seaborne and airborne troops finally arrived around noon they found only a puppet government formed by Quisling, which had no authority over the rest of a country that continued to owe allegiance to King Haakon VII.

Group Four, led by the *Karlsruhe*, was first delayed by fog, then met such fierce fire from the forts guarding the approaches to Kristiansand, despite bombing by the *Luftwaffe*, that Captain Rieve was compelled to retire seawards under cover of smoke. When he next tried to force an entry the visibility was so poor that he all but ran his ship ashore. But his third attempt, towards noon, was successful because the commander of the forts was tricked into doing nothing by a false message: 'British and French destroyers coming to your help. Do not fire.' By 1700 the town had been occupied by German troops. Further to the north, the Norwegian destroyer *Sleipner*, which had received the *Pol III*'s alarm, sighted the German freighter *Roda* off Stavanger. Dissatisfied with the reason which she signalled for entering the port, the *Sleipner*'s captain did not hesitate to sink her. But the loss of this Trojan Horse did not prevent the seizure of Norway's finest airfield to which the *Luftwaffe* soon transferred several squadrons of dive-bombers.

Group Three was more fortunate. The fog saved its approach to Bergen from being detected by a Coastal Command plane in the afternoon of the 8th, when Edwards-Collins' force could have brought it to battle before nightfall. Admiral Schmundt was able to deceive the coast defences into believing that his ships were British until after daylight and he was very near the town. Then the *Königsberg* suffered three damaging 8-inch shells hits and the gunnery training ship *Bremse* one, before the Germans finally entered the port and landed troops who overcame all further resistance by 0900.

Group Two was most fortunate of all. The forts guarding the approaches to Trondheim had received no orders to be on the alert. With the *Hipper* flashing deceptive messages in English, Captain Heye led his ships past them at 25 knots before a shot was fired. The city was in German hands by 0800, although it took two further days to overcome the spirited but belated resistance of the forts which had failed to bar the *Hipper*'s way.

Bad weather and faulty British dispositions, above all the Admiralty's withdrawal of the minelaying destroyers from the entrance to Vest Fiord at the crucial moment, allowed Group One to make its final approach during the night without hindrance and undetected. At 0410 Commodore Bonte's destroyers carrying troops of General Dietl's mountain division entered Ofot Fiord. There Bonte detached three ships to deal with supposed (in reality non-existent) forts defending the Ramnes Narrows, and four to occupy the township of Elvegaard in Herjangs Fiord, whilst in his own ship, the *Heidkamp,* he led the *Arnim* and *Thiele* on to the town of Narvik.

Dead on zero hour, at 0515, he saw its harbour ahead crowded with merchant ships of many nations. First he dealt with the Norwegian coastal defence vessel *Eidsvold,* Commander Willoch, completed as far back as 1900 with two 8-inch and six 6-inch guns, by sending an officer over to demand a free passage. In the interval he trained his torpedo tubes on her. When the German officer fired a red Very light to indicate that passage had been refused, two torpedoes sent the *Eidsvold* to the bottom with Willoch and all but a handful of his crew. The explosion awakened her sister ship, the *Norge,* Commander Askim. Seeing the *Arnim* going alongside a jetty with her decks crowded with troops, Askim opened fire. But his ship's old guns were no match for modern 5-inch weapons; nor could they protect her from German torpedoes: she was quickly sunk with few more than 50 survivors. After this Bonte met no further resistance because the commander of the garrison proved to be a Quisling traitor who ordered his troops to lay down their arms, leaving Dietl in firm control well before noon.

In sum, Raeder's and von Falkenhorst's plan had been almost wholly successful—so far. By a combination of surprise, boldness, speed and ruthlessness, German ships and troops had captured Norway's capital, her chief ports, and her principal airfields, all in the space of a few hours, with only one serious casualty, the unnecessary loss of the *Blücher.*

But this was not the end of the story. By 0630 on 9 April both the Admiralty and Forbes were at last certain of Germany's real purpose. Because the bulk of the Home Fleet was then concentrating some 90 miles to seaward of Bergen, their first reaction was to try to save this port. Parting company at 1130, Layton intended to send his seven destroyers up this fiord at dusk while his four 6-inch cruisers remained in support off its entrances. Had he continued his mission he might have sunk the *Köln,* whom he would have met as she was leaving for her return to Germany, and the damaged *Königsberg* and *Bremse.* But the Admiralty had second thoughts during the afternoon; when they received an aircraft report of two German cruisers lying in Bergen harbour they cancelled the operation and ordered Layton to rejoin his C-in-C.

Meantime both Forbes' and Layton's forces were subjected to attacks by the *Luftwaffe.* Fortunately these were by high-level bombers—the Germans had yet to appreciate the difficulty of hitting a fast-moving target from above 10,000 feet—because the British ships had to depend on their inadequate AA gun armaments for their defence. They were too

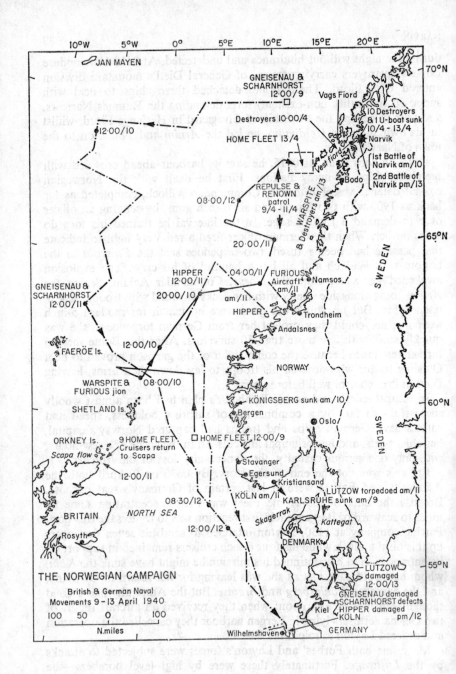

THE NORWEGIAN CAMPAIGN

British & German Naval
Movements 9–13 April 1940

100   50   0   100

N. miles

far from Scotland's airfields to be covered by RAF fighters. The *Southampton* and *Glasgow* were damaged by near-misses, the *Rodney* was hit by a heavy bomb which splintered her armoured deck but failed to explode, and the destroyer *Gurkha* was sunk, which was enough to persuade Forbes that his fleet would have to operate further to the north. But first he steered west to join up with two substantial reinforcements, the battleship *Warspite,* Captain V. A. Crutchley, recently recalled from the Mediterranean, and the aircraft-carrier *Furious* which had by this time embarked her aircraft and sailed to join him.

The German ships in Bergen were attacked by 24 RAF high-level bombers on the evening of the 9th without result. Early next morning Fleet Air Arm planes from Hatston in the Orkneys were more successful.

Seven led by Captain R. T. Partridge, Royal Marines, and nine led by Lieutenant W. P. Lucy, RN, loaded with 500 lb bombs, wallowed east, nursing every yard of the 300 miles to the Norwegian shore. A few minutes after 0700, they hit the Norwegian coast opposite Bergen as a blood-red sun rose over the hills. They climbed to 8,000 feet. Soon they could see the *Königsberg.* The two squadrons went into line astern. Then Lucy tipped the leading plane into a sixty-degree dive. The Germans had been caught unawares. Their first hint of danger was the roar of Lucy's bombs. The *Königsberg* was lifted half out of the water, then flung violently against the mole. And before her crew could recover their wits the *Königsberg* had been smothered in fifteen hits and near misses.

As soon as the Germans woke up to what was happening, a fair volume of fire was thrown up from the encircling hills, and from the cruiser herself and the ships in harbour. Three planes were hit: one badly. But the *Königsberg* suffered a great deal more. Three bombs were direct hits on 'A' turret, on the port quarter, and amidships. She became a blazing wreck. As the last plane disappeared to seaward, she rolled on to her side. Within minutes the flames got to her magazines. There was a heavy explosion and the *Königsberg* broke in half, capsized and sank.

The planes set course for home. After a flight of four hours and thirty minutes, Partridge touched down at Hatston. Several of them hadn't enough fuel in their tanks to cover an up-ended penny.[1]

The *Königsberg* was the first major warship to be sunk by bombing in war. This attack was followed on the 11th by one on Trondheim by torpedo-bombers from the *Furious.* Unhappily, like the *Köln* from Bergen, the *Hipper* had already sailed; and the waters in which the German destroyers remained awaiting a tanker to refuel them, were so shallow that the British torpedoes exploded harmlessly on the bottom.

Forbes now had to send many of his ships back to Scapa for fuel. With the rest he moved north in the hope of saving Narvik, which brings us to the two battles which are the prime subject of this chapter. But first to summarize the achievements of Max Horton's submarines; of which three were in the Kattegat, three in the Skagerrak and three off the west coast of Denmark, with six more covering the approaches to ports in the Heligoland Bight. The *Orzel's* attack on the *Rio de Janeiro* has been noted already. The *Trident* was as successful against the German tanker *Posidonia* on the same date, 8 April. Next day the *Sunfish* sank the laden transport *Amasis*. More important, at 1900 the *Truant*, Lieutenant-Commander C. H. Hutchinson, torpedoed and sank the *Karlsruhe* on her way back from Kristiansand. The *Truant's* subsequent escape from German A/S craft which depth-charged her remorselessly for many hours, was some compensation for the loss of the *Thistle* to a torpedo from *U4*.

At 0430 on 10 April the *Triton*, Lieutenant-Commander E. F. Pizey, sank the steamers *Friedenau* and *Wigbert* with the 900 troops destined for Oslo, and with a third torpedo destroyed one of their escort. The *Triton* owed her subsequent escape from A/S craft which dropped as many as 78 depth charges uncomfortably close, to the *Spearfish* which by some unwary movement revealed her presence in the adjacent patrol area. Hunted even more remorselessly until half-an-hour after midnight, she had not been long on the surface, to recharge her batteries and clear the foul air from within her hull, when Lieutenant-Commander J. G. Forbes chanced to sight the *Lützow* returning to Germany at high speed. And one of his torpedoes struck Thiele's pocket-battleship right aft, wrecking her propellors and rudder and leaving her a helpless hulk. With her batteries still too low for his submarine to be able to dive, and unaware that Thiele had sailed for Germany without an A/S escort, Forbes could not stay to admire his handiwork, let alone delay whilst his tubes were reloaded for a *coup de grâce*. The nearly sinking *Lützow* was eventually towed back through the Belt to Kiel, but a full 12 months elapsed before she was repaired and again ready for sea.

Other British submarine successes included the sinking of the transport *Ionia* by the *Triad* in the mouth of Oslo fiord on 11 April, the supply ship *August Leonhardt* by the *Sealion* in the Kattegat that afternoon, the tanker *Moonsund* next morning by the *Snapper*, and the transport *Florida* by the *Sunfish* on 14 April. But the *Sterlet* was not so lucky: after sinking the gunnery training ship *Brummer* on the 15th, she was counter-attacked and destroyed with all hands. Nonetheless the British submarine service had well-earned the Admiralty's signalled commendation, 'You are all doing magnificent work'—even though their targets did not include the *Gneisenau*, *Scharnhorst*, or *Hipper*.

After escaping from the *Renown* early on 9 April, Lütjens judged that his battlecruisers' best chance of eluding the British fleet, which would now be closing Norway's ports, when his task of covering the landings was done, would be to steer well to the west. Not until noon on the 10th did he turn south down the middle of the North Sea, to be joined by the *Hipper* early on the 12th and by the *Köln* later that day. All four ships thus eluded sightings by Forbes' ships or by Horton's submarines. They were, however, located early on the 12th by the RAF which sent 92 bombers to attack them. Unfortunately these could not find their target, so that all four German ships reached Wilhelmshaven safely on that evening, albeit with three of them in need of substantial repairs before they could again be used for operations.

Having so quickly captured Narvik, Commodore Bonte should have sailed his 10 destroyers at high speed back to Germany on the evening of 9 April, before they could be caught by the British fleet. But having already steamed 900 miles to the north they could not face this journey without refuelling, which they were unable to do in such a short time because one of the expected tankers had failed to arrive. All were required to use the *Jan Willen* in turn so that Bonte was obliged to defer sailing until the 10th. Meantime he arranged for one destroyer to patrol the entrance to Ofot Fiord, for two to be berthed off Ballangen 10 miles west of Narvik, for others to be berthed in Herjangs Fiord, and the rest to lie in Narvik harbour where the *Jan Willen* was anchored. These arrangements settled, Bonte turned in for the night of 9–10 April expecting a peaceful sleep, because *U51* had reported sighting five British destroyers in Vest Fiord at 2022 steering south-west, *away* from the entrance to Ofot Fiord.

Those ships were the *Hardy*, Captain B. A. Warburton-Lee, the *Hunter*, Lieutenant-Commander L. de Villiers, the *Havock*, Lieutenant-Commander R. Courage, the *Hotspur*, Commander H. F. Layman, and the *Hostile*, Commander J. P. Wright, which Forbes had ordered into Narvik 'to make certain that no enemy troops land'. They were expected to reach the port at 2000, but on the way Warburton-Lee reflected that such intelligence as he had received—that 'one German ship had arrived and landed a small force'—was so sketchy that he would be wise to stop at the entrance to the fiord and seek news from the pilot station before he went on 'to sink or capture enemy ship and land forces if you think you can recapture Narvik from number of enemy present'.

There, around 1600, he received intelligence which altered the picture; that at least six German destroyers, which he knew to be larger and more powerfully armed than his own, plus a U-boat, were in Ofot Fiord, whose entrance they might have mined. But this did not deter him from prompt action; signalling Whitworth and Forbes 'Intend[2] attacking at dawn high water' (which should give him the advantage of surprise and enable his ships to pass safely over any mines), he turned south-westwards to steam down Vest Fiord until after dark so as to mislead any enemy who might sight him—such as *U51* which, as already mentioned, duly lulled Bonte into a false sense of security.

At 2100 the Admiralty approved Warburton-Lee's attack and added, 'Good luck'. But they also instructed him to establish a patrol at the entrance to Ofot Fiord to ensure that the German ships did not make their escape during the night. Fortunately he turned a blind eye to this order which must have resulted in an encounter with Bonte's destroyer patrolling the entrance and lost him the value of surprise. Nor did he change his plans when the Admiralty had second thoughts and, supposing that Warburton-Lee's operation might be too hazardous, signalled: 'Norwegian coast defence ships *Eidsvold* and *Norge* may be in German hands: you alone can judge whether in these circumstances attack should be made. We shall support whatever decision you take.' Thus did the Admiralty rightly leave the final decision to 'the man on the spot', although, by the time he received this potentially disturbing message, Warburton-Lee was already feeling his way through snow storms into Ofot Fiord.

This intervention by the Admiralty was nonetheless unfortunate: on receiving Warburton-Lee's signal giving the German strength in Narvik, Whitworth, whose flagship had now been joined by the *Repulse*, *Penelope* and several destroyers, considered adding the cruiser *Penelope* and more destroyers to the Narvik force. He decided against doing so, in part because this would have required Warburton-Lee to delay his attack, in part because he was reluctant to confuse an issue which the Admiralty appeared to have taken out of his hands. He was not alone, in the light of subsequent events, in regretting this. The *Penelope*'s 6-inch guns would have clinched the annihilation of Bonte's force. But, at the time, he could not know this. His decision is, moreover, very understandable in view of the considerable extent to which both Forbes (legitimately) and the Admiralty (questionably) were issuing orders direct to units which were under his command as senior officer in the Narvik area.

TABLE 31: Ships Involved in the First Battle of Narvik

Ship	Displacement (tons)	Speed (knots)	Guns	Torpedoes	Remarks
Hardy	1,505	36	5 4·7in	8 21in	Sunk
Havock					—
Hostile	1,340	35	4 4·7in	8 21in	—
Hotspur					Damaged
Hunter					Sunk
Wilhelm Heidkamp					Sunk
Hermann Künne					Disabled
Hans Lüdemann	2,411	38	5 5in	8 21in	Damaged
Deither von Roeder					Seriously damaged
Anton Schmitt					Sunk
Bernd von Arnim					Seriously damaged
Erich Giese					—
Erich Koellner	2,230	38	5 5in	8 21in	—
Georg Thiele					Seriously damaged
Wolfgang Zenker					—

At 0100 on 10 April the British ships passed Tranöy pilot station in the order *Hardy, Hunter, Havock, Hotspur, Hostile,* steaming slowly in single line ahead through visibility reduced by falling snow, which caused them more than one anxious moment as first they narrowly avoided running ashore, and next averted collision with a local passenger ferry. Their way was not, however, barred by the patrolling *Roeder* as they turned east into Ofot Fiord: her captain, misreading his instructions, had withdrawn without waiting for the relieving *Lüdemann.* Nor, because of the snow and mist, were they seen by the destroyers anchored off Ballangen and in Herjangs Fiord. So Warburton-Lee achieved the surprise which he had planned: his ships reached the entrance to Narvik harbour without the Germans receiving any report of their approach. There the *Hotspur* and *Hostile* were detached to watch for, and if necessary neutralize, the batteries believed (erroneously) to be mounted on the north shore. The *Hardy* herself went ahead into the harbour, leaving the *Hunter* and *Havock* to follow.

At 0430 the white silence of that Norwegian dawn was suddenly rent by the *Hardy*'s broadsides as seven of her torpedoes sped towards the shipping in the anchorage. The sleeping Bonte and most of the crew of the *Heidkamp* met their deaths as one of these exploded in her after magazine. Two more sank the *Schmitt.* The other four struck merchant vessels or exploded against the rocky shore. All this in under five minutes in which not a shot was fired by the Germans. They only manned their guns as the *Hardy* was withdrawing to allow the *Hunter* and *Havock* to take her place. These dealt with the *Lüdemann,* which was fuelling from the *Jan Wellen,* as she hurriedly slipped her wires, putting a gun out of action and starting a blaze aft which required the magazine to be flooded. The other fuelling destroyer, the *Künne,* escaped harm because, with her engines put out of action by the concussion from the torpedo explosions which sank the *Schmitt,* she was unable to move clear of the tanker. Assisted by the *Hotspur* and *Hostile,* which had found the shore batteries to be a figment of some intelligence officer's imagination, the *Hunter* and *Havock* then reduced the *Roeder* to such a blazing wreck that her captain was obliged to beach her.

Having located and engaged decisively all but one of the six German destroyers he expected to meet, without significant damage to his own force, Warburton-Lee considered occupying the town, but realized that his handful of seamen would be no match for Dietl's troops, especially when he could not use his ships' guns to support them without endangering Norwegian lives. Since his only alternative was to withdraw, his five ships headed west at 0530 down Ofot Fiord at fifteen knots, with ample ammunition remaining but with their torpedo outfits considerably reduced.

The luck which so often favours the brave then turned against the British. As they passed Herjangs Fiord to starboard, the *Zenker, Giese*

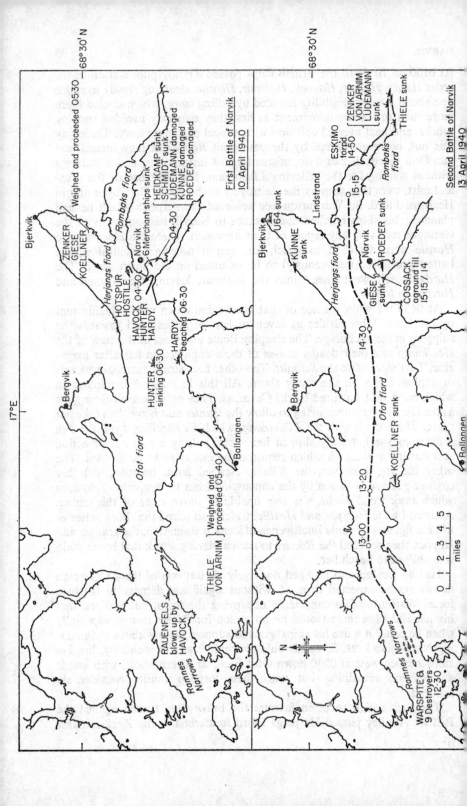

First Battle of Narvik
10 April 1940

68°30′N

Bjerkvik

ZENKER
GIESE
KOELLNER } Weighed and proceeded 0530

Herjangs fiord

HOTSPUR
HOSTILE } 04·30

Narvik 6 Merchant ships sunk

HEIDKAMP sunk
SCHMIDT sunk
LUDEMANN damaged
ROEDER damaged

Rombaks fiord

04·30

HAVOCK 04·30
HUNTER
HARDY

HARDY beached 06·30

HUNTER sinking 06·30

Bergvik

Ballangen

Ofot fiord

Ballangen

RAUENFELS
blown up by
HAVOCK

Ramnes
Narrows

THIELE
VON ARNIM } Weighed and
proceeded 05·40

17°E

N

0 1 2 3 4 5
miles

Second Battle of Narvik
13 April 1940

68°30′N

ZENKER
VON ARNIM
LUDEMANN } sunk

THIELE sunk

ESKIMO
torpd
14·50

15·15

Rombaks
fiord

Bjerkvik

U64 sunk

Lindstrand

KÜNNE
sunk

Herjangs fiord

Narvik
ROEDER sunk

GIESE
sunk

COSSACK aground till 15·15/14

14·30

13·20

13·00

Ofot fiord

Bergvik

KOELLNER sunk

Ballangen

Ramnes Narrows

WARSPITE 8
9 Destroyers
12·30

and *Koellner*—two more German destroyers than they had expected to meet anywhere in Ofot Fiord—were seen leaving this anchorage, belatedly because they had received no news of events in Narvik harbour until 0515. Mistaking them for a cruiser and three destroyers, Warburton-Lee increased speed to 30 knots as both sides opened fire. And he should have escaped from them because they had not yet refuelled and could not maintain such a high speed. But the ghost of Commodore Bonte held two more cards in his hand, the destroyers *Thiele* and *Arnim*.

Anchored for the night in Ballangen Fiord, and delayed by fog in getting under way until 0540 after receiving the alarm from Narvik, these now appeared ahead of the *Hardy*. Not only were the British ships trapped between the two German forces, but the first of many accurate German salvoes struck this flotilla leader's bridge.

Captain Warburton-Lee was hit, a bad blow, Lieutenant Cross was killed, Lieutenant-Commander Gordon-Smith was badly wounded. Paymaster Lieutenant Stanning took command. By this time we were in a worse condition than anybody else. But we had guns left and kept them working against the big German destroyers. Soon the steering wouldn't work. We ran into shallow water and grounded on the rocks about 300 yards from the shore. Then we got our last order from Captain Warburton-Lee, the last he was to give: 'Abandon ship. Every man for himself. And good luck'.

We piled overboard. Lieutenant Heppell saved at least five men by swimming backwards and forwards between the ship and the shore. Finally we got ashore, about 170 of us. Seventeen had been killed in the fight, and another two were missing. Two hundred yards away there was a house. We ploughed through nearly six feet of snow to it. A woman and her daughter did all they could for us. Captain Warburton-Lee had been towed ashore on a float, but when he reached the shore he died. The Norwegians buried him there.[3]

Meantime the *Hunter* had been left leading the British line. Receiving the enemy's full attention, de Villiers' ship was quickly set on fire and disabled. Layman in the *Hotspur*, who was next astern, gave the wheel order which would take his ship clear of her, but a German shell cut the controls before it could be applied: the *Hotspur*'s bow crashed into the hapless *Hunter*. As the enemy poured a hail of fire into the two helpless British destroyers, Layman managed to find his way from bridge to after steering position; and from there he extricated his much damaged ship from the now sinking *Hunter* and once more headed down the fiord at high speed.

The Germans' decision to concentrate their fire on the leading British ships had left the *Havock* and *Hostile* virtually undamaged. Having cleared the interlocked *Hunter* and *Hotspur,* and engaged the *Thiele* and *Arnim* at point blank range as they ran past eastwards to join up with the

Zenker, Giese and *Koellner,* Courage turned back intending to support the *Hunter* and *Hotspur* with gun fire and by screening them with smoke. But as he boldly headed his two ships towards the German five, Courage found that the enemy was in no mood to continue the fight. Three were too short of fuel; the *Thiele* had two guns out of action and had flooded a magazine; the *Arnim* had a boiler room out of action. All headed up the fiord towards Narvik whither it would have been rash to have followed them.

The score in this first battle of Narvik is memorable. Of Bonte's ten destroyers two (*Heidkamp* and *Schmitt*) had been sunk, three (*Roeder, Thiele* and *Arnim*) so seriously damaged that they were virtually unseaworthy, whilst one (*Lüdemann*) had a flooded magazine and another (*Künne*) had disabled engines. Only the *Zenker, Giese* and *Koellner* remained undamaged, but with little fuel in their tanks and only half their ammunition remaining. Against such destruction Warburton-Lee's smaller force had lost only the stranded *Hardy,* and the *Hunter* sunk in mid-fiord where the icy waters claimed many of her company before 50 could be rescued by the Germans. For achieving so much at the cost of his own life Warburton-Lee was awarded a posthumous Victoria Cross.

But this was not quite the end of the battle. As the *Hostile* led the *Havock* and the damaged *Hotspur* through the Narrows towards the sea, Wright sighted a large merchant ship entering the fiord. She was quickly brought to with a shot across her bows. A second hit her and compelled her crew to abandon ship. They were picked up by the *Havock* which sent a boarding party over to identify her as the German supply ship *Rauenfels.* To sink her Courage needed only two HE shells. The second detonated her cargo with a shattering roar and sent debris skywards for more than 3,000 feet. The surviving German destroyers were left with no source from which to replace the ammunition which they had expended.

Warburton-Lee's last signal, reporting a cruiser and three destroyers coming out of Herjangs Fiord, reached Whitworth at 0600. He immediately ordered Captain Yates to take the *Penelope* and eight destroyers to support the retirement of the five 'H' boats, after which he was to patrol the entrance to Vest Fiord 'to prevent further enemy forces reaching Narvik'. Yates fulfilled his first task by meeting the three surviving British destroyers and agreeing that the *Hostile* should escort the *Hotspur* to the shelter of Skjop Fiord, in the Lofoten Islands, for repairs to make her seaworthy. Adding the *Havock* to his own force Yates then established a patrol whose purpose, 'to prevent reinforcements reaching Narvik,' was confirmed by an Admiralty signal around noon, which also ordered him to 'allow no force from Narvik to escape'.

'Lose not an hour', wrote Nelson. Belief in this dictum gained Warburton-Lee his victory, but it was too seldom remembered by other British commanders during these anxious days. The Admiralty and

Forbes had hesitated before taking any action to prevent the German assault on Norway. So, too, with their subsequent cancelled decision to send Layton's cruiser and destroyers into Bergen. Now they and Whitworth allowed precious hours to slip by before following up Warburton-Lee's success. Not until the evening of the 10th did the Admiralty signal Yates: 'If you consider it a justifiable operation, take available destroyers in the Narvik area and attack enemy tonight or tomorrow morning'.

Here was Yates's golden moment. He would have found Captain E. Bey making desperate efforts to get the eight surviving German destroyers battleworthy. The *Giese* and *Zenker* were ready by the afternoon, and the *Koellner* would be finished by midnight, but the *Roeder* was too badly damaged to do more than defend the harbour from alongside the jetty, and the other four needed two days work to make them seaworthy. An immediate attack must have annihilated them. But Yates replied: 'Consider attack justifiable although surprise has been lost. Navigation dangerous from wrecks sunk today eliminate chances of successful night attack'. So far so good. But his signal continued: 'Propose attacking at dawn *Friday [12th] since operation orders cannot be got out and issued for tomorrow in view of present disposition of destroyers on patrol'*. Italics are well justified for this excuse for giving the Germans a further 24 hours in which to regird their loins.

Exasperated by this further example of the Admiralty taking direct control of his forces, Whitworth pointed out that such an attack conflicted with his orders to prevent Narvik being reinforced by sea. However, Churchill and Pound were not to be deflected from approving Yates's plan to attack early on 12 April. But on the afternoon of the 10th Bey received orders from Berlin to leave Narvik that night with such of his ships as were seaworthy. With only the *Giese* and *Zenker* he sailed down Ofot Fiord soon after dark. As he emerged into Vest Fiord he sighted the *Penelope* and two destroyers, without himself being seen. He immediately returned to Narvik, and next day signalled Berlin that the British forces in Vest Fiord made any attempt to return to Germany impossible, even though more of his ships would soon be ready for sea.

Meantime, during the night of the 10th, a chance incident had an untoward effect on Yates's plans. *U25* fired torpedoes at his destroyers patrolling outside the entrance to Ofot Fiord—torpedoes which were exploded by their defective magnetic pistols harmlessly short of the *Bedouin*, Commander J. A. McCoy. *U25* supposed she had sunk two enemy vessels: McCoy, believing that his ships had strayed into a controlled minefield, withdrew from the area and signalled that an attack on Narvik 'could no longer be carried out'. Around the same time Whitworth received seemingly important news from the *Hostile*, guarding the damaged *Hotspur* in Skjop Fiord. According to the Norwegian police a German warship was lying in Tennholm Fiord, 50 miles down the coast, waiting to bring a large tanker north, and to collect several transports from Bodö,

all destined for Narvik. Early on the 11th Yates was ordered to take the
Penelope and two destroyers first to Bodö, and then to Tennholm Fiord,
to destroy enemy vessels in both these places, which was to 'take pre-
cedence over attack on Narvik'.

The consequences were near disastrous for Yates. Failing to find a pilot
at Tranöy he sailed south, with the *Eskimo* and *Kimberley*, without one.
And at 1500, on the way to Bodö, the *Penelope* struck an uncharted rock
and was so badly damaged that she had to be towed by the *Eskimo* back
to Skjop Fiord. And this near loss of a 6-inch cruiser was all in vain: the
Kimberley went in to Bodö to find it empty and to learn that the only
merchant ship to call there recently was the German supply ship *Alster*,
which had been captured already by the destroyer *Icarus* in Vest Fiord.
The British were not, however, alone in suffering misfortune. By the
evening of the 11th seven out of Bey's eight remaining destroyers were
seaworthy, but he heard nothing of the accident to the *Penelope*, whose
presence in Vest Fiord was his chief reason for refusing Raeder's recall to
Germany. And that night, whilst manoeuvring in Narvik harbour, the
Koellner and the *Zenker* ran aground, the first to incur irreparable
damage, the latter to cut her speed to 20 knots.

Since the *Penelope's* accident rendered impossible an attack in force on
Narvik at dawn on the 12th, the Admiralty ordered Forbes to mount
another for the 13th, this time headed by a battleship. Early on the 12th
his flagship, with the *Warspite, Valiant* and *Furious* in company, was
joined by the *Renown* and *Repulse*. That evening planes from the
Furious delivered their already mentioned abortive raid on Trondheim,
while Whitworth transferred his flag to the *Warspite* and, with four
'Tribals' and four other destroyers, parted company with orders to attack
Narvik next day. Simultaneously Forbes learned that, to follow up this
attack, half a battalion of Scots Guards was being rushed from Scapa
Flow in the *Southampton*, to be followed next day by the remainder of
the Guards Brigade and the 146th Brigade in five transports, for whose
escort the *Valiant* and *Repulse* were detached.

Overall command of this expeditionary force was given to Admiral of
the Fleet the Earl of Cork and Orrery, who hoisted his flag in the 6-inch
cruiser *Aurora* in no doubt that the Admiralty intended that he should
occupy Narvik immediately after Whitworth had destroyed the German
destroyers in Ofot Fiord. But the expedition's military commander,
Major-General P. J. Mackesy, left London to take passage in the *Southampton* (instead of in the same ship as the Earl) with War Office orders
which said that 'it is not intended that you should land in the face of
opposition'. This combined operation's potential success also suffered the
handicap that in the short time available it had been impossible to load
the troops, weapons, ammunition and stores tactically, since they had
only recently been unloaded from Layton's cruisers.

TABLE 32: Ships Involved in the Second Battle of Narvik

Ship	Displacement (tons)	Speed (knots)	Guns	Torpedoes	Remarks
Warspite	30,600	24	8 15in 12 6in	—	Carried four aircraft
Bedouin *Cossack* *Eskimo* *Punjabi*	1,870	36	8 4·7in	4 21in	—
Forester *Foxhound*	1,375	35	4 4·7in	8 21in	—
Hero	1,340	35	4 4·7in	8 21in	—
Icarus	1,530	36	4 4·7in	10 21in	—
Kimberley	1,690	36	6 4·7in	10 21in	—
Hermann Künne *Hans Lüdemann* *Deither von Roeder*	2,411	38	5 5in	8 21in	All sunk or otherwise destroyed
Bernd von Arnim *Erich Giese* *Erich Koellner* *Georg Thiele* *Wolfgang Zenker*	2,230	38	5 5in	8 21in	

Germany's 'B' Service enabled Raeder to give Bey ample warning that a strong British force could be expected to enter Ofot Fiord on 13 April. He responded by ordering his battle-worthy destroyers to Ballangen and Herjangs Fiords, from where they might be able to trap Whitworth's ships, as some had come so near to catching Warburton-Lee's. But like many British commanders during these days he forgot the Nelsonian maxim: 'Lose not an hour'. As late as 1300 the damaged *Koellner* was being escorted by the *Künne* towards Lindstrand, where she was to lie in ambush, when Whitworth's ships were sighted entering the Narrows, while Bey's other destroyers were still at anchor off Narvik, without steam in their boilers. Not until after receipt of the *Künne*'s enemy report did the *Lüdemann*, followed by the *Zenker* and *Arnim* get under way, whilst the *Thiele* and *Giese* were unable to move until later, leaving the disabled *Roeder* to guard the anchorage. Whitworth, be it noted, had decided to attack during the afternoon rather than at dawn, because he could not expect to surprise the enemy, and on the advice of the *Havock*'s captain, Lieutenant-Commander Courage, that ships in the side fiords were less likely to be obscured by poor visibility, which even now was restricted to six miles.

On seeing the *Warspite* the *Künne* immediately retired up the fiord, leaving the *Koellner* to head for Bjervik Bay. There she might have remained hidden had not Crutchley already catapulted a float plane to scout ahead. Its observer first reported both destroyers, then flew on to sight *U64* on the surface of Herjangs Fiord where she was promptly sunk with a direct hit from a 350 lb bomb. Almost as quickly the guns and torpedoes of the *Bedouin* and *Eskimo*, followed by 15-inch salvoes from the *Warspite*, sent the *Koellner* to the bottom, after she had missed the British ships with her torpedoes.

Petty Officer Reardon, gunner's mate of the *Warspite*'s 'A' turret recalls:

An early dinner today, before action stations sounds. Our gun-house crew is soon correct. The turret officer tells me I can load. We hear the cages come up with a thud, and out go the rammers. We can feel that we have increased speed. Heavy explosions shake the ship; the destroyers are attacking a submarine. Suddenly comes the order, 'Salvoes', and the right gun comes to the ready. Our guns are nearly horizontal, so the range must be short. Then the 'ding-ding' of the fire gong, the right gun moves a little, comes steady and there is a 'woof' which rocks the turret. The left gun is now at the ready, and fires while the right gun is reloading. The turret officer calls out, 'We have hit a destroyer and she is burning nicely'. Then the trainer reports, 'Blimey, another one has got it'. Sixteen rounds from each gun so far. After a while 'check fire' is ordered and, 'Crews may go on top of turrets', and what a sight—burning and sinking enemy ships all around us, and our own destroyers searching into every corner that might hide something.

Further up Ofot Fiord Whitworth's force met the *Künne, Lüdemann, Zenker* and *Arnim* which fought a gallant fight as they retreated before an onslaught that they could not hope to stem, and from which they suffered heavy damage. Nor were the British ships their only enemy: down through the low clouds came 10 planes which Forbes had ordered off the *Furious*. But these scored no hits for the loss of two shot down.

Having been unable to replenish their magazines since 10 April the German destroyers were now running out of ammunition. The *Eskimo* pursued the *Künne* into Herjangs Fiord where her captain beached his ship so that his crew could escape ashore before Commander Micklethwait completed her destruction with a well-aimed torpedo. The *Zenker* and *Arnim* retired up Rombaks Fiord. Meantime the British destroyers had not escaped damage: the *Punjabi*, in particular, had been hit several times and Commander H. T. Lean and his crew were busy trying to extinguish fires when she was abruptly stopped by a fractured main steam pipe which took an hour to repair.

As the rest of Whitworth's ships came in sight of Narvik harbour, they were met by the *Giese* which was quickly reduced to a burning, drifting hulk. The *Roeder* was the target, first for the *Warspite*'s guns and then for the *Cossack*'s, before she blew up just as Lieutenant-Commander Peters was leading the *Foxhound* towards her with orders to board and take her. But the *Cossack* had suffered eight hits which severed all leads between bridge and engine room: out of control she ran aground on the south shore. Fortunately Dietl's troops had not yet received any heavy artillery so that Commander R. St V. Sherbrooke's crew suffered nothing more than occasional field gun fire as they struggled to effect damage repairs for the next twelve hours.

Micklethwait, having seen German destroyers retiring up Rombaks Fiord, went after them with the *Eskimo, Bedouin, Forester, Hero* and *Icarus*. The *Warspite*'s plane warned him that whilst two had gone to the head of this fiord, two more were waiting only three miles inside the 500 yards wide entrance from where they fired their torpedoes. One from the *Thiele* blew off the *Eskimo*'s bows before the *Thiele*'s wounded captain ran his ship on to the rocky shore where she capsized. By skilful manoeuvring the other British destroyers avoided the torpedoes fired by the *Thiele* and the *Lüdemann*. The latter, having expended her ammunition, was pursued up to the head of the fiord where the *Arnim* and *Zenker* were found scuttled in shallow water and abandoned by their crews. So, too, with the *Lüdemann*, although British boat crews had time to board her and hoist the white ensign over the Nazi flag before deciding that salvage was impracticable, and she was finally destroyed by a torpedo.

Thus the second battle of Narvik ended with the almost total destruction of Bey's force, a débâcle which he might have avoided had he sailed his seaworthy ships back to Germany 36 hours earlier, in accordance with Raeder's instructions. In the circumstances he was lucky to escape with his life and with his reputation untarnished. We shall meet him again flying his flag as a rear-admiral in a more important command.

One writes 'almost total destruction', because one unit escaped. *U51*, in Narvik harbour when the British attack began, had quickly submerged and escaped to sea. In so doing she wrought no damage to the British force: nonetheless her presence influenced subsequent events. Whitworth, having triumphantly fulfilled his mission and revenged Warburton-Lee's heroic death, was faced with deciding whether he should retire from the fiord or whether he should remain off Narvik and land seamen to hold the town from which Dietl's troops had fled into the mountains. He chose the former course because he doubted whether a few hundred seamen could defend Narvik once Dietl's 2,000 troops, reinforced by as many men from the sunken German destroyers, came to their senses. This must be before the *Southampton* arrived in 48 hours time with her advance party of Mackesy's troops. Moreover, he learned from the *Foxhound* that a German prisoner from the *Giese* had said that there were submarines—in the plural—in the fiord, and only one had been sunk. When Britain had so few capital ships, the *Warspite* was too valuable a unit to be hazarded to gain the town of Narvik—and such destroyers as could be left, after discounting the crippled *Cossack, Eskimo* and *Punjabi*, and providing the battleship with an A/S escort, were too few for such a task.

Nonetheless Whitworth waited, after embarking the wounded from the *Eskimo* and *Cossack* and committing their dead, only twelve, to the deep of Ofot Fiord, for the *Cossack* to be refloated at 0315 next morning and sent down the fiord, escorted by the *Forester*, to Skjel Fiord for further repairs. The *Eskimo*, which had also grounded after losing her bows, had already been towed off by the *Forester* and *Punjabi* and sailed for this haven. Whitworth stayed also to embark the survivors from the *Hardy*, when he learned from the *Ivanhoe* that these had been succoured and hidden from German troops by the brave people of Ballangen. From there the *Ivanhoe* also rescued the crews of the British merchant ships which had been caught in Narvik by the German seizure of the port. After being imprisoned in the ss *North Cornwall* which, to their good fortune, was one of the few vessels to escape being sunk by the first British attack, they had managed to make good their escape during the second battle. The *Hunter*'s survivors were almost as fortunate: put ashore by the German destroyer which had picked them up after the first battle, a kindly German indicated the road to neutral Sweden, a hint which they put to good use during the panic and confusion of the second battle.

All this done, the *Warspite* and her destroyers left Narvik on the evening of 13 April for the open waters of Vest Fiord where Whitworth signalled: 'Enemy forces in Narvik were thoroughly frightened by today's action. I recommend that town be occupied without delay by main landing force'. But this could not arrive for another 48 hours. Next day Whitworth signalled again: 'Norwegian sources estimate 1,500 to 2,000 [German] troops. I am convinced Narvik can be taken by direct assault without fear of meeting serious opposition'. Lord Cork, heading for Vest Fiord in the *Aurora*, readily accepted this appreciation. But Mackesy, in the *Southampton*, had no intention of taking any such risk. He decided to land at Harstadt, in Vaags Fiord, to the north of Ofot Fiord, and there to unload and sort out his troops' equipment before ordering them to advance southwards, which would take much longer than the hour which Nelson—and Napoleon—counted so precious. Although Warburton-Lee's and Whitworth's two battles had destroyed as many as 10 German destroyers at the cost of only two British, the other fruits of the former's initiative and the latter's success were thrown away, chiefly by Whitehall where the War Office had failed to give Mackesy orders as resolute as those with which Churchill and Pound inspired Lord Cork.

Between 14 April and 2 May the Allies attempted to recapture Trondheim, with 30,000 troops landed at Aandalsnes and Namsos, which was aborted by the overwhelming air superiority enjoyed by the *Luftwaffe*, notably its terrifying dive-bombers, and by German troops better trained to operate over snow-covered terrain. A futile attempt to deny Germany the use of Stavanger airfield by sending the *Suffolk*, Captain J. Durnford, to bombard it on 17 April, ended in this 8-inch cruiser limping home to Scapa so badly damaged by dive-bombing that her quarterdeck was awash.

The advance on Narvik did not begin until 24 April, and the port was not finally captured, by the French General Béthouart, before 28 May, after Mackesy had been replaced by General C. J. Auchinleck. Both these assaults were, however, amphibious operations which fall outside the scope of this book. It must suffice to mention that the Allied Navies' involvement cost them the large cruiser *Effingham*, which was stranded in Vest Fiord, one other cruiser and 10 destroyers and sloops, with as many damaged, most of them by dive-bombing attack—losses which would have been considerably larger but for the continued failure of the magnetic pistols on the many torpedoes fired by German U-boats. Subsequent events must, however, be told because these included one further significant naval engagement.

The long delay in capturing Narvik had incalculable consequences. By the time the port was occupied, and the remnants of Dietl's troops all but pursued into Sweden, Germany had not only overrun the Low Countries but was rapidly advancing into France. The need for every available man to stem this Nazi invasion required the Allied Governments to evacuate Norway as soon as Narvik's port facilities had been destroyed, with the consequence that King Haakon and his Government had to leave their country in German hands for the subsequent duration of hostilities, for all of which Hitler had to offset the gain of Norway's fiords with the need to deploy several of his best divisions against the possibility (never seriously contemplated) that the Allies might launch a major operation to recover them.

The evacuation from Narvik required 15 large troopships and a number of storeships. Six fast liners left for home on 7 June, and the others on the 9th, after safely embarking 25,000 Allied troops under an air umbrella provided by RAF fighters using Bardufoss airfield, and by planes from the *Ark Royal* and *Glorious* which had arrived in the area from the Mediterranean on 2 June. Group One was escorted only by the repair ship *Vindictive*, but Group Two had the *Ark Royal*, the cruisers *Southampton*, flying Lord Cork's flag, and *Coventry*, plus five destroyers. Other home bound movements included two slow convoys of storeships, Cunningham's flagship, the *Devonshire*, proceeding independently to Scapa with King Haakon and his Government, and the *Glorious*, commanded by Captain G. D'Oyly Hughes, a World War One VC. Her own complement of planes had been reduced so that she could embark the RAF machines from Bardufoss. Nonetheless, because she was short of the fuel required for high speed steaming, Lord Cork agreed with her captain's proposal that this valuable ship should sail home escorted only by the destroyers *Acasta*, Commander C. Glasfurd, and the *Ardent*, Lieutenant-Commander J. F. Barker.

All these movements should have been covered by a battle force provided from the British Home Fleet. Unhappily, on 5 June, a false report of two unidentified warships 200 miles north-east of the Faroes again led Forbes to suppose that German ships were about to break out into the Atlantic. He sent the *Renown, Repulse, Newcastle* and *Sussex* on a wild goose chase after them. Since the *Rodney* had to be at short notice to proceed south in event of any German move to disrupt the now vital cross-Channel link, Forbes was left with only the *Valiant* to cover the many vessels returning from Narvik. She met the liners of Group One on the 8th and saw them safely past the Faroes, then turned east to meet the ships of Group Two on the 10th.

And all would have been well but for the ironic chance that the Admiralty had by this time taken steps to render its ciphers more secure. Raeder learned nothing of the Allied evacuation of Narvik from his 'B' Service, or from any other source. Lacking this intelligence, he decided to reverse the disastrous situation facing Germany in the Narvik area by ordering an attack in force on Allied shipping in Vaags Fiord. For this he sailed the *Scharnhorst*, flag of Admiral W. Marschall, *Gneisenau, Hipper* and four destroyers from Kiel on 4 June. And, favoured by misty weather their movement north was not detected by any Allied source.

Marschall was bent on attacking Vaags Fiord during the night of 8–9 June, until, on the evening of the 7th, he began receiving *Luftwaffe* reconnaissance reports of Allied ships from which he suspected that Narvik was being evacuated. Turning a blind eye to contrary orders from Berlin, which did not accept his new appreciation of the situation, he changed his object to the destruction of Group One. But he underestimated the speed of these liners so that, instead of finding them, his force sighted, early on the 8th, the lone oil tanker *Oil Pioneer,* escorted by a single trawler. Shortly after sending these to the bottom, one of his catapult planes found the liner *Orama,* which had not been required for the evacuation and had been sent back to Scapa alone in company with the hospital ship *Atlantis.* The *Hipper*'s 8-inch shells soon sank the *Orama*: the *Atlantis*'s immunity under the Geneva Convention was respected. No news of these incidents reached the Allies, because the German ships successfully jammed their victim's enemy reports, and because the *Atlantis* could not, without breaching the Geneva rules, use her radio. Nonetheless, since Marschall could not expect his presence in the area to remain a secret for much longer, he decided to use only the *Scharnhorst* and *Gneisenau* to hunt for the most valuable prizes which the *Luftwaffe* had now reported, the aircraft-carriers *Ark Royal* and *Glorious,* and ordered the *Hipper* and his destroyers into Trondheim.

The German battlecruisers surprised the *Glorious* around 1600 on 8 June. Although the British carrier quickly turned away at her best speed, they had her within range of their 11-inch guns by 1630 and opened fire. She failed to launch a torpedo-bomber strike, her only effective defence, before shell hits set the aircraft in her hangars ablaze. Although the *Acasta* and *Ardent* gave her considerable protection by laying a smoke screen, a shell hit her bridge around 1700 leaving her out of control, and soon after this a devastating hit aft made it clear that she could not long survive. The order was given to abandon ship and she eventually sank at 1740, taking D'Oyly Hughes and all but 43 of her crew, as well as a number of officers and men of the RAF, with her.

But the two British destroyers did not allow the German ships to escape unscathed. The *Ardent* was the first to attempt a torpedo attack. By causing the *Scharnhorst* and *Gneisenau* to turn away she gave the *Glorious* a brief respite, but after her torpedoes had missed their target, the *Ardent* was overwhelmed by gunfire and speedily sunk with only two survivors. Then it was the *Acasta*'s turn, as described by her only survivor, Leading Seaman Carter:

The captain had this message passed to all positions: 'You may think we are running away from the enemy; we are not; our chummy ship [*Ardent*] has sunk, the *Glorious* is sinking; the least we can do is make a show'. We then altered course into our own smoke screen. When we came out of it I had my first glimpse of the enemy. I fired two torpedoes, the foremost tubes fired theirs. From one of the ships a yellow flash and a great column of smoke and water shot up. We knew we had hit.

After we had fired our torpedoes we went back into our smoke screen. 'Stand by to fire remaining torpedoes.' This time, as soon as we poked our nose out the enemy let us have it. A shell hit the engine-room. I was blown to the after end of the tubes. The ship stopped with a list to port. I fired the remaining torpedoes. The *Acasta*'s guns were firing the whole time. The enemy hit us several times and one big explosion took place right aft. The captain gave orders to abandon ship, and when I was in the water I saw him leaning over the bridge, take a cigarette from a case and light it. He waved, 'Goodbye and good luck'—the end of a gallant man.

Glasfurd's action saved the *Ark Royal* and every other Allied ship that was then at sea between Narvik and Britain. The torpedo which struck the *Scharnhorst* not only flooded her starboard and centre engine rooms, reducing her speed to 20 knots, but put her after turret out of action and killed two officers and 46 men. Marschall immediately headed for the safety of Trondheim.

Enemy jamming prevented news of this reaching Forbes. Only the *Devonshire* intercepted part of an enemy report from the *Glorious* which was so obscure that Cunningham did not consider it justifiable to risk the lives of his very important passengers by breaking radio silence to pass it on. The first ship to tell Forbes anything was the *Valiant* when she met the *Atlantis* early on 9 June and learned from her of the *Orama*'s fate by visual signal. Not until then, after Marschall had reached Trondheim, were the *Rodney, Renown* and *Repulse,* with two cruisers and several destroyers ordered—too late—to cover the shipping homeward bound from Narvik.

For the serious damage to the *Scharnhorst* Raeder blamed Marschall and ordered his supersession, categorizing his destruction of the *Glorious* as an extraordinary stroke of luck. But Admiral Lütjens, who replaced him, was no more fortunate. When he made a sortie with the *Gneisenau* and *Hipper* on 29 June, to distract British attention while the *Scharnhorst* limped her way home, a torpedo from the submarine *Clyde,* Lieutenant-Commander Ingram, struck the *Gneisenau*'s bows. Both German battle-cruisers were thus put out of action for many months to come.

It is not easy to allocate responsibility for the loss of the *Glorious*. She might have put up a stouter defence, just as the US escort carriers managed to do so successfully at the battle of Samar which is described later in this book. A better organized air department might have been able to launch a torpedo-bomber strike more quickly against the enemy, just as Rear-Admiral Clifton Sprague's 'baby flat-tops' did against Vice-Admiral Kurita's force of capital ships and 8-inch cruisers in Leyte Gulf on 25 October 1944. As Flag Officer Narvik Lord Cork was at fault for accepting D'Oyly Hughes' ill-judged suggestion that such an important but weakly armed ship should be sailed with no more than a small A/S escort. But, as C-in-C Home Fleet, Forbes was responsible for sending the bulk of his available major units on a wild goose chase instead of using them to cover the sizeable number of large vessels returning from Narvik. The ultimate responsibility lies with the Admiralty, in particular for appointing as Flag Officer Narvik an admiral of the fleet senior to Forbes who was consequently led to treat Narvik as lying outside his sphere. Thus there arose a system of divided control which is always a potential source of disaster, for which reason the Admiralty decided against blaming anyone for the *Glorious*' loss. But after Lord Cork hauled down his flag at midnight on 9 June 1940, they did not again make the mistake of appointing an admiral of the fleet to a subordinate operational command.

Two, above all, of the timeless principles of war are underscored by the naval aspects of this campaign. Without a plan characterized by boldness and surprise Germany could not have overrun Norway so swiftly. The prize, fiords from which Germany's surface ships and U-boats, helped by the *Luftwaffe,* were to prove such a menace to the Allies, especially to the Arctic convoys which were needed to sustain the USSR after she was attacked by her Nazi 'friends', was worth the cost. The losses and damage suffered by the German Navy, almost all *after* it had put the German Army ashore, were no greater than Raeder expected. So, too, with the first battle of Narvik. Warburton-Lee's initiative, though it cost him two of his ships as well as his own life, delayed the departure of Bey's destroyers until a stronger British force could annihilate them all.

The value of time is well illustrated by Bey's fatal delay in sailing back to Germany such of his ships as were seaworthy, and by Yates's failure to seize his golden moment when ordered to attack Narvik, because he believed that it would take 24 hours to distribute the orders for it. Above all, however, was the muddle and hesitancy so conspicuously shown during the first weeks of the campaign by the Admiralty, personified in Churchill and Pound, on the one hand, and by the British C-in-C Home Fleet, Forbes, on the other. That the latter should have hesitated in deciding how best to counter this fresh German offensive when a bold and immediate response might have halted it, is understandable if not excusable. But the confusion which occurred because the Admiralty would not leave operations in the hands of the C-in-C and of his principal subordinates, notably Whitworth, merits further comment because this was not the first time that they so intervened (*e.g.* the *Altmark* affair), nor was it to be the last nor the most disastrous (*e.g.* the destruction of much of Arctic Convoy PQ17).

Except during the first months of World War One, when the recently formed Naval Staff at the Admiralty was ill-organized and inexperienced, so that naval operations were directed personally by two men so dynamic as the young Churchill and the ageing Fisher, there was seldom such interference with operations by the Grand Fleet: Jellicoe and Beatty made it abundantly clear that they would not suffer it. But by September 1939 the Naval Staff, though now well trained and experienced, was no match for a Churchill who had not forgotten 1914 (nor the Dardanelles campaign whose failure had been his downfall) and a Pound who, for all his merits, was always reluctant to delegate.

Defenders of the Admiralty advance three arguments. With the C-in-C Home Fleet at sea they wished to save him from breaking radio silence. Secondly, they sometimes held vital intelligence not available to the C-in-C which they could not pass on to him in a cipher whose security was suspect without the risk of compromising a sensitive source. Thirdly, they could save vital time by issuing orders direct to individual units, as against the delay which must ensue if they first passed the relevant information to the C-in-C and left him to issue the orders. And undoubtedly there were occasions to which these arguments applied; but since there were many more to which the progression, order, counter-order, disorder, applied, some other solution should have been found before hostilities were a year old instead of leaving it until after the war was over.

In World War One all the more important North Sea operations were carried out by the Grand Fleet as a whole, or by a major part of it, notably the Battlecruiser Force, in expectation of meeting the High Seas Fleet. Jellicoe and Beatty were therefore, right to fly their flags afloat.

World War Two was a very different story because Britain and Germany opposed much smaller forces over a much wider area than the North Sea. When Rear-Admiral R. H. C. Hallifax, commanding the Home Fleet's destroyers from the 6-inch cruiser *Aurora*, represented that he could not control 30 or more widely dispersed vessels from a flagship employed singly on patrol for periods of 10 days or more during which she could not break radio silence, it was agreed that he should transfer his flag to a depot ship at Scapa, except when he was required to take direct command of some specific operation.

The value of a C-in-C flying his flag ashore had been so far proved in 1914 (when the C-in-C China Station, Admiral Sir Martyn Jerram, finding that he could not control the widespread hunt for von Spee's East Asiatic Squadron from a cruiser required to maintain radio silence, hoisted his flag at Singapore) that by 1939 it was agreed that all British Cs-in-C overseas should set up war headquarters ashore, *e.g.* at Bermuda, Freetown, Colombo and Singapore. Even so great a fighting seaman as Admiral Sir Andrew Cunningham was persuaded to do so at Alexandria before the war with Italy was many months old (albeit with considerable reluctance), after which he only accompanied his fleet for specific operations. So should the C-in-C Home Fleet have set up headquarters ashore at Scapa Flow or Rosyth, where he would at all times have been in direct, instant and secure communication with the Admiralty, without restriction on his use of radio, as well as being in a position to co-operate closely with the area commander of the RAF's Coastal Command. Forbes, and his successors, could then have insisted that orders to Home Fleet units should always be issued by the C-in-C and *not* by the Admiralty.

But neither Forbes, nor his successor, Admiral Sir John Tovey, suggested doing this, even though Tovey found that he could best control the Arctic convoys from his flagship lying at moorings in Scapa Flow. Nor did the Admiralty argue that this was a misuse of one of Britain's few capital ships. Tovey's successors, Admiral Sir Bruce Fraser and Admiral Sir Henry Moore, had the advantage of a First Sea Lord, Cunningham, who understood the art of delegation and seldom allowed the Admiralty to 'interfere'. That the proper solution was for the C-in-C to have his headquarters ashore is well illustrated by the fact that some years after the war was over, he transferred his flag to Northwood in north London, alongside the headquarters of the RAF's maritime commander. And there he remains today as C-in-C Fleet, except for such short periods as he deems it necessary to go afloat, or to take to the air, to visit the ships and bases of his now world-wide command.

As Cominch and CNO (the equivalent of Britain's First Sea Lord), America's Admiral King, who had long preached the need to delegate, very seldom (and never to any consequence) issued orders from his Washington, DC, headquarters direct to units taking part in operations. He left their conduct to his Cs-in-C who from the outset of hostilities transferred their flags to shore headquarters, notably Cinclant at Norfolk, Virginia, and Cincpac at Pearl Harbour, where they were always in direct, secure communication with Washington and enjoyed the unfettered use of radio.

To be fair, although all Germany's Group (*i.e.* Area) commanders-in-chief had their headquarters ashore, neither Raeder nor, later, Dönitz, refrained from issuing orders from Berlin direct to seagoing units, with such consequent confusion as that which led to Marschall's supersession. (Raeder and Dönitz were, of course, even more subject to Hitler's interventions into matters which were their professional responsibility than Pound and, later, Cunningham, was to Churchill's, whereas, under Roosevelt, King was largely his own master.) Japan's solution was, in effect, for Yamamoto to combine the roles of 'Cominch' and 'Cincpac', which worked well enough in 1941–42, even when he flew his flag afloat. But it proved disastrous in 1944 when his successor, Toyada, tried to control the battles of Leyte Gulf, in the Philippines, from distant Tokyo.

The above criticism of Britain's system must not, however, be allowed to obscure the notable part which the Admiralty, and Pound in particular, played in the different battle described in Chapter 7, for the proper reason that more forces than the Home Fleet were involved in it. But first we must turn to events in another sea, the Mediterranean.

NOTES

[1] From *Wings of the Morning* by Ian Cameron.
[2] Note Warburton-Lee's bold use of *intend*. In British naval parlance this means, 'I shall do it unless you, my superior, forbid'. The alternative word would have been *propose,* meaning, 'I await instructions as to whether I shall or shall not do it'.
[3] *Everyman's History of the Sea War* by A. C. Hardy.

6 *Matapan*

In none of the seas in which World War Two was fought were lessons of history more clearly demonstrated than in the Mediterranean. The role played by Italy's Navy in World War One was the reverse of impressive. Although it out-matched Austria-Hungary's Fleet by six dreadnoughts and five pre-dreadnoughts against four and three, one of her imposed conditions for joining the Allies on 24 May 1915 was that her fleet, based on Taranto, should be strengthened by four pre-dreadnoughts, with a French battle squadron stationed at Corfu. But despite this preponderance of maritime power, Italy pursued a supine strategy. The Austrian battle fleet might be limited to raids from Pola and Kotor across the Adriatic (and a planned sweep to roll-up the Allied patrols across the Straits of Otranto which was aborted by an Italian motor-torpedoboat (MTB) attack that sank the dreadnought *Szent Istvan*). But Italy's was seldom used for anything more than covering convoys supplying the Serbian Army (and, after its defeat, evacuating it to safety), and supporting her cruisers and smaller craft which, with similar British and French vessels, laid and patrolled the Otranto barrage (*cf.* the Dover barrage) designed to pen Austrian and German U-boats, based on Pola and Trieste, within the Adriatic. Indeed, in only one sphere did the Italian Navy take the offensive; in the development and use of MTBs which, in addition to the aforementioned sinking of the *Szent Istvan* off Premuda in June 1918, helped to mine the *Viribus Unitis* in Pola harbour in November of the same year.

Was it, therefore, to be expected that little more than 20 years later, in 1940, this timid leopard would have changed its spots; that its materially strong and modern Fleet would play a more adventurous role when Italy came into the war on the Axis side on 10 June? Since the C-in-C of the British Mediterranean Fleet, Admiral Sir Andrew Cunningham, had spent the greater part of World War One in these waters, where he was well placed to appreciate the inadequacies of Italy's strategy, it would have been understandable if he had discounted Mussolini's braggadocio, and believed that his Navy would present no serious threat to Allied control of the Mediterranean—exercised in the eastern half by a fleet based on Alexandria (because more urgent needs elsewhere had prevented Britain from providing any air defences for Malta despite its vulnerability to attack from Sicilian airfields), and in the western half by Force H based on Gibraltar. In the event, he neither made the mistake of underestimating Italy's potential, nor was he overawed by it—even after the French withdrawal from the war on 22 June 1940 had reduced the Allied strength to five capital ships, two aircraft-carriers, and 10 6-inch cruisers, widely divided between Gibraltar and Alexandria, against four capital ships, seven 8-inch and 14 6-inch cruisers, concentrated in the central Mediterranean, where they were backed by the full strength of the *Regia Aeronautica,* whereas neither British force could call on carrier-borne or shore-based fighters for its defence.[1] To quote Pound's sober warning of 20 May: 'The one lesson we have learned here [at the Admiralty] is that it is essential to have fighter protection over the fleet whenever it is within range of enemy bombers. You will be without such protection but I do not see any way of rectifying it.'

But Cunningham was not the man to be alarmed at such a prospect. 'You may be sure,' he wrote on 6 June, 'that all of us are imbued with a burning desire to get at the Italian Fleet.' In other words, he intended to take the offensive. For two reasons this was not easy. Although Mussolini directed his Navy to conduct 'the offensive at all points in the Mediterranean and outside,' his Chief of Naval Staff, Amiral Cavagnari, believed that this strategy would involve irreplaceable losses (whereas any losses inflicted on the Allies could be replaced from outside the Mediterranean). That the Italian Navy should act on the defensive seemed to be demonstrated as soon as the first month of hostilities when his submarine force of more than 100 boats suffered losses (10 were sunk before the end of June) out of all proportion to their few successes, even though these included the AA cruiser *Carlisle* torpedoed by the *Bagnolini,* Commander Tosoni-Pittoni.[2] But to accept this lesson was to fly in the face of a much more important one, demonstrated by the Anglo-French wars of the seventeenth and eighteenth centuries, as well as by World War One in the North Sea; that whilst it may sometimes be necessary for a weaker fleet to act as a fleet-in-being (as the British Eastern Fleet did in 1942 whilst the US Pacific Fleet was being rebuilt after the Japanese attack on Pearl Harbour), this strategy cannot win a war.

Secondly, Cunningham, who could not know of Cavagnari's decision to restrict his fleet, based on Taranto, to covering convoys supporting Italy's North African and Dodecanese colonies, instead of employing it for offensive operations such as an early assault on Malta, lacked all but a handful of RAF long-range flying-boats, divided between Gibraltar, Malta and Alexandria, which were not enough to ensure giving him news of Italian naval movements. In his own words: 'reconnaissance over the sea was fitful, and large areas were necessarily left unsearched'.[3] In sharp contrast his own ships' movements were usually (but not always) well reported by the *Regia Aeronautica*.

When, therefore, Cunningham decided, very soon after Italy joined the war, to run two convoys from Malta to Alexandria, a fast one carrying all *'les bouches inutiles'* who could be persuaded to leave the beleaguered island, and a slow one with urgently needed naval stores, he arranged to cover them with most of his fleet. On 7 July the flagship *Warspite*, Captain D. B. Fisher, with two other battleships, the *Royal Sovereign*, flying the flag of Rear-Admiral Henry Pridham-Wippell, and the *Malaya*, the aircraft-carrier *Eagle*, five 6-inch cruisers and 17 destroyers sailed from Alexandria to the west. And at 0800 next morning the submarine *Phoenix* reported two Italian battleships, the *Conte di Cavour*, flagship of Vice-Admiral Campioni, and the *Giulio Cesare*, 200 miles east of Malta, supporting a convoy of five supply ships to Libya.

Cunningham promptly headed for this prey, holding his course despite numerous high level bombing attacks by Italian aircraft from the Dodecanese, one of which wrecked the cruiser *Gloucester*'s bridge, killing her captain, F. R. Garside. Nor was he deterred by an RAF flying-boat report, at 1510, that the Italian force had been augmented by six cruisers: nor by a further report next morning, 9 July, that the number of Italian cruisers had been increased to 12. (In truth they numbered as many as six 8-inch and 12 smaller cruisers.) He was more concerned to know that they were all heading back towards Taranto.

To ensure intercepting them he decided, at 1200 when he was still 90 miles to the east of the enemy, to leave the slower *Malaya*, *Royal Sovereign* and *Eagle* to follow whilst he pressed on in the *Warspite*, at her best speed of more than 24 knots, in support of his cruisers which were already heading for the enemy at 30. To quote Cunningham's chief of staff: 'ABC felt that with the Italian battle fleet at sea any risks were justified in order to get at it. This was when he first showed himself the master of the calculated risk.'[4]—a lesson which he had learned from the tactically indecisive battle of Jutland, for which Jellicoe's insistence on keeping his battle fleet concentrated was in part responsible.

Twice—at 1145, and again four hours later—the *Eagle*, Captain A. M. Bridge, flew off 15 strike planes in the hope that their torpedoes would cut the speed of at least one of the larger Italian vessels, but none scored a hit. However, with the visibility of a fine Mediterranean day, Vice-Admiral John Tovey's cruisers, spread 10 miles ahead of the *Warspite*, managed to sight the enemy's light forces shortly before 1500, and 10 minutes later the *Neptune* reported: 'Enemy battle fleet in sight'. Another six minutes and Tovey's ships were in action with four Italian 8-inch cruisers, of which the *Bolzano* was damaged. But 'the Italians' shooting was very good and our cruisers and the *Warspite* were continually straddled at 28,000 to 30,000 yards'.[5] However, they scored no hits before this engagement was ended at 1530 by the *Warspite* opening fire with her 15-inch, which persuaded the Italians to retire behind a smoke screen.

Twenty minutes later the British flagship came within sight and range of the Italian battleship, *Giulio Cesare*. According to Cunningham, the *Warspite*'s

shooting was consistently good. At 1600 I saw the great orange-coloured flash of a heavy explosion at the base of the enemy flagship's funnels, and I knew that she had been hit at the prodigious range of 13 miles. This was too much for the Italian admiral. His ships turned away and, having discharged 17 salvoes in all, the *Warspite* ceased firing, the whole horizon being overlaid with a thick pall of smoke behind which the enemy was completely hidden.[6]

And that single 15-inch shell from one British battleship had a moral effect out of all proportion to the damage done; not only did it put a superior Italian force to flight in this battle of Calabria, but it ensured that Italian battleships never again willingly faced an engagement with their own kind. 'A pity, really, for so long as an Italian battle fleet existed we had to maintain something comparable in the Mediterranean in case they faced up to a fight.'[7]

Although the British ships worked round to the north of the smoke screen which concealed the retiring Italians, and pursued them to within 25 miles of their own coast, Cunningham was, by 1735, faced with the fact that he could not hope to bring them to action again before they reached the safety of the Straits of Messina. From 1640 to 1925 his ships were subjected to numerous high level bombing attacks. So too was the retiring Italian force. Fortunately the accuracy of the *Regia Aeronautica*, though an improvement on that of the *Luftwaffe* in the North Sea, was no better against their own ships than it was against the British: although Cunningham described it as 'most frightening', none of his ships was hit. And his force continued to cruise to the south of Malta for the next 36 hours, until 0800 11 July, before it headed back to Alexandria, suffering further bombing from Libyan airfields en route. But with the exception of several casualties in the cruiser *Liverpool* from a near miss, these caused no damage. It was the same story with the slow convoy, while the fast one eluded the enemy's attention to reach its destination without incident.

This action was followed 10 days later by the battle of Cape Spada. At daylight on 19 July five British destroyers, patrolling to the north of Crete, found two Italian cruisers which immediately opened fire. The British vessels at once retired, pursued by the enemy, towards their own supporting 6-inch cruiser, HMAS *Sydney*, Captain J. Collins, RAN, which was some 40 miles away. On receiving the destroyers' enemy reports Collins steamed towards them at full speed, and soon had the dual satisfaction of bringing the Italian ships to battle and of seeing them turn away and try to escape him, despite their superior strength. But the *Bartolomeo Colleoni*, Captain Novaro, could not elude the *Sydney's* salvoes: after a prolonged engagement lasting some two hours this Italian 6-inch cruiser went to the bottom. And the *Giovanni delle Bande Nere*, Captain F. Maugeri, flagship of Rear-Admiral Casardi, only managed to escape after being repeatedly hit, because the Australian ship was running out of ammunition.

In the next two months the Italian Fleet made no serious attempt to impede British operations: they were opposed only by the *Regia Aeronautica*. At the beginning of August the old aircraft-carrier *Argus*, escorted by Admiral Sir James Somerville's Force H, came from Gibraltar as far as the south of Sardinia to fly off the first modern fighters for Malta's defence. In the middle of the month the *Warspite, Malaya* and *Ramillies* bombarded the Libyan port of Bardia, and Fort Capuzzo, an Italian strong-point above Sollum. At the beginning of September, in response to Cunningham's urgent pleas for another fast battleship which, like the *Warspite,* had been rebuilt to give her main armament a greater range, and for a modern aircraft-carrier to provide his fleet with fighter protection, the Admiralty sent out the *Valiant* and the *Illustrious,* Captain D. W. Boyd, flagship of Rear-Admiral A. L. St. G. Lyster, both of which, together with two AA cruisers, passed safely through from Gibraltar to Alexandria. At the end of September the 6-inch cruisers *Liverpool* and *Gloucester* carried nearly 2,000 troops to reinforce the garrison of Malta. Several convoys with supplies were also run to the island. The 8-inch cruiser *Kent* was damaged on 17 September, and the 8-inch cruiser *Liverpool* on 10 October, both by Italian torpedo-bombers. But in November Cunningham's fleet gained the battleship *Barham* and the cruisers *York, Berwick* and *Glasgow,* by which time he had the additional commitment of carrying troops and supplies to Greece (and Crete) when that country was threatened by an Italian invasion through Albania.

None of these operations was, however, carried out without the considerable risk of meeting the Italian Fleet which was now headed by six battleships. Indeed, on more than one occasion five of them were reported at sea and a potential danger to the operation in hand. But there was no contact, chiefly because of shortcomings in both sides' air patrols for which only the RAF could justly plead shortage of planes. So Cunningham determined to strike his enemy in the way that Beatty had planned to deal with the Jade-bound German High Seas Fleet when he had a sufficiency of aircraft-carriers and torpedo-bombers in 1919. Soon after the arrival of the *Illustrious* carrying 12 fighters and 22 torpedo-bomber and reconnaissance machines, he began preparations for a surprise attack on Taranto, using this ship and the *Eagle,* on Trafalgar Day 1940. A fire in the former's hangar compelled a postponement. Even so, two days before sailing the *Eagle* developed defects which prevented her from taking part. Five of her torpedo-bombers, with their crews, were however transferred to the *Illustrious*.

Cunningham sailed this carrier from Alexandria on 6 November towards the central Mediterranean, in company with the *Warspite*, *Valiant*, *Malaya* and *Ramillies*, seven cruisers and 13 destroyers. During the next five days their movements were reported by the *Regia Aeronautica*, but never with sufficient clarity for Campioni to hazard a sortie against them. He paid dearly for his timidity. On 11 November an RAF flying-boat from Malta observed all six Italian battleships berthed in Taranto's outer harbour. Cunningham thereupon ordered his ships to execute an operation which he had first planned before Italy came into the war. The *Illustrious*, escorted by the 8-inch cruisers *Berwick* and *York*, and the 6-inch cruisers *Glasgow* and *Gloucester*, headed for a position 180 miles to the south-east of Taranto: Pridham-Wippell took the 6-inch cruisers *Ajax*, *Orion* and *Sydney* north for a diversionary raid on the Strait of Otranto: Cunningham's battle fleet remained where it could best cover both these forces.

That night Pridham-Wippell's ships found an Italian convoy off Valona and sank all four of its ships after they had been abandoned by their destroyer escort. The *Illustrious* flew off two strike forces, one of 12 torpedo-bombers led by Lieutenant-Commander K. Williamson at 2040, the other of nine led by Lieutenant-Commander J. W. Hale at 2130. Both achieved complete surprise. Despite anti-torpedo nets, a balloon barrage and heavy AA fire from ships and shore batteries, these obsolescent Swordfish planes dropped their torpedoes so effectively by the light of flares that they sank the *Littorio* with three hits and the *Conte di Cavour* and the *Caio Duilio* each with one. One half of Italy's battleship strength was eliminated for the loss of only two British planes: the rest returned safely to the waiting *Illustrious*.

It was an epic operation which reflected the greatest credit on the Fleet Air Arm pilots and observers and the organization of the carrier. It seemed incredible that a well-protected fleet could be successfully attacked in harbour by single-engined biplanes with a maximum speed of 130 knots. It appeared that the Italians could not believe they could be so slow and that most of their AA fire passed ahead of them.[8]

In a flying time of about six and a half hours 21 aircraft had done more damage to the Italian Fleet than was inflicted upon the German High Seas Fleet by the whole of Britain's Grand Fleet at Jutland. How richly, then, did the *Illustrious*, especially her aircrews, deserve the signal which by Cunningham's order all his ships flew when the carrier rejoined them next day, that classic understatement which is the Royal Navy's greatest praise: 'Manoeuvre well executed'. Among the signals which Cunningham himself received was this characteristic one from Somerville: 'Congratulations on successful debagging. If this goes on Uncle Benito

[Mussolini] will soon be singing alto in the choir'. (Cunningham could be wittier. When Somerville, already a Knight of the Bath, was created a Knight of the British Empire, he received this signal: 'Fancy, twice a knight and at your age. Congratulations'.)

The effect of this successful raid, the first of its kind in all history, was profound; not only was one sunken battleship, the *Cavour*, a write-off, but it took the best part of a year to salvage and repair the other two. As important, the Italians removed the survivors of their battle fleet away from Taranto to the greater safety of Naples, which so reduced its threat to Allied movements through the central Mediterranean that Cunningham was able to release the *Malaya* and *Ramillies* for service in other seas. (Half the world away the success of this raid was marked by the C-in-C of the Japanese Fleet, Admiral Isoruko Yamamoto—who put its lesson to good use when Japan decided to join the war on 7 December 1941.)

For his next opportunity to strike a decisive blow against the Italian Fleet, Cunningham had to wait for more than four months, during which his ships were kept busy supporting the British Eighth Army along the Libyan coast, bombarding the Albanian port of Valona, carrying troops and supplies to Greece, and providing escorts for convoys to and from Malta, during one of which the *Illustrious* was seriously damaged by German dive-bombers, the *Luftwaffe*'s first appearance on the Mediterranean scene. Fortunately she was able to struggle as far as Malta for temporary repairs, and to survive further heavy bombing whilst there in the dockyard, before escaping to Alexandria and proceeding through the Suez Canal to Norfolk, Virginia, for a major refit. But until she was replaced by the recently completed *Formidable*, carrying fighters and torpedo-bombers, on 10 March 1941, Cunningham's battle fleet could not safely operate in the central Mediterranean. The British offensive against Italian convoys bound for north Africa had to be left in the hands of the Malta Striking Force, a small handful of cruisers and destroyers, and of British submarines likewise based on Malta.

On 16 March two German torpedo-bombers attacked a small British force 30 miles to the west of Crete. With the exaggeration characteristic of more air forces than the *Luftwaffe*, their pilots reported hits on two units, 'probably battleships'. This encouraging news persuaded Admiral Riccardi, who had succeeded Cavagnari in Rome, to bow to German demands for an offensive against the convoys which the British were running from Alexandria to Crete and Greece. (Hitler was planning to send troops into Greece in April to enable the Axis to gain the victory over her which the Italians were unable to achieve on their own.)

A week later Vice-Admiral A. Iachino, flying his flag in the battleship *Vittorio Veneto*, Captain Sparzani, left Naples to join the 8-inch cruisers *Zara*, Captain L. Cossi, flag of Rear-Admiral C. Cattaneo, *Pola*, Captain

1 The German pocket-battleship *Admiral Graf Spee*, 12,100 tons, six 11-inch guns, scuttled off Montevideo on 17 December 1939

2 and 3 The victors of the Battle of the Plate, December, 1939. HMS *Exeter* (*above*), 8,390 tons, six 8-inch guns, hoisting out a Walrus amphibious plane; HMS *Ajax* (*below*), 6,985 tons, eight 6-inch guns, in action

4 (*top*) A victim of the 1930 London Naval Treaty: the British battleship *Emperor of India*, 26,400 tons, ten 13·5-inch guns, completed 1914, scrapped 1931

5 (*middle*) The British Washington Treaty cruiser *Berwick*, 9,750 tons, eight 8-inch guns, as first completed in 1927 with short funnels which failed to carry fumes clear of the after part of the ship

6 (*bottom*) HMS *Rodney*, 33,900 tons, nine 16-inch guns, which with her sister, the *Nelson*, were the only battleships allowed to be built by the 1921 Washington Naval Treaty

7 and 8 ALLIES. *Above*, the US fast battleships *South Dakota* and *Alabama*, 35,000 tons, nine 16-inch guns, serving with the British Home Fleet in 1943. On right the British aircraft-carrier *Furious*, 22,450 tons, 33 planes. *Below*, the US cruiser *Wichita*, 10,000 tons, nine 8-inch guns (left) in company with the British *London*, 9,850 tons, eight 8-inch guns (the only County class cruiser to be rebuilt with two funnels)

9 The German *U968* under attack by a Liberator of RAF Coastal Command on 19 July 1944

10 A British midget submarine (X-craft)

11 A British human torpedo ('Char

12 The British destroyer *Glowworm*, 1,345 tons, sinking on 8 April 1940, after ramming the German cruiser *Hipper*, 13,900 tons (taken through one of the *Hipper*'s gunsights)

13 The German cruiser *Blücher*, 13,900 tons, eight 8-inch guns, capsizing in Oslo Fiord on 9 April 1940 after being torpedoed by Norwegian coast defence batteries

14 (*left*) Flagship at the second ba
of Narvik and at the battle of Mata
the British battleship *Warspite*, 30
tons, firing a broadside with her e
15-inch guns

15 (*middle*) The Italian cruiser *Bartolomeo Colleoni*, 5,200 tons, being destroyed
by the Australian cruiser *Sydney*, 6,830 tons, on 19 July 1940. Both ships
were armed with eight 6-inch guns

16 (*bottom*) Torpedoed and sunk during the British carrier-borne air attack on
Taranto, 11 November 1940 the Italian battleship *Conte di Cavour*, 26,140
tons, ten 12·5-inch guns

17 The British battleship *Barham*, 31,100 tons, eight 15-inch guns, sinking after being torpedoed by *U331* in the eastern Mediterranean on 25 November 1941

18 The surrender of the Italian Fleet, 10 September 1943. *Left to right*, battleship *Vittorio Veneto*, cruisers *Duca d'Aosta* and *Eugenio di Savoia*, battleship *Italia*

19 Captured Japanese Zeke fighter-bomber with US markings

20 British Swordfish torpedo-bomber spotter-reconnaissance

MARITIME AIRCRAFT OF
WORLD WAR TWO

21 British Sunderland long-range reconnaissance flying-boat

22 German Me.109 fighter-bomber

23–25 SOME NAVAL LEADERS. *Top left:* Germany's Admiral Karl Dönitz. *Top right:* Japan's Admiral Isoroku Yamamoto. *Below,* left to right: US Cominch Admiral Ernest King, Prime Minister Winston Churchill, First Lord A. V. Alexander and First Sea Lord Admiral Sir Dudley Pound

26 The British battlecruiser *Hood*, 42,100 tons, eight 15-inch guns, sunk by the German battleship *Bismarck* on 24 May 1941

27 The *Bismarck*, 41,700 tons, eight 15-inch guns, down by the bows after being hit by the guns of HMS *Hood* and *Prince of Wales* on 24 May 1941

28 A typical Atlantic convoy photographed from an escorting aircraft

29 The aircraft-carrier *Ark Royal*, 22,000 tons, 72 planes, sinking after being torpedoed by *U81* in the Mediterranean on 13 November 1941 (destroyer *Legion* standing by)

30 The cruiser *Dorsetshire*, 9,975 tons, eight 8-inch guns, sinking after attack by Japanese dive-bombers off Ceylon on 5 April 1942

31 The aircraft-carrier *Hermes*, 10,850 tons, 15 planes, sinking after attack by aircraft from the same Japanese carrier force 9 April 1942

32 One of the explosions which sank the torpedoed US aircraft-carrier *Lexington*, 36,000 tons, 90 planes, in the battle of the Coral Sea on 7 May 1942

33 One of the two largest warships ever built, the Japanese fast battleship *Yamato*, 64,170 tons, nine 18-inch guns

34 The Japanese aircraft-carrier *Hiryu*, 17,300 tons, 73 planes, on fire after being attacked by US aircraft in the battle of Midway on 5 June 1942

35 The Japanese cruiser *Mikuma*, 12,400 tons, ten 8-inch guns, destroyed by US planes in the battle of Midway on 6 June 1942

36 The US aircraft-carrier *Yorktown*, 19,900 tons, 100 planes, abandoned on 4 June 1942 during the battle of Midway and subsequently sunk by the Japanese U-boat *I168*

37 The US cruiser *Birmingham* (left), 10,000 tons, twelve 6-inch guns, playing her hoses on the burning US aircraft-carrier *Princeton*, 11,000 tons, 45 planes, before she was destroyed by an internal explosion during the battles of Leyte Gulf, 24 October 1944

38 One of the many US-built escort carriers, 8,000–11,000 tons, 21–34 planes, which served in the British and US Navies during World War Two, of which 18 acquitted themselves so valiantly at the battle of Samar on 25 October 1944

39 Damaged by a Japanese *kamikaze* attack in January 1945: the Australian 'County' class cruiser *Australia*, 9,870 tons, eight 8-inch guns

M. de Pisa, and *Fiume*, Captain G. Giorgis, *Trieste*, flag of Rear-Admiral L. Sansonetti, *Trento* and *Bolzano* and the 6-inch cruisers *Duca degli Abruzzi*, flag of Rear-Admiral A. Legnani, and *Giuseppe Garibaldi*, plus 10 destroyers, to the south of the Strait of Messina on 27 March. Iachino intended to attack a British convoy as it passed Crete en route for the Piraeus. If he met any opposition it should not amount to more than a couple of British cruisers with a handful of screening destroyers.

Unfortunately for the Italian C-in-C not only was he grievously misled by the two bomber pilots but Cunningham had his own more useful sources of intelligence. He knew that the Germans were about to move into Greece; he expected an Italian attack on one of his convoys; radio intelligence indicated a significant movement by the Italian Fleet; and an RAF flying-boat reported three Italian cruisers south of Crete. Having recalled the only convoy which was at sea, and postponed the sailing of others from Alexandria and the Piraeus, Cunningham left Alexandria in the *Warspite*, Captain D. B. Fisher, at 1900 on 27 March (after dark so that neither Italian reconnaissance aircraft nor agents ashore would report his departure before next morning), accompanied by the *Barham*, Captain G. C. Cooke, flagship of Rear-Admiral Henry Rawlings, and *Valiant*, Captain C. E. Morgan, with the aircraft-carrier *Formidable*, Captain A. W. La T. Bissett, in which Douglas Boyd of the *Illustrious* now flew his flag as a rear-admiral, screened by nine destroyers.

All headed for a position to the south of Crete where they might find the enemy, albeit without much confidence that they would make contact with a foe who had proved so elusive. And there Pridham-Wippell in the cruiser *Orion*, Captain G. R. B. Back, which was in the Aegean with the *Ajax*, Captain D. B. McCarthy, *Gloucester*, Captain H. A. Rowley, and *Perth*, Captain Sir P. W. Bowyer-Smith, and four destroyers, were ordered to meet them.

Throughout that night the British battle fleet headed north-westward towards a position south of Gavdo Island, while Pridham-Wippell led his cruiser force out of the Aegean by way of the Kithera Channel to the west of Crete. During the same hours Iachino's flagship was steering east towards the same area, with Sansonetti's three cruisers some 20 miles on the *Vittorio Veneto*'s port bow and Cattaneo's and Legnani's twice this distance away on the same bearing. At dawn 0600 on the 28th, the *Formidable* launched a flight of reconnaissance planes: an hour and 20 minutes later one of these found Sansonetti's squadron: nine minutes later another reported Cattaneo's and Legnani's ships. Since both groups were only some 20 miles apart to the south of Gavdo Island, there was initial doubt as to whether they were the same or different ones. Cunningham steered 310 degrees for their positions, nearly 150 miles away, at his flagship's best speed.

The British cruiser force was much closer to the enemy: at 0745, after passing ahead of the Italian fleet, Pridham-Wippell sighted the *Trieste*,

E

TABLE 33: Major Units Involved in the Battle of Matapan

(R) indicates fitted with warning Radar

Ship	Type	Date of completion	Displacement (tons)	Speed (knots)	Guns	Torpedoes	Thickest armour
Barham	Battleship	1915	31,100	24	8 15in 12 6in	—	13in
Valiant (R)	Battleship	1916	32,700	24	8 15in 20 4·5in	—	13in
Warspite	Battleship	1915	30,600	24	8 15in 8 6in	—	13in
Formidable (R)	Aircraft-carrier	1940	23,000	31	16 4·5in Also 36 fighters and torpedo-bombers	—	4½in
Ajax (R)	Cruiser	1935	6,985	32	8 6in	8 21in	4in
Gloucester	Cruiser	1939	9,400	32	12 6in	6 21in	4in
Orion (R)	Cruiser	1935	7,215	32	8 6in	8 21in	4in
Perth	Cruiser	1936	6,980	32	8 6in	8 21in	4in
Vittorio Veneto	Battleship	1940	41,167	28	9 15in 12 6in	—	14in
Bolzano	Cruiser	1933	11,065	34	8 8in	8 21in	4in
Fiume	Cruiser	1931	11,700	29	8 8in	—	6in
Zara	Cruiser	1931	11,700	29	8 8in	—	6in
Pola	Cruiser	1932	11,700	29	8 8in	—	6in
Trieste	Cruiser	1928	10,500	31	8 8in	8 21in	4in
Trento	Cruiser	1929	10,500	31	8 8in	8 21in	4in
Duca degli Abruzzi	Cruiser	1937	9,959	31	10 6in	6 21in	5½in
Giuseppe Garibaldi	Cruiser	1937	9,387	31	10 6in	6 21in	5½in

Trento and *Bolzano* coming up over the horizon astern. Because these three ships were armed with 8-inch guns, as opposed to his own 6-inch, he altered course to 140 degrees and increased speed to 28 knots, intending to lead them towards the British battle fleet—despite the possibility, indicated by the *Formidable*'s aircraft reports, that the way might be barred by the *Zara, Fiume, Pola, Garibaldi* and *Abruzzi,* which were over the horizon to the north-east.

At 0812 Sansonetti's three faster cruisers opened fire on the *Gloucester* but scored no hits. Not until the range was down to 23,500 yards were the British ships able to retaliate. Both sides then fought a long-range action without effect until 0855, when Iachino ordered Sansonetti to turn his squadron away to the north-west, so that it drew out of range. Rightly believing that it was his duty to maintain contact with the enemy, Pridham-Wippell turned to follow, not knowing that Iachino designed to lure the British cruisers within range of the *Vittorio Veneto*'s heavy guns. Nor did Iachino know that his flagship was heading for Cunningham's battle fleet, because he dismissed a report by a reconnaissance aircraft from Rhodes, containing an inaccurate position, as being of his own fleet, despite the fact that it referred to an aircraft-carrier and two battleships, as well as cruisers and destroyers.

Meantime, at 0849, Cunningham had ordered Maleme Naval Air Station at the west end of Crete to send a strike against Sansonetti's cruisers. Because of signal delays its three available planes did not take the air until 1050; and when these dropped their torpedoes shortly after noon the Italian cruisers successfully avoided them. Before this, however, at 0956, the *Formidable* flew off a six plane torpedo strike, led by Lieutenant-Commander G. Saunt, to attack the same force. But before they could reach their objective Pridham-Wippell sighted a ship which transformed the situation. At 1058 he identified the *Vittorio Veneto* 16 miles away almost due north. Immediately he made three emergency signals to his force: 'Make smoke', 'Turn together to 180 degrees', and 'Proceed at your utmost speed'. Intercepted by the *Warspite,* these were enough to tell Cunningham that an Italian battle fleet had been sighted.

As the *Veneto* opened fire Sansonetti swung his cruisers round to south-east to engage the British cruisers. Threatened from both quarters by faster and more powerful ships, Pridham-Wippell was in a critical position. Fortunately, 29 salvoes from the Italian 15-inch guns at a range of some 12 miles achieved no more than near misses. More fortunately still, at 1127, the *Formidable*'s strike arrived on the scene. According to Lieutenant F. H. E. Hopkins, Saunt's observer:

> We sighted one large warship, escorted by four destroyers, steaming towards our cruisers. Since the battleship was steaming at 30 knots, it was clear that our cruisers were in for trouble. Unless we could do something quickly they would be picked off one by one by the *Vittorio.* The trouble was that we were abaft her beam, so that since our air speed was only 90 knots we were catching up at a relative speed of only 60.

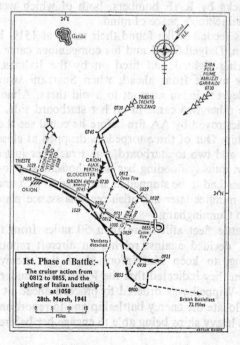

1st. Phase of Battle:-
The cruiser action from
0812 to 0855, and the
sighting of Italian battleship
at 1058
28th. March, 1941

0 5 10 15
|___|___|___|___|
Miles

British Battlefleet
72 Miles

It took the best part of 20 minutes to creep up to a suitable attacking position. The first flight of three dived to the starboard bow of the target and dropped torpedoes. As the *Vittorio* turned to comb the tracks she was caught beam on by the second flight.[9]

The *Veneto* eluded all these torpedoes, but she had such a narrow escape that Iachino decided that his fleet was too near to Cretan airfields, and to a possible British aircraft-carrier, for its health. He reversed course to west-north-west away from the scene at 18 knots. Before Pridham-Wippell could appreciate what had happened, the Italian flagship and Sansonetti's cruisers had disappeared over the horizon. In view of his squadron's inferiority, he did not attempt to relocate them, but held his southerly course until, at 1224, the *Gloucester* made contact with the British battle fleet coming in from the east, when the cruisers were ordered to take station at maximum visibility distance ahead of the *Warspite*.

To Cunningham there appeared to be only one way by which his slower fleet might catch the enemy, another strike by the *Formidable*'s aircraft. At 1225, having survived a torpedo attack by a flight of Italian machines, Bissett's ship flew off her remaining five planes, led by Lieutenant-Commander J. Dalyell-Stead. But before they could find their objective the validity of Iachino's decision to retire to the westward was seemingly reinforced by the aforementioned torpedo attack from Maleme, and by high-level attacks by RAF bombers, both of which were too near to scoring hits for Iachino's peace of mind.

Formidable's second strike found their target at 1519. Having worked up into the sun, Dalyell-Stead and his companions came down to 5,000 feet before being sighted and fired on by the Italians. Three planes delivered their attack from ahead, when Sparzani swung the *Veneto* through 180 degrees in an attempt to avoid them. Almost immediately afterwards the other two came in on her starboard side. Dalyell-Stead's machine was destroyed by AA fire before he could see the success of his skilful leadership. Out of three torpedoes dropped at close range to port of the *Veneto* and two to starboard, one struck her just above her port outer propeller, quickly flooding her with thousands of tons of water. At 1530 her engines had to be stopped as she listed to port and settled by the stern. Twenty minutes later a British reconnaissance plane reported her predicament to Cunningham.

With his battle fleet still more than 50 miles from the enemy, the British C-in-C decided against relying on aircraft reports, which were often confusing, to keep him informed of the enemy's movements, especially when they indicated that the *Veneto* was under way again. At 1644 Pridham-Wippell was ordered to proceed ahead at his squadron's best speed, to locate the enemy battleship and to report on the chances of Cunningham's heavy ships being able to engage her before nightfall. And

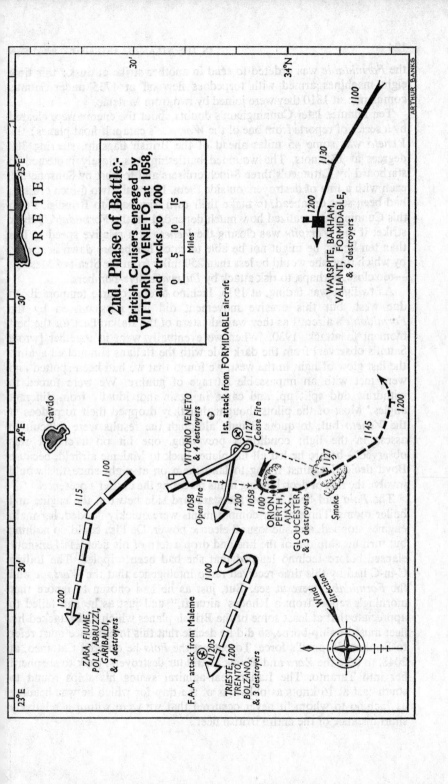

2nd. Phase of Battle:-
British Cruisers engaged by
VITTORIO VENETO at 1058,
and tracks to 1200

CRETE

34°N

ARTHUR BANKS

Gavdo

WARSPITE, BARHAM,
VALIANT, FORMIDABLE,
& 9 destroyers

1100

1130

1200

1100

1st. attack from FORMIDABLE aircraft

1115

1200

1100

1200

1058
Open Fire

1127
Cease Fire

VITTORIO VENETO
& 4 destroyers

1200

1058

1100

1127

Smoke

1145

1200

ORION,
PERTH,
AJAX,
GLOUCESTER,
& 3 destroyers

ZARA, FIUME,
POLA, ABRUZZI,
GARIBALDI,
& 4 destroyers

1100

Wind
direction

F.A.A. attack from Maleme

1205

TRIESTE, 1200
TRENTO,
BOLZANO,
& 3 destroyers

0   5   10   15
Miles

23°E   30'   24°E   30'   25°E

the *Formidable* was ordered to send in another strike at dusk: this time eight machines armed with torpedoes flew off at 1735 under Saunt's command: at 1810 they were joined by two from Maleme.

Ten minutes later Cunningham's doubts about the enemy were cleared by a series of reports from one of the *Warspite*'s catapult float planes: the *Veneto* was some 45 miles ahead of the British flagship, steering 300 degrees at 13 knots. The wounded battleship was closely protected to starboard by Cattaneo's three 8-inch cruisers and to port by Sansonetti's, each with a line of destroyers outside them. Legnani's two 6-inch cruisers had been sent on ahead, to make their own way back to Brindisi. From this Cunningham realized how much depended on the *Formidable*'s dusk strike; if the *Warspite* was closing the *Veneto* at a relative speed of less than ten knots, he might not be able to catch her before dawn next day, by which time she would be less than 250 miles from the Strait of Messina —too close, perhaps, to risk attack by *Luftwaffe* dive-bombers.

As twilight was fading, at 1915, Iachino altered course temporarily to due west, but this evasive movement did not pass unseen by the *Formidable*'s aircraft as they waited astern of the Italian fleet for the best moment to attack, 1930. 'When we eventually went in together [wrote Saunt's observer] from the dark side with the Italians silhouetted against the last glow of light in the west, we found that we had been spotted and were met with an impassable barrage of gunfire. We were forced to withdraw and split up, and came in again individually from different angles.' Most of the pilots thought that they dropped their torpedoes at the *Veneto* but, to quote Saunt, 'although the results were difficult to assess in the light conditions prevailing, one hit on a cruiser was observed'—before he led all his planes back to Maleme airfield, because Boyd decided against trying to land them on at night since this would involve the risk of deck landing lights revealing the carrier's presence.

The *Pola* had been hit on the starboard side between the engine and boiler rooms. Three of her compartments were quickly flooded, her main engines stopped, and she lost all electric power. De Pisa could do nothing but turn his ship out of the line and drop astern of his fleet. Half-an-hour elapsed before Iachino learned that she had been crippled. The Italian C-in-C had by this time received radio intelligence that the *Warspite* and the *Formidable* were at sea. But, just as he had chosen to ignore that morning's report from a Rhodes' aircraft,[10] and just as he had failed to appreciate that at least some of the British planes which had attacked his fleet must be ship-borne, so did he decide that this intelligence must refer to Pridham-Wippell's force. To protect the *Pola* he ordered Cattaneo, at 2048, to take the *Zara* and *Fiume*, with four destroyers, back to shepherd her into Taranto. The Italian rear-admiral swung his ships round to south-east at 16 knots as oblivious of the trap for which he was heading as Iachino to whom 'it never occurred that we were within a relatively short distance of the entire British fleet'.

No C-in-C could have made a more disastrous appreciation. Conversely when, shortly after 1900, Pridham-Wippell, who was some 20 miles ahead of the *Warspite,* reported sighting 'two unknown vessels' right ahead distant about 10 miles, Cunningham judged that the whole fleet was standing by the crippled ship.

Now came the difficult moment of deciding what to do. I [Cunningham] was fairly well convinced that having got so far [to the south of Cape Matapan] it would be foolish not to complete the *Vittorio Veneto*'s destruction. At the same time it appeared that the Italian admiral must be aware of our position. Any British admiral would not have hesitated to use every destroyer he had, backed by all his cruisers fitted with torpedo tubes, for attacks on the pursuing fleet. Some of my staff argued that it would be unwise to charge blindly after the retreating enemy with our three heavy ships, and the *Formidable* also on our hands, to run the risk of ships being crippled within easy range of enemy dive-bombers at daylight. I paid respectful attention to this opinion and told them I would have my evening meal and see how I felt afterwards.[11]

One of his staff recalls the actual words Cunningham used: 'You're a pack of yellow-livered skunks. I'll go and have my supper now and afterwards see if my morale isn't higher than yours'. These epitomized Cunningham's fighting spirit. To quote the same officer: 'As soon as he came on deck every available sound destroyer—eight in all—was sent ahead to form the attacking force under Captain P. J. Mack in the *Jervis,* while the battle fleet prepared to engage the enemy by night, screened by only four destroyers'.[12]

At 2037 Mack received the order: 'Attack enemy battle fleet with torpedoes'. He at once steered 300 degrees at 28 knots for the enemy's estimated position. He expected to find Iachino some 30 miles ahead. But this assumed that the *Veneto*'s speed was only 15 knots, when it was, in truth, nearer to 20. Moreover, at 2048, Iachino altered course from 300 to 323 degrees. At 2115 Mack signalled that he intended to pass up the starboard side of the damaged battleship beyond visibility range, prior to delivering an attack from ahead.

He planned to divide his force into two divisions, to come down on opposite courses and pass between the battleship and the cruisers on each side at a range of 500 yards. He hoped to throw the enemy into confusion so that they would fire at each other. It was a bold plan, in keeping with the C-in-C's known belief in Nelson's maxim, 'Engage the enemy more closely'. But this was not to be. At 2200 Mack altered course to 285 degrees. Shortly afterwards the *Ajax* reported three unidentified ships on her radar screen bearing between 190 and 252 degrees distant five miles. Although these were Cattaneo's ships returning to the crippled *Pola,* the

Jervis's plot indicated that they must be the rest of Pridham-Wippell's force, so Mack ignored them.

The eight British destroyers maintained their course until 2320, shortly after Mack had been puzzled to receive this signal from Cunningham: 'All forces not engaged in sinking the enemy retire north-eastward'. He turned accordingly, then asked whether this applied to his ships. When Cunningham replied: 'After your attack', Mack altered back to the west. Twenty minutes later he estimated that he was sufficiently far ahead of the *Veneto* to turn to 200 degrees. But he found nothing, because the *Veneto* was more than 30 miles further ahead and to the north of where he supposed her to be. Subsequently Cunningham criticized his decision to pass to the north of the *Veneto* as 'most unfortunate' because it 'left the southern flank of the enemy open for escape' and because it 'cramped the cruiser squadron', of which the first point was less than just, in that Iachino's only route to safety lay to the north-west.

On the other hand Pridham-Wippell's ships had begun pursuing the Italian fleet at 30 knots, spread on a line of bearing 020–200 degrees, seven miles apart. But as soon as the *Orion* reported two unknown vessels 10 miles ahead at 1915, the vice-admiral concentrated his squadron in line ahead. Half-an-hour later darkness reduced visibility to four miles and he lost sight of the enemy. But at 2014 the *Orion* obtained a radar echo six miles ahead from which Pridham-Wippell was able to report, at 2040, an unknown ship lying stopped. He considered that if it was the damaged *Veneto*, it was Mack's task to finish her off. (In fact the *Jervis* did not receive this report.) Alternatively, if it was some other ship, it was still his task to regain touch with the enemy's main fleet.

This required him to work round to the north of the stopped *Pola* before again heading west, when he realized that Mack's destroyers were on a converging course. And when he received the *Ajax*'s already mentioned report of three unidentified ships at 2155, he decided that they must be Mack's force (just as Mack supposed them to be Pridham-Wippell's). To avoid a clash he turned further north, to 340 degrees, intending to alter back to the west when he was well clear. But before this he received Cunningham's signal to withdraw to the north-east, so he turned his cruisers to 060 degrees, whereby he missed finding the *Veneto* and her escort by 35 miles, just as Mack missed them by 30.

Before this much had happened elsewhere. About an hour earlier, to quote one of Mack's destroyer officers: 'On the port quarter a flash showed up over the horizon and a star-shell hovered in the sky. Then another and greater flash. And then to starboard of the first flash a great tower of flame shot up into the air, lighting up the whole sea. The battle fleet had evidently walked into something'. Hoping that the stopped ship was the *Veneto*, Cunningham had ordered his battle fleet, at 2100, to steer 280 degrees for her position 20 miles ahead at 20 knots, in the order *Warspite*, *Valiant*, *Formidable* and *Barham*, with the destroyers *Stuart* and *Havock* one mile to starboard and the *Greyhound* and *Griffin* one mile to port. At 2203 the *Valiant*'s radar detected the stopped vessel six miles on her port bow. Handling his heavy ships with all the skill of an experienced destroyer commander, Cunningham immediately swung them 40 degrees to port together, then ordered the *Greyhound* and *Griffin* to join the *Stuart* and *Havock* on his starboard side where they would be clear of the expected contact.

With their crews at action stations and with their turrets trained and all guns loaded, the three British battleships bore down on the enemy in quarterline until, at 2223, the *Stuart* suddenly signalled that she had sighted darkened ships on her starboard bow. Steaming across the course of the British fleet from right to left, distant about two miles, were the destroyer *Alfieri* leading the *Zara*, followed by the *Fiume* and the destroyers *Gioberti, Carducci* and *Oriani*. A moment later these were seen from the *Warspite*'s bridge, when Cunningham swung his fleet back into line ahead, on to a course almost parallel but opposite to the enemy's 130 degrees. At 2227 both the *Warspite* and the *Valiant* opened fire with their main and secondary armaments at ranges between 3,000 and 4,000 yards.

> One heard the 'ting-ting-ting' of the fire gongs. Then came the great orange flash and the violent shudder as the big guns were fired. The *Greyhound* switched her searchlights on to the *Alfieri*, showing her up as a silvery-blue ship in the darkness. Ours shone out with the first broadside and provided full illumination for a ghastly sight. I saw our great projectiles flying through the air. Five hit a few feet below the level of the *Fiume*'s upper deck and burst with splashes of brilliant flame. The Italians were quite unprepared. Their guns were trained fore and aft. They were helplessly shattered before they could put up any resistance.[13]

For allowing his ships' companies to be in their hammocks instead of at their action stations Cattaneo was to pay a heavy price. (To be fair he was not the only commander to make this error of judgment during World War Two: a later chapter of this book will recall the night when an Allied naval force paid as dearly for the same error of judgment.) Aflame for most of her length Gingis's cruiser turned out of the line listing heavily to starboard, her after turret blown over the side. Three quarters of an hour later, at 2315, she sank.

After her first devastating broadside the *Valiant* shifted target to the *Zara*, as did the *Warspite* after two. Both poured 15-inch shells into Cattaneo's flagship which, like the *Fiume*, was caught wholly unprepared for battle. The *Barham* did likewise after the *Formidable* had hauled clear of the line to starboard, and after firing one broadside into the *Alfieri*, leaving her a burning wreck. The boilers of the blazing *Zara* then exploded and a forward turret was blown overboard.

E*

A few minutes later, at 2231, Cunningham saw the three destroyers astern of the Italian cruisers turn to port and fire torpedoes. He responded with an emergency turn of 90 degrees to starboard together, away from the enemy, and shifted his battleships' guns on to these vessels. Then he released his four destroyers to finish off the enemy, following this with the signal which has been mentioned twice already.

> In the general melée [wrote one of his staff officers] it was clear that our battleships were liable to be torpedoed by the enemy destroyers or by our own. For that reason I wrote out a signal saying 'all ships not engaged in sinking the enemy steer to the north-eastward'. The C-in-C agreed and we led the battle fleet round to this course. This was a most unfortunate signal since it led Pridham-Wippell to give up his shadowing task. This had never been envisaged by me or by the C-in-C since all our peace-time training had stressed that in no circumstances should cruisers give up touch.[14]

According to Cunningham:

> The order was intended to ensure withdrawal on parallel tracks clear of the destroyer melée and was made under the impression that Pridham-Wippell's cruisers and Mack's striking force were in contact with the enemy. Unfortunately they were not so engaged and the vice-admiral accordingly withdrew to the north-east. He had sighted a red

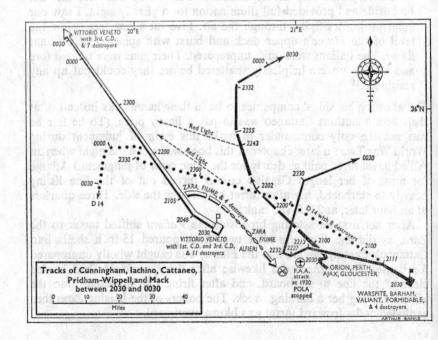

Tracks of Cunningham, Iachino, Cattaneo, Pridham-Wippell, and Mack between 2030 and 0030

pryotechnic signal some distance to the north-west some 30 minutes earlier and was about to spread to investigate. This red signal was sighted simultaneously by Mack who, seeing it in the direction of Pridham-Wippell and knowing from his alarm signal that he had seen it, forbore to investigate it. This must have been the remainder of the Italian fleet withdrawing to the north-west.[15]

'Forbore to investigate it': in view of Cunningham's adverse comments on Mack's performance, already quoted, one would have expected him to have been even more critical of Pridham-Wippell, since the vital import- ance of cruisers maintaining touch with the enemy was one of the more important lessons learned by the Grand Fleet in World War One. Be this as it may, the *Formidable* rejoined the line at 2320 as the battle fleet steamed north-east through the night, leaving its destroyers to 'finish the job'.

In an action that had lasted only three minutes Cattaneo's three leading ships had been reduced to blazing wrecks, the destroyer *Alfieri* by two broadsides from the *Barham*, the cruiser *Zara* by four from the *Warspite* and five from the *Valiant*, and the cruiser *Fiume* by two from the *Warspite* and one from the *Valiant*, all at under 4,000 yards—which impelled Cunningham to write later (albeit with tongue in cheek): 'The right range for any ship in the Mediterranean Fleet to engage the enemy is *point blank, at which range even a gunnery officer cannot miss'*. His victims had not only been caught unprepared for battle; contrary to the lesson of Jutland, so well learned from the Germans by the British, Japanese and US Fleets, they were neither equipped nor trained to fight a night action.

There remained three Italian destroyers. The *Greyhound*, Commander W. R. Marshall-A'Deane, and *Griffin*, Lieutenant-Commander J. Lee-Barber, went after them but only managed a brief engagement around 2320 before their targets were hidden behind a smoke screen. HMAS *Stuart*, Captain H. M. L. Waller, RAN, fired her torpedoes at the stricken *Zara*, scoring at least one hit, then sank the already crippled *Alfieri* by gunfire around 2315. The *Havock*, Lieutenant C. R. G. Watkins, fired four tor- pedoes at the *Carducci*, scoring a disabling hit before sinking her by gunfire, at 2330; then fired her other four at the still burning *Zara*.

Half-an-hour later Watkins discovered the hapless cause of all this trouble for the Italian fleet, the disabled *Pola*, powerless to move and with all her guns trained fore and aft. In the light of the *Havock's* single searchlight he first supposed her to be a 'Littorio' class battleship. Having already expended his torpedoes, he withdrew and radioed her position. On receiving this at 0030, Mack understandably believed her to be the ship he had been ordered to attack and swung his eight destroyers round to east-south-east. Ten minutes after his first signal Watkins corrected his report to read one 8-inch cruiser. But this did not reach Mack until after

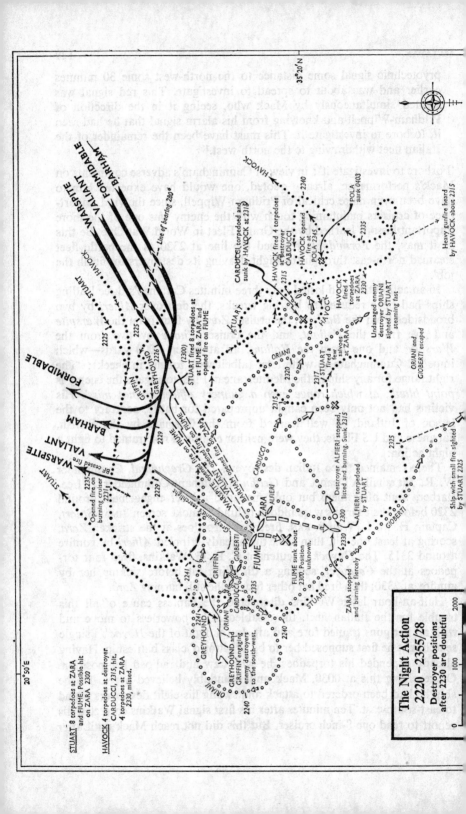

The Night Action 2220 – 2355/28
Destroyer positions after 2230 are doubtful

0130, by which time his flotilla had been steaming at high speed away from Iachino's flagship for more than an hour. Appreciating that he was now too far, nearly 100 miles, from the *Vittorio Veneto* to catch her, Mack decided against turning back to the west, and around 0200 arrived on the scene of the action. Finding the sea full of boats, rafts and swimming men, he ordered his rear destroyers to pick up survivors. The *Jervis* then closed the abandoned *Zara* and fired five torpedoes at her, scoring three hits. These were followed by a massive explosion after which the Italian cruiser turned over and sank at 0240.

Meanwhile the *Greyhound* and *Griffin* had joined the *Havock*'s watch on the helpless *Pola* whose crew could be seen crowding her decks, thoroughly demoralized, and longing to surrender, although her ensign was still flying. How best to deal with a ship so much larger than themselves in such a condition was epitomized by Watkins' signal enquiring whether he should 'board or blow off her stern with depth charges'. Mack's solution, when he appeared on the scene at 0325, is told in the words of the *Jervis*'s first lieutenant:

> After circling round, Captain Mack said 'I am going alongside—tell the first lieutenant to prepare wires and fenders starboard side'. 'A' gun's crew armed themselves with cutlasses and prepared to capture by boarding. A perfect approach, and over went a heaving line accompanied by the cry 'Take this, you b–gg–rs'. Uttering blood-curdling cries, 'A' gun's crew swarmed on board. They came back with a story of chaos. The officers' cabins had been looted and empty Chianti bottles lay everywhere. Only 256 of a ship's company of 1,000 remained, and they were huddled on the forecastle; the remainder had already jumped overboard. They filed on board in an orderly fashion followed by the commander and captain. A number showed unmistakable signs of inebriation. After about 20 minutes I was able to report that everybody was on board. Casting off, the *Jervis* steamed slowly round and illuminated the dead cruiser with her searchlight. Captain Mack then ordered the *Nubian* to finish her off with a torpedo, after toying with the idea of towing her back to Alexandria, some 500 miles. He reluctantly dismissed it owing to the certainty of heavy air attack next day.[16]

The *Nubian*, Commander R. W. Ravenhill, fired two torpedoes, and at 0403 the *Pola* blew up and sank. Of Cattaneo's force of three 8-inch cruisers and four destroyers only two of the latter, the *Gioberti* and *Oriani*, had escaped that night's holocaust to return safely to their base. With the *Fiume*, *Pola*, *Zara*, *Alfieri* and *Carducci* perished the Italian rear-admiral and some 3,000 of his officers and men.

With only three hours to go before daylight, when the battle fleet must have a destroyer screen, Mack called his ships off the task of rescuing Italians from the water and headed north-east at 20 knots. By 0700 all 12

British destroyers had rejoined their battle fleet. So, too, had Pridham-Wippell's cruisers. At 0800 the whole force headed back to the scene of the battle and in little over an hour during the forenoon of 29 March brought the number of rescued Italians up to 905. Then a German air-craft appeared—sufficient warning that an attack by shore-based bombers could be expected. A dawn air-search by the *Formidable*'s planes having discovered nothing—Iachino's fleet was by now more than 200 miles away—Cunningham was obliged to stop his humanitarian task and shape course for Alexandria. But he did not forget to radio the position of the remaining swimmers to the Italian Admiralty so that another 160 officers and men were rescued two days later by the hospital ship *Gradisca*. Before this 110 more were picked up by Greek destroyers, who would have taken part in the battle but for a ciphering error in a signal which directed them to 'await tankers' instead of 'await orders'.

The expected air attack on Cunningham's fleet did not materialize until after 1500. Then it was limited to 12 dive-bombers which were beaten off by the *Formidable*'s fighters and a heavy barrage of gunfire. And by the next morning the British ships were beyond the range of air attack. That evening they berthed in Alexandria harbour, not only triumphant but, almost miraculously, having suffered neither damage nor casualties, apart from the crew of one of the *Formidable*'s planes. How well earned was this signal to Cunningham from King George VI: 'My heartiest congratulations to all ranks and ratings under your command on your great victory'. But there was also disappointment: as Cunningham wrote in his despatch: 'The results of the action cannot be viewed with entire satisfaction since the damaged *Vittorio Veneto* was allowed to escape. The failure of the cruisers and destroyers to make contact with her during the night was unlucky and is much to be regretted'. But to suggest how he might have completed the destruction of Iachino's damaged flagship would serve no more purpose than reiterating his admission that his withdrawal signal was unfortunate. For, in his own words:

> Looking back I am conscious of several things which might have been done better. However, calm reflection in an armchair in the full knowl-edge of what actually happened is a very different matter from conduct-ing an operation from the bridge of a ship at night in the presence of the enemy. Instant and momentous decisions have to be made in a matter of seconds. With fast moving ships at close quarters and the roar of heavy gunfire, clear thinking is not easy. In no other circum-stances than in a night action at sea does the fog of war so completely descend to blind one to a true realization of what is happening.

And there can be no doubt that he richly deserved the award of the GCB because

we could claim substantial results. Those three heavy Italian cruisers with their 8-inch guns were armoured against 6-inch gunfire and were always a threat to our smaller and more lightly armed ships. More important still, the inactive attitude of the Italian Fleet during our subsequent evacuations of Greece and Crete was directly attributable to the rough handling they received at Matapan. Had the enemy's surface ships intervened in these operations, our already difficult task would have been well nigh impossible.[17]

to which he could have added the much longer task of reinforcing and supplying Malta in which Force H also played a major role, with the consequence that although beleaguered for much of three years this brave little island, so close to Sicily and the heel of Italy, never had to surrender.

Nine months elapsed before Nemesis struck Cunningham's battle fleet, before history repeated itself and the Italian Navy had their revenge in just the way that they had decimated the Austrian battle fleet near the end of World War One. First, on 25 November 1941, Lieutenant von Tiesenhausen in *U331* penetrated the British destroyer screen north of Bardia and struck the *Barham* with three torpedoes. As she capsized her magazines exploded. Cooke and 861 of his officers and men perished: Pridham-Wippell and 450 others were rescued. Secondly, during the night of 18–19 December the Italian submarine *Scirè*, Commander Prince Borghese, launched three chariots, 'captained' by Lieutenant-Commander de la Penne, Captain Marceglia and Captain Martellotta, just outside Alexandria harbour. These managed to pass through the boom in the wake of destroyers entering harbour and fix their charges under the *Queen Elizabeth,* the *Valiant* and the tanker *Sagona.* All three were severely damaged and, but for shallow water which brought them to rest on the bottom, might have sunk. This left the eastern Mediterranean bereft of battleships when, with the need to send capital ships to the Indian Ocean to counter the threat presented by Japan, no replacements could be provided.

Fortunately, when Admiral Riccerdi eventually learned of this success, he made no significant attempt to exploit it. His strategy remained supine. And his capital ships were not only hampered by a growing shortage of oil fuel but remained under the command of Iachino who feared to lose them even when their movements were restricted to the central Mediterranean; who at the first and second battle of Sirte (17 December 1941 and 22 March 1942), more especially the latter, failed to come to grips with a handful of British cruisers escorting convoys to Malta, when they were skilfully and courageously handled by the redoubtable Rear-Admiral Philip Vian.

Wars are not won without taking the offensive, nor battles gained without taking calculated risks. Of all the admirals who commanded

British ships in World War Two, none demonstrated this better than he who was to become Admiral of the Fleet Viscount Cunningham of Hyndhope. No other so well deserved, after death, the eminence of a bust beside those of Jellicoe and Beatty in the shade of Nelson's column in London's Trafalgar Square.

NOTES

1 The two aircraft-carriers, *Ark Royal* and *Eagle*, stowed only spotter-reconnaissance and torpedo-bomber planes.

2 They were no more successful when, later, some of them sortied into the Atlantic. Indeed, U-boat operations in the Mediterranean were only a serious threat after Germany began sending hers through the Straits of Gibraltar in October 1941.

3 In *A Sailor's Odyssey*.

4 Admiral of the Fleet Sir Algernon Willis in his unpublished *War Memoirs*.

5 Willis *op. cit.*

6 Cunningham *op. cit.*

7 Willis *op. cit.*

8 *Ibid.*

9 Quoted in S. W. C. Pack's *The Battle of Matapan*.

10 Since when the *Regia Aeronautica* had failed to provide him with further air reconnaissance reports just as it had failed to give his fleet fighter protection. Nor, for that matter, did the *Luftwaffe* help him, notwithstanding its success against the *Illustrious*. To quote the Italian admiral: 'I felt pretty well deceived by the lack of co-operation'.

11 Cunningham *op. cit.*

12 Quoted in Pack *op. cit.*

13 Cunningham *op. cit.*

14 Quoted in Pack *op. cit.*

15 Cunningham *op. cit.*

16 Quoted in Pack *op. cit.*

17 Cunningham *op. cit.*

7 'Hood' and 'Bismarck'

On 8 April 1805 Villeneuve's Toulon fleet escaped through the Straits of Gibraltar and headed for the West Indies with Nelson's Mediterranean fleet in pursuit. After spending a month attacking British trade and possessions in the Caribbean, and having waited in vain for Ganteaume's Brest fleet to join him (because it was unable to break Cornwallis' blockade), the French admiral headed east for the Bay of Biscay, hoping that he might meet Ganteaume there and, as a combined force, command the Straits of Dover so that Napoleon's *Grande Armée* could invade England. Nelson followed Villeneuve, after sending news of his return on ahead to the Admiralty by a fast brig, which reached England in time for Lord Barham to send orders to Cornwallis to detach a sufficient force to intercept the returning enemy. Calder's action off Ferrol on 22 July was indecisive, but it served to divert Villeneuve, first into Ferrol and then south to Cadiz, from which he only emerged to be virtually annihilated off Cape Trafalgar on 21 October. In short, the greater part of the British Fleet in Home waters, the Atlantic and Mediterranean was engaged in hunting down a powerful Franco-Spanish force for some six months before it was destroyed. For two particular reasons this took so long; the slow speed of sailing ships-of-the-line, and the lengthy time then required to convey intelligence and to transmit orders.

This chapter tells the story of a similar operation, fought over much the same wide area of ocean, during which, with the benefit of steam turbines, aircraft and radio, a powerful German force bent on attacking Allied trade in the north Atlantic was hunted down and destroyed in just five days in May 1941. As the earlier story is worth recalling for the intuitive reactions of the several British commanders involved, under the general direction of the Admiralty, to such news as they could obtain of the French Fleet's movements, which were crowned by Nelson's greatest triumph, so is this one to be remembered for the way in which both the Admiralty and the C-in-C Home Fleet directed the operations of eight capital ships, two aircraft-carriers, and 11 cruisers, as well as aircraft of both Coastal Command and the Fleet Air Arm, towards their final goal.

The loss of the *Graf Spee* was enough to deter Raeder from sending another warship into the Atlantic for almost a year. The *Admiral Scheer*, Captain Krancke, was at large from 23 October 1940 until 1 April 1941 during which she sank 99,059 tons of shipping and the armed merchant cruiser *Jervis Bay*. Within the same period the *Admiral Hipper*, Captain Meisel, made a three weeks' sortie from 5 December 1940, during which she attacked troop convoy WS5A on the 25th to the 27th, being beaten off by its cruiser escort, and a second sortie from 1–15 February 1941 during which, on the 12th, she attacked convoy SLS64, sinking seven of its 19 ships. The *Gneisenau*, Captain Fein, and *Scharnhorst*, Captain Hoffmann, were also out from 3 February–22 March, under Admiral Lütjens, a period notable for the way in which he was deterred from attacking convoy HX106 by the presence of HMS *Ramillies* on 8 February, and convoy SL67 on 7 March by HMS *Rodney*, before seeking sanctuary in Brest.

Since on other occasions during this sortie Lütjens' ships sank as much as 115,622 tons of shipping, he was ordered to hoist his flag in the new 15-inch gun *Bismarck*, Captain Lindemann, when Raeder decided to send out this pride of his Fleet, accompanied by the 8-inch cruiser *Prinz Eugen*, Captain Brinkmann. (Raeder had intended to employ also the *Gneisenau* and *Scharnhorst*, but both had been too heavily damaged by RAF attacks on them in Brest for this to be possible.) They sailed from Gdynia on 18 May 1942, passed through the Sound on the 19th, called at Kors Fiord, near Bergen, for fuel on the 21st, and thence headed to pass well to the north of the Faroes at 25 knots. The *Bismarck* was to attack Allied convoys with battleship escorts, whilst the *Prinz Eugen* tackled other prey. Seven tankers and supply ships were deployed ready to replenish them.

The C-in-C of Britain's Home Fleet, now Admiral Tovey, received first warning of this sortie on 20 April when the ships were sighted in the Kattegat by the Swedish cruiser *Gotland* and her report was passed to the Admiralty by the British naval attaché in Stockholm. Twenty-four hours later Coastal Command discovered the *Bismarck* and *Prinz Eugen* in Kors Fiord, and subsequently tried to bomb them, but without success. Tovey sailed the *Hood*, Captain R. Kerr, flying the flag of Vice-Admiral L. E. Holland, and *Prince of Wales*, Captain J. C. Leach, accompanied by six destroyers, for Iceland's Hvalfiord to be ready to back up his cruisers patrolling the gaps to the north and south of this island. The 8-inch cruiser *Norfolk*, Captain A. J. L. Phillips, flying the flag of Rear-Admiral W. F. Wake-Walker, was on her way to relieve the *Suffolk*, Captain R. M. Ellis, patrolling the Denmark Strait, while the 6-inch cruisers *Arethusa*, *Birmingham* and *Manchester* were patrolling the wider Iceland-Faroes passage.

The rest of Tovey's immediately available ships, the *King George V*, Captain W. R. Patterson, and the 6-inch cruisers *Galatea*, flag of Rear-

Admiral A. T. B. Curteis, *Aurora, Kenya* and *Neptune*, plus the 5·25-inch *Hermione* and five destroyers (to which by cancelling a WS convoy the Admiralty added the aircraft-carrier *Victorious*, Captain H. C. Bovell, and the battlecruiser *Repulse*, Captain W. G. Tennant) were brought to short notice for steam in Scapa Flow. The *Prince of Wales*, be it noted, was so newly completed that she had not yet finished working-up. Moreover the contractors were still working on her 14-inch turrets. To this extent she was not battleworthy, but confronted with so great a danger, she had to be used.

Bad visibility deprived Tovey of further news until the evening of the 22nd, when a single Fleet Air Arm machine from the Orkneys penetrated Kors Fiord and investigated Bergen harbour. When its experienced observer, Commander G. A. Rotherham, reported at 1909 that the enemy had sailed, Tovey left with his main force at 2245 and headed for the best position to back up his cruisers on both sides of Iceland. The same bad weather which had delayed news of the Germans' departure from Kors Fiord prevented *Luftwaffe* reconnaissance planes reporting the Home Fleet's absence from Scapa Flow. It also hampered Coastal Command's efforts to locate the enemy. But, according to one of the *Suffolk*'s officers :

> Suddenly at 1922 one of our look-outs sighted the *Bismarck* and the *Prinz Eugen* emerging from a snow-squall between the *Suffolk* and the ice in the Denmark Strait. The enemy ships were moving fast in a south-westerly direction parallel to our own. 'Action stations' was immediately piped, full speed rung to the engine-room, and a sharp alteration of course made away into the enveloping mist as the first of a stream of sighting reports was sent out. It was more important that we should maintain contact with our radar than be annihilated. About an hour later HMS *Norfolk* joined us and began to shadow too. The pursuit continued at high speed throughout the night, moving roughly parallel to the coast of Greenland.

Phillips' ship came briefly, but harmlessly, under fire at a range of 13,000 yards before retiring under cover of smoke to radio the first enemy report to reach Tovey, whose main fleet was then some 600 miles to the southeast. Holland, whose two ships were much closer, had already received the *Suffolk*'s report and was heading for the enemy at 27 knots.

During much of the night the British cruisers, helped by radar, admirably performed their prime duty of shadowing a more powerful force despite rain, snow and ice, from outside gun range, whilst the *Hood* and *Prince of Wales* were coming up from the south. Expecting to gain contact with the enemy at any time after 0140 on 24 May, Holland cleared for action, ready for a night engagement. Unfortunately, during this crucial period Wake-Walker's cruisers lost contact, leaving Holland uncertain of the enemy's movements. Supposing that Lütjens might have made a large alteration of course, he turned from west to north, with the consequence that he lost bearing on an enemy who was still heading south-west.

At 0031 Holland signalled his heavy ships to concentrate their fire on the *Bismarck*, intending to leave Wake-Walker to deal with the *Prinz Eugen*. But since he did not wish to hazard revealing his approach to Lütjens by breaking radio silence, he did not inform the cruisers who were unaware that Holland's force was so close. (For the same reason Holland did not allow the *Prince of Wales* to use search radar, with which the *Hood* had not yet been fitted.) He did not therefore learn that Lütjens had ordered the *Prinz Eugen* to lead his line, so that the *Bismarck* was in the best position to deal with the British shadowers if they ventured too close. Nor did Wake-Walker attempt to reduce the range from which he was shadowing the enemy ships, so that when these joined action with Holland, his cruisers were some 15 miles away, too far to take part in it.

At 0203 Holland, still uncertain of Lütjens' whereabouts, turned his heavy ships to the south to await full daylight, while his destroyers continued searching to the north with the consequence that they were not available to carry out a torpedo attack during the coming battle. At 0247 the *Suffolk* regained contact and fed the *Hood* with a steady flow of reports of the enemy's position, course (SW) and speed (28 knots). At 0340 Holland increased to this speed and turned on to a converging course. The visibility was then some 12 miles. The *Prince of Wales* tried to fly off her reconnaissance aircraft but found that its fuel was contaminated by salt water.

Holland now made two cardinal errors. For one, he led the line in the *Hood* instead of ordering the better armoured *Prince of Wales* to do so where she would have drawn the brunt of the enemy's fire. Tovey was strongly tempted to radio Holland of the need to do this but, to his subsequent regret, forbore to 'interfere' with the man on the spot. For another, which was contrary to a lesson taught by Jutland, Holland kept his two ships in close order (600 yards) under his own control, instead of ordering open order (1,000 yards) and giving Leach freedom of manoeuvre.

More important, however, was the consequence of his two hour alteration of course to the north during the night. Knowing the weakness of the *Hood* compared with the *Bismarck*, he planned to close the range rapidly to some 12,000 yards at which the flat trajectory of the German shells would strike her side armour instead of plunging through her inadequately protected decks. And had he done this from fine on the enemy's bow his ships' superior gun power might have been decisive. But when he first sighted the enemy distant 17 miles and almost abeam at 0537, he could only close relatively slowly on a course on which his ships could bring only half their armament to bear, four 15-inch instead of eight and five 14-inch instead of nine (one of the *Prince of Wales'* forward guns being out of action); in effect no more than the eight 15-inch which the *Bismarck* brought to bear when both sides opened fire at 0553 at a range of 26,500 yards.

TABLE 34: Ships Involved in the Destruction of HMS *Hood*

Ship	Date of completion	Displacement (tons)	Speed (knots)	Guns	Thickest side armour	Thickest deck armour
Hood	1920	42,100	31	8 15in 12 5·5in	12in	3¾in
Prince of Wales	1941	35,000	29	10 14in 16 5·25in	15in	6in
Norfolk	1930	9,925	32	8 8in	—	4in
Suffolk	1928	9,800	31½	8 8in	5in	1½in
Bismarck	1940	41,700	30	8 15in 12 6in	12¾in	7¾in
Prinz Eugen	1940	14,240	32	8 8in	3¼in	3¾in

Nor was this all: while both German ships concentrated their fire on the *Hood*, and the *Prince of Wales* rightly chose the *Bismarck*, the *Hood* selected the relatively harmless *Prinz Eugen* because she was leading the enemy line and because all the larger German ships had similar profiles. The situation was, therefore, much in the Germans' favour—four 15-inch engaging the *Prinz Eugen* and five 14-inch engaging the *Bismarck*, whilst eight 15-inch and eight 8-inch engaged the *Hood*. Neither side's gunnery radar sets seem to have been effective at this range. The German ships relied on their stereoscopic rangefinders; the British on their less accurate coincidence ones, because in the post-World War One years the Admiralty, whilst recognizing the greater value of the former, rejected their adoption on the inadequate grounds that they needed exceptionally skilled men to operate them.

The consequence was that while none of the *Hood*'s salvoes seriously endangered the *Prinz Eugen,* and the *Prince of Wales* failed to find the *Bismarck*'s range until after her sixth salvo, the German battleship immediately straddled the British battlecruiser. Moreover, her second and third salvoes struck Holland's flagship amidships whilst those from the *Prinz Eugen* started a fire among her ready to use AA ammunition. And at 0600, just as the British squadron was altering course to bring all guns to bear, the *Hood* was hit again by shells which pierced her decks and detonated her after magazines. A tremendous explosion followed, and she blew up and disappeared almost before it was necessary for the *Prince of Wales* to alter course to avoid the wreckage. With her perished Holland, Kerr, and all 95 officers and 1,324 men of her crew except for one midshipman and two ratings who were rescued by the destroyer *Electra*. The distinguished actor Esmond Knight, then a Lieutenant RNVR, was serving in the *Prince of Wales*:

Suddenly there appeared the topmasts of two ships. 'Enemy in sight!' Silently the director towers swung in that direction, followed by the great fourteen-inch guns. The minutes raced by. There they were, in sharp silhouette on the horizon—*Bismarck* and *Prinz Eugen*, steaming in smokeless line ahead. The range was closing at an alarming speed. The two enemy ships, travelling at about thirty knots, were practically crossing our bows. At last came a signal from *Hood*—'Open fire!' Great orange flashes and huge clouds of black smoke belched from the forward turrets of the *Hood* as she fired her first salvo.

This fell just astern—one could see the great columns of water spurting into the air. Almost simultaneously we saw those brilliant flashes and the same jet-black smoke belching from *Bismarck*. Now followed those desperate and precious seconds while guns were reloaded and the enemy's first salvo was roaring to meet us. One became conscious of a noise growing in a gradual crescendo, suddenly to cease as the first great spouts of water rose just astern of *Hood*. It was impossible to measure time as we got off salvo after salvo; and again that horrible rushing noise, and an enormous geyser of water rising on our starboard side as a shell from *Bismarck* fell just short.

I saw a big fire burning on the boat-deck of the *Hood*. Then the incredible happened: a great explosion issued from her centre, tongues of pale-red flame shot into the air, while clouds of whitish-yellow

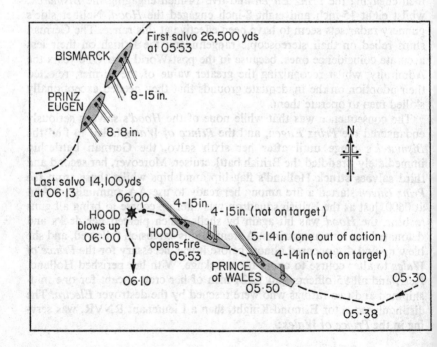

smoke burst upwards, gigantic pieces of brightly burning debris being hurled in the air. *Hood* had been blown to pieces.[1]

Such was the disastrous end of the fourth of Lord Fisher's ill-conceived all big-gun cruisers: as three were sunk at Jutland, now was the *Hood* lost because of his false belief that speed is armour. And to quote Admiral of the Fleet Lord Chatfield, who as First Sea Lord from 1933–38 had fought hard to have Britain's older capital ships modernized: 'The *Hood* was destroyed because she had to fight a ship 22 years more modern than herself'; 22 years in which 'engineering science and the power-weight ratio have changed beyond imagination'.[2]

The *Hood*'s swift end allowed Lütjens to turn his ships' main and secondary armaments on to the *Prince of Wales* at a range of 18,000 yards. Almost at once, at 0602, the British vessel's bridge was hit, killing or wounding almost all who were there, except for her captain. This blow was followed by four more 15-inch shells and three 8-inch. With the range down to 14,500 yards and with five of his 14-inch guns out of action, Leach decided to break off his engagement with a superior enemy. At 0613 he turned away under cover of smoke, intending to use his now damaged and defective vessel to help Wake-Walker's cruisers to maintain contact with the enemy until Tovey could reach the scene. He could not know that his newly-commissioned ship had obtained three hits on the *Bismarck*, one of which had caused a tell-tale leak of oil from two fuel tanks, and contamination of others. At 0800 Lütjens decided to abandon his sortie and head for the safety of St Nazaire, the only port on the Atlantic coast of France with a dry dock large enough to take his flagship. To return via the Denmark Strait to Germany was too hazardous now that much of the British Fleet must be hunting for him. But nor did Lütjens know of the *Prince of Wales*' deficiencies: had he done so his decision must have been to close and sink her.

As the two German ships continued to steer south-west, they were shadowed by the *Norfolk* and *Suffolk*, supported by the *Prince of Wales*. The nearest other force was Tovey's, the *King George V*, *Repulse*, *Victorious*, four cruisers and nine destroyers. Since these were 330 miles away to the south-east, the earliest time at which they could make contact was 0700 next morning, the 25th. They were not, however, the only ships heading for the scene. The Admiralty had ordered Somerville's Gibraltar-based Force H, which was covering a Clyde-Cape troop convoy, to head north; the *Rodney*, Captain F. H. G. Dalrymple-Hamilton, and three destroyers, which were on escort duty 550 miles to the south-east, to close the enemy; the *Ramillies* to leave her convoy for a position to the west of the enemy; and the *Revenge* to sail east from Halifax, while the *Edinburgh* on patrol in mid-Atlantic joined the shadowing cruisers. Even so, despite the help he could expect from reconnaissance planes of Coastal

Command and, of greater significance, despite the news which he received from Wake-Walker at 1320 that the *Bismarck* had turned south and cut her speed to 20 knots, Tovey calculated that she could still elude the net which he and the Admiralty had spread across the north Atlantic.

In an attempt to prevent this, he decided at 1440 on the 24th to send the *Victorious,* escorted by Curteis' cruisers, to launch an air strike from a position within 100 miles of the enemy. Because she had been about to ferry a cargo of fighters to Malta this aircraft-carrier's operational planes were limited to nine torpedo-bombers and six reconnaissance machines which were flown off at 2210. Flying through scudding rain clouds they obtained radar contact at 2327. Three minutes later the *Bismarck* was sighted, then lost again, but not before the planes had been seen by the battleship's crew. The shadowing British cruisers redirected them on to their quarry by midnight, after they had been led on a false scent by the chance presence of a neutral US coastguard cutter in the area, when they carried out their attack, with the disadvantage that they had lost the value of surprise. Even so they achieved one torpedo hit amidships, although it did no significant damage, before returning to the *Victorious* and landing on safely in the dark, except for two of the shadowing planes which were lost, although their crews were saved.

They had found only the *Bismarck* because around 1830 Lütjens had detached the *Prinz Eugen* to continue her ordered foray alone, enabling her to do so unobserved by allowing his battleship to fall back temporarily on his British pursuers and engaging them in a brief gun action. A further similar engagement around 0100 on the 25th was followed by a potential disaster: at 0401 Ellis reported that the *Suffolk* had lost radar contact with the enemy, and all his attempts to regain it failed because they were based on the concept that the *Bismarck* had turned away to the west when she had, in fact altered to south-east for St Nazaire. Tovey, whose flagship was now only 100 miles away, was thus deprived of his hopes of bringing the German battleship to action in some three hours time.

Although Lütjens passed safely within this distance at 0800 and later passed still closer to the *Rodney* and *Edinburgh,* the net was nonetheless tightening around him. The *Norfolk* and *Suffolk* were seeking him to the west and south-west of his last known position. The *Victorious* was ordered to send out air searches to the north-west, which were to be backed up by Curteis' cruisers. Since he could not know Lütjen's destination, Tovey thought it likely that he planned to rendezvous with a tanker south of Greenland to refuel before attacking Atlantic trade. The south-eastern sector towards which the German battleship was actually heading was not, however, unguarded. Here were the *Rodney,* the *Ramillies* and the *Edinburgh,* which the Admiralty had already ordered to the scene, the *Dorsetshire,* Captain B. C. S. Martin, escorting a south-bound convoy, and, 1,300 miles away, Somerville's flagship, the *Renown,*

Captain R. R. McGrigor, with the *Ark Royal*, Captain L. E. H. Maund, and the *Sheffield*, Captain C. A. A. Larcom.

During the forenoon a misreading of Admiralty bearings of the *Bismarck*'s radio transmissions persuaded Tovey that she was heading for the Iceland-Faroes passage, with the result that, at 1047, his flagship and many of the other searching vessels steered at high speed on this false scent, whereby they lost ground on the enemy. And not until 1924 did the Admiralty go so far as to instruct Tovey's ships that Lütjens must be heading for Brest, although the C-in-C had reached the same conclusion an hour earlier, when he altered course accordingly. But when the *King George V* turned she was as much as 150 miles astern of her quarry, with no good reason for Tovey to suppose that he would be able to catch her. Fortunately the Admiralty had given the same instructions much earlier, at 1100, to Somerville, whose ships were already steaming at high speed to the north to intercept.

Meantime, exhaustive searches by a Coastal Command aircraft in deteriorating weather had failed to find the *Bismarck* throughout the 25th. Fortunately these were directed with persistence and skill by a C-in-C who was as experienced in the ways of the sea as of the air. Air Marshal Sir F. W. Bowhill had begun his career in the Royal Navy, and for most of World War One had served in the RNAS before, in 1918, transferring to the newly formed RAF. And after more than 24 most anxious hours for Pound and Tovey, one of his planes[3] spotted the *Bismarck* at 1030 on the 26th, when she was less than 700 miles west of Brest, which she could be expected to reach late on the next day. Before this, however, she would receive strong cover by the *Luftwaffe* in waters dominated by Doenitz's U-boats which had been withdrawn from the trade routes, so that only 24 hours remained for the British to catch her. Tovey had already detached both the *Prince of Wales* and the *Repulse* with Curteis' cruisers and all his screening destroyers to Iceland and Newfoundland to refuel, but the *Rodney* had taken their place. Yet, against the advantage of superior gun power, nine 16-inch and ten 14-inch against eight 15-inch, he had to offset the latter ship's maximum speed of only 22 knots and the fact that both she and the *King George V* would soon have to leave the scene to refuel. His chances of success were slim.

All depended on Somerville's ships. When the *Bismarck* was relocated on the 26th, Force H was just 70 miles to the east, barring her way. The *Renown* could not be expected to engage her (indeed, the Admiralty ordered her not to do so), but the *Ark Royal*'s planes might be able to reduce the enemy vessel's speed enough for Tovey's two battleships to deal with her. Despite heavy weather, in which the aircraft-carrier's flight deck pitched to an extent which normally precluded flying operations, search planes took off, found the *Bismarck* and kept in touch with her, while the *Sheffield* was detached to help them. At 1450 the *Ark Royal*

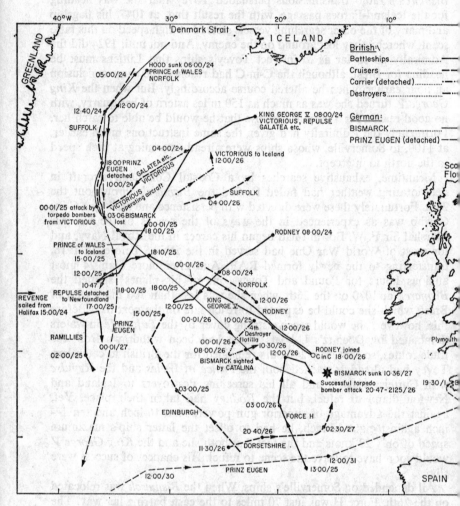

11 Pursuit of the *Bismarck*, 24–26 May 1941

Within the map:

GREENLAND

40°W   30°W   20°W   10°W

Denmark Strait

ICELAND

Scapa Flow

British:
Battleships ....
Cruisers ....
Carrier (detached) ....
Destroyers ....

German:
BISMARCK ....
PRINZ EUGEN (detached) ——

HOOD sunk 06·00/24
PRINCE of WALES
NORFOLK
05·00/24
12·00/24

12·40/24
SUFFOLK

KING GEORGE V 08·00/24
VICTORIOUS, REPULSE
GALATEA etc.

04·00/24

VICTORIOUS to Iceland
12·00/26

18·00 PRINZ EUGEN
detached
10·00/24
GALATEA etc.
VICTORIOUS

SUFFOLK
04·00/26

00·01/25 attack by
torpedo bombers
from VICTORIOUS
VICTORIOUS
operating aircraft
03·06 BISMARCK
lost
00·01/25
18·00/25

RODNEY 08·00/24

PRINCE of WALES
to Iceland
15·00/25
12·00/25
10·47

18·10/25
00·01/26
08·00/24
NORFOLK
12·00/26

REVENGE
sailed from
Halifax 15·00/24
REPULSE detached
to Newfoundland
17·00/25
18·00/25
18·00/25
12·00/25
KING
GEORGE V
00·01/26
10·00/25
RODNEY
12·00/26

RAMILLIES
PRINZ
EUGEN

00·01/27
02·00/25
15·00/25

4th
Destroyer
flotilla
00·01/26
08·00/26
10·30/26
RODNEY joined
OinC 18·00/26
12·00/26

BISMARCK sighted
by CATALINA

★ BISMARCK sunk 10·36/27
Successful torpedo
bomber attack 20·47–21·25/26

Plymouth

19·30/1

EDINBURGH
03·00/25
03·00/26
FORCE H

02·30/27

20·40/26
11·30/26   DORSETSHIRE

12·00/31

12·00/30   PRINZ EUGEN   13·00/25

SPAIN

launched 14 torpedo-armed planes, but with their crews unaware of the *Sheffield*'s mission. Flying over a stormy sea, and using radar, they came down through low cloud to drop their weapons before they recognized their target. Fortunately none scored a hit, in part because the *Sheffield* took drastic avoiding action, in part because of faulty magnetic pistols.

As soon as these planes had returned to the *Ark Royal*, Maund sent off a second strike of 15 planes at 1910. Learning the lesson of the first attack their torpedoes were fitted with contact pistols. They were also ordered to locate the *Sheffield* and rely on her to direct them on to their proper target. They found her soon after 2030. Poor visibility, low cloud, half-a-gale, rough seas and fading daylight, plus heavy AA fire from the *Bismarck*, combined to prevent co-ordinated attacks. Although spaced over more than half-an-hour, they were pressed home so that out of 13 torpedoes dropped two scored hits. Like that from the *Victorious'* strike, one struck the battleship's armour belt amidships where it did no damage; but the other hit right aft, wrecking her steering gear and jamming her rudders 15 degrees to port. Lütjens soon realized the consequences: at 2140 he signalled Berlin: 'Ship no longer manoeuvrable. We fight to the last shell. Long live the *Führer*'.

Shortly after this success, five destroyers, under the redoubtable Captain Vian in the *Cossack*, came on the scene. The Admiralty had detached them from escorting a convoy to replace the destroyers screening Tovey's battleships. Intercepting Coastal Command's sighting report that morning, Vian had decided that he would do better to steer for the enemy. His intuition sealed the *Bismarck*'s fate. His ships shadowed her throughout the night, providing Tovey with frequent and accurate reports of his damaged enemy. And by coming in to close range again and again on different bearings to fire torpedoes despite heavy radar-controlled gunfire, they further slowed a wounded battleship that could no longer steer a steady course.

Tovey's initial reaction to the success of the *Ark Royal*'s attack had been to turn his two battleships south in the hope of bringing his quarry to action against the afterglow of sunset; but the light failed before he could find her. Subsequently he decided against a night action: it was so evident that the *Bismarck* could not now escape him that he warned Somerville, who was planning another strike from the *Ark Royal* for daylight on the 27th, to keep clear.

As day dawned on 27 May, Tovey ordered the *Rodney* to assume open order (1000 yards) from the *King George V*, and gave Dalrymple-Hamilton freedom of manoeuvre. Then he brought both ships down from the north-west, followed by the *Norfolk* and *Dorsetshire* which joined them, on a course opposite to the *Bismarck*'s slow and erratic progress. She was sighted at 0843 at a range of 25,000 yards. Four minutes later, according to an eye-witness, 'there was a crackling roar to port; the *Rodney* had opened fire, and an instant later the *King George V* follows.

TABLE 35: Ships Involved in Sinking the *Bismarck*

Ship	Date of completion	Displacement (tons)	Speed (knots)	Guns	Thickest armour
King George V	1940	35,000	29	10 14in 16 5·25in	16in
Rodney	1927	33,900	23	9 16in 12 6in	16in
Norfolk	1930	9,925	32	8 8in and 8 21in TT	3in
Dorsetshire	1931	9,975	32	8 8in and 8 21in TT	3in
Bismarck	1941	41,700	29	8 15in 12 6in	14in

I have my glasses on the *Bismarck*. She fires all guns from her forward turrets. The Germans have a reputation for hitting with early salvoes. It seems to take about two hours for their shells to fall opposite but beyond the *Rodney*'s forecastle'.[4] Subsequently the *Bismarck*'s gunnery became more and more erratic at both British battleships as, soon after 0900, with the range down to 16,000 yards, 'both forward turrets were put out of action. A further hit wrecked the forward control position; the after control position was wrecked soon after'.[4] But it took another hour and a quarter of gun fire at point blank range, during which 'the coppery glow of our secondary armament shells striking her upper works became more and more frequent, and one fierce flame shot up from the base of the burning structure, enveloping it as high as the spotting top for a flickering second'.[4] 'For some time the *Bismarck*'s after turrets fired singly, but by about 1000 all the guns were silent.'[4] She had been reduced to a burning but still floating wreck, which says as much for her strength as it tells against British gunnery. The *King George V* had fired 339 14-inch shells, the *Rodney* 380 16-inch of which only a small proportion scored hits. Tovey was sufficiently exasperated to tell his fleet gunnery officer that he would have a better chance of hitting if he threw his binoculars at her.

As the British battleships withdrew, undamaged but seriously short of fuel, the *Norfolk*, followed by the *Dorsetshire*, closed and fired torpedoes into the wallowing hulk. But whether these or scuttling charges gave her the *coup de grâce* is open to question. To quote one of her officers:

The noise of combat became more irregular until it sank to a series of sporadic crashes. The control bells from the bridge stopped ringing. All three turbine rooms were filled with smoke. At about 1015 I received the order: 'Prepare the ship for sinking'. Slowly the ship sank deeper and we knew that she would eventually capsize. After a triple '*Sieg heil*', I ordered, 'Abandon ship'. Hardly were we free of her when she keeled over to port. Then the bows rose in the air and, stern first, the *Bismarck* slipped to the bottom.[4]

To quote Tovey's report: 'The *Bismarck* had put up a most gallant fight against impossible odds, worthy of the old days of the Imperial German Navy, and she went down with her colours flying', at 1036, taking Lütjens, Lindemann, and all his crew of almost 2,400 men with her except for 119 who were subsequently rescued. The *Luftwaffe*'s attempts to aid the *Bismarck* did no more than sink the *Mashona* and badly damage another 'Tribal' destroyer, while Dönitz's U-boats achieved nothing of import. Lieutenant-Commander Wohlfarth of *U556*, for example, experienced the chagrin of sighting Force H from an ideal firing position, after he had expended all his torpedoes against less valuable targets.

To destroy this impressive monument to the skill of German ship designers the British forces expended 71 torpedoes, of which at least eight, and possibly 12, scored hits, as well as a large quantity of armour-piercing shell. Tovey gave the credit to 'the co-operation, skill and understanding displayed by all forces during this prolonged chase. Flag and Commanding Officers of detached units invariably took the action I would have wished, before and without receiving instructions from me'; and to 'the accuracy of the information supplied by the Admiralty and the speed with which it was passed which was remarkable. The balance struck between information and instructions passed to the forces out of touch with me was ideal'.

On the whole operation, which involved so many separated units, both on the sea and in the air, it would be difficult to improve on this judgement:

> Without a Coastal Command flight the *Bismarck* would not have been sighted in the Norwegian fiord. Without a Fleet Air Arm flight her departure would not have been discovered. Without cruisers in the Denmark Strait she would not have been sighted on her way through that passage. Without heavy ships to engage her next morning she would not have been hit and her course brought round to where the *Victorious*' aircraft could torpedo her. Without Coastal Command aircraft she might not have been resighted after being lost. Without the aircraft from the *Ark Royal* she would not have been decisively slowed-up. Without the destroyers it would have been difficult to keep track of her during the night. And without the battleships she would probably not have been sunk.[5]

For the operation's ultimate success praise is due, above all, to three men. Throughout an anxious week Pound not only restrained his inborn tendency to usurp the functions of the C-in-C (and dissuaded Prime Minister Churchill from his greater tendency to do so[6]) but played as great a part in the *Bismarck*'s destruction as Barham played in ensuring that Villeneuve was brought to battle in 1805. Nor must Bowhill be forgotten for the ready and effective co-operation of Coastal Command. But the greatest credit goes to Tovey. He was of the same breed as Nelson. He led a band of brothers in a long chase which, after the initial loss of the *Hood,* ended in the only triumph which satisfied Nelson, annihilation. One is therefore glad to record that, despite subsequent differences with both Pound and Churchill,[7] especially over the conduct of the Arctic convoys, this was duly recognized by his inclusion in the very short list of British admirals who were honoured with a peerage shortly after the war was over.

After parting company with the *Bismarck* on the 24th, the *Prinz Eugen* headed south to refuel in mid-Atlantic. Five days later she developed engine defects so serious that Brinkmann decided to end a fruitless sortie. A Coastal Command patrol sighted the cruiser heading for Brest on the 27th but, thereafter, when so many British warships were in port refuelling and replenishing their magazines after sinking the *Bismarck,* she managed to reach this French port safely on 1 June.

Although the Allies could not know it, this was the end of Raeder's attempts to use his surface warships to disrupt Allied trade in the Atlantic. The forays by the *Hipper* and *Prinz Eugen* had shown that the 8-inch cruisers were unsuited to such operations. The *Gneisenau* and *Scharnhorst* were immobilized in Brest. By the time the ill-fated *Bismarck*'s sister, the *Tirpitz,* was ready for sea later in 1941, and the two battlecruisers with the *Prinz Eugen* had made a successful high speed escape up Channel back to Germany on 12–13 February 1942, Germany's heavy ships were required to play a different role. They were moved north to Norway's fiords to operate against Allied convoys carrying supplies to the USSR, with the compensating advantage of freeing many of Britain's battleships from the tedious task of escorting Atlantic convoys to proceed to eastern waters, where they were required to counter Japan's intervention on the side of the Axis Powers.

NOTES

[1] In *Enemy in Sight.*
[2] In *The Times,* 26 May 1941.
[3] Since its co-pilot was Ensign L. B. Smith of the 'neutral' US Navy on leaselend to the RAF, one is irresistibly reminded of the incident in 1859 when Flag Officer Josiah Tattnall, USN, in the frigate *Mississippi,* gave assistance beyond the bounds of neutrality to a British warship in difficulties with China's Pei-ho forts, with the excuse: 'Blood is thicker than water'.
[4] Various eye-witness accounts from both sides.
[5] Captain Russell Grenfell, RN in *The Bismarck Episode.*
[6] With a few exceptions, notably this singular message to Tovey which Churchill initiated: '*Bismarck* must be sunk at all costs and if to do this it

is necessary for *King George V* to remain on the scene, she must do so even if it means subsequently towing her home'. In the event it reached Tovey after the *Bismarck* had been sunk, but had he had to obey it, both the *King George V*, and the *Rodney* towing her at six-eight knots, must have been sacrificed to the *Luftwaffe* and Dönitz's U-boats. Pound, be it added, subsequently apologised to Tovey for having allowed this signal to be sent.

[7] Angered by the loss of the *Hood* and the subsequent near escape of the *Bismarck*, Churchill persuaded Pound to require Tovey to charge Admiral Wake-Walker, of the *Norfolk*, and Captain Leach, of the *Prince of Wales*, before courts martial for failing to engage the *Bismarck* during her run south. To his credit Tovey had the moral courage to refuse to be an accomplice to such an injustice. He went so far as to threaten to haul down his flag so that he might act as prisoner's friend for both these distinguished officers, which persuaded Pound to retract.

8 *Convoys*

Towards the end of September 1941, just three months after Hitler's treacherous invasion of the USSR, the first Allied convoy sailed to Archangel. For the rest of the year successive mercantile convoys, each with a close escort of destroyers and other A/S craft and a small covering force of one or two cruisers, all provided by the British Home Fleet, continued to run without hindrance to and from this Soviet port or, after winter froze the White Sea, Murmansk in the Kola Inlet. But by the end of the year Germany realized the extent to which the war supplies carried by this route were helping the USSR to stem and turn back the Nazi onslaught. (On 4 October 1941 Britain and the USA agreed to send *per month* 400 planes, 500 tanks and 200 Bren-gun carriers, 22,000 tons of rubber, 41,000 tons of aluminium, 3,860 tons of machine tools and large quantities of food, medical supplies and other raw materials. Up to March 1942 110 merchant ships sailed in these convoys and only one was lost.) In January 1942 Raeder began moving his surface vessels and U-boats to the fiords around Trondheim, so that they, in conjunction with the *Luftwaffe*, could launch a rising crescendo of attacks on these convoys, with the advantage that they were compelled by geography and the Arctic ice edge to pass through a corridor only 250 miles wide round North Cape in the Barents Sea.

This required the Allies to augment their close escorts with escort carriers and AA vessels, and to include capital ships in their covering forces. Convoy PQ18, of 46 merchant ships, which left Scotland's Loch Ewe on 2 September 1942, was closely escorted by one escort carrier, three AA vessels, and as many as 20 destroyers, and covered by the battleship *Duke of York* and four cruisers. Nonetheless it suffered the loss of 13 merchant ships to U-boat and air attack before the remainder reached Archangel, albeit a more favourable figure than its immediate predecessor PQ17 which lost all but 10 of its 33 ships. With the onset of winter, with the long nights and stormy weather of the Arctic, Tovey argued that such large convoys ran the risk of being split up into scattered groups which would be easy prey for the enemy. Pound reluctantly agreed that the next convoy, whose designation was changed for security reasons from PQ19 to JW51, should sail in two parts.

The 16 merchant ships of JW51A left Loch Ewe, escorted by seven destroyers and five small A/S vessels, on 15 December. JW51B, of 14 merchant ships escorted by six destroyers and five small A/S vessels, left a week later. Both were covered by the 6-inch cruisers *Sheffield,* Captain A. W. Clarke, flying the flag of Rear-Admiral Bob Burnett, and *Jamaica,* Captain J. L. Storey, and, from a greater distance, by the battleship *Anson* and the 8-inch cruiser *Cumberland.* JW51A was not sighted by the enemy, and reached Kola Inlet safely on Christmas Day. But JW51B was less fortunate: in a gale on the sixth day five merchant ships and two of the escort lost touch. The minesweeper *Bramble* was detached to search for them. Four of these merchant ships and one escort subsequently rejoined the convoy, but the other merchant ship and the A/S trawler *Vizalma,* Lieutenant J. R. Angleback, RNVR, proceeded independently to their destination.

Meantime, Burnett, having taken his cruisers through to Kola Inlet with JW51A, and refuelled them there, sailed again on 27 December to cover JW51B. He first swept well to the west, then back to the east, to the south of the convoy's route. On the 30th, he turned north-west, aiming for a point about 40 miles astern of the convoy, because he expected enemy surface vessels trying an attack to search along its route from west to east. In the event, because the position of the convoy signalled to him by the C-in-C at 1600 on the 29th put it as much as 150 miles east-north-east of its true position, Burnett's cruisers crossed its route well ahead, and by 0830 on the 31st were some 30 miles to the north of it, without knowing that they were unfavourably placed to deal with an approaching enemy.

Despite the unfavourable conditions of bad weather and very few hours of daylight, a *Luftwaffe* reconnaissance plane sighted and reported JW51B to the south of Bear Island on 24 December. So did Lieutenant-Commander K. Herbschleb in *U354.* The Germans at once ordered its destruction. During the afternoon of 30 December Vice-Admiral O. Kummetz took his flagship, the 8-inch cruiser *Admiral Hipper,* Captain H. Hartmann, with the pocket-battleship *Lützow,* Captain R. Stange, and six large destroyers out of Alten Fiord. He was under orders not to risk a night action with escorts which might use their torpedoes against him, and by day only to engage a force weaker than his own. He was further hampered by the knowledge that, on completion of his operation the *Lützow* was to make a sortie into the Atlantic.

Kummetz planned, as Burnett assumed, to overtake the convoy from astern. The *Hipper* and three destroyers were to come down from the north-west, the *Lützow* and the other three destroyers up from the south-west. A commander who divides his force is open to the criticism that he gives a weaker enemy a chance to destroy each part of it separately. But Kummetz's decision to do so would have been amply justified had not

F

Stange been so concerned to avoid damage to the *Lützow* before her planned Atlantic sortie. Stange was, indeed, handicapped by a divided aim, which is seldom a recipe for success.

At 0830 on 31 December the British ships in the area were split into four groups. The main convoy of 12 merchant vessels and eight escorts was steering east; one merchant ship and the A/S trawler *Vizalma* were about 45 miles to the north; the minesweeper *Bramble* was about 15 miles to the north-east; and Burnett's two cruisers were some 30 miles to the north. At this time the *Hipper* and her destroyers crossed the convoy's route 20 miles astern of it; the *Lützow* and her destroyers were 50 miles to the south and closing it. The weather was clear except during snow storms, the visibility ranging between seven and ten miles. But the destroyers and other small ships were handicapped by the icy temperature which froze the spray that swept over them when they steamed at more than 20 knots, making it difficult to fight their forward guns.

The corvette *Hyderabad*, Lieutenant S. C. B. Hickman, RNVR, was the first to sight the approaching enemy, at 0820. Supposing the *Hipper*'s destroyers to be expected Russian reinforcements, she made no report— an unfortunate mistake. Ten minutes later the destroyer *Obdurate*, Lieutenant-Commander C. E. Sclater, on the convoy's starboard beam, reported ships passing astern to the escort commander in the flotilla leader *Onslow*, but without identifying them. Captain R. St V. Sherbrooke promptly ordered Sclater to investigate; but although he closed at the *Obdurate*'s best speed, it was not until she was within four miles of them, at 0930, that he knew that they were the enemy because they opened fire. He promptly turned away, and Kummetz's destroyers made no attempt to follow.

Having made his intentions in event of an enemy surface attack clear before sailing, Sherbrooke swung the *Onslow* round to join the *Obdurate*, followed by the *Obedient*, Lieutenant-Commander D. C. Kinloch, and the *Orwell*, Lieutenant-Commander N. Austen. This left only the *Achates*, Lieutenant-Commander A. H. T. Johns, and three smaller escorts to protect the convoy by a smoke screen.

An hour before the *Obdurate*'s sighting, Burnett had learned the convoy's true position and turned his cruisers south towards it. His approach was, however, delayed between 0900 and 1000 while, in the continuing darkness, he investigated a contact which proved to be the *Vizalma* and her single merchant ship proceeding independently. Moreover, although he saw gun flashes over the horizon at 0930, Burnett supposed them to be British AA fire at a German plane. That something much more serious was menacing the convoy did not become apparent until 0946 when, just as he received the *Onslow*'s 0941 enemy report, heavy gunfire was seen to the south. Only then did Burnett increase speed and radio Sherbrooke that he was coming to his support.

This gunfire was aimed by the *Hipper* at the *Achates*. Seeing it, Sher-

TABLE 36: Ships Involved in the Battle of Barents Sea

Ship	Type	Date of completion	Displacement (tons)	Speed (knots)	Guns	Torpedoes
Sheffield	Cruiser	1938	9,600	32	12 6in	6 21in
Jamaica	Cruiser	1941	8,000	33	12 6in	6 21in
Onslow	Flotilla leader	1941	1,550	36	4 4in	8 21in
Obdurate	Destroyer					
Obedient	Destroyer	1942	1,540	36	4 4in	8 21in
Orwell	Destroyer					
Achates	Destroyer	1931	1,350	35	4 4·7in	8 21in
Bramble	Minesweeper	1939	875	17	1 4in	—
Hyderabad	Corvettes	1941	925	11	1 4in	—
Rhododendron						
Ocean Gem	Trawler	?	?	11	1 4in	—
Vizalma	Trawler	1940	?	11	1 4in	—
Lützow	Pocket-battleship	1933	11,700	26	6 11in 8 6in	8 21in
Admiral Hipper	Cruiser	1939	14,050	32	8 8in	12 21in
Friedrich Eckoldt	Destroyer	1938	2,239	38	5 5in	8 21in
Richard Beitzen	Destroyer	1937	2,232	38	5 5in	8 21in
Theodor Riedel	Destroyer	1938	2,171	38	5 5in	8 21in
Z29	Destroyers	1942	2,603	38	5 6in	8 21in
Z30						
Z31						

brooke, in the *Onslow*, and the *Orwell* at once engaged her, and continued to do so intermittently in and out of smoke, often threatening her with their torpedoes, for the next half-hour. The *Obedient* and *Obdurate* went back to join the *Achates* in protecting the convoy against the other known threat, Kummetz's three powerful destroyers. Fortunately the *Hipper*'s gunnery at the *Onslow* and *Orwell* fell below the usual German standard, being 'aimless and erratic', albeit in difficult light conditions, until at 1020 when, according to Kinloch, 'she suddenly pulled herself together', and found the *Onslow*'s range. Half the latter's armament was then put out of action, her engine room holed and the ship set on fire. Moreover, Sherbrooke suffered serious wounds which obliged him to turn over command of the escort to Kinloch in the *Obedient*, although he refused to leave the *Onslow*'s bridge until assured that Kinloch had done so at about 1035, when the *Hipper* suddenly disappeared into a snow squall.

As the *Sheffield* and *Jamaica* came south at 30 knots, Burnett glimpsed the action between the *Onslow* and *Orwell* and the *Hipper*, but could not decide which were British ships and which were German. Moreover, at 1032 he turned away to investigate two unidentified radar contacts until he again saw heavy gunfire on the *Sheffield*'s starboard bow: the searching *Bramble*, of only 850 tons and armed with a single 4-inch gun, had blundered into the *Hipper* and was being blasted to the bottom with 8-inch salvoes, taking with her Commander H. T. Rust and all his crew. At 1045 Burnett glimpsed Kummetz's flagship briefly for himself, but did not immediately pursue her, because the whole situation, as observed from, and plotted by radar in, the *Sheffield,* appeared confused.

As soon as the *Hipper* disappeared Kinloch ensured that all his five destroyers, including the damaged *Onslow,* rejoined the convoy, which had altered course to south-east at 1020. Around 1040 the *Hyderabad* sighted unidentified ships to the south and again failed to report them. (The *Hyderabad* was, incidentally, the only ship to receive the hapless *Bramble*'s enemy report which she failed to pass on.) Fortunately the *Rhododendron* saw them at 1045—the *Lützow* and her three powerful destroyers which were only two miles away. Stange was now in the best of positions to destroy the convoy, but he allowed this chance to go by the board: when a snow squall temporarily obscured his target he stood away 'to wait for the weather to clear'.

Around 1100 the British destroyers again sighted the *Lützow*'s group to the south. Kinloch manoeuvred his ships so that they were between this enemy force and the convoy which they shrouded in smoke. Then the *Hipper* reappeared to the north and with a few well-aimed salvoes crippled the *Achates,* causing many casualties including the death of her captain, Lieutenant-Commander Johns. Next Hartmann shifted his 8-inch guns to the *Obedient,* but with less success: these salvoes did no more than put Kinloch's radio out of action, though this was enough for him to turn over command of the escort to the *Obdurate*'s captain. Threatened by the British destroyers' torpedoes, the *Hipper* then hauled off, only to find herself suddenly straddled by multi-gun salvoes from the north. The *Sheffield* and *Jamaica* had sighted her and opened fire at 1130 with all 24 of their 6-inch guns at a range of 14,000 yards, with sufficient accuracy to score a hit that reduced the *Hipper*'s speed to 28 knots.

Hartmann was so surprised by Burnett's unexpected appearance that he was slow to react. Before he could turn the *Hipper* away she received two more hits. Realizing that he was caught between British cruisers to the north and destroyers to the south, Kummetz seems to have thought only of his strict instructions not to engage anything but an inferior force. He ordered all his ships to retire to the west. But they did not escape retribution. At 1143 two German destroyers suddenly appeared within 4,000 yard's of Burnett's cruisers. The *Sheffield*'s guns reduced the *Eckoldt,* Captain A. Schemmel, to a burning wreck. The *Jamaica*'s gunnery was less sure: the *Beitzen* was able to escape into the snow squall which had already obscured the *Hipper.*

Around the same time the *Lützow* opened fire on the convoy from the safe range of 18,000 yards, damaging one merchant ship before the commodore could order an emergency turn away. Sclater promptly led his three surviving destroyers out to the attack as they laid more smoke. As

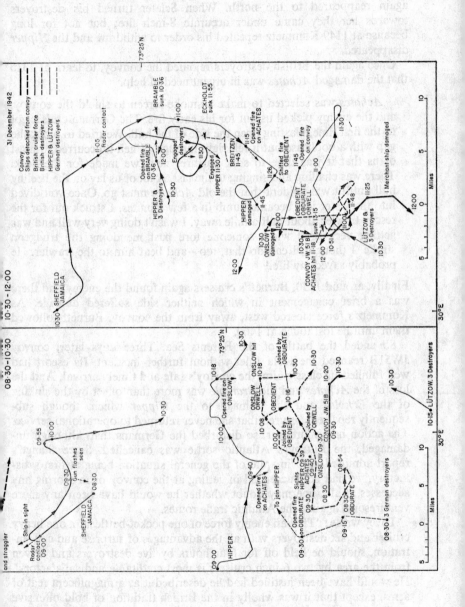

promptly the *Lützow* ceased fire, which was as well because the *Hipper* again reappeared to the north. When Sclater turned his destroyers towards her they came under accurate 8-inch fire; but not for long because at 1149 Kummetz repeated his order to withdraw and the *Hipper* disappeared.

Once again the British destroyers rejoined the convoy, to learn at 1315 that the damaged *Achates* was in urgent need of help.

> *Achates* was selected to make a smoke-screen to shield the convoy, and the enemy picked us out for his early fire. The German cruiser got us the first time, blasting open the side of the hull. We tried to block the gap with a bookcase but it fell right through. When it occurred to most of us that it was time to seek pastures new, we made for the deck. There was chaffing and singing to the last. A lot of us lay on the heeling hull until it was evident that the old *Achates* must go. Once you dived into the water you became numb in a few minutes. I struck out for the rescue trawler about half a mile away. I wasn't doing very well and was getting very tired when someone tore past me doing the trudgeon stroke. I thought, I can do that, too—and beat him to the trawler. He probably saved my life.[1]

Finally, around 1230, Burnett's cruisers again found the enemy and there was a brief engagement in which neither side suffered damage. As Kummetz's force steered west, away from the convoy, Burnett followed them until he lost touch at 1400.

So ended the battle of the Barents Sea. Three days later, convoy JW51B reached the Kola Inlet without further incident. Its escort had well fulfilled its classic aim, the convoy's safe and timely arrival. And the loss of the *Achates* and the *Bramble* was more than offset by the sinking of the *Eckoldt* and the damage to the *Hipper* which, though subsequently repaired, ensured that she never returned to operational service. The action had, moreover, so disturbed the Germans that, although undamaged, the *Lützow*'s Atlantic sortie was cancelled. Since Stange's report admitted that 'in spite of the general situation being at first satisfactory, we had not succeeded in getting at the convoy or in scoring any successes at all', one may doubt whether he would have been any more venturesome against the Atlantic trade routes.

Tovey wrote: 'That an enemy force of one pocket-battleship, one heavy cruiser and six destroyers with all the advantages of surprise and concentration, should be held off for four hours by five destroyers and driven from the area by two 6-inch cruisers is most creditable and satisfactory'. He would have been justified had he described it as a magnificent feat of arms, except that it was wholly in the British tradition of bold offensive tactics, carried out with undaunted determination, and matchless courage against heavy odds. In sharp contrast, and even allowing for the crippling restrictions imposed upon them by Berlin, the German ships were handled with singular timidity. This is especially true of the *Lützow* and her group of destroyers.

For his gallant and determined leadership and the skill with which he had shielded JW51B from destruction by a more powerful German force for the best part of an hour (to which Kummetz paid tribute in his report) Sherbrooke was awarded the Victoria Cross. 'There was never anything finer in the annals of the Royal Navy', said First Lord A. V. Alexander. So one is glad to be able to record that at a later date the Admiralty remembered Nelson: although Sherbrooke's wounds healed he never recovered the use of one eye, yet he was in due time promoted to flag rank.

Tovey and the Admiralty criticized Burnett for being so long in coming south to protect the convoy after receiving the *Onslow*'s enemy report—which rankled until the end of his career as C-in-C Plymouth after the war, although before 1943 was out he was given another chance to be in at the kill of bigger prey.

The battle had significant reactions in the Third *Reich*. In one of his ungovernable rages Hitler told Raeder that his larger surface ships were clearly contributing nothing to a German victory and that it was his 'firm and unalterable resolve' that they should be paid off and their crews used elsewhere. When Raeder protested to the point of submitting his resignation, Dönitz was appointed in his stead. Ironically enough, this distinguished U-boat leader was able to do more than persuade Hitler to recant; he was allowed to give senior officers in command of future operations greater freedom than had been allowed to the hapless Kummetz.

From one convoy battle to another of a very different but more frequent kind. Of all the actions fought by the Allies against German U-boat packs in the turbulent waters of the Atlantic Ocean, that which defeated the attacks on convoy ONS5 merits telling not only as an example of this kind of warfare, but because it marked the turn of the tide. Henceforward the long-drawn battle of the Atlantic, which above all threatened Britain's survival, was won.

Convoy SC122 of 60 merchant ships, which left New York on 5 March 1943, and the faster HX229 of 40 vessels which sailed three days later, faced a swarm of more than 40 U-boats as they headed east across the Atlantic. Although both were escorted by British or US destroyers, frigates and corvettes throughout their voyage, and by shore-based air patrols for much of it, they lost as many as 21 merchant ships in a mid-Atlantic battle fought between 16 and 19 April, whereas the Germans lost only *U384*, sunk by an RAF flying-boat. Dönitz might note that 'nearly all his other boats suffered from depth-charges or bombs and two were seriously damaged', but it was clearly a German victory.

Convoy ONS5, of 40 merchant ships under Commodore J. Brooks,

RNR, passed out of the Irish Sea little more than a month later. This was accompanied by Escort Group B7, comprised of the destroyer *Duncan*, Commander P. W. Gretton, the frigate *Tay*, and the corvettes *Sunflower*, *Loosestrife*, *Snowflake* and *Pink*, which were later joined by the destroyer *Vidette* with three merchant ships from Iceland. For the first five days Gretton's escort and their 'sheep' steamed slowly westward through a roaring gale and mountainous seas which tended to scatter them. By the time the weather improved slightly on 27 April one merchant vessel had been damaged in a collision requiring her to be detached to Iceland for repairs, and another was missing, being so slow that she had dropped astern. But the *Duncan*, of low endurance, was able to refuel from a tanker instead of having to leave the convoy for an Icelandic port.

On the next day a U-boat sighted and reported the convoy. Whilst this was Dönitz's cue to order a 'wolf pack' to concentrate ahead of the convoy's route, its intercepted radio signal also warned Gretton to be ready for trouble. Shortly before dark his huff-duff gave the bearing of a U-boat transmission. He at once headed the *Duncan* and *Tay* in this direction. They were in time to sight her on the surface, but the sea was too rough to obtain sonar contact after she dived. Gretton could do no more than leave the *Tay* to keep the U-boat down until after dark. Flying-boats hastily dispatched by Coastal Command had better luck. They found three U-boats on the surface to the south of the convoy heading towards it, of which they sank *U710* and compelled the others to submerge.

Six times during the ensuing night U-boats tried to attack Brooks' convoy but each was detected by the escort's radar, chased and forced to dive. Judging the chances of success in such weather to be small, Dönitz then called off his pack, ordering it to head south-west to join up with another which was gathering further along the convoy's expected route, and that of the eastbound convoy SC128 of whose sailing he had learned from Germany's 'B' service. All, that is, except for one U-boat which, having missed this signal, lay in wait just ahead of ONS5 and delivered a successful submerged attack during the 29th which cost the convoy its first ship. Otherwise this day passed without incident except for worsening weather.

The threat ahead of both convoys was now sufficiently clear, from Britain's 'Y' service, for the C-in-C Western Approaches in his Liverpool headquarters, Admiral Sir Max Horton, to sail the Third Escort Group of five destroyers, led by the *Offa*, from St John's Newfoundland, to re-inforce Gretton's ships. For the next five days ONS5 and its escort were virtually hove to, battered by a tempestuous storm which saved them from further U-boat attacks. SC128, in the same area but on a route further to the south, was not only similarly secure but, having the gale force wind and mountainous seas on its quarter, able to make better progress.

At 2000 on 2 May the Third Escort Group joined ONS5. Next day, because the *Duncan* could not refuel in such conditions, Gretton was forced to part company for St John's, leaving command of his group to Lieutenant-Commander R. E. Sherwood, RNR, of the *Tay*. One day more and three of the *Offa*'s group had to seek harbour to replenish their tanks. To replace these absentees, Horton ordered the First Escort Group under Commander G. N. Brewer in the sloop *Pelican*, with three frigates and a US Coastguard cutter lease-lent to the RN, out of St John's. On this day, too, when the weather moderated, came concrete warning of what was about to happen. Royal Canadian Air Force planes sighted and attacked several U-boats closing ONS5 from the north, but they sank only *U630* with a stick of well-placed depth-charges.

The real battle between the British vessels escorting ONS5, limited to the *Tay*, the destroyers *Offa* and *Oribi* and four corvettes, and Germany's U-boats began that night, 4–5 May. A pack of 30, which was more by chance than design on its route rather than SC128's, attacked with torpedoes and was counter-attacked with depth charges time and again, reducing ONS5 from 30 to 26 ships. Not until four more had been sunk during daylight on 5 May did one of the escorts, the corvette *Pink*, Lieutenant R. Atkinson, RNR, manage to do anything towards repaying this debt by sinking *U192*. Not surprisingly *Offa*'s captain was moved to record that by that evening 'the convoy seemed doomed to certain annihilation': all the escort vessels' commanders were suffering the strain of many days of fearful weather followed by sleepless nights defending their charges against odds of six to one.

Fortunately these were shortened during 5 May by the arrival of Brewer's group. And the combined escort soon hit back. Because ONS5 would soon come under an air umbrella provided by RCAF planes from Newfoundland, Dönitz ordered his pack to make an all out effort that night. 'About 24 attacks took place from every direction except ahead: the battle continued without a stop until 0420.' But although 'the situation was confused', Brewer's ships struck in no uncertain manner: 'all showed dash and initiative. None required to be told what to do'. Not only were all the attacks repulsed but four of the enemy were sunk, *U638* by the corvette *Loosestrife*, Lieutenant Stonehouse, RNR, *U125* by the *Vidette*, Lieutenant R. Hart, *U531* by the *Oribi*, Lieutenant-Commander J. C. Ingram, and *U438* by Brewer in the *Pelican*.

This was the end of Dönitz's attempts to destroy ONS5: with daylight and, for the convoy and its escort the welcome concealment of fog, the U-boat pack was ordered to proceed to the east ready to attack other prey. On that day, too, the exhausted escort vessels were relieved by the western local escort, which took all that remained of the convoy safely to its destination. Twelve merchants ships had been lost. But, far more important, so had as many as nine U-boats, because in addition to seven sunk by British ships and aircraft, two had collided with each other whilst chasing the convoy in the dark. Moreover, several more had been damaged by relentless depth charge and hedgehog attacks. For the first time in the battle of the Atlantic the Germans had suffered a serious defeat.

Nor was this all. The pack was now ordered south to attack convoys HX237 and SC129 which, in the mid-Atlantic gap that Coastal Command could not cover, enjoyed the protection of aircraft from the escort carrier *Biter*. HX237 lost only three ships for the same number of U-boats destroyed; SC129 lost only two for two U-boats sunk. These German failures were followed by the proverbial final straws. SC130, whose 38 ships left Halifax on 11 May protected by Gretton's Escort Group, reached its UK destination without loss; but *U954* and *U258* were sunk by Coastal Command, *U209* by the frigate *Jed* and the erstwhile US Coastguard vessel *Sennen*, *U381* by Gretton's *Duncan* and *U273* by an RAF plane. During the same period Convoy HX239 and its escort had a like success, its victims falling to aircraft from HMS *Biter* and USS *Brogue*.

To quote Churchill:

> The battle of the Atlantic was the dominating factor all through the war. Never for one moment could we forget that everything happening elsewhere, on land, at sea, or in the air, depended ultimately on its outcome. Our merchant seamen displayed their highest qualities and the brotherhood of the sea was never more strikingly shown than in their determination to defeat the U-boat.[2]

And in May 1943 that battle was won. Faced with the loss of as many as 33 U-boats since 1 May, Dönitz ordered their withdrawal on the 22nd, only to lose eight more before the month was out. The Admiralty noted 'the sudden cessation of U-boat activity on or about 23 May. SC130 was the last convoy to be seriously menaced'. More telling are Dönitz's words: 'The overwhelming superiority achieved by the enemy defence was finally proved beyond dispute in the operations against Convoys SC130 and HX239'. To quote the British Official Historian: 'After 45 months of unceasing battle of a more exacting and arduous nature than posterity may easily realise, our convoy escorts had won the triumph they so richly merited'.[3]

This was not, however, the end of the battle. 'Again and again,' wrote a desperate Dönitz, 'we debated whether a continuation of the U-boat campaign was justified in the face of these heavy losses. But in view of the vast enemy forces which our U-boats were tying down, we came always to the same conclusion. The U-boat campaign must be continued with the forces available. Losses which bear no relation to the success achieved must be accepted, bitter though they are.' So the battle of the Atlantic went on, albeit more to the south where the chief successes were scored by US escort groups, especially after the Allied invasion of North Africa.

But never again, after the victory gained by the escorts of ONS5, did an Atlantic convoy suffer serious loss.

Back to the Arctic. In the German attack on convoy JW51B in the Barents Sea, the heavy element of the covering force, the battleship *Anson* and 8-inch cruiser *Cumberland*, played no part. They were too far to the west to be able to intervene when Kummetz's ships were reported, because they could not be hazarded, without good reason, to air attack from German bases in northern Norway.

It was otherwise with JW55B and RA55A in December 1943. After an interval during the summer of this year, when no Allied convoys were run to the USSR because it was judged too dangerous when there was daylight for much, sometimes all, of each 24 hours, RA54A, of 13 empty merchant ships, was brought home from Archangel in November without incident. JW54A and JW54B, totalling 32 merchant ships and both outward bound from Loch Ewe later in the same month, were as successful. So, too, was JW55A of 19 ships. But by the time JW55B, also of 19 British and US merchant ships, began its 2,000 miles journey from the same assembly point on 20 December, and RA55A of 22 ships sailed for Britain from Kola Inlet three days later, each with an escort of 10 British destroyers and three or four smaller vessels, Dönitz had learned that the Allies had resumed running these convoys. He had issued a directive that they were to be attacked not only by his 24 U-boats based on Bergen and Trondheim, with the now reasonably effective co-operation of the *Luftwaffe*, but by Germany's surface ships.

The largest of these now operational in Norwegian waters was the battlecruiser *Scharnhorst*,[4] Captain F. Hintze, which, in the absence of Kummetz on leave, flew the flag of Rear-Admiral Bey, who as a captain had been fortunate to escape with his life and reputation but not his ships, from the two battles of Narvik. After RA55A and JW55B had both been reported by the *Luftwaffe*, Bey sailed in the *Scharnhorst* with five destroyers at 1400 on Christmas Day and headed north, his prey being one or other of these convoys early on Boxing Day. He was to 'exploit the tactical situation skilfully and boldly' but 'disengage if heavy units are encountered'. In short he was to achieve success without taking risks, never a good recipe for success.

At 0901 on 25 December, a time of year when there is no more than twilight between 0900 and 1530, *U601* made contact with JW55B and thereafter shadowed it, despite several attempts by its escort to drive her off, which was a stroke of fortune for Bey since the *Luftwaffe*'s reconnaissance planes were now grounded by bad weather. Bey subsequently learned that this convoy was being covered by three cruisers, the *Belfast*, Captain E. R. Parham, flying Admiral Burnett's flag, with the *Sheffield*, Captain C. T. Addis, and the *Norfolk,* Captain D. K. Bain. But he did not know that it was also to be covered by the C-in-C Home Fleet, now

Admiral Sir Bruce Fraser, in the battleship *Duke of York,* Captain the Hon. G. H. Russell, with the cruiser *Jamaica,* Captain J. Hughes-Hallett, and four destroyers, which had sailed from Iceland.

Moreover, by Christmas Eve Fraser was sufficiently convinced that the *Scharnhorst* would come out to increase the speed of his force to 19 knots towards a position close to JW55B. Since he thought it likely that this convoy would be attacked rather than RA55A, he detached four destroyers from the latter to reinforce the former's close escort, which should suffice to drive off the *Scharnhorst,* and perhaps damage her enough for her to fall a victim to the *Duke of York.* By way of confirmation, as the British battle force headed east through a gale from the south-south-east and a rising sea during the night of 25–26 December, news came from the Admiralty's 'Y' service that in all probability the *Scharnhorst* was now at sea.

TABLE 37: Ships Involved in the Battle of North Cape

Ship	Type	Date of completion	Displacement (tons)	Speed (knots)	Guns	Torpedoes	Thickest armour
Duke of York	Battleship	1941	35,000	29	10 14in 16 5·25in	—	16in
Jamaica	Cruiser	1941	8,000	33	12 6in	—	3½in
Belfast	Cruiser	1939	11,550⁵	32	12 6in	6 21in	4½in
Sheffield	Cruiser	1938	9,600	32	12 6in	6 21in	4in
Norfolk	Cruiser	1930	9,925	32	8 8in	8 21in	4in
Matchless	Destroyer }	1942	1,920	36	6 4·7in	8 21in	—
Musketeer	Destroyer						
Opportune	Destroyer	1943	1,540	37	4 4·7in	8 21in	—
Saumarez	Destroyer						
Savage	Destroyer						
Scorpion	Destroyer	1943	1,710	37	4 4·7in	8 21in	—
Stord	Destroyer						
Virago	Destroyer						
Scharnhorst	Battlecruiser	1939	31,800	32	9 11in 12 6in	6 21in	14in

By 0400 that morning RA55A, which was about to be scattered by the gale, had cleared North Cape and was away to the north-west of it, without the enemy being aware of its movements since 22 December, whereas JW55B would soon pass about 100 miles to the north of the cape. Burnett's cruisers were 150 miles to the east of it, the *Duke of York*'s group 200 miles to the south-west, both closing at their best speed in the prevailing weather, but the *Scharnhorst* and her destroyers were in the advantageous position of being little more than 50 miles to the south-west and, with the wind well abaft the beam, coming up to it rapidly.

At 0730 Bey ordered his destroyers to spread and search ahead for JW55B. Unhappily a signalling error led to these five vessels losing touch with their flagship, so that they took no part in subsequent events: they were, indeed, ordered to return to harbour at 1418. As unfortunate for Bey, Germany's 'B' service failed to provide him with intelligence of the trap for which he was heading, although Fraser and his ships used radio several times, notably to ensure that they were all aware of each other's positions.

At 0815 Burnett was heading west for the convoy at 24 knots. Twenty-five minutes later first the *Norfolk*'s and then the *Belfast*'s radar obtained an echo from the *Scharnhorst* at 35,000 yards bearing slightly north of west, when she was only 30 miles from the convoy. Closing rapidly on an interception course the *Sheffield* glimpsed the German battlecruiser through the stormy darkness at 0921 at a range of 13,000 yards. Three minutes later the *Belfast* tried to illuminate her with starshell before the *Norfolk* and *Sheffield*, followed by the flagship, opened fire with their 8-inch and 6-inch guns using radar control. Their salvoes scored three hits, one of which put the *Scharnhorst*'s port 6-inch control system out of action, before Bey, after retaliating with a few harmless 11-inch salvoes, turned away to the south-east.

The cruisers gave chase, but in the prevailing weather the larger enemy vessel was able to work up to a higher speed and soon drew away from them. At 0955 Bey altered back to the north-east in further search of his prey. Knowing his prime duty to be the protection of the convoy, Burnett altered to north-west so as to place his squadron between JW55B and the enemy. As a result he lost contact at 1019.

Meantime, at 0940, Fraser had intervened to the extent of temporarily turning the convoy north and ordering the escort commander, Captain J. A. McCoy in the *Onslow*, to detach four of his destroyers to join Burnett's force. He sent the *Musketeer*, Commander R. L. Fisher, with the *Opportune*, *Virago* and *Matchless*. Having stationed his squadron 10 miles ahead of the convoy by 1045, Burnett used this reinforcement to screen his cruisers. Learning that he had lost contact with the enemy, Fraser replied that 'unless touch can be regained there is no chance of my finding the enemy'. But in his subsequent report he did not criticize Burnett's decision against using his ships to search for the *Scharnhorst*.

Fraser's difficulties, which included the fact that his destroyers were running low in fuel, were resolved shortly after 1200 when the *Belfast* regained contact. Burnett's judgement that the enemy was still bent on attacking the Allied convoy was proved sound. Again it was Addis who, at 1221, signalled, 'Enemy in sight', and all three of Burnett's cruisers opened fire with full broadsides at 11,000 yards whilst his destroyers moved out to attack with torpedoes. Unfortunately they were unable to gain a firing position before the action ended 20 minutes later with the *Scharnhorst* retiring rapidly to the north-east. By this time the *Norfolk*, which bore the brunt of the battlecruiser's 11-inch salvoes, had one turret and all her radar out of action, and the *Sheffield* had suffered splinter damage. Against this the British had scored a number of hits on their

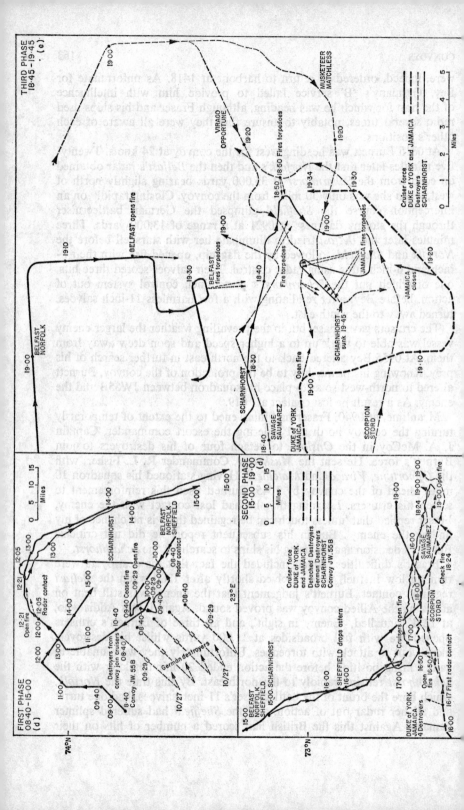

powerful opponent, including one abreast 'A' turret and one on the quarterdeck.

Thereafter the *Belfast* maintained radar contact as the *Scharnhorst* hauled round on to a south-south-easterly course, Burnett judging that she had now abandoned her attempt to attack the convoy. Bey had, indeed, been sufficiently intimidated against doing so by his encounter with the three cruisers. Of the fact that he thereby greatly facilitated the inexorable approach of the *Duke of York* he remained in blissful ignorance. Russell's radar obtained an echo at 1617, when the *Scharnhorst* was more than 20 miles away to the north-north-east. As the range closed rapidly the screening destroyers *Savage*, Commander M. D. G. Meyrick, *Saumarez*, *Scorpion* and the Norwegian manned *Stord* moved out ready to attack with torpedoes.

At 1650 Fraser ordered the *Belfast* to illuminate the enemy with starshell. Almost simultaneously Bey was surprised by the guns of the *Duke of York* and *Jamaica*. 'When the starshell first illuminated the enemy,' wrote one of the *Scorpion*'s officers, 'I could see that her turrets were fore-and-aft. Almost at once she was obliterated by a wall of water from the *Duke of York*'s first 14-inch salvo. When she reappeared her turrets wore a different aspect.'

According to one of the *Jamaica*'s officers:

I think we had fired two or three broadsides before the reply came. Her first retaliation was by star-shell. In their light the sea was lit up very brightly. After what seemed like an age her star-shell dimmed and guttered out in a shower of bright sparks. Just as we had again been plunged into the comforting gloom I saw the angry wink of her first 11-inch broadside. There was a vague flash off the port bow then—crack, crack, crack, and the drone and whine of splinters passing somewhere near. Another 6-inch broadside, and a few seconds later the same angry wink on the horizon. This time I saw her shells burst, the splashes, mast-high and unpleasantly near the *Duke of York,* who was steadily crashing away with her full broadsides.[6]

From Burnett's squadron (reduced to two ships by shaft trouble in the *Sheffield*) engaging him from the north, and from Fraser's force to the south, Bey attempted to escape. And for a time he managed to open the range. But not for long; at 1724 he radioed: 'Am surrounded by heavy units'. The *Scharnhorst*'s 11-inch guns were aimed at the *Duke of York*. Having been taken by surprise, their fire was initially erratic but once they had settled down, they scored many straddles at 17,000–20,000 yards, but no hits except on the British flagship's masts whose plating was too thin to detonate armour-piercing projectiles. Contrariwise the *Duke of York*'s gunnery was admirable, 52 broadsides scoring 31 straddles, with enough hits to put the enemy's 'A' and 'B' turrets out of action and, more important to the outcome, rupturing steam pipes which reduced her speed, so that Bey could not hope to escape Fraser's clutches.

By 1740 the fight had been reduced to a duel between the two heavy ships, both of which relied on radar to aim their guns at targets of which they could seldom see more than their gun flashes. The *Scharnhorst* was now beyond the range of Burnett's two cruisers, whilst the *Jamaica* ceased firing because Hughes-Hallett judged that the expenditure of 6-inch shell against a heavily armoured vessel at extreme range was not warranted.

It was a slogging match between giants, appalling in their might and fury. Every time the *Duke of York* fired there came the vivid flicker of the *Scharnhorst*'s reply, the lazy flight of the fourteen-inch tracer, followed by the crack, crack of the 11-inch reply in the sea, and the drone of splinters. At one moment I thought the *Duke of York* was hit. Simultaneously with the burst of three 11-inch close to her, a red glow blossomed from somewhere for'ard and lit up her entire bridge super-structure. However, it turned out to be the flash of her reply from 'A' turret, suffused in billowing cordite smoke.[7]

At 1824 Bey radioed: 'We shall fight to the last shell', as the third of the *Scharnhorst*'s 11-inch turrets was put out of action. Seeing this, and realizing that the *Duke of York*'s 14-inch shell, fired at short range with a flat trajectory, were unlikely to pierce the enemy's armour, Fraser ordered his flagship to check fire and turn away to the south-east.

By 1840 the *Savage, Saumarez, Scorpion* and *Stord* had managed to close within five miles of the enemy. Under heavy fire from the *Scharnhorst*'s secondary armament, the first two came in from the north-west firing starshell. The other two came in to 3,000 yards unseen from the south-east to fire their torpedoes at 1849. Too late, Hintze turned the *Scharnhorst* away to port and engaged these adversaries: at least one of the *Scorpion*'s torpedoes scored a hit. And Hintze's turn gave the *Savage* and *Saumarez* their chance: out of their 12 torpedoes three hit their target and further reduced her speed before the *Saumarez* suffered damage from the enemy's gunfire.

As these British destroyers retired under cover of smoke, the *Duke of York* and *Jamaica* again closed in from the south-west and re-opened fire at 1901 at little more than 10,000 yards. Soon afterwards Burnett's cruisers joined in. The *Scharnhorst* 'must have been a hell on earth. The 14-inch from the flagship were hitting or rocketing off from a ricochet on the sea. Great flashes rent the night, and the sound of gunfire was contin-uous, and yet she replied, but only occasionally now with what armament she had left'.[8]

By 1930 the *Scharnhorst* had been reduced to a wreck unable to steam at more than five knots. 'Finish her off with torpedoes', Fraser signalled his cruisers. Closing in on both sides, they scored several hits. Fisher's destroyers then arrived on the scene; closing the enemy on both quarters the *Musketeer, Opportune, Virago* and *Matchless* fired their torpedoes at some 2,000 yards from the dull glow which was all that they could see of the burning enemy through a thick pall of smoke. These sealed the *Scharnhorst*'s fate: at about 1945 she blew up and went to the bottom, leaving only 36 of her crew of 1,968 officers and men to be rescued by the British ships from the icy, wreck-strewn sea.

Bey paid the penalty of poor planning, weak intelligence and timid execution but, as with the *Bismarck,* his crew fought to the end with steadfast gallantry against a superior British force. So, too, is a tribute due to her designers since she withstood at least 30 14-inch shell hits scored by 80 broadsides and did not sink until she had been struck by 11 torpedoes out of 55 fired.

For this British victory the chief credit goes to the accuracy of Fraser's intelligence and the good use which he made of it, and for his masterly control of widely-separated forces. Credit, too, to Burnett for his cruisers' shadowing which allowed the *Duke of York* to gain the scene: he had worthily redeemed his failure in the battle of the Barents Sea. Nor must the skill and courage with which the destroyers pressed home their attacks be forgotten. But, to quote Fraser's report, the *Duke of York* 'was the principal factor in the battle. She fought the *Scharnhorst* at night and she won'. It was, indeed, one of the last occasions on which a capital ship triumphed over one of her own kind in a gun duel fought in the old way, without the intervention of submarines or aircraft. No aircraft-carrier was present, although their paramount importance was now recognized, because in this part of the world, at this time of year, flying operations were seldom possible.

To this account of the battle of North Cape it remains to add only that convoy JW55B, with its escort and covering forces, reached Kola Inlet safely on 27 December, and that never again did Germany's surface ships attempt an attack on an Arctic convoy. Nor, within the terms of reference of this book, was there another surface action in the Atlantic or the Arctic because none of Dönitz's 8-inch cruisers nor his larger warships were now operational. This left Britain free to reduce the strength of her Home Fleet in order to build up an effective force to fight Japan in the Pacific.

NOTES

[1] Ordinary Seaman Ted Cutler in *The Listener.*
[2] In *The Second World War,* Vol.V.
[3] Captain Stephen Roskill in *The War at Sea,* Vol. II.
[4] The *Tirpitz* had been put out of action by British midget submarines on

22 September. The *Lützow* was undergoing a refit. The *Gneisenau*, *Admiral Scheer* and *Admiral Hipper* had been paid off.

[5] Her tonnage was increased from 10,000 to this figure while she was being repaired after breaking her back on a magnetic mine in the Firth of Forth on 21 November 1939.

[6] Lieutenant B. B. Ramsden, Royal Marines, of HMS *Jamaica* in *The Sinking of the Scharnhorst*.

[7] *Ibid.*

[8] *Ibid.*

9 *Midway*

Germany's excepted, no major Fleet has had a shorter history than that of the Imperial Japanese Navy. None has derived more benefit from a close study of the history, traditions, and skills of another country, Britain, by whom it was trained and provided with most of its ships down to 1914. And none has scored more significant victories within the brief span of less than a quarter of a century. There was no Japanese Fleet to impede the arrival of Commodore Biddle's American squadron in 1846, nor of the better known Commodore Perry's seven years later, events which persuaded Japan to open the Treaty Ports that began her lightning transformation from feudal isolation into a world Power. Nor was there a Japanese Navy to prevent the punitive bombardment and burning of Kagoshima by a British squadron in 1862. But within 30 years of that incident the Japanese Fleet destroyed a stronger Chinese Navy in the Sino-Japanese War of 1894–95, chiefly at the battle of the Yalu River. And by 1904 it had produced in Count Heihachiro Togo an admiral who was such an assiduous student of Nelson that he successfully blockaded the Russian Far East Fleet in Port Arthur, where the bulk of it was sunk, and subsequently annihilated Admiral Rozhdestvenski's Baltic Fleet at Tsushima, the only major fleet action of the pre-dreadnought era.

But these triumphs pale beside the Imperial Japanese Navy's record in 1941–42. To the people of the USA Pearl Harbour may be remembered as 'a date which will live in infamy', but it cannot obscure the achievements of Admiral Isoroku Yamamoto who, more than any other naval commander of his generation, realized that the range and destructive power of a carrier task force far exceeded that of a battle fleet, especially after the British attack on Taranto in 1940. His Combined Fleet inflicted a near mortal wound on the US Pacific Fleet on the morning of 7 December 1941. With the advantage of total surprise, 374 torpedo-bombers and dive bombers escorted by 79 fighters, flown off Vice-Admiral Chuichi Nagumo's six aircraft-carriers, backed by two battlecruisers, sank or inflicted serious damage on eight out of nine of Admiral Husband Kimmel's battleships in an attack that lasted little more than two hours.

Only by circumstances against which Yamamoto could not plan did this attack fail also to destroy Kimmel's three carriers. The *Enterprise* and *Lexington* were absent delivering fighter reinforcements to the islands of Midway and Wake; the *Saratoga*, like the surviving battleship *Colorado*, was on the west coast of America. (The USA's other five battleships were in her Atlantic Fleet, ready for hostilities with Germany.) Two days later Britain's recently formed Far East Fleet, headed by the battleship *Prince of Wales* and the battlecruiser *Repulse*, was as swiftly annihilated in the South China Sea by Rear-Admiral Sadaichi Matsunaga's 22nd Air Flotilla from the airfields which Japan had occupied in Vichy French Indo-China—in part because Admiral Sir Tom Phillips (with the confidence of a gunnery specialist who lacked previous experience of the war at sea) ignored the lesson learned by the British Fleet in Home waters and in the Mediterranean, that battleships could not safely operate within range of air attack unless they were provided with fighter cover.

And these two Japanese victories were only the prelude to a whole series of amphibious operations, on a scale which the Allies did not mount in any theatre before the end of 1942, by which their forces captured Hong-Kong, marched down the Malay peninsula from the beaches of Singora and Kota Bharu to capture the great port of Singapore with its important British naval base, invaded and obtained the surrender of Borneo, occupied the Philippines, and seized Guam, Wake and Rabaul, all by 23 January 1942. Just over a month later, on 27–28 February, the last substantial Allied naval force in the Far East, of a dozen cruisers and destroyers flying the British, Netherlands and US ensigns, under the Dutch Admiral Karel Doorman, was virtually wiped out in the battles of the Java Sea and Sunda Strait. Another week and the last of the Netherlands East Indies, the island of Java, capitulated. In only 90 days, instead of the 150 which they had allowed to do so much, Japan had conquered the territories needed to supply her with oil, rubber, tin and the other vital war materials of which she had been deprived by the sanctions imposed by the USA, with British and Dutch support, early in 1940 in a move to abort her invasion of China begun in 1937.

No maritime campaign has been more successful. It did not, however, lead to the negotiated peace on which the Japanese Cabinet gambled when they decided to take the offensive in the Pacific. As soon as 1 February 1942, the Allies began to hit back with their only available weapon, 'air'. The Marshall and Gilbert Islands suffered raids by Vice-Admiral William Halsey's Task Force (TF), headed by the *Enterprise*, and by Rear-Admiral Frank Fletcher's which was headed by the *Yorktown* and *Lexington*. These were followed two days later by one on Wake, and another by Australian shore-based planes on Rabaul. Although too small to do much damage, these attacks so worried Japan that she began to extend her defensive perimeter to a great arc running from the western Aleutians round through Midway, Samoa, the Fiji Islands, New Caledonia and Port Moresby in the Pacific, to the Andaman Islands in the Indian Ocean, and to Burma (all with singular disregard for the sea transport problems which would be involved in keeping so many islands supplied).

And these further operations, which were presaged by a damaging carrier-borne raid on Darwin in northern Australia on 19 February, did not all go according to plan. Although the Andamans were taken on 23 March, Nagumo's five aircraft-carriers, escorted by four battleships, came up against tougher air defences (under the spirited command of Admiral Sir Geoffrey Layton) than Singapore's when they raided Colombo on 5 April and Trincomalee four days later. They were also threatened by a new British Eastern Fleet, headed by five battleships and three aircraft-carriers, which was so well handled by Admiral Sir James Somerville that it not only avoided losing little more than the small carrier *Hermes* and two 8-inch cruisers, but from its base at Kilindini on the east coast of Africa, helped to deter the Japanese from again sending any substantial force into the Indian Ocean.

More important, however, were the defeats which Japan suffered to the south and east. Her control of the Bismarcks was completed in April 1942 with landings in the Solomon Islands. But her subsequent attempt to invade New Guinea was a different story. Under the overall command of Vice-Admiral Shigeyoshi Inouye on board the cruiser *Kashima* at Rabaul, Japan launched two amphibious landings, the first on Tulagi Island in the South Solomons to establish an air base from which to dominate the Solomon Sea, the second to capture Port Moresby in Papua. The smaller force for the first of these assaults was headed by the mine-layer *Okinoshima,* flagship of Rear-Admiral Shima: the larger for the second included a dozen transports and was not only headed by the small cruiser *Yubari,* flagship of Rear-Admiral Kajioka, but covered by Rear-Admiral Aritomo Goto with the small aircraft-carrier *Shoho* and four 8-inch cruisers.

While these three forces, the first two from Rabaul and the third from Truk, were to enter the Solomon Sea from the north, Vice-Admiral Takeo Takagi, with the large aircraft-carriers *Shokaku* and *Zuikaku,* accompanied by two 8-inch cruisers, was to enter the area from the east, by way of the Coral Sea, to ensure that no Allied Navy interfered with these landings. For lack of trained pilots after casualties suffered during the first months of the war—855 planes lost—Japan's other aircraft carriers were not available; but this did not trouble the Japanese because they supposed that there was only one US carrier in the South Pacific.

Kimmel having been made a scapegoat for the débâcle at Pearl Harbour, had been relieved as Cincpac by Admiral Chester Nimitz. And from radio intelligence Nimitz knew enough of Inouye's plans by 17 April to order Rear-Admiral A. W. Fitch to take the *Lexington* and two 8-inch cruisers out of Pearl Harbour to rendezvous in the Coral Sea with Fletcher's *Yorktown* and three 8-inch cruisers, and with Rear-Admiral J. G. Crace's two Australian and one US cruiser. The principal units which thus came to be in the Coral and Solomon Sea areas at the beginning of May 1942—only a small part of the Japanese Fleet but almost all that was available to Nimitz—are best tabulated for comparison.

TABLE 38: Allied and Japanese Ships in the Coral and Solomon Seas in May 1942

	Allies	Japanese
Large aircraft-carriers	2	2
Small aircraft-carriers	—	1
8-inch cruisers	7	6
Smaller cruisers	1	3
Destroyers	13	15

Fitch and Fletcher, the latter being the senior officer, met on 1 May; Crace joined them three days later. By then the Japanese had won the first round: Shima's force occupied Tulagi unopposed on 3 May, and not until 1900 on that date did Fletcher know this from shore-based reconnaissance planes. Because US carriers were not equipped with the necessary lighting and other gear needed to operate aircraft by night, nor were their pilots trained to do so, the *Yorktown* and *Lexington* had to wait until next morning before launching 99 planes to raid Tulagi harbour, where they sank one Japanese destroyer and three small minesweepers. This operation encountered no opposition because Inouye, with that disregard for the value of time, which is so often disastrous in war, had delayed the arrival of Takagi's carriers by two days so that they could first deliver a mere nine fighters to Rabaul. Not until 5 May did the opposing carrier forces begin groping for each other, albeit without success because of poor visibility on both that day and the next, although at one time they were within 70 miles of each other.

There followed on 7 May a tragi-comedy of errors which highlighted a lesson that Britain, Germany and Italy had already learned, the fallability of aircrews. A dawn reconnaissance by planes from the *Shokaku* and *Zuikaku* found the US tanker from which Fletcher's ships had already refuelled, and her escorting destroyer—and reported them to be an aircraft-carrier and a cruiser, with the consequence that as many as 60 torpedo-bombers and dive bombers escorted by fighters were sent to sink them at 0930. But if Fletcher's force thereby escaped attack, its exploits were little more adroit. At 0815 a reconnaissance plane from the *Yorktown* signalled a report of two heavy cruisers and two destroyers, which was wrongly coded as two aircraft-carriers and four heavy cruisers, with the result that the *Lexington* and *Yorktown* sent 93 bombers and torpedo-bombers with fighter escort to attack around noon what proved to be

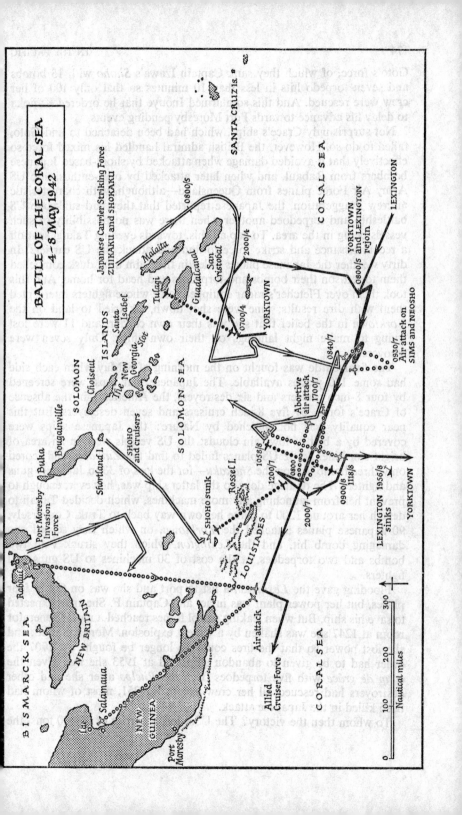

BATTLE OF THE CORAL SEA
4 – 8 May 1942

Japanese Carrier Striking Force
ZUIKAKU and SHOKAKU

SANTA CRUIZ IS.

CORAL SEA

BISMARCK SEA

Rabaul

NEW BRITAIN

Salamaua

NEW GUINEA

Port Moresby

SOLOMON ISLANDS

Buka
Bougainville

Shortland I.

Choiseul

Santa Isabel

The New Georgia Is.

Malaita

Guadalcanal

San Cristobal

Tulagi

SHOHO and cruisers

SHOHO sunk

Rossel I.

LOUISIADES

Port Moresby Invasion Force

Allied Cruiser Force

Air attack

Air attack

CORAL SEA

YORKTOWN and LEXINGTON rejoin

LEXINGTON

0800/5
2000/4
0700/4
0840/7
0800/5
0930/7 Air attack on SIMS and NEOSHO

Abortive air attack
1700/7

1058/8
0800
1200/7
2000/7
0900/8
1118/8
YORKTOWN
1956/8
LEXINGTON 2000/7 sinks

Nautical miles
0   100   200   300

Goto's force, of which they sank Captain Izawa's *Shoho* with 13 bombs and seven torpedo hits in less than 10 minutes so that only 100 of her crew were rescued. And this so alarmed Inouye that he ordered Kajioka to delay his advance towards Port Moresby pending events.

Not surprisingly Crace's ships, which had been detached to find Goto, failed to do so. However, the British admiral handled his mixed force so effectively that it avoided damage when attacked by shore-based Japanese bombers from Rabaul, and when later attacked by over-enthusiastic US Army Air Force planes from Queensland—although, with characteristic aircrew exaggeration, the Japanese reported that they had sunk one US battleship and torpedoed another when there was no possibility of such vessels being in the area. To cap all this, towards evening Takagi sent off a reconnaissance and strike force to find and attack the US carriers. In dirty weather the Japanese planes failed in their aim until dusk compelled them to jettison their bombs and torpedoes and head for home. And this took them over Fletcher's radar equipped force whose fighters intercepted them with dire results; nine were shot down, six tried to land on the *Yorktown* in the belief that she was their own carrier, and 11 were lost trying to make night landings on their own ships. Only seven were recovered.

The final battle was fought on the morning of 8 May when each side had some 120 planes available. The Japanese 'flat tops' were screened by four 8-inch cruisers and six destroyers, the American, in the absence of Crace's force, by five 8-inch cruisers and seven destroyers. But this near equality was not matched by Nature: the Japanese ships were covered by a belt of low rain clouds; the US vessels were in an area of bright sunshine. So 82 US planes failed to find the *Zuikaku*, and scored only three bomb hits on the *Shokaku*—for the loss of 33 to Japanese guns and fighters. The damage done to the latter ship was, however, enough to prevent her from launching any more machines, which decided Takaji to detach her around 1200 to make her own way back to Truk. Conversely, 90 Japanese planes attacked the *Yorktown*, on which they scored one damaging bomb hit, and the *Lexington*, which they struck with two bombs and two torpedoes, at the cost of 30 machines to US guns and fighters.

Flooding gave the *Lexington* a list to port and she was on fire in four places, but her power plant was intact and Captain F. Sherman expected to save his ship. But when leaking petrol fumes reached a motor generator room at 1247 she was shaken by a violent explosion. More followed, and she lost power so that the fires could no longer be fought. At 1707 the order had to be given to abandon ship, and at 1953 she was given the *coup de grâce* with five torpedoes from the *Phelps* after she and other destroyers had rescued all her crew except for 251, most of whom had been killed in the Japanese attack.

To whom then the victory? The USA lost a carrier of 36,000 tons, the

Japanese one of only 11,260. Both Japan and the USA had a large carrier damaged, but the latter's was repaired by the beginning of June, whereas the former's was in dockyard hands for two months. Moreover, the *Zuikaku* took more than a month to replace her lost planes and aircrew. As a result the *Yorktown* was available to take part in a much more crucial battle soon to be fought elsewhere, whereas neither the *Shokaku* nor *Zuikaku* could be present. And if this is not enough to count the battle of the Coral Sea an Allied victory, albeit one which reflects no great credit on either side, there remains Inouye's reaction. Fearing to risk Kajioka's assault force against Port Moresby without air cover, he ordered it to return to Rabaul. For the first time since 7 December 1941, the Japanese advance to the south was checked.

Such then was the first naval battle in all history between two fleets at sea whose ships never sighted each other, which were indeed never within 50 miles, and in which the chief weapon was the carrier-borne aircraft, armed with bomb and torpedo, and not the shell-firing gun. Of incidental interest, it was also the first battle in which the senior officers afloat, Fletcher and Takagi, both of whom flew their flags in 8-inch cruisers, transferred tactical command (OTC) of their forces to their aircraft-carrier commanders, Fitch in the *Lexington* and Rear-Admiral Chuichi Hara in the *Zuikaku*, because these officers were in a better position to order the frequent manoeuvring required by carriers to operate their aircraft.

Yamamoto's plan to invade Midway, an atoll six miles in diameter and long enough for an aircraft runway, just one month later was designed to do more than seize this strategic island within shore-based air range (1136 miles) of Pearl Harbour: he hoped also to annihilate the remaining units of the US Pacific Fleet, notably its aircraft-carriers, which had not only escaped the holocaust of 7 December 1941 but which had prevented the capture of Port Moresby. For this he employed the greater part of the Japanese Fleet, and arranged a diversionary attack on the Aleutians.

For the latter Vice-Admiral Moshiro Hosogaya was given a force headed by the aircraft-carriers *Ryujo* and *Junyo*, three 8-inch and three smaller cruisers. With the former he bombed Dutch Harbour, the US base in the Aleutians on 3 and 4 June. Three days later uninhabited Attu and Kiska in the western Aleutians were occupied, the first by 1200 troops landed by Rear-Admiral Sentaro Omori, the latter by 1,250 landed by Captain T. Ohno. Air Force bombers foiled an attempt to seize Adak, but otherwise this diversion encountered no opposition.

From radio intelligence Nimitz had learned enough of Yamamoto's plans by 27 May[1] to strengthen his North Pacific Force, based on Dutch Harbour, to two 8-inch and three 6-inch cruisers. But its commander, Rear-Admiral R. A. Theobald, made two related errors of judgement. He mistrusted Cincpac's intelligence; he preferred to believe Hosogaya aimed to seize Dutch Harbour. And being more concerned to protect this base than a couple of uninhabited islands, he deployed his force 400 miles to the south of Kodiak instead of towards the western Aleutians. In effect he chose a defensive posture instead of an offensive one, so that he was in no position to deal with the Attu and Kiska invasion forces; nor in the poor visibility prevalent in these northern latitudes, did he find the two Japanese aircraft-carriers. Perhaps fortunately, this latter reason also cloaked his own ships from discovery by the enemy's planes.

Against Midway Yamamoto, who flew his flag in the giant battleship *Yamato*, employed the following forces:

TABLE 39: Japanese Forces in the Battle of Midway

Force	Capital ships	Large aircraft-carriers	Small aircraft-carriers	8-inch cruisers	Smaller cruisers	Destroyers
Main Body (Admiral Yamamoto, Vice-Admiral Shiro Takusu)	7	—	1	—	3	21
Carrier Strike Force (Vice-Admiral Nagumo, Rear-Admirals Tamon Yamaguchi and Hiroaki Abe)	2	4	—	2	1	12
Invasion Force (Vice-Admirals Nobutake Kondo, Takeo Takagi and Takeo Kurita)	2	—	1	8	2	20
Totals	11	4 (272 planes)	2 (32 planes)	10	6	53

Yamamoto also deployed 15 U-boats between Midway and Pearl Harbour to give him warning of the approach of US forces. And he could call on Rear-Admiral Minoru Maeda's 24th Air Flotilla of 72 fighters, 72 torpedo bombers and 18 flying boats shore-based at Aur, Jaluet, Kwajalein and Wotje, but in the event very few of these played any part in the coming battle.

Against this formidable armada of ships and aircraft Nimitz sailed from Pearl Harbour on 28 May only the following puny forces.

TABLE 40: US Forces in the Battle of Midway

Task Force (TF)	Large aircraft-carriers	8-inch cruisers	Smaller cruisers	Destroyers
16 (Rear-Admiral Raymond Spruance)	2	5	1	11
17 (Rear-Admiral Frank Fletcher)	1	2	—	6
Totals	3 (233 aircraft)	7	1	17

Nimitz was also able to sail Rear-Admiral Anderson's two battleships from San Francisco on 31 May and an additional large aircraft-carrier, Fitch's flagship *Saratoga,* from San Diego on 1 June, but these could not reach the Midway area in time. However he had 115 planes shore-based on the island. Despite the great disparity between the ships on each side,[2] their aircraft strengths were about equal, the better performance of the Japanese machines being offset by radar with which only the US ships were equipped.

Thus David faced Goliath—a David who had more than one pebble in his sling. One was Nimitz's foreknowledge of Yamamoto's plans, which enabled him to order his two task forces to a position 200 miles north of Midway, in an area where they were unlikely to be sighted by Japanese carrier-borne reconnaissance planes before their ships were spotted by the longer range, Midway based machines, and one which happened to be outside the arc covered by Yamamoto's 15 patrolling U-boats. The other lay in the quirk of Nature which at this critical moment sent the proper commander of TF16, Vice-Admiral William Halsey, into hospital. Just as the death of General Gott, the destined new commander of the British Eighth Army in North Africa in August 1942 (the plane flying him to Cairo was shot down) gave General Montgomery his chance to show his mettle at the battle of Alamein, so was Raymond Spruance to show his. 'You will,' Nimitz wrote to him and Fletcher, 'inflict maximum damage by employing strong attrition tactics. You will be governed by the principle of calculated risk, the avoidance of exposure of your force to attack by superior enemy forces without good prospect of inflicting greater damage on the enemy'. No instructions could have been wiser; none more intelligently carried out.

To begin with, however, as with other men's best laid plans, Nimitz's went 'agley'. Low cloud prevented his Midway planes sighting Nagumo's Carrier Strike Force until 3 June, when it was 200 miles to the north-west of Midway, only four days before the island was due to be invaded; and a hastily launched night strike from this atoll secured only one hit, on a Japanese tanker, at 0143 on 4 June. Moreover, the first news of this sighting did not reach Fletcher and Spruance until shortly after 0600 that morning by which time flying operations—the need to turn into the wind—had placed the former's *Yorktown* further from the enemy than the latter's *Enterprise* and *Hornet.* Fletcher promptly ordered Spruance to head south-west and launch a strike as soon as Nagumo's ships could be located, adding that the *Yorktown* would give her support after she had recovered her dawn reconnaisance machines.

Meantime, shortly before sunrise, and wholly unaware of the near presence of these US carriers, Nagumo (whose intelligence foretold that only one might be in the area) had gone ahead with the first part of his own plan. The *Akagi, Hiryu, Kaga* and *Soryu* had launched 108 planes (torpedo-bombers and dive-bombers escorted by fighters) from a position

200 miles to the northward of Midway, to neutralise the island's defences. Radar detection at 93 miles saved its planes from being caught on the ground, but its fighters were too few and too slow to break up the attack which lasted for 20 minutes from 0630 and did considerable damage.

A too confident Nagumo then made a mistake which was to lose him the battle. Because his returning planes reported that the island needed a further strike, an assessment confirmed by the arrival of a Midway-based US air strike of 52 torpedo-bombers and dive bombers, which lost 17 of its strength and scored no hits, and because his dawn reconnaissance planes had sighted nothing, he ordered his remaining 93 planes to be struck below and rearmed with incendiary and fragmentation bombs—which were the most suitable for attacking the island's runways, but the least effective against ships. Fifteen minutes later he was disconcerted to receive a report from a cruiser's search plane of 10 enemy ships to the north-east; but because this did not mention the presence of a carrier, a further quarter-of-an-hour elapsed before he made up his mind to reverse his previous order. His planes in their hangars had not, therefore, been rearmed with torpedoes and armour-piercing bombs by the time, 0835, that his initial Midway strike required to land on.

Moreover, in Spruance, the US Navy had a commander whose nimble mind was more than a match for Nagumo. Looking 'over the hill', as a good commander should, he reckoned that the golden moment to attack the Japanese carriers, of which he had received a reconnaissance report at 0534, would be when they were refuelling their planes for a second strike against Midway. Between 0700 and 0800 the *Enterprise*, Captain G. D. Murray, and *Hornet*, Captain Mark Mitscher, from a position 175 miles to the north-east of the enemy, flew off 116 torpedo-bombers and dive bombers with fighter escort. These were followed an hour later by 35 planes from the *Yorktown*, Captain E. Buckmaster.

However, around 0917, as the last machine from Nagumo's Midway raid was flying-on to refuel and rearm, and before all the others had finished rearming, the Japanese admiral ordered his force to alter course to north-north-east 'to contact and destroy the enemy'. (His four carriers were in a box formation screened by two capital ships, three cruisers and 11 destroyers. This was similar to the circular disposition which the US Pacific Fleet adopted when, later, it had a sufficiency of aircraft-carriers —with one notable difference. Instead of using all his capital ships and cruisers to screen his carriers against air attack as the USA and the British were to do, Yamamoto made the tactical mistake of keeping those which he had not sent north to support the attack on the Aleutians many miles to the westward with Kondo's Invasion Force, despite the known fact that there were only two US battleships operational in the Pacific at this time.)

As a result of this alteration of course the *Hornet*'s dive-bombers and

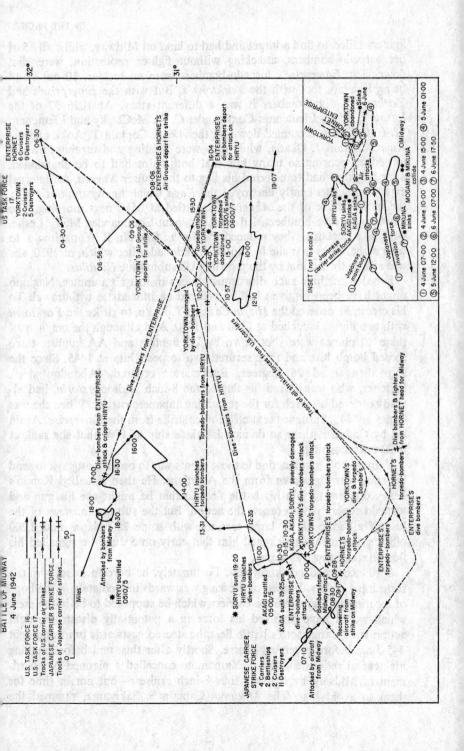

BATTLE OF MIDWAY
4 June 1942

U.S. TASK FORCE 16 ——————
U.S. TASK FORCE 17 ——————
Tracks of U.S. carrier air strikes ——+—+—
JAPANESE CARRIER STRIKE FORCE —·—·—·
Tracks of Japanese carrier air strikes ···········

Miles
0   50

JAPANESE CARRIER
STRIKE FORCE
4 Carriers
2 Battleships
2 Cruisers
11 Destroyers

Attacked by aircraft
from Midway
07·10

KAGA sunk 19·25
dive-bombers
AKAGI scuttled
05·00/5
SORYU sunk 19·20
HIRYU launches
dive-bombers

HIRYU launches
torpedo-bombers

13·31

14·00

16·30

18·00
18·30
17·00 dive-bombers from ENTERPRISE
attack & cripple HIRYU

1600

12·35

1·00

12·10
12·00

10·57

Torpedo attack
on YORKTOWN

YORKTOWN's Air Group
departs for strike

Track of all striking forces from U.S. carriers

Dive-bombers from HIRYU

Torpedo-bombers from HIRYU

Dive-bombers from ENTERPRISE

YORKTOWN damaged
by dive-bombers

Attacked by bombers
from Midway

HIRYU scuttled
05·10/5

Dive bombers & fighters
from HORNET head for Midway

Dive bombers & fighters
from HORNET head for Midway

HORNET's
torpedo-bombers

ENTERPRISE's
torpedo-bombers

ENTERPRISE's
dive bombers

YORKTOWN's
dive & torpedo
attack

HORNET's
dive & torpedo
attack

ENTERPRISE's torpedo-bombers attack
09·28
YORKTOWN's torpedo-bombers attack
ENTERPRISE's dive-bombers attack
10·15 - 10·30
KAGA, AKAGI, SORYU, severely damaged
10·30
Bombers from
Midway attack
08·30   09·17
09·28
Recovering
aircraft from
strike on Midway

ENTERPRISE's
dive-bombers

U.S. TASK FORCE
17
YORKTOWN
2 Cruisers
5 Destroyers

ENTERPRISE
HORNET
6 Cruisers
9 Destroyers

06·30

04·30

06·56

09·06   08·06
ENTERPRISE & HORNET's
Air Groups depart for strike

15·30

16·04
ENTERPRISE & HORNET's
dive-bombers depart
for attack on HIRYU

19·07

14·40
YORKTOWN
torpedoed
13·30/6 sinks
06·00/7

YORKTOWN
abandoned
15·00

10·00

32°

31°

INSET (not to scale)

YORKTOWN

HORNET   ENTERPRISE

YORKTOWN
abandoned
6 June

YORKTOWN
Sinks
6 June

Air
attacks

HIRYU sinks

SORYU sinks
AKAGI sinks
KAGA sinks

Japanese
carrier strike force

Japanese
main body

MIKUNA
sinks

MOGAMI & MIKUNA
collide

○Midway I

Japanese
invasion force

① 4 June 07·00   ② 4 June 10·00   ③ 4 June 15·00   ④ 5 June 01·00
⑤ 5 June 12·00   ⑥ 6 June 07·00   ⑦ 6 June 17·50

fighters failed to find a target and had to land on Midway, whilst all 15 of
her torpedo-bombers, attacking without fighter protection, were shot
down. The *Enterprise*'s torpedo-bombers were no luckier, 10 out of 14
being lost. So, too, with the *Yorktown*'s. But with the *Enterprise*'s and
Yorktown's dive-bombers it was a different story. At 1026 37 of the
former's, led by Lieutenant-Commander C. W. McClusky and Lieutenant
W. E. Gallaher, screamed down on the *Akagi,* Captain T. Aoki, and the
Kaga, Captain J. Okada, while they were twisting and turning to avoid
torpedoes, scoring so many hits that both ships had to be abandoned,
after Nagumo had transferred his flag to the cruiser *Nagara.* An internal
explosion subsequently destroyed the *Kaga* which finally sank at 1925:
the useless hulk of the *Akagi* was scuttled at 0510 next morning. The
Yorktown's dive-bombers, led by Lieutenant-Commander M. F. Leslie,
were as successful: they reduced the *Soryu,* Captain R. Yanagimoto, to
such a shambles that she had to be abandoned, after which, at 1920, she
was sent to the bottom by the prowling US submarine *Nautilus.*

Faced with three such disastrous attacks in just six minutes, Nagumo
might have been forgiven had he ordered an immediate withdrawal. To
his credit, he ordered the *Hiryu,* Captain T. Kaku, to strike the *Yorktown*
with two flights launched at 1100 and 1330. And although the majority of
these 40 planes were shot down by US fighters and AA gunfire, three
scored bomb hits and four secured two torpedo hits at 1445. Since the
ship then listed 26 degrees, Buckmaster ordered, 'Abandon ship'.
Fletcher, who transferred his flag to the 8-inch cruiser *Astoria,* had already ordered a search for the remaining Japanese carrier. When she was
found at 1445, Spruance sent off another strike from the *Enterprise.* Again
led by Gallaher, these so damaged Kaku's ship at 1700 that she sank at
0500 next morning.

Yamamoto's first reaction to these events was to order Hosogaya to send
his small carriers down from the Aleutians. He then signalled Kondo's
heavy cruisers to join his battle fleet so that he might use his gun and
torpedo superiority to renew the action. But the subsequent news of the
loss of all four of his large carriers, with some 250 planes and 2,200
officers and men, so sickened him that early on 5 June he signalled his
fleet to retire towards Japan.

Spruance could not know this. Fortunately, he bore in mind Nimitz's
restraining orders. Instead of pressing westwards immediately in the hope
of locating further Japanese carriers which he supposed to be in the area,
which would have involved his force in a potentially disastrous night
action with Yamamoto's battle fleet, he steered eastwards until midnight
4–5 June before reversing course. Shortly after this, and before making
his general retirement signal, Yamamoto cancelled a planned bombardment of Midway by Kurita's four 8-inch cruisers—but not in time for
them to avoid loss. The *Mikuma,* Captain S. Sakiyama, rammed the

Mogami, Captain A. Soji, while both were making an emergency turn to avoid attack by the US submarine *Tambor*. The two cripples were subsequently located by a US reconnaissance plane, attacked unsuccessfully by planes from Midway, and at 0800 on 6 June struck by Spruance's dive-bombers. The *Mikuma* was then sunk, but the heavily damaged *Mogami* managed to struggle back to Truk.

On receiving news of the US carrier strike against these two ships Yamamoto ordered a powerful cruiser force to locate and destroy the *Enterprise* and *Hornet*, and turned his battle fleet east in support. But Spruance, whose conduct throughout was so outstanding, had no intention of being trapped by any such force; he was already heading east to refuel from his fleet train with the consequence that on 7 June Yamamoto called off the hunt and next day abandoned the whole operation.

The end of the damaged *Yorktown* remains to be told. The Japanese U-boat *I168*, Commander Tanabe, found her in tow of the minesweeper *Vireo* during daylight hours on 6 June, more than 24 hours after the Japanese air attack, proving that she had been prematurely abandoned, and put two torpedoes into her, and one into the destroyer *Hammann* which was alongside trying to supply power for her salvage crew, which sank her. Even so the 'Waltzing Matilda', as the *Yorktown* was affectionately known, remained afloat until 0600 on 7 June before finally plunging to the bottom in 2,000 fathoms—a sad end since it is clear that, like the British *Ark Royal*, torpedoed in the Mediterranean on 13 October 1941, she could have been saved had the use of speedy counterflooding to correct an apparently dangerous list been properly appreciated.

So ended the first major victory for the US Navy in World War Two. Nimitz's able deployment of his limited forces, Spruance's clever handling of his two aircraft-carriers and the skill and matchless courage of few more than 200 pilots,[3] did much more than frustrate an invasion of Midway. They annihilated the core of the Japanese Fleet, its Carrier Strike Force. Never in the field of naval warfare was such a mighty armada defeated by one so small. Nor was further proof needed that battleships had been effectively supplanted by aircraft-carriers in little more than two decades since their inception. But most importantly, Midway was a disaster from which, despite desperate efforts, Japan could never recover. This was the end of her aggression. Time was now on the side of the USA with its immense industrial resources; the time needed to rebuild her battle fleet and to create the carrier task forces and the amphibious ships and craft required to invade and capture Japan's ill-gotten gains in the Pacific and, ultimately, to bring the war so near to Japan's homeland that, after the USSR's belated declaration of war in August 1945, she realized her cause to be hopeless and agreed to surrender.[4]

But, on the day that Midway was fought and won, that final victory was more than three long years away.

NOTES

[1] Of incidental interest the Japanese signals referred to their principal objective as 'AF'. To confirm that this was Midway, Nimitz instructed the island to radio in plain language an appeal for fresh water. Shortly afterwards a Japanese cipher message reported that 'AF' was short of water.
[2] Because the *Saratoga* was undergoing damage repairs and the only other US carrier, the *Wasp*, was on her way back from the Mediterranean after flying off fighter reinforcements for Malta, King asked Pound on 19 May to reinforce Nimitz's fleet with a British carrier. Pound had to reply that none was available. In any case the nearest was 11,000 miles away, a distance which could not have been covered in time to take part in the battle of Midway, even if King had revealed earlier to Pound that a Japanese attack on the island was imminent. However, after the *Hornet* had been sunk later in the year Pound made the *Victorious* available to work with the US Pacific Fleet for six months in 1943, when only chance denied her any opportunity to show her mettle against the Japanese.
[3] In this action, as in the Coral Sea, they even overcame an obstacle of their own making. By filling the ether with exuberant, but anti-productive chatter, they seriously handicapped effective control by their radar fitted carriers. Fortunately for the future, Spruance's annihilating victory did not prevent the US Navy learning from it the importance of strict discipline on voice radio.
[4] The atomic bombs dropped on Hiroshima and Nagasaki served to reinforce this decision. But since up to this time there remained a significant number of Japanese sufficiently fanatical to wish to continue the war, it is arguable that if the two bombs had not been dropped a far greater number would have lost their lives post-August 1945 than were killed in the Hiroshima and Nagasaki holocausts (or died later), large though these numbers were.

10 Guadalcanal

From two actions in which the chief weapons were carrier-borne aircraft, we turn to more conventional naval battles—battles which were, moreover, not all won by the Allies, proving that the Japanese victory in the Java Sea (a surface ship action in which their forces had the distinct advantage of having been well trained to work together whereas the mixed Allied one had never done so) was no flash in the pan. They could fight their ships as well as their opponents, and their Long Lance torpedoes were more deadly than the gun.

After Midway had stemmed the rising tide of Japanese aggression the Allies, among whom the USA were much more than *primus inter pares* in the Pacific, turned to the task of rolling it back. Their general strategy was clear enough; in the words of Cominch, Admiral King, written as soon after Pearl Harbour as February 1942: 'to set up "strong points" from which a step-by-step advance can be made through the New Hebrides, Solomons and the Bismarck Archipelago'. In effect to launch an amphibious assault against some point on Japan's defensive perimeter, and when this had been gained, against another—and another, each nearer to the Philippines and then to Japan itself—island hopping, as it came to be called. But putting this strategy into effect against the toughest of enemies with the very limited forces at the disposal of the Allies in the Pacific theatre in 1942 was no easy matter.

For their first objective the US Chiefs of Staff agreed on the British island of Guadalcanal in the Solomons, on the northern fringe of the Coral Sea. This was nearly 600 miles from Rabaul, where the Japanese had established a base from which, after their defeat in the battle of the Coral Sea, they planned to capture Port Moresby by a land campaign across New Guinea. Here by the last week of July 1942 was deployed their Eighth Fleet under Vice-Admiral Gunichi Mikawa, Nagumo's second-in-command during the Pearl Harbour raid. This comprised five 8-inch and two smaller cruisers plus a handful of destroyers and seaplane tenders, and Rear-Admiral Yamada's 25th Air Flotilla of 24 bombers and 30 fighters. The Japanese Main Fleet, including its three surviving aircraft-carriers, was far away in Home waters: the nearest force to Mikawa's was Inouye's Fourth Fleet of two cruisers and four destroyers at Truk, some 1,000 miles to the north. As much of this as matters was known to the Allies from air reconnaissance and other intelligence sources.

The Allied amphibious armada, which included almost all of the then available ships of the US Pacific Fleet, was under the overall command of Vice-Admiral Robert Ghormley, who had charge of the South-West Pacific Area with headquarters in New Zealand. The assault had been planned for later in the year but was brought forward, on King's insistence, when it became known that the Japanese, having established a seaplane base at Tulagi, had started to bulldoze an airstrip, to be known as Henderson Field, out of the jungle near Lunga Point on the north side of Guadalcanal. As soon as 26 July the US and Australian ships assembled in the Koro Sea, 400 miles to the south of the Fiji Islands. Rear-Admiral Richmond Turner's TF (Task Force) 62, of 19 transports carrying 19,000 US Marines under Major-General Alexander Vandegrift, was escorted by TG (Task Group) 62·2 of three 8-inch and one 6-inch cruiser, plus nine destroyers, under Rear-Admiral Victor Crutchley, a Royal Navy VC (awarded for his part in the unsuccessful attempt to block the Ostend entrance to the Bruges canal in May 1918), and accompanied by two fire support groups, TG 62·3 of three 8-inch cruisers and four destroyers, and TG 62·4 of one 5-inch cruiser and two destroyers.

Turner would be helped by US and Australian search planes based on Queensland and Port Moresby, and by Rear-Admiral John McCain's bombers and fighters. But the latter's support, ordered from his headquarters at Noumea, was limited to the extent that all his bases were outside fighter range of Guadalcanal and Tulagi. For close air support during the assault TF 62 would depend on TF 61 operating to the south-east of Guadalcanal. Under the command of Fletcher, who was Turner's senior, this was headed by the carriers *Saratoga, Enterprise* and *Wasp*, escorted by the new fast battleship *North Carolina* and six 8-inch cruisers.

D-day having been brought forward to 7 August, Vandegrift's Marines were able to carry out only one unsatisfactory practice landing on Fiji and, in the event more important, there was too little time for Crutchley to organize and train his Australian and US ships into a homogeneous force. To begin with, however, all went reasonably well; not until 0725 on 7 August did Mikawa learn that TF 62 had arrived off Tulagi and Guadalcanal, by which time US Marines were landing on both islands. Effectively protected by TF 61's aircraft against Yamada's planes, 6,000 men captured the former island by the afternoon of 8 August, by which time 11,000 had landed on the latter. But because of interruptions caused by enemy air attacks, the transports had not completed unloading by nightfall on this, the second day. Another 24 hours would be needed, half of it when fighter protection would not be available if Fletcher carried out his intention to withdraw TF 61 before any of its precious carriers were lost to Japanese air attack.

Shortly after TF 62's arrival on 7 August TGs 62·2, 62·3 and 62·4 were reorganized. Rear-Admiral Norman Scott, with the 5-inch cruiser *San Juan* (flag) and the Australian 6-inch cruiser *Hobart* plus two destroyers, was ordered to give such protection as he could to the two transport forces anchored off Tulagi and Lunga Point against the relatively unlikely possibility of a Japanese intrusion from the east, for which purpose he established a patrol midway between them. To guard against an attack from the west, Crutchley was given the six 8-inch cruisers and six destroyers.

With this force he had two alternatives. He could have concentrated his cruisers some 20 miles to the west of Savo Island, where there was plenty of sea room, and disposed his destroyers as a warning screen further to the west. He chose to take up a position immediately to the east of Savo where his movements were confined within the 20 mile wide strait between Tulagi and Guadalcanal, and where geography compelled him to divide his cruisers into two separate groups.

With HMAS *Australia,* Captain H. B. Farncomb, RAN (flag) and *Canberra,* Captain F. E. Getting, RAN, and the USS *Chicago,* Captain H. D. Bode, he himself guarded the channel between Cape Esperance and the small offshore Savo Island. The USS *Vincennes,* Captain F. L. Riefkohl, *Quincy,* Captain S. N. Moore, and *Astoria,* Captain W. G. Greenman, were ordered to guard the channel between Savo and Tulagi. Crutchley kept four of his destroyers to provide inadequate A/S screens for each cruiser group. He stationed the remaining two as radar pickets, the *Ralph Talbot* to the north-west of Savo and the *Blue* to the south-east, where their movements were not co-ordinated. If the *Blue* happened to be at the southern limit of her beat when the *Ralph Talbot* was at the northern end of hers, a sizeable gap was left in their radar coverage midway between them. Thirdly, Crutchley omitted to give his ships, notably Riefkohl who was senior officer of the northern group, clear instructions as to how they should operate if an enemy attack developed.

Daylight air raids excepted, 7 August and the ensuing night passed without significant incident. The next day was a different matter. The area between Guadalcanal and Rabaul was believed to be covered by Allied shore-based search planes, not to mention several US submarines. And these produced nothing more significant than reports of enemy ships in the St George's Channel, near to Rabaul, and, one of a force well to the east of Rabaul. The latter report was, however, delayed by some eight hours because the pilots of the two planes involved attached undue importance to maintaining radio silence. Not until 1845 did Turner and Crutchley learn that this force included three cruisers; but because these were said to be accompanied by two seaplane tenders, both admirals concluded that it must be bent on establishing a new seaplane base on one of the islands, rather than on an offensive mission. That evening they were under the impression that an attack by Japanese surface craft was not to be expected during the coming night when, in truth, both planes had sighted the whole of Mikawa's cruiser force hell-bent on just such a task.

Turner was chiefly worried by another signal which he received little more than an hour later. Despite the fact that unloading the transports needed another day, Fletcher, with vivid memories of losing the *Yorktown* and *Lexington* in previous battles, intended to withdraw the whole of TF 61 that night; a withdrawal which Ghormley approved (and against which Turner, as Fletcher's junior, had already protested to no effect) although the transports off Tulagi and Guadalcanal would be left without air cover next day, 9 August. Turner and Vandegrift were so disturbed by this that the former summoned Crutchley, at 2032, to a conference onboard the transport *McCawley*, anchored off Lunga Point.

Having been lulled into a sense of security which was to be proved as false as that which cost the Italians the loss of three 8-inch cruisers during the battle of Matapan, Crutchley obeyed to the extent of weakening the group to the south-east of Savo by taking his flagship, HMAS *Australia*, away from its patrol instead of making the 20 miles journey to Lunga Point in one of his destroyers. He left command of his group in the hands of Bode of the *Chicago*, but he omitted to inform Riefkohl of the *Vincennes*, who was now the senior officer in the Savo area, of his absence. Moreover, he left his ships with only half their guns manned their crews being in their bunks and hammocks.

How grim the reality behind all this. Mikawa had no sooner learned of the US landing on 7 August than he called in his outlying ships and, later in the day, headed east with the 8-inch cruisers *Chokai*, Captain M. Hayakawa (flag), *Aoba*, Captain Y. Hisamune (flagship of Rear-Admiral Goto who had lost the *Shoho* in the battle of the Coral Sea), *Kinugasa*, Captain M. Sawa, *Furutaka*, Captain T. Araki, and *Kako*, Captain Y. Takahashi, and the smaller cruisers *Tenryu*, Captain S. Asno, and *Yubari*, Captain M. Ban, plus one destroyer. Lieutenant-Commander Munson in the US submarine *S38* saw them that night, but he was too close to fire torpedoes, and, because of the darkness, radioed a report which considerably underestimated their strength.

Omitting the *Australia* (and Scott's four ships), five Japanese cruisers armed with 34 8-inch guns and 48 24-inch torpedo tubes were heading for the same number of Allied cruisers armed with 44 8-inch guns but only 16 21-inch torpedo tubes. On paper this was no great disparity in strength. In truth, the Japanese had the considerable advantage of surprise by a homogeneous force against a divided one, as well as their Long Lance

TABLE 41: Ships Involved in the Battle of Savo Island

Ship	Displacement (tons)	Speed (knots)	Guns	Torpedo
HMAS *Australia* (flag)	9,870	31	8 8in	8 21in
HMAS *Canberra*	9,850	31	8 8in	8 21in
USS *Chicago* (SO)	9,300	31	8 8in	—
USS *Patterson*				
USS *Bagley*	1,500	36	4 5in	16 21in
USS *Blue*				
USS *Vincennes* (SO)	9,400	32	9 8in	—
USS *Quincy*	9,375	32	9 8in	—
USS *Astoria*	9,950	32	9 8in	—
USS *Helm*				
USS *Wilson*	1,500	36	4 5in	16 21in
USS *Ralph Talbot*				
USS *San Juan* (flag)	6,000	32	16 5in	8 21in
HMAS *Hobart*	7,150	32	8 6in	8 21in
USS *Monssen*	1,630	37	5 5in	10 21in
USS *Buchanan*	1,630	37	4 5in	5 21in
Chokai (flag)	13,160	34	10 8in	16 24in
Aoba (flag)	9,380	33	6 8in	8 24in
Kako	9,150	33	6 8in	8 24in
Kinugasa	9,380	33	6 8in	8 24in
Furutaka	9,150	33	6 8in	8 24in
Tenryu	3,230	33	4 5·5in	6 21in
Yubari	2,890	35	6 5·5in	4 24in
Yunagi	1,270	37	4 4·7in	6 21in

torpedoes. Moreover, although they lacked radar, they were otherwise well equipped and trained for a night action. Conversely, whilst several of the Allied ships were fitted with some form of radar, none had fired their guns at night during the previous eight months, and some not for more than a year.

Through the dark hours of 7–8 August Mikawa led his ships past Buka Island so that during the forenoon of the 8th they were to the north of Bougainville. There he received air search reports of the disposition of the Allied ships which decided him to descend upon them during the coming night. At 1300 he increased speed to 24 knots and headed his ships southward into the Slot, as the Americans called the long sea channel running east and west between the two chains of islands comprising the Solomons. He intended to come down from the west 'like a wolf on the fold', overcome any opposition offered by Allied warships, then wreak havoc, first among the transports off Guadalcanal and subsequently among those off Tulagi. 'Let us attack with certain victory in the traditional night attack of the Imperial Japanese Navy. May each one calmly do his utmost', he signalled his eight ships shortly before the

G*

darkness of a clouded sky enveloped them. Although he had no news of the US carriers, he accepted the possible risk of being attacked by their planes during his subsequent daylight withdrawal.

At 2313 the *Chokai, Aoba* and *Kako* catapulted their floatplanes to locate enemy vessels and illuminate them with flares. These were heard by several of the Allied warships shortly after midnight, but were rashly assumed to be friendly and allowed to continue overhead unhindered, as the *Canberra* and *Chicago* patrolled in line ahead, with the *Patterson* and *Bagley* screening on each bow, at 12 knots along a line to the south-east of Savo, and the *Vincennes, Quincy* and *Astoria,* screened by the *Helm* and *Wilson,* did a square patrol to the north-east.

By 0100 Turner, Vandegrift and Crutchley had agreed that, for lack of fighter protection, the transports would have to withdraw soon after dawn. Crutchley then returned to the *Australia* where he decided against trying to rejoin his group to the south-east of Savo during such a dark night; he would remain off the transport anchorage. But this decision was of no importance because the die had already been cast against the Allies. At 0054 the *Chokai* sighted the radar picket *Blue* distant five miles on her starboard bow. Mikawa immediately cut his speed to reduce his ships' tell-tale bow waves and hauled off to port—only to sight the *Ralph Talbot* five miles on his flagship's port bow. Since there had been no reaction from the *Blue*—which had neither sighted the Japanese squadron nor detected it by radar (the *Ralph Talbot* did no better)—Mikawa resumed his previous course and increased speed so that by 0130 he was heading through the seven mile wide channel between Savo and Guadalcanal.

Four minutes later the Japanese ships sighted the destroyer *Jarvis* limping at eight knots towards Sydney for repairs to damage inflicted during the previous day's air attacks and, because they were not seen by her, again held their fire. However, Mikawa detached the destroyer *Yunagi* to ensure that neither she nor other Allied destroyers should disrupt his plans. By this time those on the bridge of the *Chokai* could see through their powerful night glasses two much larger targets, the *Canberra* and *Chicago,* at a range of 18,000 yards. And at 0138 the first Japanese torpedoes headed for these two cruisers. Not for another five minutes did the *Patterson, Bagley* and *Canberra* sight the Japanese ships dead ahead and so jam the ether with the warning, 'strange ships entering harbour', that no Allied vessel received it.

Both US destroyers turned to fire torpedoes but, having been taken by surprise, only the *Bagley* managed to launch four of hers, albeit after she had swung past the firing course. Simultaneously Mikawa's aircraft dropped their flares on Turner's transports, which silhouetted the *Canberra* and *Chicago* whilst the Japanese cruisers remained nearly invisible against the dark shape of Savo Island. Half the *Canberra*'s crew were tumbling out of their hammocks and hurrying to their action stations in

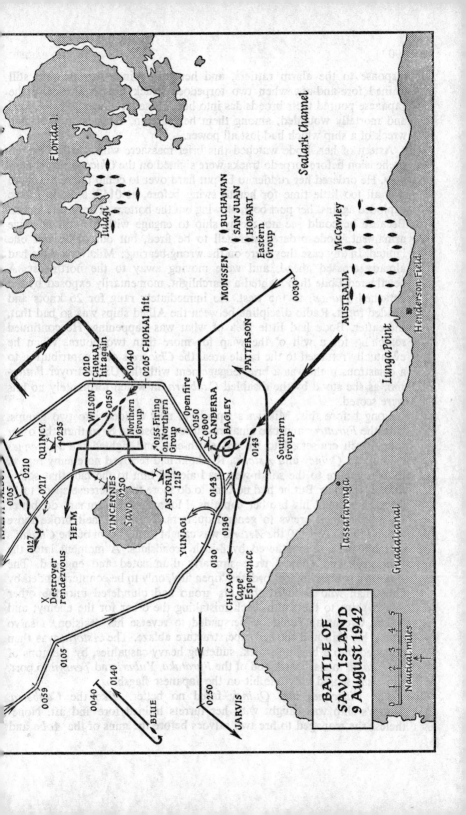

BATTLE OF
SAVO ISLAND
9 August 1942

Nautical miles
1 2 3 4 5

response to the alarm rattlers, and her four 8-inch turrets were still trained fore-and-aft, when two torpedoes struck her forward and the Japanese poured their broadsides into her. These left a shambles of dead and mortally wounded, among them her captain, Getting, in a blazing wreck of a ship which had lost all power.

Astern of her, Bode watched this brief massacre with startled incomprehension before torpedo tracks were sighted on the *Chicago*'s starboard bow. He ordered her rudder to be put hard over to comb them, but there was all too little time for her to swing before, at 0147, a Long Lance exploded against her port bow, blowing out the bottom of her cable locker. Because he could see no enemy ship to engage with his still effective armament, Bode ordered starshell to be fired, but out of 16 not one ignited. In any case they were on the wrong bearing: Mikawa's ships had already crossed ahead, and were moving away to the north-east. A bewildered Bode then sighted a searchlight, momentarily exposed by the detached *Yunagi*, to the west. He immediately rang for 26 knots and headed for it. Radio discipline between the Allied ships was so bad that, thereafter, Bode had little idea of what was happening. He continued searching for a will o' the wisp for more than two hours. When he eventually returned to the battle area, the *Chicago*'s only contribution to a disastrous night was a brief engagement with the US destroyer *Patterson*, as she stood by the disabled *Canberra*, in which fortunately no hits were scored.

Long before this, Mikawa's squadron, now divided into two groups, with the *Furataka* and two smaller cruisers closer to Savo than the other four 8-inch cruisers, had steered north-east and sighted the *Vincennes* leading the *Quincy* and *Astoria*. Riefkohl had received no enemy report, though gunfire to the south-west had alerted him to the fact that something was amiss. But he had no time to do more than increase speed to 15 knots, nor could his brother captains, Moore and Greenman, do better than order their crews to general quarters, before all hell broke loose around them. At 0150 the *Astoria* was caught in the beam of the *Chokai*'s searchlights, and smothered by 8-inch broadsides. A moment later the *Vincennes* and *Quincy* were similarly illuminated and engaged. The *Astoria*'s gunnery officer ordered 'open fire', only to be countermanded by Greenman who believed that his group had blundered into the other Allied ships to the south, each mistaking the other for the enemy; and before Greenman could be persuaded to reverse his decision, a salvo struck his ship and set her superstructure ablaze. The *Astoria* was then pounded into a blazing wreck, suffering heavy casualties, by the guns of the *Chokai* to starboard, and of the *Furataka*, *Yubari* and *Tenryu* to port, while she scored only one hit on the Japanese flagship.

The *Vincennes* and *Quincy* fared no better. Like the *Canberra*, Moore's ship was caught with her turrets trained fore and aft. Nonetheless she managed to fire two salvoes before the guns of the *Aoba* and of the *Furataka* group destroyed one of them and reduced her bridge structure to a shambles. A torpedo then struck abreast her port engine room, so that at 0235 she capsized and sank taking Moore and many of his crew with her. Riefkohl's ship likewise managed to fire two salvoes, of which one damaged the *Kinugasa,* before she, too, was staggering under the blows of Japanese broadsides. As shell after shell struck her, a torpedo exploded against the port side of her hull and completed the devastation. When the enemy ceased fire at 0215 the *Vincennes* was another burning wreck, whose crew tried vainly to fight the flames before, at 0300, she capsized and took many of them down with her.

These Allied ships were not, however, lost to no purpose. In the confusion and turmoil of a battle which lasted for less than an hour, Mikawa's squadron lost cohesion. The Japanese admiral found himself unable to lead it towards Turner's transports. In order to regain control he headed the *Chokai* northward and ordered his ships to withdraw with her. In so doing the *Furataka, Yubari* and *Tenryu* came across the *Ralph Talbot* to which they did much damage before she was hidden by a rain squall. By the time Mikawa had gathered his squadron together he decided that he was not justified in returning to attack Turner's transports when he might well be subjected to heavy air attacks by Fletcher's carrier-borne planes soon after daylight. He continued back up the Slot at high speed for Rabaul. He did not, however, reach this base without incident: his course took him through the area in which the US submarine *S44* was patrolling, allowing Lieutenant-Commander J. R. Moore to sink the *Kako* with four torpedoes.

Not until 0250, when Bode brought the *Chicago* back from her wild goose chase, did Crutchley learn that she had been torpedoed and that the *Canberra* was a burning wreck. But although he immediately ordered his seven destroyers to concentrate on the *Australia,* his signal was misinterpreted to mean proceed to a rendezvous five miles to the north of Savo, where they could do nothing. Nor was it until daylight on 9 August that the Allies learned the full extent of the disaster they had suffered; that the *Vincennes* and *Quincy* had been sunk; that the *Astoria* and *Canberra* were burning hulks. Turner ordered the last named to be sunk at 0630, but since she proved so stoutly built that it required some 300 shells and five torpedoes from the destroyers *Selfridge* and *Ellet* to send her to the bottom, many Australians believe that she was needlessly sacrificed, more especially since Greenman was allowed to continue trying to save the *Astoria* until she suffered a magazine explosion around noon, and then capsized and sank. (By way of appeasing Australia the USA subsequently named a new cruiser *Canberra,* and Britain gave her the 8-inch cruiser *Shropshire.*)

The disasters of the night put paid to Turner's decision to withdraw his transports soon after dawn: there were too many survivors, many of them wounded, to be succoured. While unloading continued throughout 9

August fortune favoured them: Tanaka's planes were more concerned to find and strike at Fletcher's carriers. Not surprisingly they failed because TF 61 was already far to the south of Guadalcanal. Their only victim was the hapless *Jarvis* which was sunk with all hands.

Turner finally withdrew his transports to Noumea at dusk on the 9th, escorted by the *Australia, Chicago, Hobart* and *San Juan*. They left behind them some 18,000 US Marines, short of food and of all the munitions of war with which to face a precarious future on the islands of Tulagi and Guadalcanal, more especially the latter on which the small Japanese garrison remained concealed in the hills.

The story of this Allied disaster may be rounded off with these telling statistics:

TABLE 42: Battle of Savo Island: Statistics

	Allied Force		*Japanese Force*	
Rounds fired	107 8-inch		1,020 8-inch	
	385 5-inch		176 5·5-inch	
			592 4·7-inch	
Torpedoes fired	8		61	
Ships sunk	Four 8-inch cruisers (*Canberra, Astoria, Quincy, Vincennes*) [One destroyer (*Jarvis*)]		[One 8-inch cruiser (*Kako*)]	
Ships damaged	Two destroyers (*Ralph Talbot, Patterson*)			
Killed	*Canberra*	85	*Chokai*	34
	Chicago	2	*Kinugasa*	1
	Astoria	216	[*Kako*	34]
	Quincy	370		
	Vincennes	332		
	Ralph Talbot	11		
	Patterson	8		
	[*Jarvis*	247]		
Wounded	*Canberra*	55	*Chokai*	48
	Chicago	21	*Kinugasa*	1
	Astoria	186	*Tenryu*	2
	Quincy	166	[*Kako*	48]
	Vincennes	258		
	Ralph Talbot	11		
	Patterson	11		

The victor did not return in triumph: Mikawa was justly criticized by Yamamoto for withdrawing after the night action instead of going on to decimate the anchored transports. A bolder decision would not have greatly increased the risk which he had accepted when he made his plans, of being attacked by Fletcher's planes during the following daylight hours; a risk which, with TF 61's withdrawal, ceased to exist.

The Allies learned many more lessons, some as old as war. To the shortcomings of Crutchley's force and his errors of judgement, to Bode's curious absence from the battle, and Fletcher's pusillanimous handling of TF 61 (when Nimitz wrote: 'The simultaneous departure of all the carriers was most unfortunate', Fletcher replied: 'The decision to withdraw was believed sound in view of the presence of 40 enemy planes equipped with torpedoes'), the exhaustive enquiry conducted by Admiral Arthur Hepburn added others after an honest Crutchley had written:

> The fact must be faced that we had adequate forces placed with the very purpose of repelling surface attack, and when that was made it destroyed our force. The transports were defended, but the cost was terrific, and I feel that it should have been the enemy who should have paid, even though at night the odds are in favour of the attacker.

The Allied flag and commanding officers were more exhausted than the Japanese by the debilitating climate, and were in no way 'battle-minded'. They had, for example, too readily believed that the Japanese cruisers' floatplanes were friendly. There was excessive confidence in air reconnaissance: as scouting cruisers could not in the past be sure to report an approaching enemy, one could not now be certain of aircraft or radar. Communications were inadequate: not all the radio equipment in the Australian cruisers was compatible with that in the US ships. Like the Royal Navy the former depended on strictly disciplined morse for manoeuvring and enemy reports: the latter had adopted TBS (voice) whose greater speed and clarity was nullified by ill-disciplined chatter. And both Turner and Crutchley made their plans on the basis of what they thought the Japanese *would* do, instead of what they *could* do: on the assumption that Mikawa's ships *would* not attack until daylight on 8 August, when they *could* attack during the preceding hours of darkness.

Four men paid the price for this disaster. Early in September, albeit after he had nearly lost the *Saratoga* to a torpedo from the Japanese U-boat *126* on 31 August, Fletcher was relieved and, to quote the caustic words of the US official historian, 'during the rest of the war received commands more commensurate with his abilities'[1]—of the remote North Pacific Ocean Area.[2] In October Nimitz ordered Ghormly's relief by Halsey; it is well that he did so on the grounds of failing health with the consequence that he lacked the offensive spirit, because it is difficult to fault him over Savo, except perhaps for approving Turner's premature withdrawal. Riefkohl, who suffered the delusion that his three cruisers had saved the transports from annihilation and that he was therefore responsible for an American victory, was not given another sea command. Bode, who had previously suffered the shock of losing the battleship *Oklahoma* during a night whilst he was on shore leave at Pearl Harbour, was so conscience-striken by his inglorious part that he committed suicide.

The two flag officers who set the stage for this disaster were more fortunate. In the vital interests of Allied unity, the usually anglophobic

King overrode his Chief of Staff's criticisms—notably: 'the fallacy of dividing defending forces is as old as war'—and endorsed Ghormley's report with these words before sending it on to Pound: 'I deem it appropriate and necessary to record my approval of the decisions and conduct of Rear-Admiral R. K. Turner, USN, and Rear-Admiral V. Crutchley, RN. In my judgement these two officers were in no way inefficient, much less at fault, in executing their parts of the operation'. Turner went on to command other amphibious forces with undoubted success. Crutchley continued to lead the Australian Squadron for the normal term, and to command for as long the small British contribution to the war in the Pacific—until the Royal Navy was able to deploy, in 1944, a sizeable force of battleships and aircraft-carriers to work with the US Pacific Fleet.

Six months elapsed before the US Marines finally over-ran the island of Guadalcanal; six months of bitter fighting through stinking swamp and humid jungle during which air power, sometimes from aircraft-carriers, at others from the all-important Henderson Field, gave the Americans control over these narrow waters by day, and sea power enabled the Japanese to control them by night, so that both sides were able to supply and reinforce their men on the island. These involved numerous high speed, hair-raising runs by ships of both sides up and down the Slot—and more naval battles than in any previous campaign of comparable length in history, except for the Anglo-Dutch wars of the seventeenth century. They cost the USA two carriers, nine cruisers and 18 destroyers as well as various transports and auxiliary craft, while the Japanese lost two capital ships, two carriers, eight cruisers, 37 destroyers and many smaller vessels. But the space available in this selective work will not allow more than one of these actions to be described in detail. The rest must be briefly outlined in order to bridge the gap between the disaster of Savo Island and the battle named after the islands of Guadalcanal.

Shortly after Savo, Yamamoto moved the major part of his Combined Fleet down to Truk. Radio intelligence warned Ghormley that the Japanese intended to run a 'Tokyo Express'—a convoy of destroyers and fast transports—carrying 1,500 reinforcements, under Rear-Admiral Raizo Tanaka, to Guadalcanal. This was to be covered by Nagumo's three carriers, *Ryujo, Shokaku* and *Zuikaku,* supported by the battleship *Mutsu,* the battlecruisers *Hiei* and *Kirishima,* and ten cruisers under Admiral Kondo. Fletcher was ordered out of Noumea with the carriers *Saratoga, Enterprise* and *Wasp,* the fast battleship *North Carolina* and nine cruisers to intercept this convoy and its covering force. But before he could do so he was misled by faulty intelligence into detaching the *Wasp* and three cruisers to refuel. They were, therefore, absent on the morning of 24 August when planes from the *Saratoga* and *Enterprise* found and quickly sank the *Ryujo,* but not the other Japanese carriers. And also when planes from the *Shokaku* and *Zuikaku* struck back that afternoon, seriously damaging the *Enterprise*. This 50 per cent reduction in the operational strength of Fletcher's carrier force, and the failure of his planes to find the two large Japanese carriers, impelled him to withdraw —which allowed Tanaka to land his troops on Guadalcanal, albeit at the cost of his flagship, the small cruiser *Jintsu,* sunk by planes from Henderson Field.

This indecisive battle of the Eastern Solomons was followed on 31 August by an attack on the *Saratoga* by the Japanese submarine *I26*. Commander Yokota's torpedoes put her out of action for the next three months. A fortnight later, on 15 September, Commander Narahara fired a salvo of six torpedoes from the *I19* at a force covering US transports. Three sank the *Wasp*: the others missed the *Hornet* but damaged the *North Carolina,* and the destroyer *O'Brien* which subsequently sank.

There followed the battle of Cape Esperance. Turner's two transports and eight destroyers, all carrying reinforcements for Guadalcanal, were covered by three groups, one under Rear-Admiral G. D. Murray headed by the *Hornet* and four cruisers, a second under Rear-Admiral Willis Lee, headed by the new fast battleship *Washington* and two cruisers, and the third under Scott with the 8-inch cruisers *San Francisco* and *Salt Lake City* and the 6-inch cruisers *Boise* and *Helena,* plus five destroyers. On the afternoon of 11 October a US shore-based search plane reported the 8-inch cruisers *Aoba,* flying Goto's flag, *Furataka* and *Kinugasa,* with two destroyers, heading for Guadalcanal. They were covering Rear-Admiral Joshima's 'Tokyo Express' of two seaplane carriers and six destroyers, likewise taking supplies and reinforcements to the island.

Speeding to intercept Goto to the west of Savo Island, Scott achieved complete surprise when, shortly before midnight, he opened fire on the *Aoba* at 4,800 yards. In a brisk gun action that lasted for little more than half-an-hour, in which Goto was killed and in which the Japanese ships had no chance to fire their torpedoes, the *Furataka* and the destroyer *Fubuki* were sunk, and the *Aoba* badly damaged. Since on the US side only the destroyer *Duncan* was mortally wounded (by American gunfire), and the *Boise* and the destroyer *Farenholt* damaged, Scott was clearly the victor. He was, however, unable to prevent Joshima achieving his purpose during that night, albeit for the loss of two destroyers to air attack, any more than Goto's force, having been put to flight, could stop Turner effecting his on 13 October.

It was immediately after this battle that Halsey succeeded Ghormley in command of the South-West Pacific Area, and Thomas Kinkaid replaced Fletcher in the US carrier force which now comprised the *Hornet* and the hastily repaired *Enterprise*.

In mid-October Yamamoto ordered the greater part of his Combined Fleet to cover and support a major land attack designed to seize Henderson Field, which was begun on 22 October. When this air strip was prematurely reported to have been captured from its stout-hearted US Marine defenders, the Japanese ships moved southwards. Kondo led the Advance Force headed by the battlecruisers *Haruna* and *Kongo,* the carrier *Junyo,* and four 8-inch cruisers. Nagumo led the Striking Force headed by the carriers *Shokaku, Zuikaku* and *Zuiho,* and the 8-inch cruiser *Kumano.* Rear-Admiral Abe led the Vanguard Force, headed by the battlecruisers *Hiei* and *Kirishima* and three 8-inch cruisers. To these, on 21, 23 and 24 October, Japanese shore-based search planes repeatedly reported Lee's TF 64, headed by the fast battleship *Washington* and three 8-inch cruisers, which was one part of the fleet which Nimitz and Halsey had ordered out of Noumea to frustrate the Japanese move. But they failed to locate Kincaid's TF 61, headed by the carrier *Enterprise,* the new fast battleship *South Dakota* and two cruisers, or Murray's TF 18, headed by the carrier *Hornet* and four cruisers, as they steered to meet the Japanese Vanguard Force after it was reported by shore-based planes on 23 October. Not until the 26th did a catapult plane from the cruiser *Tone* sight the two US carriers. A strike of 138 planes was then launched against them by all four Japanese carriers. Almost half of these were shot down by US fighters, but the rest scored several bomb hits and three damaging torpedo hits on the *Hornet*; also three bomb hits on the *Enterprise* which did no significant damage. The 8-inch cruiser *Portland* was lucky to survive three torpedo hits : all failed to detonate.

Meantime 16 dive bombers on an armed reconnaissance from the *Enterprise* had sighted Abe's and Nagumo's groups. These obtained two damaging hits on the *Zuiho* which put her flight deck out of action just as, on receipt of their radio reports, the *Enterprise* and *Hornet* launched a strike of 73 planes. These, which suffered fewer losses to Japanese fighters and AA fire, obtained three bomb hits on the *Shokaku,* that put her out of action for the next five months, and five on the 8-inch cruiser *Chikuma.* But when, towards evening, Abe and Kondo were reported to be heading towards the stricken American carriers, Kinkaid ordered Murray to abandon his attempt to have the *Hornet* towed to safety by the 8-inch cruiser *Northampton,* and to leave her to be sunk by Japanese destroyers (after US destroyers had failed to do so), and to retire the rest of his battle-scarred force to the south-eastwards. Fortunately Abe and Kondo failed to press their pursuit whereby they missed a golden opportunity to destroy the 'Big E' (for *Enterprise*).

Although this action, known as the battle of Santa Cruz, was a tactical victory for the Japanese, they were unable to exploit it because the US Marines remained in possession of Henderson Field. Having lost more than 100 planes as well as suffering damage, Nagumo's large carriers lacked the force to eliminate them : they were, moreover, short of fuel. So they returned to Truk.

The next battle, named after Guadalcanal Island, is the one chosen for a more exhaustive account because one phase of it has the special interest of being among the last naval actions to be fought between 'ships-of-the-line' mounting 'great guns'. In mid-November both sides launched operations to land reinforcements on the island; Yamamoto planned to oust the tenacious US Marines from Henderson Field: Halsey intended to foil this.

Turner's TG 67.1, the transport *McCawley* (flag) and three others carrying 6,000 men, escorted by the 8-inch cruisers *Pensacola* and *Portland,* left Noumea on 8 November. They were followed 24 hours later by Scott's TG 62·4 of three transports carrying 1,500 men, escorted by his flagship, the 5-inch cruiser *Atlanta.* Rear-Admiral Daniel Callaghan's TG 67·4, headed by his flagship, the 8-inch cruiser *San Francisco,* the 6-inch *Helena* and the 5-inch *Juneau,* sailed from Espiritu Santo to cover both transport groups. These joined Turner on the night of 11 November, when Kincaid's covering TF 16 left Noumea, headed by the latter's flagship, the carrier *Enterprise* (whose forward lift was still under repair, which restricted her ability to operate aircraft), the 8-inch cruiser *Northampton* and the 5-inch *San Diego,* supported by Lee's TF 64, which comprised his flagship the fast battleship *South Dakota* and her sistership, the *Washington.*

Twenty-four hours after Turner sailed, Kondo left Truk with the Japanese Second Fleet; the battlecruisers *Kongo* and *Haruna,* the carriers *Junyo* and *Hiyo,* the 8-inch cruisers *Atago, Takao* and *Tone,* and the 5·5-inch *Sendai.* From a position north-east of the Solomons these ships were to cover Abe's two battlecruisers, the *Hiei* (flag) and *Kirishima,* screened by the 5·5-inch cruiser *Nagara* and 14 destroyers, when they bombarded Henderson Field very early on 13 November—and Rear-Admiral Nishimura's 8-inch cruisers *Maya* and *Suzuya,* screened by the 5·5-inch cruiser *Tenryu* and four destroyers when they repeated the shelling early next morning. Both these groups were supported by Mikawa with the 8-inch cruisers *Chokai* and *Kinugasa* and the 5·5-inch *Isuzu.* The bombardments were designed to allow Tanaka to run in yet another 'Tokyo Express', this time of 11 transports carrying an infantry division, with a screen of 11 destroyers.

The US transports arrived first. Early on 11 November, Scott's TG 62·4 anchored off Lunga Point and began disembarkation. This was successfully completed under air cover provided from Henderson Field, except for an attack by planes from the *Hiyo,* which damaged one transport while the Eleventh Air Fleet, based on Rabaul, was bombing Henderson Field, after which TG 62·4 steamed away to the south-east. Next morning Turner's TG 67·1 arrived and began disembarkation while Callaghan's TG 67·4 also anchored off Lunga Point. Likewise provided with an air umbrella from Henderson Field, because the *Enterprise* had not yet arrived within fighter range, a Japanese air attack during the afternoon did no more than damage the *San Francisco* and the destroyer *Buchanan*.

Air reconnaissance then reported the approaching Japanese forces. On the reasonable supposition that they boded ill for his ships, Turner broke off disembarkation and withdrew to the south-east. Callaghan took the bold decision to intercept Abe's force, although it was stronger than his own, because Lee's battleships were as yet too far away to intervene: he had to do his best to frustrate the Japanese plan with the ships that he had.

TABLE 43: Ships Involved in the Battle of Guadalcanal on 12–13 November 1942

Ship	Type	Displacement (tons)	Speed (knots)	Guns	Torpedoes	Remarks
Cushing	Destroyer	1,465	36	5 5in	12 21in	Sunk
Laffey	Destroyer	1,620	37	4 5in	5 21in	Sunk
Sterrett	Destroyer	1,500	36	4 5in	16 21in	Damaged
O'Bannon	Destroyer	2,050	37	5 5in	10 21in	
Atlanta	Cruiser	6,000	32	16 5in	8 21in	Sunk
San Francisco	Cruiser	9,950	33	9 8in	—	Damaged
Portland	Cruiser	9,800	33	9 8in	—	Disabled
Helena	Cruiser	10,000	34	15 6in	—	
Juneau	Cruiser	6,000	32	16 5in	8 21in	Sunk
Aaron Ward	Destroyer	1,630	37	4 5in	5 21in	Disabled
Barton	Destroyer	1,630	37	4 5in	5 21in	Sunk
Monssen	Destroyer	1,630	37	5 5in	10 21in	Sunk
Fletcher	Destroyer	2,050	37	5 5in	10 21in	
Nagara	Cruiser	5,170	36	7 5in	8 24in	
Amatsukaze	Destroyer	2,033	35	6 5in	8 24in	
Asagumo	Destroyer	1,961	35	6 5in	8 24in	
Akatsuki	Destroyer	2,090	38	6 5in	9 24in	Sunk
Harusame	Destroyer	1,580	34	5 5in	8 24in	
Ikazuchi	Destroyer	2,090	38	6 5in	9 24in	
Inadzuma	Destroyer	2,090	38	6 5in	9 24in	
Murasame	Destroyer	1,580	34	5 5in	8 24in	
Sumidare	Destroyer	1,580	34	5 5in	8 24in	
Terutzuki	Destroyer	2,701	33	8 4in	4 24in	
Yudachi	Destroyer	1,580	34	5 5in	8 24in	Sunk
Yukikaze	Destroyer	2,033	35	6 5in	8 24in	
Hiei	Battlecruiser	31,720	30	8 14in 14 6in	—	
Kirishima	Battlecruiser	31,980	30	8 14in 14 6in	—	

Heading for the channel to the south of Savo, Callaghan formed his force into a long single line ahead, four destroyers leading his five cruisers, followed by four more destroyers, all in the order given in Table 43. It has been argued that he adopted this unwieldy formation to facilitate navigation in restricted waters; but it placed half his destroyers in a

position where they were unlikely to be able to use their torpedoes. Moreover, Abe had no difficulty in bringing his force through this channel in
the better formation of two battlecruisers in line ahead with the *Nagara*
and 12 destroyers forming an orthodox A/S screen, whence all could be
detached to carry out torpedo attacks. Nor was this Callaghan's only
error of judgement: he also failed to signal either an appreciation of the
situation or a battle plan to his captains who were left in the dark, both
figuratively and in the reality of a clouded tropical night, as to what to
expect and, if an enemy should be encountered, how they were to act.

When the *Helena* obtained the first radar contact of the approaching
Japanese ships at 0124, distant 15 miles, they were already in Ironbottom
Sound to the east of Savo. At 1030 Scott's flagship reported that she was
closing an enemy steering a reciprocal course at a combined speed of
more than 40 knots. Callaghan could have swung his force to starboard to
gain the tactical advantage of crossing the 'T'. Instead he held on until, at
0141, his leading destroyer, the *Cushing*, sighted the darkened shapes of
the Japanese destroyers *Yudachi* and *Murasame* only 1,500 yards ahead
and about to cross her bows. To avoid a collision Lieutenant-Commander
Parker swung his ship hard-a-port. This turn threw the rest of the
American line into such confusion that, for fear of hitting their own ships,
they withheld their fire. Abe's gunners thereby gained a benefit denied to
Crutchley's at the battle of Savo Island: they had nine minutes in which
to man all their guns and to change their immediately available ammunition from shells intended for shore bombardment to ones designed to be
used against ships. Nor was Callaghan helped by the US Navy's besetting
sin, ill-disciplined use of their voice radio. Not until 0150 did the first US
ship, the *Atlanta*, Captain S. P. Jenkins, open fire on a Japanese
destroyer's searchlight, when she was promptly overwhelmed by the 14-
inch guns of the two battlecruisers, which killed Scott and left her a
disabled wreck.

The action was thereafter a confused melée, aptly described by the US
Official Historian as

'an infernal spectacle. Greenish light from flashes and starshell dimmed
that of the silent stars. Red and white tracer shells arched and criss-
crossed overhead, magazines exploded in blinding bouquets of white
flame, oil-fed fires sent up twisted columns of yellow flame and black
smoke. Around the horizon smouldering hulks of abandoned ships now
glowed dull red, now blazed up when fires reached fresh combustibles.
Geysers from shells that missed their targets rose from the surface of
the sea, now fouled with oil and flotsam.'[8]

All this was accompanied by a fortissimo cacophony of ear-shattering
sound and, for the US ships, the constant raucous chatter of their TBS
circuit.

As a surprised Abe, who had not expected to meet any opposition, swung to port, intending to withdraw round Savo Island, Callaghan led his remaining cruisers between the two Japanese heavy ships, while his leading destroyers sought targets for their torpedoes. The *Hiei* sank the *Cushing* and damaged the *Laffey,* after the latter had killed the battlecruiser's captain with machine gun fire. The *Laffey* was sunk by a Japanese destroyer's torpedo. The *Sterrett* sank the *Yudachi* before she herself was put out of action. Under the concentrated fire of the American cruisers, against which her 8-inch armour belt afforded little protection, the *Hiei* was reduced to a burning wreck.

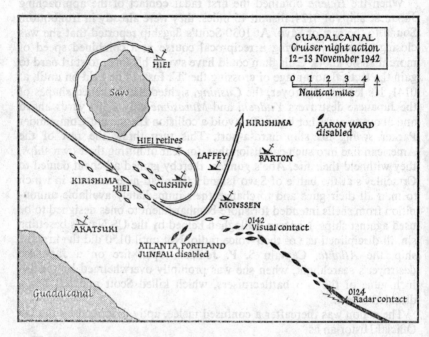

GUADALCANAL
Cruiser night action
12–13 November 1942

0 1 2 3 4
Nautical miles

The *Kirishima* was more fortunate. Informed that his flagship, the *San Francisco,* Captain C. Young, was firing at the disabled *Atlanta,* Callaghan misguidedly ordered his ships to cease fire. This allowed the *Kirishima* to overwhelm the *San Francisco* with her 14-inch guns, killing her admiral and her captain. The *Portland,* Captain L. DuBose, was hit by a torpedo which forced her out of the column. The *Juneau,* Captain Swenson, was put out of action by a Japanese torpedo which tore open her forward engine room (she sank next day), after the *Barton* had been sunk by two equally deadly Long Lances, and the *Monssen* had been reduced by 37 shell hits to a burning hulk which subsequently blew up and sank. Since the *Aaron Ward* was seriously disabled by gun fire, only the *Helena*'s guns were left to speed the enemy's flight.

At 0226 her captain, H. G. Hoover of the Helena, who was now senior officer, ordered all American ships to retire. The *San Francisco*, the *Juneau* and three destroyers were the only ones that could obey, and as they did so Swenson's cruiser was sent to the bottom by the Japanese U-boat *I26*, Commander Yokota. The *Atlanta* was subsequently found to be so badly disabled that she had to be scuttled. For these losses the Americans had their revenge. A small strike from the *Enterprise*, led by Lieutenant J. F. Sutherland, found the *Hiei* trying to limp home to the north of Savo, and with four torpedoes left her lying dead in the water. At 1800 she was so effectively hit by US heavy bombers from Espiritu Santo that she had to be abandoned by her crew and scuttled.

The losses in this first phase of the battle of Guadalcanal amounted to two US cruisers and four destroyers against one Japanese battlecruiser and two destroyers. These may be judged about equal, but there is no doubt who was the victor. Callaghan's decision to take the offensive against a superior force, although it cost him his life[4] and that of Scott, and though it was by no means faultlessly executed, was as successful as Harwood's decision to engage the *Graf Spee* off the River Plate. As the German pocket battleship's career was ended, so was Abe's mission foiled.

Mikawa and Nishimura were not daunted by Abe's defeat, for which, incidentally, he was relieved of his command and not again employed at sea. They did their best to retrieve the situation. Nishimura brought the *Maya* and *Suzuya* in past Savo Island to bombard Henderson Field from off Lunga Point early next morning, 14 November, while Mikawa, with the *Chokai* and *Kinugasa*, provided cover from the west. But neither met any opposition because there was now no US force in the area. Although Halsey had ordered Kinkaid to detach TF 64 during the previous afternoon, he was operating too far to the south of Guadalcanal—350 miles— for Lee's two battleships to reach the scene before Nishimura had completed his mission and, with Mikawa, was retiring to the north-west.

A half-hour bombardment by two 8-inch cruisers could not, however, do as much damage as Abe's 16 14-inch weapons might have done. Eighteen aircraft were destroyed and as many as 32 damaged, but Henderson Field could still be used. Soon after dawn US planes took off, and by 0700 they had located the retiring Japanese. An hour later 13 torpedo-bombers went in to the attack, holing and setting on fire the *Kinugasa* and damaging the smaller cruiser *Izuso*. The *Enterprise*, now only 200 miles to the south, also launched a strike of 17 torpedo-bombers, and their attack sent the *Kinugasa* to the bottom and damaged both the *Chokai* and the *Maya*.

In the meantime US reconnaissance planes had found an important target. Tanaka's heavily-laden transports were steaming down the Slot on their way to land an infantry division to seize Henderson Field, which they supposed to have been neutralized by bombardment, and in the mistaken belief that the 'Big E' was still undergoing action damage repair at Noumea. A fighter umbrella provided by the *Hiyo* and *Junyo* was unable to protect this convoy from attack, first by torpedo planes and dive-bombers from Henderson Field and from the *Enterprise,* and subsequently by heavy bombers from Espiritu Santo. By nightfall Tanaka had lost all but four of his transports, after the bulk of their troops had been taken off by their escorting destroyers, at a cost of only five American planes. With the remainder the Japanese admiral pressed on for his objective as darkness brought relief from air attack. Would he still be able to disembark his division during the coming night and seize Guadalcanal's vital airfield?

Kondo intended that he should. Since 1000 he had been bringing a powerful Emergency Bombardment Force down from the north. His flagship, the *Atago* led the *Takao* and the *Kirishima,* screened by the *Nagara,* flag of Rear-Admiral Hashimoto, the *Sendai,* flag of Rear-Admiral Kimura, and eight destroyers. But these were reported during the afternoon by the US submarine *Trout* after she had made an unsuccessful torpedo attack. And this was enough for Lee, who was then about 100 miles to the south of Guadalcanal, to head his two battleships, screened by four destroyers, at flank speed for the western end of the island, in a determined attempt to intercept.

TABLE 44: Ships Which Took Part in the Battle of Guadalcanal, 14–15 November 1942

Ship	Type	Displacement	Speed	Guns	Torpedoes	Notes
Walke	Destroyer	1,570	38	5 5in	8 21in	Sunk
Benham	Destroyer	1,500	36	4 5in	16 21in	Sunk
Preston	Destroyer	1,480	36	5 5in	12 21in	Sunk
Gwin	Destroyer	1,630	37	4 5in	5 21in	—
Washington	Battleship	35,000	28	9 16in 20 5in	—	—
South Dakota	Battleship	35,000	28	9 16in 20 5in	—	—
Sendai	Cruiser	5,195	35	7 5·5in	8 24in	—
Ayanami	Destroyer	2,090	34	6 5in	9 24in	Sunk
Uranami	Destroyer	2,090	34	6 5in	9 24in	—
Shikinami	Destroyer	2,090	34	6 5in	9 24in	—
Nagara	Cruiser	5,170	36	7 5·5in	8 24in	—
Terutsuki	Destroyer	2,701	33	8 4in	4 24in	—
Hatsutsuki	Destroyer	2,701	33	8 4in	4 24in	—
Shirayuki	Destroyer	2,090	34	6 5in	9 24in	—
Asagumo	Destroyer	1,961	35	6 5in	8 24in	—
Samidare	Destroyer	1,580	34	5 5in	8 24in	—
Atago	Cruiser	13,160	34	10 8in	16 24in	—
Takao	Cruiser	13,160	34	10 8in	16 24in	—
Kirishima	Battlecruiser	31,980	30	8 14in 14 6in	—	Sunk

Lee had the advantage of two of the latest, heavily armoured, fast battle-ships, fitted with radar, against a lightly armoured battlecruiser and two 8-inch cruisers, without it. The Japanese had a larger destroyer force equipped with Long Lance torpedoes. The *Washington* had been some months in commission (she had served with the British Home Fleet), but the *South Dakota* was a more recent addition to the US Fleet and her crew was as yet inexperienced. And the four American destroyers came from different divisions and had not previously worked together. (Whilst this was in part imposed by a shortage of destroyers, it was also due to a failure to realize the importance of such ships being trained and accustomed to working together. It needed the forceful arguments of such destroyer squadron commanders as 'Thirty-one knot' Arleigh Burke to reverse this trend, to significant effect, *e.g.* at the battle of Empress Augusta Bay on 2 November 1943. The British Navy had to learn the same lesson with their convoy escort and support groups.)

For these reasons Lee headed for Savo in single line ahead, the destroyers leading the battleships in the order given in Table 44. This was the easiest formation to handle and minimized the possibilities of mis-taken identity. He passed Savo from the west without sighting anything, and continued eastward into Ironbottom Sound shortly before 2200 to check that the Japanese had not already arrived off Lunga Point. He could not know that Rear-Admiral Hashimoto with the *Sendai* and three destroyers forming an advance screen ahead of Kondo's larger ships, which had the *Nagara* and six destroyers as a close screen, was only seven miles astern. Confusing land echoes had prevented Lee's radar detecting this enemy force.

The *Sendai* was the first to sight anything—Lee's ships faintly illumi-nated by a setting moon. Warning Kondo of the danger ahead, Hashimoto detached the *Ayanami* and *Uranami* to circle Savo whilst the *Sendai* and one destroyer shadowed from astern. Kondo responded by ordering the *Nagara* and four destroyers to join the *Ayanami* and *Uranami*, whilst his three large ships plus one destroyer held their course. The Japanese admirals were so confident of their ships' superiority at night fighting that they deliberately divided their ships into three separate forces, tactics which might have gained them a victory had it not been for the US radar.

At 2252, having found nothing off Lunga Point, Lee reversed course intending to return to the west by the channel to the south of Savo in search of an elusive enemy. This turn was no sooner completed than the *Washington*'s radar obtained a contact nine miles to the north-north-west. A few minutes later the shadowing *Sendai* and her accompanying destroyer were sighted at a range of 14,000 yards. In both American battleships, the *Washington*, Captain G. B. Davis, and the *South Dakota*, Captain T. L. Gatch, the triple 16-inch gun turrets swivelled silently round. Inside the armoured gun houses massive machinery slid silkily to thrust huge shells and their cordite charges into the breeches. The breech blocks closed. The long, dully gleaming gun barrels rose, checked and steadied following the movements of director sights. 'Gun-ready' lamps flicked on. At 2316 Lee gave the order: 'Commence firing when ready'. With a blinding flash and a head-splitting concussion the great guns opened fire.[5]

The *Nagara* and her escort immediately made smoke and swung sharply away—but turned back down the eastern side of Savo as soon as Lee's heavy ships lost their target.

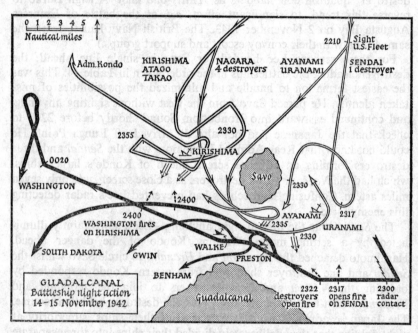

At 2322, the *Walke*, at the head of Lee's line, sighted the *Ayanami* and *Uranami* re-entering Ironbottom Sound after circling Savo. There followed a fierce gun duel between the three leading US destroyers and these two Japanese vessels. Simultaneously the *Gwin* engaged the *Nagara* which, with four destroyers, was following the *Uranami*. She was supported by the *Washington*'s secondary armament under radar control. But the *South Dakota* suffered a power failure which put her radar out of action so that she was unable to find a target at which to aim. There was no doubting the victor in this confused eight minute engagement. Japanese gunfire crippled the *Walke*, severely damaged the *Gwin* and sank the *Preston*. Conversely, only the *Ayanami* was seriously damaged. Minutes later the Long Lances took their toll: the *Walke* was sunk and the *Benham*'s bow was blown off.

Kondo's three heavy ships remained clear to the west of Savo, intending to head for Lunga Point as soon as his light cruisers and destroyers had dealt with the opposition, until at 2355 the Japanese admiral learned that the American force included battleships. With the rashness of excessive confidence he immediately headed for the fight. Blinded by her radar breakdown, the *South Dakota* had steered out of Lee's line and lost touch with the rest of his force. Alone she ran into Hashimoto's ships as they were retiring westward, and would have been sunk by some at least of the 34 torpedoes that were launched at her, but for the miracle that none scored a hit. Mere minutes later she was brilliantly illuminated by Japanese searchlights, and 14-inch shells from the *Kirishima* and 8-inch from the *Atago* and *Takao* crashed into her. Because she could reply only by aiming her 16-inch at the enemy's searchlights, she might well have suffered more than the damage which 42 hits caused to her superstructure. Fortunately the *Washington* came to her aid. Using her radar to full effect, first to plot the enemy and then to aim her main and secondary armaments, Lee's flagship opened fire at a range of 8,400 yards; and in seven minutes nine 16-inch and some 40 5-inch shells reduced the *Kirishima* to a blazing wreck.

Captain Gatch took the burning *South Dakota* away to the west, followed by the damaged *Gwin* and *Benham*, leaving Lee with only the *Washington* to deal with two 8-inch and two smaller cruisers, accompanied by eight undamaged destroyers. Boldly he steered north-west between the enemy and his crippled vessels. But Kondo had had enough; accepting that he could not carry out his planned bombardment, he ordered his force to retire at high speed. This decided Lee to regain contact with the *South Dakota*. His sharp alteration was a lucky one: by it the *Washington* just missed torpedoes fired by two of Tanaka's destroyers.

And the score? Lee had lost three destroyers, while the *South Dakota*, in addition to suffering 100 casualties, had a turret out of action and had to be sent back to the USA for action damage repairs which kept her out of the war for several months. But Kondo had lost a battlecruiser, the *Kirishima*, which had to be scuttled—his second in 48 hours—and one destroyer.

Much more important, however, than these losses and damage was Kondo's decision to call off his bombardment. This left Tanaka's four remaining transports to meet a bloody fate. Arriving at first light off Tassafaronga, where they were run ashore to speed disembarkation, they were attacked again and again by US planes from Henderson Field. All were set on fire and destroyed after they had reinforced Guadalcanal's Japanese garrison with only 2,000 men, instead of the planned 11,000, and supplied it with only a very small quantity of food and ammunition. In sum, the whole Japanese operation to land massive reinforcements and supplies on the island was a disastrous failure, frustrated by the courage and initiative of Admirals Callaghan, Scott and Lee and the officers and men of their battleships, cruisers and destroyers, and by the intrepid skill with which a small handful of American aircrew, chiefly of the US Marine Corps from Henderson Field, attacked the enemy again and again. Taken as a whole the battle of Guadalcanal was a decisive US victory—one which was to decide the fate of the island.

The campaign had, however, another two months to run, and in that time two more naval battles were fought. After the action which has just been described, the pragmatic Yamamoto wanted to abandon the place. But Prime Minister Hidaki Tojo, having switched his principal objective in the South Pacific from New Guinea to the Solomons, refused to do so. Nonetheless, the Japanese made no further attempt to send in major reinforcements: they were content with running 'Tokyo Expresses' on a scale sufficient to sustain their force already on the island.

To combat these Halsey ordered Kinkaid to organize and train a special striking force, based on Espiritu Santo, comprised of the 8-inch cruisers *Minneapolis, Pensacola, New Orleans* and *Northampton*, the 6-inch *Honolulu* and several destroyers. Kinkaid had, however, little time to do this before Nimitz recalled him for duty elsewhere, and sent Rear-Admiral Carleton Wright to relieve him. And only two days after hoisting his flag, Wright was required to sail against the redoubtable Tanaka.

The Japanese admiral planned a high speed run in to Tassafaronga with six destroyers crammed with troops. On the basis of radio intelligence Wright was ordered to intercept. Coming in from the east on 30 November, his leading destroyer's radar detected the enemy steaming along the northern shore of Guadalcanal at 2316. Wright hesitated for four vital minutes before ordering his destroyers to fire torpedoes. By the time these were launched at 2321, the Japanese ships had passed on an opposite course and were beyond their range. Before this, Wright's order to open fire gave away his column's presence to Tanaka, whose ships promptly launched 20 Long Lance torpedoes. These not only sank the *Northampton* but severely damaged the *Minneapolis, New Orleans* and *Pensacola*. Only the *Honolulu* escaped, whereas Tanaka lost just one destroyer, the *Takanami*, to US gunfire.

By the ingenuity of their crews, the three stricken cruisers were brought safely back to base for repairs. This battle of Tassafaronga was, nonetheless, 'a sharp defeat inflicted on an alert and superior cruiser force by a surprised and inferior destroyer force whose decks were cluttered with freight'[6]—one which is very much to the credit of the Imperial Japanese Navy, and very little to that of the United States Navy.

The 1st Marine Division, which had fought almost incessantly to hold

Guadalcanal for all of 17 weeks, was then relieved by the 2nd, when Vandegrift was succeeded by Major-General Alexander Patch of the US Army. One month later, on 4 January, Tojo accepted the inevitable, that he must abandon Guadalcanal. The first Japanese troops were removed by 'Tokyo Expresses'. But by 23 January US search planes reported a build up of transports, freighters and destroyers in the neighbourhood of Rabaul, and of battleships and aircraft-carriers to the north of Guadalcanal. They were being assembled in readiness for the final evacuation, but Halsey, for once short of reliable radio intelligence, assumed that the Japanese were about to send in major reinforcements.

In the hopes of tempting Yamamoto's Fleet into another major battle he sent four loaded transports in to Lunga Point as bait. To cover them Rear-Admiral Robert Giffen was given the 8-inch cruisers *Wichita*, *Chicago* and *Louisville*, three smaller cruisers, eight destroyers and, for their first operation in the Pacific, two of the new escort carriers which had recently proved their worth during the US landings at Casablanca as a part of the Allied invasion of North Africa. But Yamamoto refused to be tempted: he sent instead, from a new airstrip which the Japanese had recently completed at Munda in the central Solomons, a strong force of torpedo bombers. These attacked Giffen's force at twilight on 29 January, when they lacked fighter cover because the two escort-carriers had been detached for another unimportant purpose.

Protected only by AA gunfire the *Chicago* was hit at 1945 and so badly damaged that she lost all power. To save her Giffen ordered his whole force to retire, with the *Louisville* taking the stricken ship in tow. Next day the cripple, the towing ship and six escorting destroyers were given fighter cover by the *Enterprise*. But this was not enough to protect a target making only 5–6 knots: at 1600 on 30 January, a few miles east of Rennell Island, nine Japanese planes put four torpedoes into the *Chicago*, which sank 20 minutes later.

The four US transports landed their reinforcements without hindrance; so did five more on 4 February. But by that time the Japanese were nearly gone. On the nights of 1–2, 4–5 and 5–6 February they removed as many as 11,000 men as skilfully and silently as the Allies evacuated Gallipoli in 1916. Patch had no idea it was happening until on 9 February his Marines failed to find a single Japanese on the island. To quote from his triumphant signal to Halsey: 'Tokyo Express no longer has terminus on Guadalcanal'.

Two thousand five hundred square miles of miasmic plain and savage jungle-covered mountains were in American hands after six months of toil and suffering which stopped the enemy in his many-taloned reach for the Antipodes and concluded the first part of an arduous climb to Rabaul. Guadalcanal should ever remain a proud name in American history, recalling desperate fights in the air, furious night naval battles, frantic work at supply or construction, savage fighting in a sodden jungle, nights broken by screaming bombs and the explosion of naval shells. The jagged cone of Savo Island, forever brooding over the once blood-thickened waters of Ironbottom Sound, stands as a perpetual monument to the men and ships who rolled back the enemy tide.[7]

That cone is also a reminder of a major lesson to be learned from the Guadalcanal campaign. The US Marines, the élite of America's ground forces, took all of six months to capture the island. During that time the US Navy had to fight more sea battles than the British Navy fought in all of World War One. And of those seven actions the US Navy was the victor in only two. Of the remainder one was indecisive. But in as many as four it was defeated, in two cases—Savo and Tassafaronga—disastrously so. Why?

There is one answer which no Navy should forget. The Japanese were an aggressive nation who entered the twentieth century imbued with the *Bushido* ('cult of the warriors') traditions of the Samurai. Backed by its experience in the Russo-Japanese War, and in the whole of World War One, the Imperial Japanese Navy produced highly trained, dedicated, *professional* fighting seamen. In sharp contrast America was a peaceloving democracy. The US Navy's recent war experience was limited to the Spanish-American conflict and the post-Jutland phase of World War One in which there were no surface ship actions. With a few notable exceptions, such as Alfred Mahan, William Sims and Ernest King, its senior officers were *amateurs,* both as seamen and as fighters.

Just as the professional almost always excels over the amateur in sport and in the arts, so in war. And the next chapter will show the consequence for Japan when the US Navy, learning from its experience during 1942, produced dedicated *professionals.* This one must make the point that however much any maritime nation believes in peace, its naval commanders must be trained as professional fighting seamen.

It must also make another. Until temporarily stunned by the devastating shock of the attack on Pearl Harbour, the US Navy did not take the Imperial Japanese Navy seriously. (The British Navy was as much at fault until it suffered the loss of the *Prince of Wales* and *Repulse*.) Americans just would not *believe,* despite much evidence to the contrary, that the Japanese were building such a powerful Fleet with, in particular, the largest carrier force and strongest naval air arm in the world; nor, and in some ways more important, that the Japanese *could* be more highly skilled fighting seamen and airmen than they were. For this the US Navy paid dear from 1941–43 (and so to a lesser extent did the British Navy[8]).

Because American readers of this book may consider it presumptuous for a British writer to criticize the shortcomings of the US Navy in this way, as against praising the achievements of the Japanese, the author is grateful to the distinguished American historian, Douglas H. Robinson, for permission to quote these comments as a pertinent footnote to this chapter:

> I fully endorse your praise for the Japanese Navy: if patriotism, self-sacrifice and valour were enough, they would have won the war in the Pacific. Of course they lacked the resources for a long war, particularly the industrial base; on the other hand, their leaders, with a contemptuous attitude towards the warmaking capacity of the United States, expected we would sue for peace after the early defeats. They excelled in their advanced and sophisticated designs of aircraft and ships. Their carrier force was superior to all others at the time of Pearl Harbour. The range and combat capability of their naval aircraft exceeded ours. The *Yamato* class will forever remain the ultimate example of battleship design. And their oxygen fuelled 24-inch torpedo was well-nigh decisive in several of the night actions fought during the Guadalcanal campaign.
>
> Your judgement of the US Navy is a harsh but just one. The Imperial Japanese Navy had prepared for war with us for twenty years, had hardened their personnel in harsh manoeuvres simulating wartime conditions as closely as possible, and had not hesitated to expend material to prove their advanced weapon designs. Many of our officers foresaw war with Japan from the early 1920s, but the US Navy had many preoccupations besides readiness for war with the Japanese. Nor could we train our personnel as rigorously as they did: there would have been a public outcry if we had suffered such losses in manoeuvres as they accepted. Above all we allowed ourselves to feel superior, and the myth that the Japanese were a race of unimaginative copyists was widely prevalent.

To this the author would add these words from a singularly prophetic thesis written by Admiral King when he was at the Naval War College back in 1932: 'It is traditional (and habitual) for us [the USA] to be inadequately prepared for war. This is the combined result of a number of factors. One is democracy which tends to make everyone believe he knows it all. Another is the glorification of our victories and the ignorance of our defeats and of their causes.'

The maritime nations of the Free World would do well to remember the defeats suffered by the US Navy in 1941–42—and 'the reasons why'.

NOTES

[1] Samuel Eliot Morison in *The Two-Ocean War*.
[2] Fletcher had held his command for too long for a man who added to the

strain of war the burden of concerning himself with a multiplicity of detail which he should have left to his subordinates. In other words he was an admiral who could not leave command of his flagship in the hands of his flag captain. Vandegrift's Marines on Guadalcanal were, not surprisingly, fiercely critical of his decision to withdraw TF 61 during the night of 8–9 August, leaving them without adequate air cover. But to be fair to Fletcher there were occasions in World War Two when British troops were as critical of the RAF for seemingly failing to provide them with air cover.

[3] Samuel Eliot Morison in *The Two-Ocean War*.

[4] Perhaps fortunately. There were, and still are, Americans who hold the view that, had he survived, he would have been court martialled for mishandling the battle.

[5] Donald Macintyre in *The Battle for the Pacific*.

[6] Samuel Eliot Morison in *The Two-Ocean War*.

[7] *Ibid.*

[8] For example, as late as 1 January 1941, the British Joint Planning Staff wrote, with blithe optimism: 'The Japanese have never fought against a first-class Power in the air and we have no reason to believe that their operations would be any more effective than those of the Italians [against Cunningham's fleet in the Mediterranean]'.

11   *The Philippines*

The USA followed up their prolonged, but in the end victorious, Guadal-canal campaign with further amphibious operations against other Solomon Islands. On 30 June 1943 American troops landed on New Georgia; on 15 August on Vella Lavella; on 1 November on Bougain-ville; and on 26 December on New Britain. Before the last of these operations the forces available to Nimitz and to General Douglas MacArthur, who was in overall command of the South-West Pacific with headquarters in Australia, had so far grown in strength (for example Nimitz had nearly 20 aircraft-carriers, not counting his small escort-carriers) while the Japanese had declined (they had lost more than 8,000 planes and a large number of trained pilots), that the Americans were able to vary their strategy.

To 'island hopping' towards New Guinea, where Rabaul was their prime objective, they added 'leap-frogging' *i.e.* by-passing some of the Japanese occupied islands. To speed their progress towards the Philip-pines, Nimitz began a drive across the central Pacific to the north of the Solomons whilst MacArthur continued to ferret the Japanese out of these southern islands. The occupied British Gilberts were assaulted on 20 November, the Marshalls which had been *de facto* Japanese territory since their capture from Germany in 1914, on 31 January 1944. Saipan and Guam in the Marianas, which had likewise been mandated to Japan by the 1919 Versailles Treaty, were scheduled for June.

Having captured the Marshalls, the USA's carrier-borne planes were able to give their occupied island of Truk such a pounding that Yamamoto's successor, Admiral Mineichi Koga, withdrew his fleet west to Palau. (Yamamoto had planned to pay a flying visit from Rabaul to Bougainville on 18 April 1943. Forewarned by radio intelligence, Marc Mitscher, now a vice-admiral, ordered 16 fighters from Henderson Field to intercept the two bombers carrying Japan's foremost naval strategist and his staff. Both were shot down in flames. Koga was as unfortunate: on 31 March 1944 his plane disappeared without trace when taking him to Davao in Mindanao where he was setting up shore headquarters.) His successor, the aggressive Admiral Soemu Toyoda, was determined to wipe out the US Pacific Fleet, despite the fact that the growing number of US submarines, handled far more effectively than the Japanese U-boats, took such a toll of his tankers that he was compelled to withdraw his Fleet first to Singapore and subsequently to Brunei and Tawi Tawi, where oil supplies from Sumatra and Borneo were more sure.

By the end of April 1944 Toyoda knew enough about likely American moves to begin preparations to frustrate them. Nagumo's successor, Vice-Admiral Jisaburo Ozawa, was ordered to concentrate the First Seagoing Fleet in the Sulu Archipelago (in the strait between Borneo and the Philippines). Force A comprised three carriers, with 207 planes embarked, of which one, the recently completed *Taiho*, flew Ozawa's flag, three cruisers and nine destroyers. Rear-Admiral Joshima's Force B likewise numbered three carriers, with 135 planes embarked, one battleship, one cruiser and 10 destroyers. The powerful Van Force, under Vice-Admiral Takao Kurita, included the only two 18-inch gun battleships in the world, two battlecruisers, three carriers, with 95 planes embarked, four cruisers and nine destroyers. These three groups were to be ready to fight 'a decisive battle at the first favourable opportunity', which would arise when 'at least one third of the enemy carrier units have been destroyed by our shore-based air forces and submarines'.

Nimitz entrusted the attacks on Saipan and Guam to Spruance's Fifth Fleet, as the great part of his available ships were collectively numbered for this operation. For the actual assault on Saipan, Turner, who was by now the US Navy's most experienced amphibious force commander, sailed from Hawaii, where his transports embarked 71,000 troops, in time to arrive at the advanced anchorage of Eniwetok (to the west of the Marshalls) on 8 June. TF 52 included a bombardment group of five battleships, all Pearl Harbour veterans, and, for protection against air attack, 12 escort carriers operating more than 300 planes. For the assault on Guam, Rear-Admiral Richard Connolly brought another task force, carrying 56,500 troops from Guadalcanal and Tulagi, north to Kwajalein (in the Marshalls), likewise arriving on 8 June.

Neutralizing Japan's considerable force of Marianas-based planes, and softening up the islands' defences, were entrusted to TF 58 whose commander, Mitscher, flew his flag in the carrier *Lexington* of the new 'Essex' class. Spruance was content with the old 8-inch cruiser *Indianapolis* as his flagship. With 15 carriers, with 656 planes embarked, 17 cruisers and 53 destroyers, TF 58 comprised four carrier groups, Rear-Admiral J. J. Clark's TG 58·1, Rear-Admiral A. E. Montgomery's TG 58·2, Rear-Admiral J. W. Reeves' TG 58·3 and Rear-Admiral W. K. Harrill's TG 58·4. Also included in these groups were seven battleships, four cruisers and 13 destroyers which would form TG 58·7 when an action with enemy surface ships appeared possible.

First on the Marianas scene were several hunter-killer groups. In the latter part of May these destroyed 17 out of 25 U-boats which Toyoda deployed in the area to decimate Spruance's fleet. No less than six of them were sunk in the course of 12 days by Lieutenant-Commander W. B. Pendleton in the hedgehog armed destroyer escort *England*. This success highlights both the US Navy's acquired skill at this form of warfare and the Japanese Navy's inability to put its U-boats to good use, in part due to their excessive size, in part to their commanders' inability to handle them effectively.

Next came TF 58. Trained to a pitch of efficiency undreamed of two years before, this began operations on 11 June. By the 13th air supremacy had been gained over Toyoda's First Air Fleet based on Saipan, Guam and Taipan. Before this, on the evening of the 12th, TGs 58·1 and 58·4 were detached 650 miles to the north to attack the Bonins, the nearest islands from which Toyoda could replace his losses in the air. After they had gone, Lee's TG 58·7 and Turner's older battleships pounded Saipan with heavy shells as a final preparation for D-day which was set for 15 June, with Guam to follow on the 18th.

Before this, however, US forces had invaded Biak Island (off the north-west coast of New Guinea). And at the beginning of June Toyoda was sufficiently confident that no American operation was likely to be launched in the central Pacific in the near future, to order Rear-Admiral Ugaki to take a part of Kurita's Van Force south, both to help Biak's defenders and in the hopes of luring ships of the US Pacific Fleet within range of their great guns. The *Yamato* and *Musashi* were, therefore, in the Moluccas on 11 June when Toyoda received news of Spruance's first attacks on the Marianas. For the moment he was content to leave their defence to his First Air Fleet which he expected to inflict serious damage on the US carriers, even though his U-boats failed to do so. Not until the 13th did he recall Ugaki's squadron; and not until he received reports that TF 52 had arrived off Saipan, and that American troops were landing on the island, did he signal Ozawa's ships, much as Togo had done before Tsushima (and Nelson before Trafalgar): 'The fate of the Empire rests on this one battle. Every man is expected to do his utmost.'

At 1835 on 15 June Ozawa's main body was sighted by the US sub-marine *Flying Fish*, Lieutenant-Commander Risser, heading east after it had emerged through the San Bernardino Strait (dividing the Philippines). And at 0745 next morning the *Seahorse*, Lieutenant-Commander Cutter, reported Ugaki's battleships coming north to join Kurita. Spruance promptly postponed the landing on Guam; then, after conferring with his principal commanders, decided that, since Ozawa's ships could not reach Saipan before the morning of the 19th, unloading should continue until the evening of the 17th. The assault force would then weigh and steam off to the eastward, less several of its cruisers and destroyers which were to join TF 58, which would stay to give battle with the Japanese.

TABLE 45: Ships Involved in the Battle of Philippine Sea, 19–21 June 1944

Force	Capital ships	Fleet carriers	Light fleet carriers	8-inch cruisers	Other cruisers	Destroyers
TF 58						
TG 58·1		Hornet, Yorktown	Belleau Wood, Bataan	Boston, Baltimore, Canberra	San Juan, Oakland	14
TG 58·2		Bunker Hill, Wasp	Monterey, Cabot		Santa Fe, Mobile, Biloxi, Reno	12
TG 58·3		Enterprise, Lexington	San Jacinto, Princeton	Indianapolis	Montpelier, Cleveland, Birmingham	13
TG 58·4		Essex	Langley, Cowpens		San Diego, Vincennes, Houston, Miami	14
TG 58·7	Washington, North Carolina			Wichita, Minneapolis		13

TG 58.7 (cont.)			
Iowa			
New Jersey			
South Dakota			
Alabama			
Indiana			

| | New Orleans | | 9 |
| | San Francisco | | 9 |

First Seagoing Fleet

Van Force

Yamato			
Musashi		Atago	
Haruna		Takao	
Kongo		Maya	
		Chokai	
		Myoko	9
		Haguro	Yahagi
	Chitose		10
	Chiyoda		
	Zuiho		

Force A

Taiho	7		
Shokaku	5		
Zuikaku		8	
		7	Mogami

Force B

Junyo	8	Nagato	
Hiyo	4	Ryuho	

Summary

USA	7	8		13	66
Japan	5	4	7	1	28

Total number of carrier-borne aircraft: USA 956; Japan 473

No two fleets so large as these had clashed since Jutland was fought nearly 30 years before. Ozawa's was the weaker in every category, but he had three advantages to compensate for this if he could exploit them. Since Spruance was covering the invasion of Saipan, he could be expected to fight in its vicinity where Ozawa would have the support of the First Air Fleet: Spruance could expect no such help. Secondly, Japanese carrier-borne planes had a longer range than US ones: Ozawa's could search out to 560 miles and attack at 300, in sharp contrast to Mitscher's which were limited to 350 and 225 respectively. Thirdly, the easterly trade wind gave Ozawa the lee gauge, so that he would be closing the enemy whilst operating aircraft. In short, Ozawa should be able to choose when and where he fought Spruance, without coming within range of the US carrier-borne planes. Against this, Ozawa suffered the disadvantage that his planes lacked protection for their pilots and had no self-sealing fuel tanks. Moreover, Japanese pilots were by this date inadequately trained and lacking in experience. To quote one of their instructors: 'The Navy was frantic for pilots. Men who could never have dreamed of getting near a plane before the war were thrown into battle. We were told to rush them through their training. It was a hopeless task.'

On the afternoon of 17 April Spruance issued this battle plan to Mitscher.

> Our air will first knock out enemy carriers, then will attack enemy battleships and cruisers to slow or disable them. Battle line will destroy enemy fleet either by fleet action if the enemy elects to fight, or by sinking slowed or crippled ships if enemy retreats. Action against the enemy must be pushed vigorously to ensure complete destruction of his fleet. I shall issue general directives when necessary and leave details to you and Lee.

Contrast this delegation to his two subordinates with Jellicoe's centralized control of his large battle fleet during World War One, one reason why Jutland was indecisive.[1]

On the same day Spruance received from the submarine *Cavalla*, Lieutenant-Commander H. J. Kossler, a further report of Ozawa's east-ward advance at 20 knots. But thereafter he was ill served by his search planes. He received no further news of the enemy until late on the 18th. That evening Ozawa broke radio silence to pass orders to Kurita. Pearl Harbour fixed this transmission and at 2200 informed Spruance that an unidentified enemy force was 350 miles to the west-south-west of his position. Because Spruance had turned east at nightfall, Mitscher urged him to reverse course so that he could launch a massive air strike at dawn. But Spruance was not to be turned from his purpose—'TF 58 must cover Saipan'—by intelligence whose accuracy he doubted and which might be a Japanese ruse to lure him into a trap. Throughout that night US shore-based search planes continued to seek the Japanese fleet. One found it by radar but was unable to clear a radio report. Not until after it had returned to its base was Spruance informed, at 0900, by which time the news was too late to be of use.

Ozawa was better served. A search by seven planes from his carriers during the afternoon of the 18th enabled him to plot the enemy's disposition. TGs 58·1, 58·3 and 58·2 were to the north-west of Guam in that order on a north-south line 12 miles apart. Fifteen miles to their west, ready to combat the Japanese Van Force, was Lee in the *Washington* leading his six other battleships, with their cruiser and destroyer screen. Twelve miles to his north, to give his ships fighter cover, was TG 58·4. Calculating that the two fleets were now some 400 miles apart, Ozawa decided to maintain this distance so that he might take advantage of his aircraft's greater range. To this end he ordered an alteration of course to the southward. But before this, at 1637, the Van Force carriers launched a strike of 67 planes which could have struck TF 58 around sunset. But to conform with Ozawa's orders to prepare for a massive air strike early next morning, they were recalled before they were detected by the US ships' radar.

During the night Ozawa disposed his forces so that they were in battle order when he altered course back to north-east at 0400. One hundred miles ahead was Kurita's Van Force with its three carriers stationed 12 miles apart, each with its own circular screen of capital ships, cruisers and destroyers. Forces A and B each had their carriers concentrated in the centre of a single circular screen.

The 19 June dawned fine and clear with the US carrier groups 110 miles south-west of Saipan. Having no news of Ozawa's fleet, Mitscher accepted Spruance's suggestion that he should launch an air strike against Guam. Starting at 0830 some 33 US planes accounted for more than that number of shore-based Japanese machines. An hour and a half later US radar detected an enemy strike 150 miles to the westwards. This gave Mitscher and Lee time enough to order their ships to general quarters, and for the former's carriers to fly off a large proportion of his 300 fighter planes.

Sixty-nine torpedo bombers with fighter escort had been launched by Kurita's carriers at 0830. They were intercepted at 1036 and prevented from going further east than Lee's well disposed battle line on which they scored just one hit, on the *South Dakota*, for the loss of as many as 42 of their number. Half-an-hour after this strike had been launched, Ozawa's Force A despatched a second of 128 planes. Five minutes later, at 0905, a single well-aimed torpedo from the US submarine *Albacore*, Commander J. W. Blanchard, disabled the 33,000 tons carrier *Taiho*, which subsequently suffered a petrol explosion (the consequence of poor damage control organization), and went to the bottom at 1532 so suddenly that she took three-quarters of her crew with her, after Ozawa had transferred his flag to the cruiser *Haguro*. The *Taiho*'s planes and those from Force A's other carriers fared no better. Intercepted by US fighters at 1139, only 20 reached Lee's battleships and just six went as far as Mitscher's carriers, whilst as many as 98 were shot down.

Ozawa's third strike of 47 planes, launched by Force B at 1000, was in a sense more fortunate. Being misdirected to the north, most of these failed to find Lee's or Mitscher's ships and, when intercepted by US fighters at 1300, only seven were shot down. The fourth strike of 82 planes from Forces A and B flew off at 1130. These were likewise misdirected, this time to the south of the US fleet, so that only six managed to attack Montgomery's TG 58·2 without effect. And all except nine were destroyed, some when intercepted by US fighters at 1421, others when trying to land on Guam, where they had been directed—which was just as well since at 1135 the *Shokaku* was struck by three torpedoes fired by Kossler's submarine, the *Cavalla,* with the consequence that she went to the bottom at 1501, even earlier than the *Taiho.* Throughout this time Mitscher did not rest content with intercepting Ozawa's planes. His bombers struck Guam's airfields and defences again and again, whilst his fighters ensured that no machine from the First Air Fleet attacked his carriers.

Darkness, at 1845, ended the biggest carrier-borne air battle of World War Two. In the 'Great Marianas Turkey Shoot', as it came to be known, Ozawa lost 346 planes and two of his carriers, whereas the US fleet lost only 30 planes and suffered a single bomb hit. No victory could have been more complete. Nothing could have better demonstrated the skill and courage of the American aircrews and the ships' combat information centres which directed them, for all that it showed the consequence enforced upon Japan by her losses at Midway and in subsequent battles, the need to use hastily trained pilots with no combat experience. Nor should the skill and perseverance of the US submarines be forgotten, especially perhaps the *Albacore,* whose crew never learned of their outstanding achievement because the Japanese concealed their losses until after she had been sunk on her next patrol.

But this was not the end of the battle. At 2000 Mitscher headed his ships at 24 knots in search of the enemy whom he knew was retiring to the west, except for Harrill's TG 58·4 which remained to deal next day with what was left of the First Air Fleet on Guam and the adjacent islands. But US shore-based search planes failed 'to find and fix' the enemy for him during the night, with the consequence that not until 1540 next day, the 20th, did a carrier-borne machine report that Ozawa's fleet, having delayed to refuel at sea, was only some 275 miles away. This faced Mitscher with the need for a swift decision if the Japanese ships were not to escape during the coming night. He ordered all available strike planes to be launched at the risk of incurring losses when they returned after dark. (American carriers were still not equipped for night flight deck

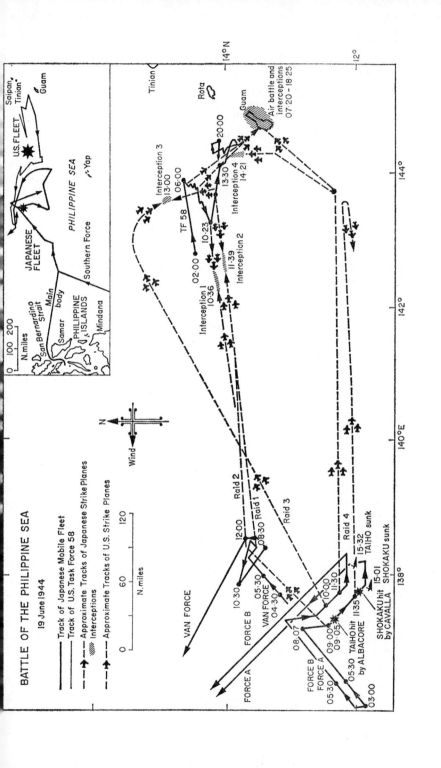

BATTLE OF THE PHILIPPINE SEA

19 June 1944

——— Track of Japanese Mobile Fleet
——— Track of U.S. Task Force 58
░░░░ Interceptions
– – – Approximate Tracks of Japanese Strike Planes
– – – Approximate Tracks of U.S. Strike Planes

operations, nor were their aircrew so trained.) At 1620 TGs 58·1, 58·2 and 58·3 sent off 131 dive-bombers and torpedo bombers and an escort of 85 fighters to fly to the limit of their range.

Shortly before sunset these found a group of six Japanese tankers, of which two were sunk. Then they attacked the three surviving Japanese carriers, with the advantage that Ozawa, greatly overestimating the damage which he had done to TF 58, had failed to dispose an effective screen around them. Two torpedoes struck and sank the *Hiyo,* while the *Zuikaku* (to which Ozawa had by now transferred his flag from the *Haguro*), *Chiyoda* and *Junyo* were seriously damaged, with the loss of a further 65 planes. So, too, were bomb hits scored on the battleship *Haruna* and the cruiser *Maya.* But Mitscher lost as many as 80 of his planes which either ran out of fuel and had to ditch, or crashed whilst trying to land on between 2045 and 2300. Fortunately all but 16 pilots and 33 other crewmen were picked up by Spruance's destroyers and by US flying-boats out of Saipan.

Mitscher's need to turn east into the wind for such a long period lost his ships so much ground that, although he resumed his westerly course at midnight, he was unable to get within air strike range of Ozawa's fleet during 21 June. Shortly after dark that day, he abandoned the chase, not least because his ships were running short of fuel, thus bringing to an end the battle of the Philippine Sea.

The Japanese had lost three large aircraft-carriers and, including those based on Guam, some 480 planes with most of their crews. For this Ozawa tendered his resignation, which Toyoda refused to accept. In the sharpest of contrasts, the USA suffered just one bomb hit on a battleship and minor damage to one or two other vessels, and lost 130 planes, but only 76 airmen. *But*—and it is a considerable *but*—the five Japanese capital ships, in particular the mighty *Yamato* and *Musashi,* escaped damage. Although Spruance's fleet scored an overwhelming victory in the air, Lee's battleships had not come within gun range of Ozawa's, nor had the latter been attacked by Spruance's destroyers. In short the US victory was not as complete as Spruance's battle orders envisaged.

In November 1940 Admiral Somerville earned the unjust anger of Churchill and Pound for his conduct of the battle of Cape Spartivento (Sardinia). Indeed, he came near to being relieved of command of Britain's Force H, because he believed the safety and timely arrival of the convoy which he was escorting to Malta was more important than pursuit of a fast retiring Italian battle fleet. So, too, was Spruance criticized for failing to allow Mitscher's ships to move westward towards the enemy, if not on receipt of the *Flying Fish*'s and *Seahorse*'s reports on 15 and 16 June, certainly after receipt of the *Cavalla*'s on the 17th: in short for adopting a defensive stance close to Saipan rather than making an offensive move towards the enemy, especially during the night of the 18th. But how much more he would have been criticized if Ozawa had outflanked him and attacked the US troops on Saipan or, worse, massacred Turner's retiring TF 52. He did not, after all, *know* that Ozawa planned only to seek battle with the US carrier groups.

Such criticism cannot, however, deny Spruance and Mitscher their due, any more than Rodney is denied credit for his victory at The Saintes, or Howe his on the Glorious First of June, because they failed to follow up and destroy De Grasse's and Villaret-Joyeuse's surviving ships. They were the victors of the biggest carrier-borne air battle of World War Two, like Midway one in which the surface forces never came within sight of each other. They destroyed half of the Japanese carrier force, whose air groups were virtually wiped out for the third time. There was no adequate Japanese fleet left to help the 25,000 defenders of Saipan so that the US forces were able to overrun the island by 9 July, after many thousands of Japanese had committed *hara-kiri,* including the naval commander, none less than Nagumo, victor of Pearl Harbour. Nor was there a Japanese fleet to impede the invasion of Guam, although this was delayed until 21 July, nor of Tinian on the 24th, with the consequence that by 12 August all the major Mariana Islands were in US hands.

Another consequence of the battle of the Philippine Sea, and the subsequent fall of Saipan, was the resignation of Tojo and his Cabinet on 18 July in tacit recognition of the inescapable fact that Japan now faced ultimate defeat.

The Philippine Sea was not, however, the last major naval battle of World War Two, nor despite the number of ships and planes involved, was it the biggest. There was another larger one fought later in 1944 which took the form of four related actions, Sibuyan Sea, Surigao Strait, Samar and Cape Engaño, which are known as the battles of Leyte Gulf. And there can be no better ending to this book than an account of this last desperate attempt by almost all that remained of a once proud and victorious Imperial Navy to halt the USA's relentless advance towards Japan. For much of it was fought 'in the old way', by ship against ship, by gun against gun, as well as by planes, and with torpedoes and bombs—for the last time in World War Two, and probably for the last time in the world's naval history, because the gun, after reigning supreme for some four hundred years, has now been succeeded by the guided missile.

MacArthur's drive north after securing New Guinea, and Nimitz's progress west across the central Pacific after taking the Marianas, made such swift progress that the US Chiefs of Staff authorized them to bring forward and undertake jointly in October, instead of in mid-December, the major task of invading and recapturing the Philippine Islands. MacArthur decided to land Lieutenant-General Walter Krueger's Sixth Army on two beaches on the eastern side of the island of Leyte immediately to the south of Samar. The assault would be directly covered by

TABLE 46: Leyte Gulf: US Seventh Fleet

Force	Capital ships	8-inch cruisers	Smaller cruisers	Escort carriers	Destroyers and destroyer escorts	Miscellaneous
TF 77 Vice-Admiral T. C. Kinkaid	—	—	—	—	—	Wasatch (Amphibious force flagship)
TG 77·2 (Fire support and bombardment) Rear-Admiral J. B. Oldendorf	Mississippi Maryland West Virginia Tennessee California Pennsylvania	Louisville (flag) Portland Minneapolis	Denver Columbia	—	15	—
TG 77·3 (Close cover) Rear-Admiral R. S. Berkey	—	HMAS Shropshire	Phoenix (flag) Boise	—	6	—
TG 77·4 (Three escort carrier groups) Rear-Admiral T. L. Sprague (in Sangamon), Rear-Admiral F. B. Stump (in Natoma Bay) and Rear-Admiral C. A. F. Sprague (in Fanshaw Bay)	—	—	—	18	20	—
TG 79·11 (Special attack group)	—	—	—	—	7	—
Totals	6	4	4	18	48	—

Kinkaid's reinforced Seventh Fleet, which included a handful of British ships, and which was under MacArthur's supreme command.

Nimitz was responsible for covering and supporting the assault force against attack by the Japanese. For this task Halsey, who had pressed for the operation to be brought forward two months, assumed command of the main body of the US Pacific Fleet, which was now numbered the Third Fleet.

The divided command, never a good recipe for success, should be noted, Kinkaid under MacArthur, Halsey under Nimitz. No one knew how to make one of these two successful commanders (more especially the ego-centric MacArthur who gulled the Great American Public into believing him to be 'next to God') subordinate to the other when the course of the war required their forces to carry out a joint operation.

TF 77, with the amphibious force for whose safety it was directly res-ponsible, assembled at Manus and other anchorages along the north coast of New Guinea early in October, in all 738 ships. TF 38 gathered at Ulithi (to the south-west of Guam). Together they made the largest and most powerful fleet ever to be employed on one operation, even if in sheer numbers it was exceeded by the Allied forces that had been employed for the invasion of Normandy in June.

TF 77's northward movement began on 10 October. On that date TF 38, having come west from Ulithi, began a week-long programme of interdicting strikes against Japanese airfields in the Philippines and on Formosa. The Japanese reacted by sending a force of torpedo-bombers to attack TF 38: at the cost of 40 shot down they succeeded only in damag-ing the cruisers *Canberra* and *Houston*. But Tokyo radio claimed as many as 11 carriers, two battleships and three cruisers sunk *plus* eight carriers, two battleships and four cruisers damaged. And Toyoda, who had moved his headquarters back to Tokyo, so far believed this as to order a force of just three cruisers and five destroyers out of the Inland Sea to mop up the crippled remnants of the US Third Fleet. Halsey offered his two damaged cruisers, which were being towed back to harbour, as bait to lure this Japanese force into the maw of his much greater strength. In the nick of time the Japanese discovered how absurd were their airmen's claims and turned for home—which impelled the ebullient Halsey to signal Nimitz that his sunken ships had been salvaged and were now 'retiring at high speed towards the enemy'. By nightfall on 16 October Japanese air strength in Formosa and the Philippines had been reduced to less than 200 planes. The Americans had lost only 90 and suffered minor damage to three carriers.

Next day, TF 77's minesweepers swept the approaches to Leyte Gulf. By noon on 18 October the small islands commanding the entrances to the Gulf, on which the Japanese had search radar stations, had been captured and Oldendorf's TG 77·2 began bombarding the beaches. Two days later Vice-Admirals Daniel Barbey and Theodore Wilkinson started

H

TABLE 47: Leyte Gulf: US Third Fleet

Force	Capital ships	Fleet carriers	Light fleet carriers	8-inch cruisers	Smaller cruisers	Destroyers
TF 38 C-in-C Admiral W. F. Halsey (flag in *New Jersey*)						
TG 38 (First Carrier Task Force) Vice-Admiral Marc Mitscher (flag in *Lexington*)						
TG 38-1 Vice-Admiral J. S. McCain		Wasp (flag) Hornet Hancock	Monterey Cowpens	Chester Salt Lake City Pensacola	Oakland San Diego	13
TG 38-2 Rear-Admiral G. F. Bogan	Iowa New Jersey	Intrepid (flag)	Cabot Independence†		Vincennes Biloxi Miami	16
TG 38-3 Rear-Admiral F. C. Sherman	Massachusetts South Dakota	Essex (flag) Lexington	Langley Princeton		Santa Fe Mobile Birmingham Reno	15
TG 38-4 Rear-Admiral R. E. Davison		Franklin (flag) Enterprise	San Jacinto Belleau Wood	New Orleans Wichita		13

TF 34
(Heavy striking Force: formed 0430 25 October out of TF 38 plus additional units marked *)
Vice-Admiral W. A. Lee

	Iowa	New Jersey	Massachusetts	*Washington (flag)	*South Dakota	*Alabama	Vincennes (flag)	Miami	Biloxi	Wichita (flag)	New Orleans	Santa Fe (flag)	Mobile	
TG 34·1 Vice-Admiral W. A. Lee														
Vincennes (flag)							8							
Miami														
Biloxi														
TG 34·2 Rear-Admiral F. E. Whiting														
Wichita (flag)										4				
New Orleans												6		
Santa Fe (flag)														
Mobile														
TG 34·3 Rear-Admiral C. T. Joy														
TG 34·4 Rear-Admiral L. T. DuBose														
Totals	6		8		8	5	9							57

† Night fighter carrier.

landing the troops from their respective northern and southern transport groups in perfect weather and against only slight opposition. 'People of the Philippines, I have returned', announced MacArthur as he waded ashore two and a half years after being compelled to withdraw from the islands. On 21 October the two nearest airfields were in US hands. By midnight that day 132,000 men and 200,000 tons of supplies and equipment had been landed, and there remained in Leyte Gulf only three amphibious force flagships (Kincaid's, Barbey's and Wilkinson's), 28 Liberty ships, and 26 tank-landing ships.

Toyoda had so far anticipated an American operation against the Philippines as to prepare four SHO (Victory) counter-plans, dependent on the island chosen for the initial landings. But from the start he suffered two disadvantages. His intelligence gave him no forewarning of MacArthur's objective: not until US minesweepers appeared off Leyte Gulf on 17 October did he know that this must be the place. Secondly, US submarines and aircraft had sunk so many of his tankers that he had been compelled to disperse his Fleet widely, from Japan's Inland Sea down to Lingga Roads, Singapore.

Compare these figures (Table 48) with those in *either* of the US fleets. If Toyoda had ordered his ships to concentrate, Ozawa would have had approximate equality with *one* of them in all *except* carriers. Of these vessels the Japanese now had only four, plus two half-converted battleships. As important, they carried only 116 planes against ten times this figure available to Kinkaid and Halsey. So SHO-1 required Ozawa's Carrier Force to come down from the Inland Sea and decoy Halsey's Third Fleet, including its carriers, up to the north, so that Kurita's First Striking Force A could come north-east from Lingga Roads to the San Bernardino Strait (dividing Samar from Luzon), and Nishimura's First Striking Force C from Lingga Roads to Surigao Strait (between Leyte and Mindanao), to pass through them and together fall upon and destroy the amphibious ships in Leyte Gulf.

In devising such a complicated plan Toyoda showed that he was not the equal of Yamamoto. It was foredoomed because of lack of 'air', because it seriously transgressed the principle of concentration of force, and because it was too dependent on first class communications to ensure that the movements of the several Japanese forces were properly co-ordinated. Specifically, the four commanders had no adequate means of communicating with each other: all were kept under Toyoda's operational control, and he could not effectively manage this from distant Tokyo. Moreover, for geographical reasons, no Japanese force could reach Leyte Gulf until after Barbey and Wilkinson had completed the critical initial landings and the bulk of the US transports had sailed. They would be too late to do more than, at best, temporarily sever General Krueger's sea supply lines. But by this stage of the war Toyoda and his compatriots were desperate men.

TABLE 48: Leyte Gulf: Japanese Fleet

Force	Capital ships	Fleet carriers	Battleship-carriers	Light fleet carriers	8-inch cruisers	Smaller cruisers	Destroyers
Carrier Force Vice-Admiral J. Ozawa	—	Zuikaku (flag)	Hyuga Ise	Chitose Chiyoda Zuiho	—	Tama Oyodo Isuzu	8
First Striking Force A Vice-Admiral T. Kurita	Yamato Musashi Nagato Kongo Haruna				Atago (flag) Takao Maya Chokai Myoko Haguro Kumano Suzuya Chikuma Tone	Noshiro Yahagi	15
First Striking Force C Vice-Admiral C. Nishimura	Yamashiro (flag) Fuso				Mogami		4
Second Striking Force Vice-Admiral K. Shima					Nachi (flag) Ashigara	Abukuma	4
Totals	7	1	2	3	13	6	31

Sailing from Lingga Roads on 18 October, First Striking Forces A and C called at Borneo's Brunei Bay for fuel. At 0800 on the 22nd Kurita's ships—the majority of Japan's battleships including the *Yamato* and *Musashi* and most of her surviving 8-inch cruisers—headed into the Sibuyan Sea for the San Bernardino Strait, whilst Nishimura's smaller force steered into the Sulu Sea for Surigao Strait. The latter was to be supported by Shima's Second Striking Force which had left the Inland Sea on the 20th, the same day that Ozawa's carriers sortied on their decoy mission undetected by any of the US submarines which Nimitz had ordered to intercept them.

The opening battle began on 23 October. Early that day First Striking Force A was detected to the west of Palawan by Lieutenant-Commander D. McClintock's submarine *Darter* and by Lieutenant-Commander B. D. Clagget's *Dace*, which were on patrol together. Both radioed reports, then gained firing positions. At 0630 McClintock sank the 8-inch cruiser *Atago* with two torpedoes and put two more into her sister, the *Takao*, which was heavily damaged. Clagget torpedoed and sank another sister-ship, the *Maya*. (The *Darter* subsequently ran aground on Bombay Shoal and had to be abandoned, but McClintock and his crew were rescued by the *Dace*.) The loss of three of his heavy cruisers, including his own flagship, did not, however, deflect Kurita from his course for the Sibuyan Sea. After all, his force included those two 18-inch gun mastodons, *Yamato*, in which he now hoisted his flag, and *Musashi*, which were reputed to be unsinkable.

Meantime, Halsey had reacted to the *Darter*'s and *Dace*'s enemy reports. By noon next day Mitscher's 11 carriers were deployed on a broad front to the east of the Philippines, Sherman's TG 38·3 to the north, Bogan's 38·2 off San Bernardino Strait and Davison's TG 38·4 some 60 miles off Samar. (McCain's TG 38·1 had been detached to Ulithi to refuel; although recalled it could not rejoin before next day, 25 October.) Mitscher's search planes had located and shadowed Kurita's force from soon after dawn: now his carrier groups launched a series of strikes with some 260 planes.

Before these could find their targets TG 38·3 was attacked by Japanese planes, possibly from Admiral Onishi's First Air Fleet from Luzon, possibly from Ozawa's force. Most of these were intercepted and shot down by Sherman's CAP, but one got through and put a 550 lb bomb into the *Princetown*, which went through several decks and started a major petrol fire. The 6-inch cruisers *Birmingham* and *Reno* laid alongside the crippled carrier, to help her fight this holocaust, but to no avail. The blaze reached the *Princetown*'s magazine. The detonation not only wrecked her, so that she had to be torpedoed and sunk by the *Reno*, but killed and wounded some 600 of the *Birmingham*'s crew, who were on deck preparing to take the wounded vessel in tow.

Mitscher's planes gained their revenge for this. Despite heavy AA fire

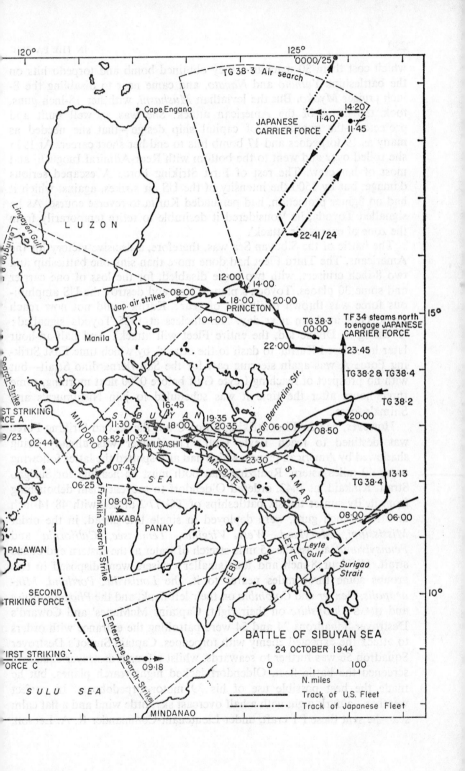

BATTLE OF SIBUYAN SEA
24 OCTOBER 1944

0   100

N. miles

———— Track of U.S. Fleet
—·—·— Track of Japanese Fleet

which cost them 30 machines, they obtained bomb and torpedo hits on the battleships *Yamato* and *Nagato*, and came near to disabling the 8-inch cruiser *Myoko*. But the leviathan *Mushashi*, with her 18-inch guns, took the brunt of the American attack. She was so well built and protected—the apotheosis of capital ship design—that she needed as many as 19 torpedoes and 17 bomb hits to end her short career. At 1935 she rolled over and went to the bottom with Rear-Admiral Inoguchi and most of her crew. The rest of First Striking Force A escaped serious damage, but by 1500 the intensity of the US air strikes, against which it had no fighter protection, had persuaded Kurita to reverse course. As he signalled Toyoda, he 'considered it desirable to retire temporarily from the zone of enemy air attack'.

The battle of the Sibuyan Sea was, therefore, a decisive victory for the Americans. The Third Fleet had done more than sink one battleship and two 8-inch cruisers, with two more disabled, for the loss of one carrier and some 30 planes. Toyoda's plan to trap and destroy the US amphibious force was thrown badly out of gear: Kurita could not now reach Leyte Gulf at dawn next day. Nonetheless at 1925 Toyoda signalled: 'Trusting in Divine aid, the entire Fleet will attack'. And half-an-hour later he ordered Kurita 'to dash to the attack', by which time First Striking Force A was again steering east for the San Bernardino Strait—but with no prospect of reaching Leyte Gulf before 0700 next morning, some three hours after the time it was scheduled to join Nishimura's and Shima's forces.

However, neither First Striking Force C nor the Second Striking Force was destined to reach Leyte Gulf. The former was already being shadowed by American planes, which had also spotted the latter following some 40 miles astern. Realizing that both must be heading for Surigao Strait, Kinkaid, at 1443, ordered Oldendorf to prevent them debouching from it. By sunset the six battleships of TG 77·2 armed with 48 14-inch and 16 16-inch guns, were deployed in single line ahead, in the order *Mississippi, Maryland, West Virginia, Tennessee, California* and *Pennsylvania*, across the 15 mile stretch of water at the eastern end of the strait. His four 8-inch and four smaller cruisers were disposed in two groups some three miles nearer to it, the *Louisville, Portland, Minneapolis, Denver* and *Colombia* on their left flank, and the *Phoenix, Boise* and HMAS *Shropshire* on their right. Captains McManes' and Coward's Destroyer Squadrons 24 and 54 were patrolling the entrance with orders to attack the expected enemy with torpedoes. Captain Smoot's Destroyer Squadron 56 was further to seawards, whilst a fourth destroyer squadron screened the battle fleet. Oldendorf lacked night search planes, but he made the best possible use of his 39 motor-torpedoboats. In perfect weather—a dark night with a half overcast sky, little wind and a flat calm sea—he sent these PT craft, under Lieutenant-Commander R. A. Leeson, to patrol inside the strait, and to the west of it, in groups of three, with orders to report all contacts and then to attack them.

So it was PT 131 which began the battle of Surigao Strait. At 2236 she obtained a radar contact of First Striking Force C and, with two other boats, attempted an attack on Nishimura's battleships after clearing a radio report. For 50 miles across the Mindanao Sea and through the Surigao Strait this Japanese force was subsequently reported, and as unsuccessfully attacked by similar groups of PT boats. All were illuminated by searchlights and driven off by gunfire, the last at 0213 on 25 October—but not before they had provided Oldendorf with the information he needed to make the best use of his battle force—to practise his own precept: 'Never give a sucker a chance'.

Three-quarters of an hour later, Nishimura encountered Destroyer Squadron 54. Coward had obtained radar contact at 0230, time enough to appreciate that First Striking Force C was disposed in single line, four destroyers two miles ahead of the *Yamashiro*, with the *Fuso* and *Mogami* following at intervals of half a mile. At 0300 he led one division, the *Remey*, *McGowan* and *Melvin* at full speed to a firing position on Nishimura's starboard bow, to launch 27 torpedoes at ranges between 8,000 and 9,500 yards. One struck the *Fuso* causing her to sheer out of the enemy line and starting an explosive fire. Half-an-hour later she broke in half and sank. Shortly after this success, Commander R. H. Phillips in the *McDermut* came in on Nishimura's port bow and torpedoed the destroyers *Yamagumo*, *Michishio* and *Asagumo*, sinking the first and crippling the other two, whilst his division mate, the *Monssen*, flooded two magazines in the *Yamashiro*. Ten minutes later McManes in the *Hutchins* led the six destroyers of Squadron 24, including HMAS *Arunta*, in to attack First Striking Force C with 19 torpedoes. One sank the disabled *Michishio*, another struck the *Yamashiro*. Nonetheless Nishimura held his course and speed: *nothing* must stop his force reaching Leyte Gulf, even though he had already lost much of it.

He cannot have known the size of the force, six battleships, eight cruisers and two destroyer squadrons, which still barred the way of his lone capital ship, his single cruiser and his one remaining destroyer. At 0323, as Oldendorf's battle force was on an easterly course, its radar began plotting the northerly course of the approaching enemy and soon allowed the US ships to appreciate that they were about to play that classic gambit, 'crossing the T'. Half-an-hour later, at 0351, the cruisers opened fire with their 8-inch and 6-inch guns at ranges of around 16,000 yards. One minute later the battleships joined in. Equipped with the latest gunnery radar, the *West Virginia* fired her first salvo at 22,800 yards, an unprecedented range for a night action. She was followed by the *Tennessee* and *California* which had the same advantage. Between them these ships fired 225 armour-piercing shells in six gun salvoes. Having an earlier type of radar, the *Maryland* had to range on the *West Virginia*'s

H*

splashes so that she fired only 48 rounds. The *Mississippi* managed only a single salvo and the *Pennsylvania* none at all, because their line of fire was obstructed by US ships.

Although Nishimura's three ships were all but overwhelmed by this devastating assault, they reacted gamely and returned the American fire, aiming at Berkey's three right flank cruisers. The destroyer *Shigure* was so ably manoeuvred that she received only one hit before retiring southwards. At 0355 the *Mogami*'s captain decided to turn away to the south whilst his battered ship could still steam. The *Yamashiro*'s 14-inch guns made only one hit, on the destroyer *Albert W. Grant*, before she turned west, ablaze from bow to stern. A few minutes later the US battle fleet and flanking cruisers reversed course to conform with this movement.

At 0401 the *Mogami* attempted an unsuccessful torpedo attack. One minute later an 8-inch salvo from the *Portland*, among Oldendorf's left flank cruisers, destroyed the Japanese cruiser's bridge, killing her captain, and so damaged her engine and boiler rooms that she came near to stopping. At 0404 Smoot's destroyers swept down to fire torpedoes at the *Yamashiro* at a range of 6,200 yards. The US gunfire did not slacken until, at 0409, Oldendorf silenced his heavy ships because they were endangering Smoot's squadron—but not before the hapless *Albert W. Grant* had been struck by fifteen American 6-inch shells.

To Nishimura—two and a half years earlier the victor in the battle of the Java Sea—and the *Yamashiro*'s officers and men, this must have seemed a God-given opportunity to escape from the terrible battering to which their ships had been subjected. Steaming at 15 knots the Japanese battleship turned southwards. But she held this course for less than 10 minutes. Just after 0411 two torpedoes fired by the *Newcomb*, of Smoot's squadron, struck her. Eight minutes later she rolled over and sank, taking Nishimura, her captain, and almost all her crew with her.

Such was the first phase of the battle of Surigao Strait.

Lowestoft, Beachy Head, Cape Chesapeake, Trafalgar, Santiago, Jutland, every major naval action of the past three centuries had been fought by classic line-of-battle tactics. In the silence that followed the roar of Oldendorf's 14-inch and 16-inch guns in Surigao Strait, one could imagine the ghosts of all great admirals, from Raleigh and De Ruyter to Togo and Jellicoe, saluting the passing of the kind of naval warfare that they understood. In the morning watch of 25 October 1944 battle line became as obsolete as the oared galley tactics of Salamis and Syracuse.[2]

(Of incidental interest Surigao Strait is also one of the very few such battles in which the senior officer did not fly his flag in one of the battleships. For more than 300 years admirals remained convinced that a battle fleet could not be effectively led from outside it. The few, such as Rodney, who tried hoisting their flag in a frigate, were quickly disillusioned.)

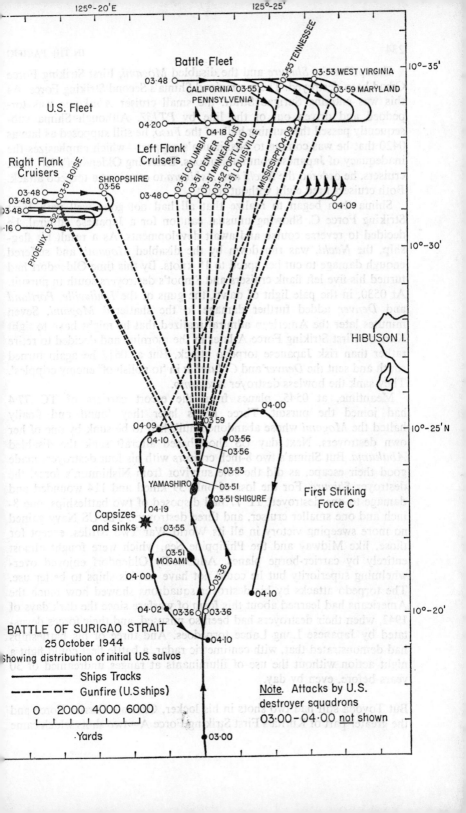

BATTLE OF SURIGAO STRAIT
25 October 1944
showing distribution of initial U.S. salvos

— Ships Tracks
- - - - - Gunfire (U.S ships)

0   2000 4000 6000
Yards

Note. Attacks by U.S.
destroyer squadrons
03·00 – 04·00 not shown

Except for the *Shigure* and the disabled *Mogami,* First Striking Force C had been destroyed. There remained Shima's Second Striking Force. As this was entering Surigao Strait, the small cruiser *Abukuma* was torpedoed and driven out of the line by *PT137.* Although Shima subsequently passed the burning hulk of the *Fuso,* he still supposed as late as 0420 that he was coming to Nishimura's support—which emphasizes the inadequacy of Japanese communications. Detecting Oldendorf's left flank cruisers, he ordered the *Nachi* and *Ashigara* to carry out a torpedo attack. Both cruisers fired eight without result.

Shima then began to realize that all had not gone well with First Striking Force C. Showing unusual caution for a Japanese admiral, he decided to reverse course and await developments. As a result his flagship, the *Nachi,* was run down by the disabled *Mogami,* and suffered enough damage to cut her speed to 18 knots. By this time Oldendorf had turned his five left flank cruisers and Smoot's destroyers south in pursuit. At 0530, in the pale light of dawn, the guns of the *Louisville, Portland* and *Denver* added further damage to the shattered *Mogami.* Seven minutes later the American admiral realized that he might have to fight Kurita's First Striking Force A later in the morning and decided to retire rather than risk Japanese torpedo attack. But at 0617 he again turned south and sent the *Denver* and *Columbia* in 'to polish off enemy cripples'. They sank the bowless destroyer *Asagumo.*

Meantime, at 0545, planes from the escort carriers of TG 77·4 had joined the pursuit. Three hours later they found and finally halted the *Mogami* whose abandoned hulk had to be sunk by one of her own destroyers. Next day US shore-based aircraft sank the disabled *Abukuma.* But Shima's two 8-inch cruisers with his four destroyers made good their escape, as did the sole survivor from Nishimura's force, the destroyer *Shigure.* For the loss of only 39 killed and 114 wounded and damage to one destroyer, TF 77 had disposed of two battleships, one 8-inch and one smaller cruiser, and three destroyers. The US Navy gained no more sweeping victory in all its World War Two battles, except for those, like Midway and the Philippine Sea, which were fought almost entirely by carrier-borne planes. Admittedly Oldendorf enjoyed overwhelming superiority but he could not have put his ships to better use. The torpedo attacks by his destroyer squadrons showed how much the Americans had learned about this form of warfare since the dark days of 1942, when their destroyers had been so misused, and their forces devastated by Japanese Long Lance torpedoes. And three of his battleships had demonstrated that, with centimetric radar, a battle fleet could fight a night action without the use of illuminants at ranges undreamed of 30 years before, even by day.

But Toyoda still had two shots in his locker, Ozawa's Carrier Force and the greater part of Kurita's First Striking Force A—two shots which came near to scoring a Japanese victory. The clock needs to be put back some 18 hours, to the afternoon of the previous day, 24 October, for the genesis of this.

Nimitz's orders to Halsey were as unwisely worded as was the US Chiefs of Staff's decision to entrust the conduct of the operation to two supreme commanders: 'In case opportunity for destruction of major portion of the enemy fleet offer or can be created, such destruction becomes the primary task' of the Third Fleet—instead of covering and supporting the Seventh Fleet. For even though the former task should be to the detriment of the latter, neither MacArthur nor Kinkaid would be able to influence Halsey's decisions: he was answerable only to Nimitz.

Throughout most of the daylight hours of the 24th this duality of tasks presented no problems. First Striking Force A was an enemy against which the shipping in Leyte Gulf needed protection *and* 'the major portion of the enemy fleet' which had been located. There was no question as to the need for Mitscher's carrier-borne planes to fight the already described battle of the Sibuyan Sea. There was also the possibility that the Third Fleet would be required to fight a surface ship action when Kurita's ships debouched from the San Bernardino Strait during the coming night. To this end Halsey signalled at 1511 that his four battleships would join Lee's two and, with six of his cruisers and 18 destroyers, form TF 34 (see Table 45 on pages 214–15).

He had, however, no sooner issued this *preparatory* instruction than a search aircraft located and reported the Japanese Carrier Force steering south in a position less than 200 miles to the north of the Third Fleet and to the east of Luzon. Halsey reckoned that Ozawa was coming to the support of the Japanese Striking Forces: he could not know that Toyoda intended him to act as a decoy. His first inclination was to form TF 34 and leave it, with one carrier group to provide air cover, to guard the exit to San Bernardino Strait, while the rest of the Third Fleet went north to tackle Ozawa. And there can be no doubt that this is what Halsey should have done. TGs 38·3 and 38·4, headed by seven carriers, reinforced by TG 38·1's five when McCain rejoined next day, would have been ample to deal with Ozawa's force. But this was not the way 'Bull' Halsey saw it: the Japanese Carrier Force was now 'the major portion of the enemy fleet' which it was his *'primary* task' to destroy, for which he should use *all* his carriers, from which he could not safely detach his battleships.

Nor did Halsey change this belief when, at 1935, a night search plane reported that Kurita's ships were again heading east for the San Bernardino Strait because, with the previously noted tendency of all aircrew to exaggerate their achievements, Mitscher's reported that First Striking Force A had suffered 'at least four, probably five battleships torpedoed and bombed, one probably sunk; a minimum of three heavy cruisers torpedoed and others bombed; one light cruiser sunk; one destroyed probably sunk and four damaged'. At 2000 Halsey ordered TGs 38·2,

38·3 and 38·4 to head north and TG 38·1 to join them at its best speed.

Around the same time Halsey signalled his intentions to Kinkaid: 'Am proceeding north with three groups to attack enemy carrier force at dawn'. He supposed that this would suffice for the commander of the Seventh Fleet to deploy some of his ships to the east of San Bernardino Strait to deal with such remnants of the supposedly battered First Striking Force A as might emerge from it. But Kinkaid had previously intercepted Halsey's signal organizing TF 34, and did not appreciate that this was only a *preparatory* instruction, to be put into effect if and when ordered. (The fault lay with Halsey's ambiguous wording since, as will be seen later, Nimitz read the signal in the same sense as Kinkaid.) He believed that, although Halsey was taking three carrier groups north, he was leaving his battleships guarding the exit from San Bernardino Strait (to the *north* of Leyte Gulf). He did not, therefore, hesitate to deploy all his own battleships and cruisers across the exit to the Surigao Strait (to the *south* of Leyte Gulf), with the decisive consequences for First Striking Force C and the Second Striking Force which have already been described.

In short, through having two *separate* fleets whose commanders were each responsible to a different commander-in-chief, with no co-ordinating authority short of distant Washington, from where, as has been previously noted, King never attempted to exercise operational control, Halsey and Kinkaid each supposed that the other was guarding the eastern end of San Bernardino Strait during the night of 24–25 October. Each *supposed*, but neither *was*. There was nothing to bar Kurita's way, nothing to stop the battleships *Yamato* and *Nagato*, the battlecruisers *Kongo* and *Haruna*, with six 8-inch cruisers and two others, plus 15 destroyers, emerging from the strait and descending upon the American amphibious shipping in Leyte Gulf, with no better protection than the Seventh Fleet's escort carriers, a task for which they were neither designed nor armed. Each mounted only one or two 5-inch guns, their speed was limited to 18 knots, and they carried at most 20 fighters and a dozen torpedo-bombers.

When Kurita brought his First Striking Force A through the Strait shortly after midnight and turned south for Leyte Gulf, he met no opposition. Nor was his approach during the first hours of daylight on 25 October spotted until he was as close as 20 miles from his objective. Kinkaid's 18 'baby flat-tops' were then deployed in three task units of six, each with a screen of three destroyers and four destroyer escorts, a short distance to seaward of Leyte Gulf; 77·4·1 ('Taffy One' for short) under Rear-Admiral Thomas Sprague in the *Sangamon* to the south, 77·4·2 ('Taffy Two') under Rear-Admiral Felix Stump in the *Natoma Bay* in the centre, and 77·4·3 ('Taffy Three') under Rear-Admiral Clifton Sprague in the *Fanshaw Bay* to the north. The last of these groups bore the brunt of Kurita's attack.

Clifton Sprague's ships, which included the *St Lo, White Plains,*

Kalinin Bay, Kitkun Bay and *Gambier Bay,* began that day with the routine launching of air patrols to cover the amphibious shipping remaining in the gulf, just as Thomas Sprague's began it with flying off a strike against Nishimura's and Shima's surviving ships fleeing from Surigao Strait. Then their crews went to breakfast. Suddenly, at 0645, the *Fanshaw Bay*'s lookouts reported AA gunfire to the north. At 0646 her radar detected unidentified ships to the north. One minute later the pilot of an A/S patrol plane reported being fired on by a force of battleships, cruisers and destroyers. One more minute and the *Fanshaw Bay*'s lookouts sighted the unmistakable pagoda-like mast structures of Japanese capital ships appearing over the horizon, of which the *Yamato* opened fire at 0648 with her 18-inch guns on Taffy Three at a range of 37,000 yards.

For what followed, an action between capital ships and heavy cruisers on the one side and puny escort carriers on the other, there was no precedent. No one could have envisaged such a seemingly unequal battle occurring. Clifton Sprague's cool, decisive handling of his unit in such daunting circumstances is one of the most notable episodes in the whole of World War Two at sea for all that he was helped by Kurita's ill-judged handling of his force. Turning east into the wind at his ships' best speed, Clifton Sprague quickly ordered them to fly off every available strike plane as soon as they could be armed with bombs and torpedoes. Simultaneously he radioed urgent appeals for help. Thomas Sprague and Stump responded by ordering off their strike planes, but the latter was 60 miles away and the former 130, half-an-hour's flying time—and they, too, had first to be armed with bombs and torpedoes. Kinkaid summoned Oldendorf's victorious battle force to the scene from the south at flank speed, but it could not arrive in less than three hours.

The six escort carriers of Taffy Three were formed in a circle with a diameter of 2,500 yards, with its destroyers and destroyer escorts patrolling the engaged sector. At 0706, to quote Clifton Sprague: 'The enemy was closing with disconcerting rapidity and the volume and accuracy of his fire increasing. It did not appear that any of our ships could survive for another five minutes.' But this did not deter him from sending his screen in to attack the enemy with torpedoes before his unit was enveloped, as if by Divine Providence, in a rain squall. Added to the smoke screen made by the American ships, this hid his escort carriers from the enemy for more than the next half hour. And during that time Kurita made the mistake of assuming that *all* US carriers were able to steam at 30 knots. Having now had the good fortune to get within gun range of some of them, without being subjected to air attack in the two hours since dawn, he determined to inflict as much damage as possible with his guns and torpedoes before their aircraft could deflect him from his purpose.

Instead of forming a battle line which would be tied to the speed of his slowest vessel, he ordered: 'General chase', thereby unleashing his ships to pursue the enemy each at her own best speed—much as Cunningham had done at the battle of Matapan. As a result, by the time Clifton Sprague's 'baby flat-tops' came out of the rain storm, he had lost control of his ships as a coherent force.

As Commander W. D. Thomas headed Taffy Three's destroyers *Hoel*, *Heermann* and *Johnston* to the north, they came under fire from the Japanese capital ships' main and secondary armaments. Nonetheless they closed to under 10,000 yards, at which range six torpedoes from the *Heermann*, Captain A. T. Hathaway, compelled the mighty *Yamato* to reverse course, taking her temporarily out of the fight. But the *Hoel* was not so fortunate: to quote Commander L. S. Kintberger, his crew 'performed their duties coolly and efficiently until their ship was shot from under them' at 0855. The *Johnston*, Commander E. E. Evans, scored a torpedo hit on the 8-inch cruiser *Kumano*, which dropped out of the battle together with the *Suzuya*, which was damaged by bombing, before being struck by three 14-inch and three 6-inch shells. These reduced her to 'a position where all the gallantry and guts in the world could not save us' from the avalanche of shells which were subsequently poured in to her. Nonetheless her crew fought on until, at 0950, she lay dead in the water and Evans ordered: 'Abandon ship'. A Japanese destroyer gave her the *coup de grâce* at 1010. Of the four destroyer escorts which took part in this attack only the *Samuel B. Roberts* was sunk.

By the time, 0743, that Clifton Sprague's escort carriers emerged from the rain squall and again came under Japanese heavy gun fire, Kurita's ships were being repeatedly attacked by the bombs, torpedoes and machine-gun fire of American planes from all 18 of the Seventh Fleet's escort carriers—attacks which continued for the next two hours and which included threatening dummy ones when they ran out of ammunition. These forced the Japanese capital ships to make such frequent evasive alterations of course that, despite their greater speed, they were only able to close the range slowly as Clifton Sprague headed away to the south. He avoided losing ground on the enemy, through turning east into the wind to land on his returning aircraft, by directing them to Stump's Taffy Two, where they were refuelled and rearmed and then flown off for a further strike.

Nonetheless the Japanese 8-inch cruisers *Chikuma*, *Chokai*, *Haguro* and *Tone* scored hits which would have been deadly but for their armourpiercing shells failing to detonate against the escort carriers' thin plating. Only an efficient damage control organization kept the *Kalinin Bay* going after she had been hit 13 times; but the *Gambier Bay*, Captain W. V. Viewag, was so badly mauled after being under fire for the best part of half-an-hour, that she capsized and sank at 0907. Revenge was exacted by four torpedo-bombers from the *Kitkun Bay*, led by Commander R. L. Fowler. With 10 hits they sent the *Chokai* to the bottom; and she was soon followed by the *Chikuma*, sunk by planes from Taffy Two. Then,

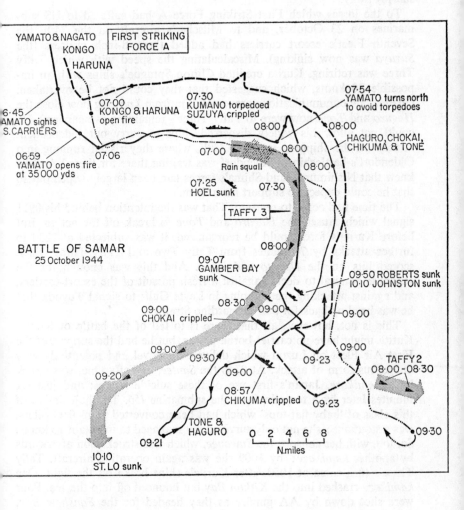

YAMATO & NAGATO
KONGO
HARUNA

FIRST STRIKING
FORCE A

6·45
AMATO sights
S.CARRIERS

07·00
KONGO & HARUNA
open fire

07·30
KUMANO torpedoed
SUZUYA crippled

07·54
YAMATO turns north
to avoid torpedoes

08·00

08·00

06·59
YAMATO opens fire
at 35 000 yds

07·06

07·00

Rain squall

08·00

HAGURO, CHOKAI,
CHIKUMA & TONE

08·00

07·25
HOEL sunk

07·30

TAFFY 3

BATTLE OF SAMAR
25 October 1944

08·00

09·07
GAMBIER BAY
sunk

09·50 ROBERTS sunk
10·10 JOHNSTON sunk

09·00
CHOKAI crippled

08·30

09·00

09·00

09·00

09·00

09·30

09·23

TAFFY 2
08·00 - 08·30

09·20

09·00

08·57
CHIKUMA crippled

09·23

09·30

TONE &
HAGURO

09·21

10·10
ST. LO sunk

0 2 4 6 8
N.miles

around 0915, almost as suddenly as the battle had begun, and as unexpectedly, Sprague's hard-pressed Taffy Three, which still expected to be overwhelmed, was greatly relieved to see the *Haguro* and *Tone* turn sharply away.

To the losses which First Striking Force A had suffered to US submarines on 23 October, and to Mitscher's aircraft on the 24th, the Seventh Fleet's escort carriers had added three 8-inch cruisers (the *Suzuya* was now sinking). Miscalculating the speed with which Taffy Three was retiring, Kurita credited Clifton Sprague's ships with an impossible 30 knots, which suggested that they could not be overtaken. (Inadequate communications prevented him from knowing how close the *Haguro* and *Tone* now were to Taffy Three's remaining five carriers). He could not allow his widely dispersed ships to carry out independent attacks on the shipping in Leyte Gulf, where they risked running into Oldendorf's battleships. (Oldendorf was waiting there for them.) And he knew that Nishimura's and Shima's forces had been largely wiped out so that he could expect no support from them.

The time had come to regroup. That was the intention behind his 0911 signal which caused the *Haguro* and *Tone* to break off the action. But before Kurita's force could be reorganized, it was subjected at 1230 to further attacks by 70 planes from Taffy Two and Taffy Three which scored hits on the *Nagato* and *Tone*. And this was enough for the Japanese admiral to decide against a fresh pursuit of the escort carriers, and against attacking the shipping in Leyte Gulf; to signal Toyoda that he was heading back for San Bernardino Strait.

This is not, however, all that there is to tell of the battle of Samar. Kurita might have no carrier-borne planes, but he had the support of the First Air Fleet on Luzon which delivered a novel and potentially very dangerous form of attack. At 0740 the *Santee*, in Taffy One, was struck by a *kamikaze*, Japan's first use of these suicide planes; and just six minutes later by a torpedo from the submarine *I56*. The hull design of this class of 'baby flat-tops' which had been converted from fleet oilers, was a stout one: she not only survived but managed to maintain 16 knots. So, too, with her consort, the *Suwanee*, which was struck soon afterwards by another *kamikaze*: by 1009 she was again operating aircraft. Taffy Three's turn came at 1050, after Kurita's ships broke off the fight. One *kamikaze* crashed into the *Kitkun Bay* but bounced off into the sea. Four were shot down by AA gunfire as they headed for the *Fanshaw Bay*, *White Plains* and *Kitkun Bay*. Two struck the *Kalinin Bay* but did little damage. But another went through the *St Lo*'s flight deck, detonating the bombs and torpedoes in the hangar, and sank her.

Kurita's retiring force was more fortunate. In response to Kinkaid's urgent appeals for help, radioed around 0800, Halsey ordered TG 38·1, as it was coming up from the south-east to join him, to launch a strike against First Striking Force A. Appreciating the urgency McCain's carriers flew off their torpedo-bombers at 1030 when Kurita's ships were as much as 350 miles away. But they could not carry heavy bombs or torpedoes for such a distance, only lighter weapons, so that when they attacked, around noon, they suffered considerable losses without inflicting damage.

Off Samar the Japanese lost three 8-inch cruisers, the Americans two escort carriers, two destroyers and a destroyer escort. Both sides also had several ships badly damaged and heavy casualties (the Americans 1,130 killed and missing plus 913 wounded). But such statistics are no measure of the result of this battle. What matters is that Kurita's First Striking Force A was prevented from carrying out its mission and compelled to retire. A powerful force of capital ships and heavy cruisers was routed by humble escort carriers, their planes and their screening destroyers. In the whole of World War Two no combatant gained a more unlikely victory. And that will always stand to the credit of Taffy One, Taffy Two and Taffy Three; to the bravery and skill of their captains and ships' companies and of their aircrews. Above all to Clifton Sprague whose handling of Taffy Three in such potentially disastrous circumstances is beyond praise. He, above all, epitomises the transformation of the US Fleet in the years 1942–44 from enthusiastic amateurs into dedicated professionals (with exceptions of which the most notable was Halsey as subsequent pages show).

What meantime of the bulk of the Third Fleet? At 2000 on the previous evening it was heading north to attack Ozawa's Carrier Force at dawn on 25 October, without regard for any enemy coming through San Bernardino Strait because 'Japanese carriers gave "Bull" Halsey blood in the eye and he was taking no chances of letting one guilty flat-top escape'.[3] Ozawa, with four carriers with 116 planes embarked (of which he flew off 40 to operate from Luzon's airfields), two hybrid battleship-carriers for which there were no planes available, three small cruisers and nine destroyers, had received reports of Sherman's TG 38·3 early on the 24th, and during the forenoon he launched all his 76 planes against it. But this strike flew to the limit of its range without finding its target. Moreover only 29 machines returned to their carriers: many of the rest landed on Luzon and around 15 ditched after running out of fuel. But Halsey, with ten carriers (not including McCain's) with 787 planes embarked, six battleships, eight cruisers and some 40 destroyers could not know that the enemy's remaining sting had thus been drawn, any more than he realized that Ozawa's purpose was only to decoy the Third Fleet away from Leyte Gulf, in which respect the Japanese admiral was singularly successful.

At dawn next day Halsey's carriers launched their first strike. Coming in on Ozawa's force in successive waves around 0800 and opposed only by intense AA fire, these planes bombed and sank the carrier *Chitose* and a destroyer, whilst a torpedo so damaged the *Zuikaku*, a veteran of Pearl

Harbour, that Ozawa was obliged to shift his flag to the cruiser *Oyodo*. A second American strike, which arrived around 0945, bombed and set on fire the carrier *Chiyoda*. Around noon a third strike frustrated the battleship-carrier *Hyuga*'s attempt to take the disabled *Chiyoda* in tow, sent the *Zuikaku* to the bottom with three torpedoes, and seriously damaged the carrier *Zuiho*. She was subsequently sunk by strike number four.

Two more American strikes, the last delivered around 1900, were less successful: they scored very few hits. In sum, 527 aircraft sorties from Mitscher's three carrier groups had sunk all four Japanese carriers and one destroyer; but they had scarcely scratched Ozawa's two battleship-carriers, his three cruisers or eight of his destroyers. Much of the credit for this must go to the accuracy of Japanese AA gunfire. But comparison with the battle of the Philippine Sea indicates that the aircrews of the US fleet carriers were more skilled at dealing with enemy planes than they were at hitting ships with their bombs and torpedoes, though why this should have been so in view of the achievements of the Seventh Fleet's aircrews is something of a mystery.

Before all but the first of these strikes, from 0822 onwards, Halsey received Kinkaid's urgent appeals for help to protect his ships from decimation by Kurita's First Striking Force A. And as already recorded, he reacted to the extent of ordering McCain's TG 38·1 to launch a strike against these Japanese ships. He did not, however, detach TF 34 to block Kurita's escape, just as he had decided against sending Lee's battleships to guard the San Bernardino Strait during the previous night. He remained resolutely determined to have *all* his heavy ships available to sink by gunfire such of Ozawa's ships as remained afloat after his planes had played their part in this battle of Cape Engaño.

In his Pearl Harbour headquarters Nimitz was not only alarmed by Kinkaid's appeals but puzzled as to how Kurita's force could be attacking the Seventh Fleet's escort carriers. Like Kinkaid he believed that Halsey had organized and detached TF 34 on the previous day to prevent any such incursion. 'Where,' he decided to radio Halsey 'is Task Force 34?' And this was the signal which should have been handed to Halsey on the bridge of the *New Jersey*. The yeoman who coded it for despatch was required, for security reasons, to increase its length with 'padding'—to add several words which were supposed to have no relation to the subject matter. Clearly distinguishable from the message itself, these would be deleted by the decoding yeoman in Halsey's flagship before the message was handed to him. Most unfortunately, since the incident involved an admiral of volatile temperament, Nimitz's yeoman was a student of the poet Tennyson, with the consequence that he chose for padding the words: 'the world wonders'.[4] And Halsey's yeoman assumed that these were a part of Nimitz's message, which reached the *New Jersey*'s bridge in the form: 'From Cincpac, action Com Third Fleet [Halsey] info Comich

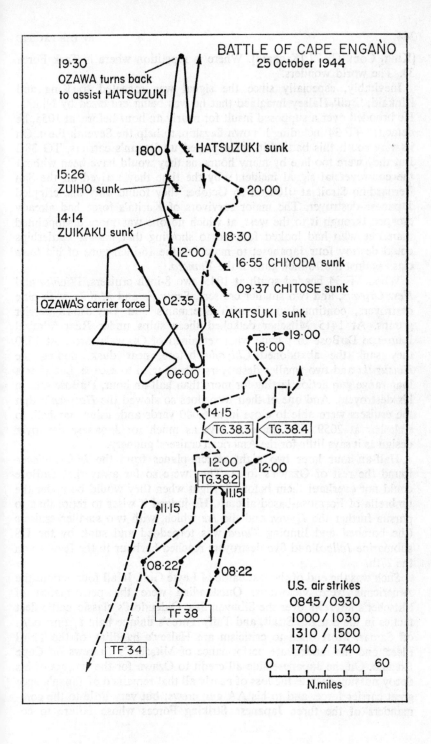

BATTLE OF CAPE ENGAÑO
25 October 1944

19·30
OZAWA turns back
to assist HATSUZUKI

1800   HATSUZUKI sunk

15:26
ZUIHO sunk   20·00

14·14   18·30
ZUIKAKU sunk
                     12·00
                     16·55 CHIYODA sunk

                     09·37 CHITOSE sunk

OZAWA'S carrier force   02·35   AKITSUKI sunk

                              19·00
                         18·00

                    06·00

               14·15
                        TG.38.3   TG.38.4

                   12·00
                        12·00
                   TG.38.2
                   11·15

          11·15

                              U.S. air strikes
                              0845/0930
          08·22   1000/1030
               08·22   1310/1500
                              1710/1740
               TF 38
                              0   60
     TF 34
                              N.miles

[King] Com TF 77 [Kinkaid]. Where is repetition where is Task Force 34. The world wonders.'

Inevitably, especially since the signal was repeated to King and Kinkaid, 'Bull' Halsey imagined that he was being criticized by Nimitz. He brooded over a supposed insult for nearly an hour before, at 1055, he detached TF 34 including his own flagship, to help the Seventh Fleet. On its way south this battleship force picked up Bogan's carriers, TG 38·2 But they were too late by many hours, as they would have been without the controversial signal incident: by the time they arrived off the San Bernardino Strait at 0100 on 26 October they found only one crippled Japanese destroyer. The major survivors of Kurita's force had already escaped through it to the west, at which no one was more disappointed than Lee who had looked forward to showing that his six battleships could destroy four Japanese; to matching the 16-inch guns of his *Iowa* class against the 18-inch guns of the *Yamato*.

When TF 34 headed south at 1045, two 8-inch cruisers, *Wichita* and *New Orleans,* and two smaller cruisers, *Santa Fe* and *Mobile,* with nine destroyers, continued north with Sherman's and Davidson's carrier groups. At 1415 Mitscher detached these ships under Rear-Admiral Laurence DuBose to pursue what remained of Ozawa's force. At 1630 they sank the abandoned *Chiyoda* before, near dusk, finding the *Hatsuzuki* and two smaller destroyers. These tried to escape, but after a long range gun action lasting for more than half-an-hour, DuBose sent in his destroyers. And one of their torpedoes so slowed the *Hatsuzuki* that the cruisers were able to close in to 6,000 yards and, using starshell, to sink her at 2059. This incident says as much for Japanese destroyer design as it says little for the American cruisers' gunnery.

Half-an-hour later two night search planes from the *Independence* found the rest of Ozawa's force. They were so far away that DuBose could not overhaul them before daylight when they would be under the umbrella of Formosa-based aircraft. He judged it wiser to retire than to pursue further the *Hyuga* and the *Ise* which, with two smaller cruisers (the bombed and limping *Tama* was torpedoed and sunk by the US submarine *Jallao*) and five destroyers reached harbour in the Ryukus on the 27th.

Such was the end of the last battle of Leyte Gulf. In all four actions the Americans were victorious. Outstanding were the performance of Mitscher's aircrews over the Sibuyan Sea, Oldendorf's classic battle fleet tactics in the Surigao Strait, and Taffy Three's unique fight against odds off Samar. Most open to criticism are Halsey's handling of the Third Fleet[5] and the inadequate performance of Mitscher's aircrews off Cape Engaño. On the Japanese side all credit to Ozawa for the success of his decoy mission despite the loss of nearly all that remained of Japan's once great carrier force, and to his AA gun crews; but very little to the commanders of the three Japanese Striking Forces whose failure to coordinate their attacks on the shipping in Leyte Gulf led them to disaster, and as little to Toyoda for conceiving and trying to conduct from distant Tokyo an almost unmanageably complicated operation.

The battles of Leyte Gulf did not end the war in the Pacific any more than the battle of North Cape ended the war against Germany. After the *Scharnhorst* was sunk on 31 December 1943, the vital battle of the Atlantic continued for the best part of another 18 months before the German delegates signed the instrument of unconditional surrender in May 1945, and Dönitz's U-boats gave themselves up to the Allies. So too, after Halsey had destroyed almost all that remained of Japan's carrier force on 25 October 1944, did the best part of a year elapse before MacArthur watched the Japanese delegates sign the surrender of their country on board Nimitz's flagship, the battleship *Missouri*, in Tokyo Bay in September 1945—a day on which Halsey (whose blunders off Cape Engaño had not dimmed the reputation for fighting leadership which he had gained during the dark hours of the Guadalcanal campaign, and which he subsequently displayed when he continued in command of the Third Fleet) joined Admiral Sir Bruce Fraser, commanding the British Pacific Fleet (which had made its significant contribution to the Allied carrier-borne air strikes against Okinawa and other objectives near to the Japanese mainland in 1945) for the impressive ceremony of Sunset on-board the battleship *Duke of York*.

Leyte was, however, the last major naval battle of World War Two. It was, too, the last in all history to be fought in 'the old way', between surface ships armed with 'great guns', as well as in the new way by carrier-borne planes. The ink was not long dry on the surrender documents before the remaining major naval Powers, when planning the future size of their Fleets, accepted that the aircraft-carrier had become the queen of the maritime chessboard and that there was no longer a viable role for the battleship. After a reign of nearly 500 years no more were laid down; those on the slips were scrapped; those that remained were sent to the shipbreakers, or preserved as floating museums, as the last great sailing ship-of-the-line, HMS *Victory*, is preserved in Britain's Portsmouth dockyard.

Those who stepped into the shoes of Dudley Pound and Ernest King, of Erich Raeder and Karl Dönitz, of Andrew Cunningham and William Halsey, of Chester Nimitz and Jack Tovey, of Bruce Fraser and Raymond Spruance, of Carleton Sprague and Philip Vian, had also to ponder the impact of nuclear weapons and guided missiles on future naval battles—and, more recently, the problems of countering the growth —wholly unforeseen when the sun set on Tokyo Bay on 2 September 1945—of a new Soviet Navy, and its transformation from a coastal defence force into a major Fleet ranging the oceans of the world.

In the spring of 1972 the headmaster of one of Britain's schools wrote in the London *Times*: 'A world war is now unthinkable'. *Unthinkable,* yes, in this age of nuclear weapons; but *impossible,* no. A future war will not necessarily be a brief nuclear holocaust. Such devastation would be of too little benefit for an aggressor nation to seek to win it in this way— unless the gods should first make its rulers mad. A fierce struggle for maritime supremacy is more likely. Man is, and always will be, dependent on the sea—for the carriage of the food by which he lives, for the raw materials and finished goods of civilized life, for fuel by which he lives and fights, and for the transport of troops and their equipment and stores with which war is waged on land; and most recently for what can be obtained from the sea itself and from its bed. The side which fails to protect its shipping, and its seabed resources of oil and gas, will face defeat. Victory will depend on the outcome of naval battles.

These will be very different from those that were fought in the past: such is the inevitable outcome of technological progress. Those who fought at Trafalgar could not have envisaged Jutland; nor could those who fought with Jellicoe and Scheer on 31 May 1916 have foreseen Midway or the Philippine Sea. *But,* just as students of World War One recognize how much was learned by the world's Navies in the days of Fighting Sail that was relevant to the Dreadnought era, so has this book shown how much was learned from World War One that was put to good use—or forgotten, sometimes disastrously—in World War Two. (For a brilliant exposé of the British Navy's shortcomings during the post-1918 decades, see *From the Dardanelles to Oran* by the American historian Professor Arthur Marder. A comparable indictment of the US Navy needs to be written.)

It may be difficult if not impossible to predict how future naval battles will be fought, but one thing is certain, that many of the lessons learned in previous wars will still be valid. In the words of the Chinese philosopher Sun Tzu: 'War is a great affair of state, the realm of life and death, the road to safety or ruin, *a thing to be studied with extreme diligence*'. And to recall Churchill's words with which this book began: 'History is the one sure guide to the future—that and imagination'. Or, to put it another way, history enshrines the wisdom of the ages.

NOTES

[1] For the same reason, slavish adherence to the dogma of fighting in a rigid single line, out of 15 consecutive engagements fought by the British Navy in the late seventeenth and the eighteenth centuries, *all* were draws. Conversely, at Trafalgar Nelson designated Collingwood as 'OTC' of half his fleet, which was a contributory factor to this overwhelming British victory.

[2] Samuel Eliot Morison in *The Two-Ocean War.*
[3] *Ibid.*
[4]   When can their glory fade?
     O the wild charge they made!
     All the world wonder'd.
           (*Charge of the Light Brigade*)
[5] For which reason Cape Engaño is sometimes known as the battle of
Bull's Run. To understand this British readers are referred to the story of
the first battle of Bull Run (1861) in the American Civil War.

POSTSCRIPTS TO CHAPTER 4

1. I welcome this opportunity to stress that Japanese aircraft were *not* able to
   carry Long Lance torpedoes, contrary to what, due to a misunderstanding, I
   stated in my monograph on *The Loss of the 'Prince of Wales' and 'Repulse'*,
   published in 1973.
2. *To page 79, note 4.* Since this book went to press more has been revealed
   about Britain's ability to decipher German radio messages. Group-Captain
   F. W. Winterbotham, in the *Ultra Secret*, tells how Britain's Secret Intelligence
   Service obtained from a source in Poland a German Enigma cipher machine
   shortly before World War Two with which, from mid-1940, a special unit
   at Bletchley Park, Buckinghamshire, was able to decipher secret German signals
   intercepted by Britain's 'Y' Service. (Further Enigma machines were subsequently captured, notably from *U570* when she surrendered to a Coastal
   Command plane in August 1941.) Winterbotham also outlines how this vital
   intelligence was disseminated only through special communication channels,
   (using secure one-time reciphering pads) to selected senior British (and, later
   US) senior commanders prefixed 'Ultra', to limit its distribution to an essential
   'must know' basis; and how they were required to refrain from acting on it
   before confirming it by some other means (*e.g.* by sending out a search aircraft),
   in order to ensure that Germany never learned that her enemies were obtaining
   this very valuable intelligence. It was Germany's failure to take comparable
   precautions with intelligence acquired by her 'B' Services, that enabled Britain
   to discover, in 1940, that her naval ciphers had been broken. Although
   Winterbotham deals chiefly with the uses to which the Army and RAF put
   'Ultra' intelligence, he mentions as examples of naval operations which
   benefited from it, the battle of Matapan, the search for the *Bismarck,* and the
   battle of the Atlantic, in particular the location and sinking of U-boat supply
   ships.

Index

Numerals in heavy type refer to figure numbers of illustrations. Abbreviations used are:
(B) = British (including Dominions); (F) = French; (G) = German; (I) = Italian; (J) = Japanese;
(N) = Netherlands; (US) = United States of America; (USSR) = Soviet Union.

Actions

Personalities

These are given their most senior rank, title, etc. mentioned in the book.

(Capital ships, Aircraft carriers and Cruisers)

Ships